SAVING THE
SECURITY STATE

NEXT WAVE New Directions in Women's Studies
A series edited by Inderpal Grewal, Caren Kaplan, and Robyn Wiegman

SAVING THE
SECURITY STATE

Exceptional Citizens in Twenty-First-Century America

INDERPAL GREWAL

DUKE UNIVERSITY PRESS
Durham and London 2017

Text designed by Courtney Leigh Baker
Cover designed by Matthew Tauch
Typeset in Arno Pro and Helvetica Neue by Westchester
Publishing Services

Library of Congress Cataloging-in-Publication Data
Names: Grewal, Inderpal, author.
Title: Saving the security state : exceptional citizens in
    twenty-first-century America / Inderpal Grewal.
Description: Durham : Duke University Press, 2017. |
    Series: Next wave | Includes bibliographical references
    and index.
Identifiers: LCCN 2017019893 (print)
LCCN 2017022469 (ebook)
ISBN 9780822372554 (ebook)
ISBN 9780822368908 (hardcover : alk. paper)
ISBN 9780822368984 (pbk. : alk. paper)
Subjects: LCSH: United States—Social conditions—
    21st century. | Neoliberalism—Social aspects—United
    States. | National security—Social aspects—United States.
    | Citizenship—United States. | Feminism—United States.
Classification: LCC HN59.2 (ebook) | LCC HN59.2 G743 2017
    (print) | DDC 306.09730905—dc23
LC record available at https://lccn.loc.gov/2017019893

COVER ART: Michele Pred, *American Red Cross*, 2005.
Airport confiscated knives. Image courtesy of the artist.

No project achieves "hegemony" as a completed project. It is a process, not a state of being. No victories are permanent or final. Hegemony has constantly to be "worked on," maintained, renewed, and revised. Excluded social forces, whose consent has not been won, whose interests have not been taken into account, form the basis of counter-movements, resistance, alternative strategies and visions . . . and the struggle over a hegemonic system starts anew. They constitute what Raymond Williams called "the emergent"— and are the reason why history is never closed but maintains an open horizon towards the future. —**STUART HALL,** "The Neoliberal Revolution"

CONTENTS

ACKNOWLEDGMENTS

I had thought this was going to be a short book. I had written an essay on "Security moms" and thought that I would just expand that into a few other directions and write a long essay on the topic of gender and security. But it turned out I had a lot to say and explore about US imperial power in the new century. Trained as a postcolonial studies scholar, but one who had become interested in the relation between postcolonial politics and transnational epistemologies and analytics, I thought US empire could be examined through a transnational lens that could critique the geopolitics of exceptionalism. Instead of a long essay, it's now a book that took almost a decade to write.

I've been fortunate over the years to have been part of many new paradigms that have come to decenter imperial knowledges and the racial and gendered hierarchies that prevented academic research on communities and identities resulting from colonial and imperial power. From colonial discourse analysis, to transnational feminist cultural studies, and then to critical security studies, examinations of racialized empire and militarism, and cultural politics—all these fields have been critical to the methods and subjects of my research. I've been privileged to work with colleagues and students who have changed fields and methods, though many of us still believe that there is more to be done. Many of these scholars are first- or second-generation immigrants, and scholars who have become diasporic, who have brought studies of European and American imperialisms to new directions through their critiques. The Cold War demarcations of areas, of North and South, are being undercut through a variety of practices of research and knowledge making. There is the joy and pleasure of seeing so many wonderful books and research projects that have contributed to my thinking and writing.

This project began when I was based at the University of California, Irvine, and was supported by researchers in both the women's studies department where I was appointed and the Critical Theory Institute that took on the challenge of thinking of security as a thematic project. My thanks to the faculty in both these groups. In women's studies, Jennifer Terry and Laura Hyun-yi Kang were my key interlocutors, along with Lilith Mahmud and Jeanne Scheper. I have great appreciation for David Theo Goldberg at the Critical Theory Institute for engaging with the project of thinking security within critical theory and cultural politics. My thanks at UCI also to Arturo Arias, Tom Boellstorf, Vinayak Chaturvedi, Susan Coutin, Jim Fuji, Doug Haynes, Ketu Katrak, Arlene Keizer, Rodrigo Lazo, Karen Leonard, Cecilia Lynch, Bill Maurer, Glen Mimura, Michael Montoya, the late wonderful Mark Poster, Jill Robbins, Kamal Sadiq, Annette Schlichter, Heidi Tinsman, Linda Vo, Mei Zhan. I was so fortunate to find a wonderful collaborator in Victoria Bernal at UCI, and she and I went on to work on NGOs and to collaborate in that exciting project. My UCI students were a key part of the UCI community and taught me so much; they inspire me and make me proud: Priya Shah, Neha Vora, Cindy Cheng, Randy Ontiveros, Donna Tong, Laura Knighton, Seo Young Park.

At Yale, I am fortunate enough to have colleagues who have been terrific scholars to think with. My thanks for comradeship and conversations to Elizabeth Alexander, Vanessa Agard-Jones, Jafari Allen, Melanie Boyd, Ned Blackhawk, Alicia Camacho, Jill Campbell, Hazel Carby, Geeta Chanda, Nayan Chanda, Michael Denning, Narges Erami, Joseph Fischel, Jackie Goldsby, David Grewal, Zareena Grewal, Kasturi Gupta, Margaret Homans, Matt Jacobsen, Amy Kapzynski, Greta Lafluer, Katie Lofton, Mary Lui, Karuna Mantena, Vida Maralani, Joanne Meyerowitz, Ali Miller, Steve Pitti, Birgit Rasmussen, Doug Rogers, K. Sivaramakrishnan, Maria Trumpler, Steven Wilkinson, Libby Wood. We lost Barny Bate from Yale and, later, from the world; he is much missed. My thanks to Rebecca Wexler for her keen eye and knowledge of legal terminologies and for sharing digital media wisdom. Thank you to Laura Wexler, who also read the manuscript despite her superbusy schedule. Deep appreciation to Craig Canfield, Maureen Gardner, and Linda Hase for support that enabled me to have time for research. And last but not least, my thanks to wonderful undergraduate students: Scott Hillier, Silia Fillipis, Rhiana Gunn-Wright, Michael Singleton, Mira Vale, Will Schlesinger, Dianne Lake, Jessica Newman, Joan Gass, and Yemurai Mangwendeza. My wonderful graduate students are inspiring and have taught me so much: Kaneesha Parsard, Najwa Mayer, Anusha Alles, Sahana Ghosh, Courtney Sato, Gavriel Cutipa-Zorn, Grace Ting, Tina Palivos, Dina Omar, Ryan Jobson, Juliet Nebolon, Tyler Rogers, Samar Al-Bulushi, Sasha Sabharwal, Jessica Newman, Fadila Habchi, Jenny Tang, Randa Tawil.

I am so lucky to have friends who read chapters and sections and gave me wonderful feedback, as well as so much else that is so important to survive in these institutions we work in. I cannot thank enough Caren Kaplan, Minoo Moallem, Jennifer Terry, Robyn Wiegman, Eric Smoodin, and Sherene Razack for their support of this project through the years. My grateful thanks to Surina Khan and Shahin Bayat, who are always ready for great conversation and discussion, whether about national politics (in many places), global conditions, or good food and wine. A special thank you goes to Liz Montegary, who sent me some great citations that became key texts for my argument. Thanks, Liz!

Elsewhere in many places I am fortunate to have these wonderful scholars and thinkers in my life: Attia Ahmad, Anjali Arondekar, Paul Amar, Srimati Basu, Tina Campt, Deb Cohler, Cathy Davidson, Karen Engle, Harjant Gill, Akhil Gupta, Janet Jacobsen, Amina Jamal, Lamia Karim, Mallika Kaur, Virinder Kalra, Melani Macalester, Arvind Mandair, Purnima Mankekar, Ghada Mahrouse, Liz Montegary, Mimi Nguyen, Geeta Patel, Kris Peterson, Ambra Pirri, Jyoti Puri, Tej Purewal, Parama Roy, Sandra Ponzanesi, Shirin Rai, Svati Shah, Nadera Shalhoub, Anu Sharma, Sima Shakhsari, Lesley Sharp, Ella Shohat, Bob Stam, Harleen Singh, Deborah Thomas, Alyssa Trotz, Toby Volkmann, and Neha Vora.

My thanks to audiences at UCLA, UC Davis, Wilfred Laurier University, University of Toronto, University of Waterloo, UT Austin, Rice University, University of Houston, University of Warwick, the Gender Institute at the London School of Economics, Northwestern University, Barnard College, Duke University, Clark University, Tufts University, Binghamton University, Birmingham University, University of Illinois, Urbana-Champaign, Purdue University, Lewis and Clark College, Punjab University, UC Irvine, Kenyon College, Texas Christian University, University of Michigan, Università degli Studi di Palermo, Casa Internationale della donna in Rome, Italy, Harvard University, Brown University, Texas A&M University, National Taiwan Normal University, Georgia State University, UC Berkeley, Columbia University, Trinity College, and University of Pennsylvania.

For research assistance, my thanks to Gavriel Cutipa-Zorn. Invaluable editorial assistance came from Cathy Hannabach, Jessica Newman, Mira

Vale, Genevieve Creedon, and Najwa Mayer. Special shout-out to Sonal Jessel, my daughter, for coming to my rescue in the copyediting stage!

Thank you to my wonderful readers at Duke University Press, who pushed me and supported the project in the most helpful ways. And at Duke University Press, Ken Wissoker has been such a great support. Ken's tireless efforts at the press have benefited all of us in expanding interdisciplinary and transnational gender studies in ways that have been invaluable to disseminating the research of so many wonderful scholars. Thanks also to Courtney Martin, Jade Brooks, and Maryam Arain for being such terrific editors. DUP has always been a home.

The Grewal and Jessel families have been such a great support, though we lost Walter Jessel, Cynthia Jessel, and Kyle Adams in the decade of the writing of this book. They are all so missed. Both Walter and Cynthia taught me so much about war, race, gender, and geopolitics; their love is always with me. Peggy Jessel, Robert Jessel and Lori Rosello, Vinnie and Anthony Jessel compose a small but close family that always gives loving support. My sister and her family have always been there for love and laughter: Kiran, Jaspal, Aneel, Rajneet, Sunny, and their partners and children. Maninder Grewal and Minty Grewal and their children, Gurmehar and Mankaran, including Jaspret and Tara, provide hospitality and wonderful company. Sukh Grewal and Paula Kavathas have been generous, kind, and loving through the years—providing food and fun, as well as passionate discussion. New Haven is always associated with you and has become a home because of you. Elena and Emily have been a joy to meet and converse with, keeping us all in touch with SF and the changes wrought by digital media. Getting to know Jasmit Rangr and Abby Dillon, and Sher, of course, has been one of the pleasures of the East Coast. I am fortunate in having so many wonderful aunts and uncles, cousins, and nieces and nephews who are great fun to be with, though often mystified by my work. The love and support of my late parents, Mehar Singh and Tej Kaur, are always with me.

I dedicate this book to Alfred, Kirin, and Sonal, the three Jessels who make life worthwhile and joyful. All three of you are the light of my life—well, maybe three lights. You inspire me to keep trying to live up to you.

An early version of chapter 2 was published as "American Humanitarian Citizenship," in *Gender, Globalization and Violence: Postcolonial Conflict Zones*, ed. Sandra Ponzanesi (New York: Routledge, 2014). A short version of chapter 4 appeared as "'Security Moms' in Early 21st Century USA: The Gender of Security in Neoliberalism," *Women's Studies Quarterly* 36, nos. 1–2

(2006). It was reprinted in an anthology entitled *The Global and the Intimate,* ed. Geraldine Pratt (New York: Columbia University Press, 2012). An excerpt from the coda appeared as "Racial Sovereignty and 'Shooter' Violence: Oak Creek Massacre, Normative Citizenship and the State," *Sikh Formations* 9 (September 2013): 187–97.

My thanks also to Steve Bell for permission to use his brilliant and evocative cartoon.

INTRODUCTION. Exceptional Citizens?

Saving and Surveilling in Advanced Neoliberal Times

> If you see something, say something.
> —*Sign created and sponsored by the*
> *Department of Homeland Security after 9/11*

> You see a girl who could do anything.
> He sees a girl he can force to do anything.
> STOPSEXTRAFFICKINGINTL.COM
> —*Sign at Tennessee rest stop, starting 2014*

How might we theorize a state that sponsors and displays both of these signs?[1] One asks individuals to be responsible for surveillance and to work for the security of state and empire. The other asks them to surveil fellow travelers to rescue victims of "trafficking."[2] This book argues that these two seemingly divergent modes of participation reveal the intertwining and co-construction of citizen-subjects of welfare and militarization in the context of American imperial power within a neoliberal era. These two modes of power—surveillance and saving—in this new century construct citizens as securitized subjects within the United States, producing "exceptional citizens" who work to save the "exceptional nation." What I call the "advanced" phase of neoliberalism has made visible insecurities concerning the waning power of the US global empire that results in protests, some progressive and some revanchist, by these exceptional citizens.

The United States, under both neoliberal and imperial policies, can be understood through the "state effect" of appearing as a security state, operating through securitization as a mode of power over its populations. Its liberalism has long been contested because of its history of what Patrick Wolfe called settler colonialism and the continuing legacy of racism.[3] It cannot be seen as a welfare or a liberal state because its remit has turned to maintaining state security in the context of ongoing wars.[4] By using terms such as "securitization" and "security state," I show how constructs of security have come to dominate everyday life in the US imperial state.[5] Relations are changing between the state and its citizens: between individuals, communities, and families; and between the state, corporations, and individuals.[6] A state of security as permanent emergency and endless war has become the hegemonic logic of governance of this neoliberal security state. Security has become the rationale for militarized cultures of surveillance and protection that lead to insecurities, threats and fears, which work at material, affective and embodied levels. Security is also a cause and effect not just of the relations of the United States with the world, but also of neoliberal policies that have contributed to the inequalities that create insecurity throughout the world, including in the United States itself.[7] In response to these insecurities of the new century, private individuals who see themselves as normative citizens become empowered to take responsibility for maintaining the imperial security state.[8] These individuals, produced as responsible and self-improving and thus products of neoliberal self-empowerment regimes, hope to repair the effects of imperial and neoliberal policies and thereby save the security state. Yet however much they try, their attempts often end in failure, thus producing more insecurity. This shuttle between security and insecurity marks the exceptional citizens of the US security state.

Neoliberal policies were implemented during the 1970s in the so-called developing world—that is, the regions formerly colonized by Europe—by the International Monetary Fund and the World Bank, which demanded that countries in debt from the rise in the price of oil in the 1970s repay their debts by slashing their welfare budgets. Many countries had to comply, and it was often the case that the cuts came from reducing welfare to the poorest of inhabitants. Called "The Washington Consensus," these policies were later jointly championed by UK Prime Minister Margaret Thatcher and US President Ronald Reagan in the 1980s, and led to similar reductions to welfare in both countries. These policies included greater belief in the work of the market to address all social issues, the reduction of welfare, the privatization of public goods, and the language of efficiency and productivity in everyday life. David Harvey describes neoliberalism as the acceptance of the idea that "human well-being can be advanced by liberating individual entrepreneurial freedoms and skills within an institutional framework characterized by strong private property rights, free markets and free trade."[9] While Harvey's emphasis lies on the market logics that are important for neoliberal policies, Nikolas Rose calls the production of an entrepreneurial self an important feature of "advanced liberalism."[10] Following Michel Foucault's theorization of the crisis of the liberal state and economism at the end of the twentieth century, Rose argues that the self-making, self-marketing, and self-improving subject is characteristic of this new phase in Western liberal democracies that are unable (or unwilling) to provide welfare to all. While considering the impact of economic policies across the globe as described by Harvey, I rely on Rose's analysis to suggest that neoliberalism also altered subjectivities; the exceptional American citizen trying to save the security state is the product of the self-empowerment regime that is central to neoliberalism in the United States.

While David Harvey, Michael Hardt, and Antonio Negri argue that neoliberalism is a global phenomenon, others note that it manifests in specific localized/national or transnational projects.[11] For instance, John and Jean Comaroff suggest the specificity of what they call "millennial capitalism" in South Africa is one example of neoliberalism being globally connected, but also having particular regional specificities.[12] Following this focus on specificities, I argue in this book that the specificity of American neoliberalism is connected to its military projects, the emergence of its Christian and humanitarian citizenship, and the rearticulation of its exceptionalism.

While theories of neoliberalism have suggested the ideologies that construct neoliberal policies were fashioned by international organizations and economists in the United States, each region and state has come to have its own history of neoliberalism, with particular impacts and differences. After many decades, we see an "advanced stage" that is also specific to each location, a stage that becomes the result of how neoliberalism manifested itself in its particularities. This "advanced" stage captures how decades of neoliberal policies have altered the social and created problems that we see across the world. In the United States, neoliberalism's "advanced" stage appears in a context that is not just economic, but incorporates both capitalism's and liberalism's late modern forms. Thus it includes wars without end, environmental and social insecurities, proliferating racial and gendered differences generated by the conjoining of militarism and capitalism. It is also manifest in the naturalization of the neoliberal individual as exceptional citizen, one who is shaped not simply by capitalism but also by a variety of social and political formations and affiliations that construct individuals, communities, nationalisms. The shift to an "advanced" form becomes visible in the emergence of contradictions and protests to neoliberalism, as well as the management of these by neoliberal subjects, militarized power, and authority. Protests find openings and possibilities in the contradictions between transnational capital and the imperial state; between neoliberal polices and imperial state powers; and between neoliberal and securitized citizen-subjects within the complex history of American exceptionalism.

Protests are not limited to the United States either. They are also globally disparate, as neoliberal policies and divergent histories contribute differentially to particular regional and national politics and powers. Just as neoliberal policies are nationally and culturally specific, protests are also specific—though globally they can collaborate, sustain each other, or clash. Not all protests take the form of a particular racial or class formation nor a religious, gendered, sexual, or racial identity. Not all are progressive, and they can be revolutionary or revanchist in heterogeneous ways, catalyzed by local and transnational events and connections, and many shift over time according to the stresses and possibilities that protestors encounter.

Protests in the United States come from concerns over waning empire, loss of racial sovereignty among whites, and economic issues as well as social movements based on race, gender, and sexuality. Imperial wars have led to declines in US global power, and neoliberal policies have shifted power from state to private individuals (including private corporations) and created economic inequalities. "Exceptional citizens" are a result of such declines. Naturalized as entrepreneurial and aspirational but also fearful and insecure, they believe that they can do more than the state and save the empire and the world. Yet they are concerned about everyday safety and security and thus turn to the security state for protection. These citizens, insecure and imperial, wish to access and maintain the privileges of whiteness to become exceptional and sovereign. Those who pass for white, or try to do so,[13] seek a strong military state yet are historically suspicious about state power. They thus both collaborate and come into conflict with the state in the work of surveillance and security.

In the United States, these decades of neoliberal policies have altered the state and its relation to people, resulting in changes in the nature of political sovereignty. While some scholars argue that neoliberalism has waned,[14] this book argues that, on the contrary, a more "advanced" stage enables its contradictions to be resolved by neoliberal and militarized means, that is, through the work of securitized, exceptional citizens. As contradictions have emerged between imperial state power and deeply unequal individuals, states, and cities, what becomes visible are the myriad insecurities that individuals must manage in order to become normative, exceptional citizens of the US empire. "Advanced neoliberalism" marks both the specificities of this stage of neoliberalism in this new century as well as its shifting mode of power in so-called advanced liberal democracies.[15] If neoliberalism's characteristics include self-responsible and self-improving citizens and the move from welfare to security, the characteristics of its advanced form include the emergence and management of protests as well as the visibility of insecurities of imperial power. Divisions between public and private become difficult to sustain, as sovereignty is claimed by white male power and privilege, and as corporations carry out the work of the military and as nongovernmental organizations take over the welfare function of the state. These changes have weakened ties between states and citizens that were enabled by welfare, so that the security state becomes a means to connect citizens to the state through militarization,[16] a project that often goes awry, or leads to consequences that create further insecurity. To manage protests, subjects are securitized in neoliberal ways—that is, made fearful through mediated panics about external threats from immigrants and terrorists as the causes of insecurity—and they take responsibility for security. These insecurities continue to try to repress the rebellious consequences of neoliberal policies, as much as they continue to generate its insurrections.

Such citizen-subjects who work to save the security state comprise individuals (or corporate entities) acting as both agents and vehicles of humanitarian welfare and surveillance, hoping to reassert the legitimacy of the United States as a model of a liberal, capitalist democracy. These entities undertake this work as imperial subjects: first, in deciding who should be improved, in claiming to make these improvements, and in making others into subjects of neoliberal empire; and second, in enabling and incorporating the practices of security through surveillance into the changing norms of family, consumer, and citizen. Transnational corporations are also increasingly claiming their own sovereignty, as they become endowed with some of the sovereign rights of citizens.[17] In addition, because a small transnational capitalist class also often governs corporations, the alliances of transnational corporations go beyond the United States. Neoliberalism's transnational scope produces contradictions, banality, and crises.

Since the US empire is not new, neither are its imperial subjects—including its white, masculine sovereignties—nor its militarisms.[18] US surveillance regimes can trace a history from nineteenth- and twentieth-century imperial projects in the Philippines.[19] Yet some subjects and modes of what has come to be called "securitization" by the neoliberal state are shifting because the endless war on terror, the failures of US invasions in the Middle East, and a changing politics of race, class, sexuality and religion have produced moral panics as well as economic precarities, adding to histories of racialization and expulsion from citizenship. There are concerns about American power and security, as well as protests against the reduction of welfare and the security state from what is seen as a past of plenty and prosperity, even if this was not uniformly available to all citizens or even available for long periods of time.[20] The resolution of these tensions and contradictions emerges as humanitarianisms and exceptional citizens struggle to save the security state.

In this book, I examine the contradictions of neoliberal empire in the United States through several securitized subjects: the "security mom" who works to privatize state security within the heteronormative and white middle-class family through parental and community surveillance; the "humanitarian," often white but including others aspiring to exceptionalism, who makes individual and consumer choices about who should get welfare and who should not in the hope that individual efforts can remedy the depredations of globalization and American racial/colonial histories; the "security feminist" who takes on the work of counterterrorism and counterinsurgency as a project of gendered empowerment to protect the security state; and the "shooter" who embodies the white, male exceptional citizen to whom sovereignty is dispersed so that he can use violence in the protection of the American empire. These figures are often struggling, tragic, or violent, and have become normative citizen-subjects of the United States as a neoliberal, imperial, security state.[21]

American Exceptionalism and Postcolonial Theories

For many who live in the United States and outside it, the history of the United States and of its geopolitics (as well as its expansion in North America) is not about claims of civilizational superiority or moral authority. Many in the United States and around the world have few illusions about the moral claims made by the US nation-state. They have long challenged its legitimacy as a proponent of freedom and democracy given its history of wars and colonialism, of being a racial settler state, and of supporting violent dictatorships in Latin America during the Cold War. More recently, many in the United States seem concerned with its waning power, and with the insecurities engendered by such loss.[22] Their concern is that the United States has lost the stature that enabled its claim of geopolitical and national exceptionalism after the Cold War.

Postcolonial theories of the state emphasize the differential power of European and American states that make claims to normative notions of liberal democracy. They critique the ability of Europe and North America to adjudicate which states are "failed" and which are successful, which are "civilized" and which are not, which are modern and which are traditional.[23] Postcolonial theories also emphasize differences between European or US imperial states and postcolonial states, even as a transnational analysis can break down the grounds of hierarchical (rather than cultural or historical) difference, especially undercutting claims of superiority and hierarchy made on behalf of the "West." Postcolonial theory has needed theories of transnationalism to examine how the making of empire within and outside are connected, and to reveal the contradictions and emptiness of claims of liberal equality in the United States.[24]

Jean and John Comaroff argue that we need a "Theory from the South," deterritorializing the concept of the "south" away from the regional demarcation of the "Global South" to understand the forms of capitalism and state power that we see globally. Recognition of the "South," its forms of power, and governance that are now the norm, decenters the norm of the modern, liberal Western state and its assertions of liberal democracy.[25] Such theories suggest that the United States and other Western countries are now following the forms of state, governance, and authority that prevail in the regions where imperial projects and policies in tandem with neoliberal capitalism have been implemented for over four decades. For it is in the Global South where emergent nationalisms, militancies, and violence appeared in the late twentieth century. "Terrorism" against the state, as many insurgencies were called, also emerged in several regions of the Global South (i.e., India, Sri Lanka, Colombia, Peru, Indonesia, Israel, and the Philippines), providing laws and security expertise for counterinsurgency campaigns by states.[26] The Global South was the laboratory of the wars against state power,[27] as well as the site for the implementation of neoliberal policies. But it was not only the Global South that became the laboratory of neoliberalism, but also many regions within the United States and Europe, where elites could extract profits while reducing welfare or use race to extract labor and profits. These were regions where the imperial state and the racial state were operating in conjoined ways producing what appeared as a security state for many minority populations.

While the notion of the "South" can highlight the connections between state practices within and outside US borders, it is nevertheless important to make some distinctions between the United States and regions outside it, as much as it is important to reveal the racialized discrepancies between US geopolitics and national politics. Geopolitics can be a site where contradictions of US power have become visible. As an imperial state, the United States and its inequities reveal it to be—as Achille Mbembe suggests of the postcolony—banal in its production of violence and inequalities as well as in the limits of its liberalism and welfare.[28] While the United States is different in its constant claim of superiority and power, it is similar to so many other global regions in its insecurity and burgeoning inequalities. Thus, the US nation-state can be understood as unexceptional despite its claims of national exceptionalism since, like so many states in the Global South, it has emerged as a security state rather than a liberal, welfare state with regard to its own populations. There are, however, limits to this equivalence. The insurgencies in the Global South, even if they were called "militancies" or "terrorism," did not have the impact that was the result of what was called terrorism in the empire. The US imperial state is different in scale and in the nature of its exceptionalism, rather than exceptional or superior from the postcolonial state. Its difference is that its claims the right to use violence globally while producing itself as normative and liberal, despite its waning power globally and its illiberalism within. Despite this difference, however, it also now seems unable to control geopolitics, or to assert itself as morally superior, or to gain legitimacy by providing welfare to its own populations.

The claim of American exceptionalism has been based on both a history of national formation within an anti-imperial teleology, and the imperial power to use violence.[29] Making visible this ideology requires consideration both of the historical construction of national exceptionalism and of the political concepts of sovereignty and the modern state. Amy Kaplan has argued that the idea of American exceptionalism has been understood as a claim to anti-colonial origins that erases viewing the United States as empire. She suggests that exceptionalism is a denial that produces America as a self-generating and autonomous nation-state that leaves out the ways that a history of American empire and imperialism has continuities with European colonialism.[30] As Jasbir Puar argues, Kaplan's critique of exceptionalism engages usefully with an understanding of the geopolitics of sexuality and American exceptionalism through the work of Giorgio Agamben and Carl Schmitt. These theories of the state and sovereignty as exception lay bare the violence of the state that is racial, gendered, and sexualized.[31] Such an engagement can usefully examine how United States as empire comes to appear as uniquely progressive by absorbing social movements such as those by US-based LGBT communities to create an emergent homonationalism.[32]

It is not just in the making of nationalism, but in what has been ideologically constructed as a security state that we can diagnose the contradictions of the claim of US exceptionalism. In previous work, I have argued that it is in the juxtaposition of necropolitics and geopolitics, the "interrelation between the sovereign right to kill and the right to rescue" that constitutes modes of state power at the end of the twentieth century.[33] This juxtaposition has particular salience for American exceptionalism. The United States has acted as a globally sovereign actor, able to suspend international law while insisting it applies only to Other (non-European, for the most part) nations, groups, or individuals. Conservative arguments supporting America's national exceptionalism rely on ideas of Western liberalism and humanism as superior characteristics of the United States,[34] or on the ideology of a nation of migrants, class mobility, and the "American dream." At the same time, critical scholarly studies have examined American exceptionalism as national fantasy,[35] where national exceptionalism enables war and violence. All of these approaches render liberalism as either strategic or a mode of power, as the US empire that calls itself a liberal democracy is able to wage war and to violate the sovereignty of other states, setting itself up as moral arbiter and police as well as proponent of freedom, democracy, and the capitalist "American Dream."[36]

Theories of US exceptionalism also have considered the problems of divergent effects of such claims. In a book of essays published in 1997, Seymour Martin Lipset argued that American exceptionalism stemmed from Alexis de Tocqueville's conceptualization of America, and from the position of the United States as a country born out of revolution. According to Lipset, the characteristics of US exceptionalism include liberty, egalitarianism, individuality, populism, and laissez-faire capitalism.[37] Yet he argued that the antielitist, populist, and individualist aspects of this exceptionalism can lead to problems of populism, some of which have become visible over the decades and in the new century. As he very presciently observed, while elite forms of power continue to shape policy, populist elements continue to challenge notions of liberal democracy creating forms of violence that undercut US geopolitical clout.

Both elites and nonelites have become concerned with America's waning power, though for different agendas and reasons. David Bromwich has argued that US exceptionalism has changed, becoming much more about the claim of being "the greatest country in the world," defending peace and democracy globally, but also being unaccountable to anyone. He believes that exceptionalism has led to moral decline.[38] While there are many who would contest the claim of the United States to the moral high ground that Bromwich's critique implicitly relies upon, his challenge that the claim of exceptionalism is a moral hazard that produces a lack of accountability is useful. It helps in understanding the US mode of empire as including a moral aspect. This moral aspect appears in the will to rescue, to save, to become humanitarians, or to wage "just war." It is this aspect that continues to be powerful in producing securitized subjects who wish to become global humanitarians, even when faced with the impacts of the neoliberal policies and wars of the United States. It is also a "moral" aspect that has been absorbed into the formation of the neoliberal entrepreneurial subject within what Didier Fassin and Mariella Pandolfi have called a "moral economy."[39] This moral striving leads exceptional citizens to continue to strive to improve themselves and others, even though such efforts may appear to be empty or futile.

Surveilling, Securitization, and the Security State

Over the last few years, journalists have revealed the extent to which the US state surveilled its citizens, especially those, such as Muslims, who are now figured as racialized national security threats.[40] This surveillance exists alongside continuing racial profiling of South Asian Muslims and those of Middle Eastern descent, as well as Latinos and African Americans; such profiling has become a method of crime and "terror" prevention.[41] Corporations also participate in surveillance by gathering consumer data, producing profiles, and predicting consumer behavior and habits.[42] Consumer data as well as political behavior and actions online that become political data are commodities that are for sale, increasing the likelihood of more surveillance by digital technology companies.[43] There is often a close relation between corporations and state security projects, as states and corporations work on surveillance either in partnership, separately, or even antagonistically. In addition, because neoliberalism often blurs divisions between public and private entities, corporations are increasingly endowed with the rights of persons. Entities and groups that claim to be outside of the state, such as NGOs, can both depend on the state and claim to be outside of it.[44] One widely noted example of the collaboration between public and private entities is the US government's privatization of state security through its use of private corporations in the invasions of Iraq and Afghanistan.[45] It is this fuzziness between public and private power through which sovereignty is shared, making some persons more secure because of power given to them and some insecure (or even targets of racial violence) because of the power exercised by these non-state sovereignties. Both race and gender are key determinants of sovereignty or lack thereof, as race emerges to enable white citizens to governmentalize security, leading to criminalizing nonwhite groups in old and new ways.[46] New technologies of profiling emerge within legal, material, and political domains that engage with the political economy of security and insecurity.

Neoliberalism relies on racial, religious, and gender exclusions as much as did liberalism. Dispersing sovereignty to particular authoritarian white masculinities and, to a lesser extent, femininities,[47] these racialized and gendered subjects feel empowered and responsible in emergent ways in this century. Some are empowered by a sovereignty given to them to claim historically racialized white power for groups not always seen as white, while others bring together race and gender to create new imperial feminisms. While some forms of racialized exclusions (such as immigration laws) seem to continue, Muslims, Arabs, and South Asians are more visibly racialized as dangerous Others who are left out even from becoming neoliberal citizens.[48] African Americans, Latinos, and Native peoples continue to be targets of a carceral state that is also part of the security state.[49] White, imperial sovereignties constitute the "soft" and "hard power" of military force, sometimes as humanitarianism and other times as police.[50] In particular, what is visible in the new century is that this "soft power" is inextricable from the "hard power" of the military. Military and consumer technologies have long been codependent, and military technologies continue to reformulate everyday life in new ways.[51] In particular, what is called the "carceral state" is constructed through military technologies to enact forms of racialized power.[52] Racial profiling and consumer profiling are both enabled by new technologies that allow public and private organizations to collect personal data.[53] State welfare agencies, banks, and retail companies all use digital technologies to collect biometric, location, DNA, consumption, Internet, and face-recognition data. Data-mining tools grow ever more sophisticated and fine tuned, though it is unclear whether they can achieve the sophisticated profiling their marketers claim.[54]

In the context of twenty-first-century US empire, what Armand Mattelart calls "the techno-security paradigm" is focused on "terrorism," a deliberately vague concept that allows violence and is not accountable to liberal constitutional ideals. Mattelart argues that the war on terror was mobilized by collaborations among "the entire information and technology complex."[55] Shadowy government agencies and private corporations wage "network-centric" cyberwar,[56] using information technology to create geopolitical advantage, with the support of nontechnological mechanisms such as state antiterror laws that enforce and popularize surveillance and secrecy technologies. The state and its exceptional subjects use these new technologies to mobilize racialized and Orientalist ideologies.[57]

In the name of enhancing personal and state security, the US government, the technology industry, and other corporations manage and proliferate risks and fears to create ever more surveillance. Internet and communication technology growth is fueled by the promise of accurate and effective profiling—and this is part of the long history of all technology. Caren Kaplan has shown how air-power technology industries have long relied on such claims of "precision bombing" while naming their targets as "collateral damage."[58] When the "profile" of a consumer, criminal, citizen, or terrorist is dynamic—created out of shifting information flows and racialized notions of security and fear—it is nothing but aporetic. Profiling does not work through accuracy but rather through its broad racial effects that are terroristic; that is, profiling itself produces terror for those it catches in its security net, and those it catches are a broad group identified by religious, gendered, and racial characteristics produced by histories of racialized imperialism. In the continued use of race and colonial regimes of Orientalism, new surveillance technologies rely on older racial and colonial ideologies embedded in Western visual histories.

One result of these twenty-first-century US surveillance practices is that the term "security" has come to index heterogeneous and unstable state, social, and economic powers, through blurred distinctions between individuals, corporations, the state, public entities, and private entities. It is precisely the transfer of technology from military to ordinary, everyday life that enables the duplicity of the term "security" for the state and for individuals; this creates the state effect of fluidity between individual, personal ideas of home, safety, and protection, as well as between those interests and national threats and state security. Security traffics in the dynamism of affect across family, home, safety and national security, in which differences can be highlighted or dissolved at different times and places.

Security can refer to welfare and militarization, and to safety and violence. It can refer to individual and biological processes of welfare and biopolitics that in the US context are based on biometrics, pathologization of new racial formations, old and new Orientalisms, and widespread surveillance. These neoliberal securitizations have, since the 1970s, supported what some scholars argue is an authoritarian populism that criminalizes on the basis of race, class, gender and religion.[59] But it can also refer to the demands made on the state for safety and protection that it cannot ensure, and which it often refuses to ensure. Security works affectively through the promise of the safety of home and of nation, but also enables the powers of protection claimed by patriarchies, fraternities, and nationalisms that work through violence. Security enables a promise of welfare that the state cannot fulfill, not because it is unable to but because its neoliberal alliances prevent it from doing so. This means that neoliberalisms alter the relations between citizens, nations, and states by shifting power and sovereignty to corporations and individuals at national and transnational scales. Such shifts create problems of state legitimacy, and have come to produce protests and frictions that mark the era of advanced liberalism.

Citizenship

US imperial insecurities within advanced neoliberalism mean that citizenship itself has shifted, as rights have been replaced by humanitarianism, and social security by state security. Citizenship becomes especially fraught for many protesting the impacts of war and inequality, especially those who will not or cannot pass for white or who are able to access its privileges and are not seen as normative Americans. Sherene Razack argues that Muslims have been cast out from US liberal citizenship through their racialization.[60] I would qualify this argument by saying that they are cast out not from liberal citizenship, but from neoliberal citizenship. What is foreclosed for Muslims in the decade since 9/11 in the contemporary United States is even the opportunity to become the exception, neoliberal economic citizen-subject of rational, flexible, and self-making practices, who makes proper investments in oneself through productive consumption and who takes responsibility for saving the security state.

In my last book, *Transnational America*, I argued that citizenship is no longer tied to liberal rights, but has become defined through technological, consumerist, and transnational modes. I rejected the notion of "global citizenship" (for its history of Western travel and empire), and showed the multiple notions of "belonging" as citizenship, suggesting that when differential mobilities shape the lives of millions around the world, our relations to place and identity become unstable and malleable.[61] In this book, I continue the discussion of the shift in liberal citizenship, arguing that under neoliberalism, rights shift as well, especially in relation to sovereignty and identity. Citizens' rights have changed as the work of welfare moves to corporations and NGOS, dissolving some ties between people and the state. These rights have become replaced by charity and privatized giving, even as the demands for welfare continue.[62] Yet rights and citizenship continue to be important, especially given the burgeoning numbers of stateless people in the new century and especially since fewer people can claim them.

Security has moved from the protection from adversities through welfare and state support to militarized security, aggrandizing the powers of the state. Yet demands for welfare and state support continue from those who see themselves as entitled exceptional citizens, though these may not be demands for rights but for special access to entitlements over others. As neoliberalism has become deeply entrenched, more and more of the population has been enlisted for humanitarian work, and more and more institutions have come to support it. In the process, poor women, children, people of color, and immigrants find it increasingly difficult to access their rights (not just to welfare but also to proper wages and protections). Yet in the phase of advanced neoliberalism, protests for rights become instead a rationale for authority and repression. Such repressions occur not just by the state but also through disparate sovereignties created by race, religion, class, and gender. This terrain of citizenship in the US security state is formed by exclusions created by new laws against terrorism, denial of citizenship to many millions, including the incarcerated, immigrants, and migrants who are Muslim or Latino, threats by powerful white neoconservative activists, and violence by antigovernment vigilantes, as well as vigorous social movements that protest violence and dispossession. What continue are also the demands for expertise and labor from the global economy and transnational corporations, though these have come to also generate protests from working-class communities in the United States. As the United States continues to wage imperial war and extract profits, populations from those targeted regions demand asylum, but most are denied entry because of opposition from groups identifying as white who scapegoat immigrants and refugees as they realize the repercussions of the waning geopolitical power of the United States.

Two seemingly contradictory ideas emerge in this new citizenship configuration: first, neoliberal authority is based on the reconfiguration of citizen-subjects by the use of state security apparatuses such as police, militarized cultures of surveillance, and carceral public and private institutions; and second, sovereignty is both devolved and still tied to the state. Yet this situation is not paradoxical. Because the notion of sovereignty has been long shared by state and citizen through the long history of the Westphalian state,[63] these notions of citizenship are not altogether new, though the globalizations of the twentieth century—those that have disempowered working classes in the United States or produced large migrations—have created new tensions. Thomas Ilgen argues that "global forces, both political and economic, pry open states and their societies in ways that complicate the task of national governance and reduce its effectiveness," resulting in a "multilayered structure of governance."[64] While Ilgen is correct in this analysis that the state has not always had a monopoly on sovereignty, his claim that these forces also "enable sub-national authorities to govern more responsibly and effectively" does not apply to many countries in the world where authoritarian regimes repress their citizens in numerous ways.[65] Brenda Chalfin, for instance, has shown that in the case of neoliberal Ghana, state sovereignty is both segmented and enhanced, and Aihwa Ong has argued for the "graduated sovereignty" available under flexible neoliberal capitalism. Ong suggests that Asian political sovereignty is both specific and flexible, in a trajectory quite different from that in the United States.[66]

In another approach to the dispersal of sovereignty, Thomas Blom Hansen and Finn Stepputat delink the assumed connection between sovereignty and territory, showing each of these as constructs of the state.[67] Their research is useful to my project, since they examine sovereignty as exercised through violence over bodies, rather than simply by control over territories. Finn and Stepputat point out that European state violence was not exceptional, as Carl Schmitt suggests, and they claim that "colonial sovereignty remained a naked version of modern sovereign power,"[68] as Achille Mbembe has also argued.[69] They suggest that postcolonial sovereignty—expressed in the Global South by many states—is consequently "fragile, eroding and contested,"[70] in part because other sovereignties have emerged, including the "economic citizenship" that Saskia Sassen suggests is linked to "global economic actors."[71] Although Hansen and Stepputat's analysis focuses on postcolonial states, rather than on the colonial ones, their insights into violence are also applicable to the United States in its national politics, suggesting that the US empire is not exceptional, having some residues from European colonial histories, including its Orientalisms and racial formations.

Their analysis of the British colonial context also applies to US empire, as territory becomes spectacle while sovereign power is exercised through threats and violence in distant regions where the United States has waged wars in pursuit of capital or geopolitical power. In US history, sovereignty has not been given to all citizens, because of the history of race, patriarchy, settler colonialism, and slavery; it has been a central aspect of white power, captured by populist and authoritarian elements in US culture, such as those males claiming whiteness who have been given the ability to use violence for control of nonwhite bodies. This white racial sovereignty continues to have power over other groups in the new century; for instance, the ability of white males to amass weapons and to use them with impunity is protected by interpretations of the Second Amendment of the US Constitution. What we can conclude is that both neoliberalism and the war on terror have added emergent characteristics to this dispersal of sovereignty as it constructs the exceptional citizens of the United States in this new century.

The Security State

Scholars suggest that the US welfare state peaked by the 1970s and that economic stagnation proliferated in North America and Western European countries by the 1980s.[72] How much this decline can be attributed to neoliberal policies is an important question. While some scholars suggest that neoliberalism is all powerful and has the ability to incorporate into its logic all sorts of differences and oppositions, others argue that neoliberalism's power is waning and power is shifting to other security projects. In his analysis of the relation between security and sexuality, Paul Amar argues that neoliberal governance has reduced the Global North's power and that governance is now being replaced by a humanitarian project of human security.[73] Amar reveals how powerful states construct human security laboratories around sexualized and gendered subjects who need saving or who wish to do the saving. This gendering and sexualizing of insecurity asks for a more textured analysis of the relation between neoliberalism, militarized security, and the politics of protest around sexuality and gender. While Amar is correct in his claim about reduced superpower exceptionalism, I argue that US neoliberalism in this advanced phase is being *enabled* (not replaced) by humanitarian governance, since it is precisely through the production of insecurity at individual and state scales that US neoliberalism requires humanitarian governance. To counter protests created by insecurities, twenty-first-century US humanitarian governance requires security through policing and military intervention, as well as the support of its exceptional citizens. Following Amar's focus on security and authority, I consider that the twenty-first-century US security state becomes visible as a set of racialized, classed, religious, and gendered institutions that use authority and violence to wage war and use neoliberal policies to benefit privileged groups. The state thus comes to appear—as the state effect theories suggest—as empire not just through military or global policing but also through "soft power," exercised transnationally by particular sets of subjects and processes that gain traction because of histories of white racial, masculinized sovereignty.[74]

The contemporary proliferation of authoritarianism, technologized mass surveillance, counterinsurgency policing, and militarization of everyday life has produced a security state that is quite different from the declaration of state emergency referred to as the "state of security," which authorizes the state to declare war and to use violence in the name of protection.[75] Scholarly work on the security state follows three main approaches. In one approach— relying on Stuart Hall and Raymond Williams's reading of Karl Marx, Louis Althusser, and Antonio Gramsci—the state is controlled by the hegemonic capitalist ruling class, predominantly white in Europe and North America. In their seminal book on neoliberalism's emergence in Britain of the 1970s, Stuart Hall et al. argue that the neoliberal state tends toward an authoritarian populism.[76] Public/private collaboration on behalf of capital require police, creating an authoritarianism that relies on racism, masculinity, and patriarchy even as it allows some groups of women, especially those considered white, to be empowered. This approach is extremely useful in understanding the legacies of racism, gender, sexuality, and class. However, it does not distinguish between different capitalist classes, nor does it explain how contemporary imperial states work geopolitically to adjudicate the states labeled "failed" or "developing." Theories of hegemony and neoliberalism also need to be modified (as Hall later did)[77] toward inclusion of postcolonial, feminist, and race theorists who focus on the gendered and racialized nature of these elites and states formed under colonialism as well as the ways that capitalist oligarchies are also patriarchies.

In a feminist approach to the security state, Iris Marion Young, for instance, argues that the security state has a "patriarchal logic": "The role of the masculine protector puts those protected, paradigmatically women and children, in a subordinate position of dependence and obedience," and they, then, come to "occupy a subordinate status like that of women in the patriarchal household." She sees the security state as having "a more authoritarian and paternalistic state power, which gets its support partly from the unity a threat produces and our gratitude for protection," while "it legitimates authoritarian power over citizens internally" and "justifies aggressive war outside."[78] Young separates "dominative masculinity" from "protective masculinity," arguing against Carole Pateman's more essentialized and heteronormative versions of women and of patriarchy that sees all women as belonging to the private sphere of the patriarchal family.[79] Yet, Young's analysis of a Hobbesian Leviathan-like security state, while useful in the analysis of the production of fear and insecurity, leaves out the geopolitics of differentiating states. It also disregards gender as intersectional, leaving aside the ways that notions of dominative and protective masculinity are differentiated *also* by race in the United States. In a geopolitical context, differential state trajectories and aspirations separate the colonial state from the postcolonial as well as the imperial state from the states that it controls and invades. Furthermore, the relation between colonialism and capitalism produces different sorts of masculinities and patriarchies, based on culture and histories of empire.

Understanding such hegemonic masculinities as articulated with race, religion, and class reveals the security state and its patriarchal authority as contingent and shifting, and its relation with global capital as transnational. Scholars deploying the second scholarly approach to the security state use Michel Foucault's theory of governmentality and state effect, theorizing securitization as incorporating state subjects in the governance project. For Foucault, security is a mode of liberal power. Colin Gordon has argued that for Foucault, even liberalism becomes an "effective practice of security" that is the "political method" of modern governmental rationality.[80] For Foucault, the state is made up of diverse governance practices, many of which go awry or do not reach their goals. Furthermore, Foucault theorizes the state as a "state effect," due to its heterogeneity and diversity of practices. This "state effect" approach accounts for the ways that security and insecurity concerns produce the state as a node of power, which is both feared and desired. As Thomas Biebricher and Frieder Vogelmann argue, Foucault's focus on governmentality explains how the state comes to be perceived in a particular way in a given period, "under what conditions, and in what form the state began to be projected, programmed, and developed . . . at what moment it became an object of knowledge and analysis . . . at what point it began to be called for, desired, coveted, feared, rejected, loved and hated."[81] While Foucault does not contend with state imperial projects, theories of governmentality have become useful in the context of neoliberal empire. For instance, Miguel de Larringa and Marc G. Doucet suggest that security has been governmentalized and encompasses not simply military defense but also new political, economic, and social spaces and processes.[82]

The contemporary neoliberal state requires a Foucauldian, Gramscian, critical race, and feminist approach, which explains the forms of equality, elitism, and power that have become visible—especially the making of patriarchal oligarchs (a masculinized and classed project) and powerful white masculinities, including the "homonationalisms" that Jasbir Puar has critiqued.[83] Many scholars—especially those studying race, gender, sexuality and empire through cultural practices or local social movements—are attentive to power and inequality. For instance, Hugh Gusterson and Catherine Besteman reveal that the emphasis on security has enabled power and wealth to be concentrated in the hands of the wealthiest Americans, leading to economic and political precariousness and the loss of civil liberties for many.[84] Jennifer Terry shows how war becomes governmentalized in medical research through war funding and war injuries.[85] What is especially useful about the Foucauldian approach is that it helps to understand how such inequalities make subjects who do not belong to ruling classes but who governmentalize the state and its powers. Foucault's idea of "state effect" also critiques the positivism in international relations literature, and allows an examination of geopolitics as a mediated and technologized project through which the state can become both alien and exceptional. It explains how the United States can be seen simultaneously as a waning empire and an exceptional power.

A third approach to the security state comes from international relations scholars who see "state security" as national security in realist terms. National security in this formulation becomes a matter of military and diplomatic geopolitics, with emphasis on the Weberian model of the state as having a monopoly on violence. More recently, scholars have critiqued this approach as too narrow and needing to be modified by adding cultural, economic, and social factors.[86] It remains powerful, however, among those who work in government, diplomacy, and media, as well as in many academic institutions. Some of these critics emphasize the importance of those nonstate and transnational actors who are often ignored in the international relations literature.

Thomas Hansen and Finn Stepputat argue that international relations scholars have produced a normative idea of the state that is increasingly out of touch with the kinds of dispersed sovereignty and governance regimes that currently operate beyond the state.[87] The dominant international relations notion of nation-states as bounded and territorialized entities has also come under critique. Joseph Nye argues that power is dispersed, divided among military, economic, transnational and non-state actors, and while the US is still dominant in military power, economic power is multipolar and diffused across many different actors. He argues for a new concept of US power that is "smart" because it is focused not on domination but on using "soft power" to set agendas that benefit the United States. He advocates that the United States take a paternal role, offering ideas and directions to attract other countries and ultimately enhance its own power.[88] He does not address, however, the violence and coercive aspects of this "soft power," which produce violence and inequality. For instance, the pressures put on states to wage a "war on terror" has made it a transnational project, with countries borrowing from each other to create laws that enable states to incarcerate and exclude without cause. While countries such as India have long-standing antiterrorism laws that derive from colonial rule and have been in operation since the 1980s—and many other countries have their own trajectories of violence and exclusion—US support (and funding) has transnationalized these projects in new ways, producing counterinsurgency and "antiterrorism" as technologies of power that connect the heterogeneous actions of actors dispersed globally.[89]

Some international relations scholars eschew realist approaches and suggest that rather than security, the project must be securitization, which may include nonstate actors.[90] Barry Buzan, Ole Wæver, and Jaap de Wilde see securitization as the shifting relations between subjects and sovereign, arguing that the traditional approach that sees security as the domain of a state-centered security apparatus as inadequate.[91] Securitization needs to address the governmentalization of security through the work of individuals and citizens and to examine the ways that particular institutions and subjects produce the "state effect."

The difference between "security state" and "national security state" approaches is made clear through examining empire and colonial histories. Scholars such as Paul Amar see the security state as an empire that is now transnational in its focus on policing and war, which uses humanitarianism as an imperial tool because neoliberal power has waned.[92] Mark Duffield argues that even development has become a technology of security, while others suggest that development (and welfare) has taken a back seat to security projects in many countries.[93] Laleh Khalili suggests, against Giorgio Agamben and Carl Schmitt, that states are unexceptional in creating zones where laws are temporarily allayed and that they work to expand their influence and power over other states and regions.[94] With a more feminist approach, the security state becomes visible as a construction of a particular masculine authority—manifest diversely as patriarchy, as a variety of racialized and uneven hierarchies of masculinities, or as patrimonial capitalism. These versions of hegemonic, racial white authority, intimately connected to elite transnational masculinities and femininities, enable state violence, capital accumulation, and its corollary insecurities. These insecurities have made visible economic and sexual violence that both oppresses and disciplines; insecurities produce violence that represses and excludes in the name of neoliberalism but can also disrupt the neoliberal project, revealing its contradictions.

Authority is constitutively a matter of gender, as well as of intersectional formations of class, race, and empire; it is visible in racialized and patriarchal masculinities that are fought over because they appear to be waning, even as they remain violent. The US security state depends on and creates not just a masculine authority, but also a white, masculine and imperial authority whose patriarchal power is aspirational to its many subjects. Its state effect becomes an exclusionary realm of white, Christian power that produces insecurity and threats to many who live within it or who wish to enter it. While the state effect displays this masculinist power, some feminine subjects are also incorporated into this state. Wishing to be seen as empowered, imperial, and white subjects, they struggle with and against this patriarchy-desiring masculinity to demand individuality, equality, and sovereignty. These struggles can be antagonistic but also collaborative, securing the nation and its exceptionalism. The United States as security state is thus a racialized and gendered imperial and neoliberal state effect that produces insecurity and securitizes populations nationally and transnationally. This effect is produced not only by the state, but also by the work of exceptional citizens—white, male, Christian—endowed with sovereignty to target black and brown Others within it and outside of it through modes of war that incorporate militarized humanitarianism and surveillance.

Media Convergence

Security is a difficult project because it cannot be ensured. All we have are the promises of security. Fears required and engendered by insecurity have a political economy in which media and culture industries are vital.[95] Such insecurities are amplified across multiple boundaries, institutions, and subjectivities. As David Campbell has argued, foreign policy and security are essential for producing national identity and the self/other divide.[96] They create commodities that gain value from circulation. Insecurity has a political economy that works via the notion that militarization and technological change will produce commodities that can in turn provide better security. Proponents of digital technologies, for instance, promise state security that is better, faster, and total, on the one hand, even as they claim to enable "democratization," insurgencies, and "commons" on the other. Despite the use of such technologies by "nonformal political actors" to "accommodate a broad range of social struggles and facilitate the emergence of new types of political subjects," as Saskia Sassen wrote in 2002,[97] the digital media that has become iconic of this new century creates value for corporate and formal networks and shapes popular culture in ways that are similar to earlier media technologies. Such control is not absolute, however, and there are failures that challenge security claims, even as those insurgent challenges lead to counterinsurgencies in turn.

Neoliberal capitalism's contradictions are not solely responsible for this insecurity around US exceptionalism. Rather, it occurs through the transnational media spectacle of US failure and audience responses to this failure. Contradictions are not simply "there" in some transparent way so they can be read as such; contradictions are *made* visible in ways that enable protests and upheavals that are narrated and understood in a variety of ways. Capitalism's contradictions appear through the agency of viewers, readers, writers, politicians, and the "international community," as well as media technologies and knowledge networks that articulate those contradictions in divergent ways—some through a concern for the loss of empire and some through the struggle for inclusion and social justice. How these become visible and how they circulate is thus a critical issue for the study of cultural politics.

In the twenty-first century, there is a struggle over the United States as a declining superpower or an exceptional nation. That the United States is a superpower is made clear by its imperial wars, through which its own temporality becomes historicized and universalized. US events are made into world events. This resonance is not magical but rather enabled by multiple forms of power generating uncontrollable violence. In *Philosophy in a Time of Terror*, Jacques Derrida explains that 9/11 was "felt" in the United States as a "singular" and "unprecedented" event, which was "to a large extent conditioned, constituted, if not actually constructed, circulated . . . by means of a prodigious techno-socio-political machine."[98] He goes on to say that " 'to mark a date in history' presupposes, in any case, that 'something' comes or happens for the first time, 'something' that we do not yet really know how to identify, determine, recognize or analyze but that should remain from here on as unforgettable: an ineffaceable event in the shared archive of a universal calendar."[99] Here, Derrida makes three points: first, the event is produced by a vast and complex machinery that disseminated images of 9/11 around the globe; second, such a machinery produces a temporality that comes to be seen and understood as universal; and third, we need to distinguish the *event* (the thing itself) from the *impression* (created through repetition by the US hegemonic machinery) and the *interpretation* (the belief that it was a major event). Derrida's distinctions are critical, suggesting that it is equally important to recognize how the individual, the nation, and the state—and many outside of the United States—all came to recognize 9/11 as an event, and an unprecedented one, at the same time. The time of terror became universal when the temporalities of these entities became globally synchronous and when the United States enlisted states around the world to join the "war on terror." Thus, one can argue that the United States and its policies create convergences through media and media corporations, ignoring or eliminating differences to gather and create new consensus.[100]

As Derrida suggests, the power of the superpower is never absolute. Corporate media's unstable representations and heterogeneous audiences, as well as its political economy that depends on a transnational reach and rapid circulation of images, unsettle the hegemon. Migrations and diasporas may (though not always) disrupt the nation and its hegemonic formations. Media audiences—whether they are US based, American nationalist, anti-colonial, antiracist, or anti-Western—use the discourses of crisis, loss of US economic power, and critique of human rights to make visible the contradictions of the imperial project; and they challenge the United States in its claims of superiority. Struggles over US power, over its state effect, become visible in new and powerful ways.

Geopolitics is produced not simply through "real" relations between states, but through multiple political projects in which media and spectacle have played important roles. Media images are always open to interpretation, as well as encoded with ideologies,[101] and can unsettle a superpower or, in other times, make it more powerful. Media's many screens send out diverse messages that can enable contradictory meanings, though their effects cannot always be controlled and may lead to protests and uprisings. Embodied political agents and diverse organizations make meanings through the repetition and circulation of specific content. In the context of digital media—while some scholars believe that capitalism's incorporation of digital media may lead to depoliticization[102]—it is also possible that the heterogeneous receptions of transnational media may produce challenges and protests as much as they produce acquiescence. Further, media does not function alone. It is always connected to a variety of institutions and subjects that give it meaning. The securitized subjects I discuss in this book become visible through these media industries, gaining agency within a transnational network that can be linked to national projects, yet is not contained by them.

The connection between protests and digital media has become an important question, as media corporations, such as Facebook, claim that they enable democratization.[103] There are many claims about new digital media technologies that were also made about older media technologies: they are global or enable globalization; they will produce democracy; they can resist power or a state; they are democratic; they can produce moral and social panics, governmentalities, and new forms of governance. At the same time, digital technology has amplified and circulated changes in social relations, subjectivities, and the ways many of us live and work—all while keeping capitalist neoliberalism alive. David Lyon has written that technology must be seen as a "mode of mediating daily life,"[104] and it is true that many people live with computers in a way they did not live with television or radio; for many, their laptops are now a prosthetic technology that makes media embodied in new ways. Digital technology reproduces security as affect that is historically specific to the period, where external threats such as terrorism, via the war on terror, produce subjects who work to contain and respond to these threats.

Much of the debate around security and new technologies has focused on surveillance, the deliberate leaking of corporate or personal secrets, and the disclosure of state secrets. Scholars have suggested that the security state signals a shift from Foucault's notion of the disciplinary society to Gilles Deleuze's notion of the society of control. While Mark Poster argues that networks create a "superpanopticon"—a vastly expanded and powerful version of Foucault's notion of panopticon, which disciplines subjects through visibility—David Lyon suggests that we have moved to a "post-panopticon" society. In a society of control, as suggested by Deleuze, there is both a panopticon and a synopticon (with many watching the few), and the media has now made surveillance part of everyday life. Greg Elmer argues that Deleuze enables us to understand how sites of control are themselves multiple and expanded, though even Deleuze assumes a stable object of surveillance rather than the networking process that creates "a range of values to objects" and "seeks to determine the meaningfulness of surveillant objects within the context of networked economies." Surveillance is thus "subject to an economy that constantly seeks to rationalize relationships among people and things to better manage the future."[105] In the US neoliberal security state, the media economy of surveillance is also an economy that manages insecurities and protests through the work of subjects who become exceptional citizens as they do this work. In so doing, however, they become subjects of both the state and of corporations, using media products to securitize themselves as well as the security state.

David Lyon's term "panopticommodity" names the ways people market themselves on the Internet as individuals.[106] As personal computers and tablets have not only become prosthetic but also dynamic repositories that bring together actions, subjects, and selves into new digital social forms, information stored on private and state websites and servers requires protection. "Networked identities" are now precious commodities. Privacy is bought and sold—desire for protection sells products. "Identity management" has become a business, as corporations manage information, passwords, and log-ins. Similar to embodied selves, digital selves are marked by insecurity. Exhortations that everything in our computers is public and news reports on hacking and corporate security breaches produce privacy as a banal project, producing public selves securitized enough to claim that they have "nothing to hide."

In contrast to normative citizens with "nothing to hide," minorities (racial or otherwise), "terrorists," and "aliens" are constituted as both public and private, having public identities with secrets, and private selves which must be uncovered. Having "nothing to hide" is not a possibility for such subjects who are constituted as already public. As public subjects, they are constructed as threats since they are assumed to have secret private selves that must be surveilled and brought to the surface. In such a context, public selves are assumed to have privacy that requires disclosure, as even the most public subjects require monitoring. Only those constituted as sovereign subjects, such as the exceptional subjects I examine in this book, can experience privacy as a tool for opposing corporate and militarized state intrusion, or are able to deploy privacy in legal and democratic struggles.

Feminist Challenges

The securitizations and insecurities that pervade the United States make feminism relevant in newly urgent ways. How do we understand what is happening when feminist discourses are used to bomb and to liberate, when feminist discourses, strategies, and injuries become available in new and unintended ways to empower, secure, and destroy?[107] How do we explain the American belief that women in the United States are better off than women anywhere else, despite gendered inequalities, cuts in welfare for women with families, and the banality of sexual violence in the United States? American exceptionalism mediates considerations of gendered inequalities and forecloses its geopolitics.[108] While most "security" expertise addresses questions of states and geopolitics while ignoring gender, race, and sexuality, many feminist scholars have critiqued masculinity and militarism by linking feminism and women with peace, victimhood, and innocence.[109] But feminists also have discussed the ways in which women and feminists have participated in nationalism and militarism as well as the ways in which domestic ideologies have supported national and imperial goals.[110] An enduring and important feminist approach has been to analyze domesticity itself as violent, since its many institutions feminize subordinate subjects.[111] Gender has an important role to play in understanding war and conflict, and women are not simply innocent victims of masculinist militarism.[112] In line with more intersectional and transnational critiques of gender and militarism, I theorize feminisms, patriarchies, masculinities, racialized and militarized violence, and terror as contingent, networked, mediated, and transnational formations that make up the US as empire and as security state. I draw on feminist theory challenging essentialized connections between militarism, the state, and masculinity, as well as those demonstrating the violence of the state, domesticity, home, and the everyday in contexts of neoliberal policies.[113]

Debates about neoliberalism demand feminist intervention because too often they assume that neoliberalism means the privatization of public goods, or that public and private are understood only in terms of states and corporations/individuals, even though the private sphere of liberal thought has been associated with family and the domestic sphere.[114] Many scholars of neoliberalism assert that the protection of the private sphere (and its ownership of property) is a central element of contemporary capitalism. For example, David Harvey has defined neoliberalism in terms of an altered relation between public and private in which contemporary capitalism accumulates by dispossession and eliminates the "commons." Gender, the family, and sexuality appear as superstructural, as consequences of globalization's new mode of production.

Feminists, however, have long argued that "public" and "private" are not useful concepts for understanding how gender works in modern societies. In classical political theory, public/private divisions have been central to the liberal social contract. Feminists such as Carole Pateman point out that the liberal public/private divide is only made possible through the control of women. The liberal "social contract" is a "sexual contract" in which the patriarchal control of the family grounds the liberal state. In liberalism, Pateman claims, women have few privacy rights over their homes or their bodies because they are always regulated by the patriarchal state.[115] Along with Charles Mills, Pateman has argued that sexual violence is also racialized. Yet these divisions are difficult to maintain in the security state.

As terms, public and private are not stable or universal, nor are the related terms of home, privacy, and domesticity. If, in neoliberal times, the term "private" has become associated with the privatization of capital and of the state, the term "public" has also undergone semantic shifts, as the state has changed through new collaborations with corporations, NGOS, and religious groups. Separations of public and private don't have good explanatory value for the messy processes of contemporary globalization. To call corporations "private," when they are publicly traded, simply exonerates them from accountability and enables corporate leaders to claim legal personhood, as the US Supreme Court confirmed in *Citizens United v. Federal Election Commission*.[116] Definitions of the terms "private," "privacy," and "secrecy," as well as associations between individual freedoms and control over female bodies, have long been debated. What counts as "private" shifts, even within liberal democratic states. The domestic space has never been private but rather constructed by the state and its sovereign masculinities, and not all masculinities have been understood as patriarchal in their control over the private sphere.

As the security state has become dominant in the United States in contrast with the welfare state, feminists' tasks include analyzing the gendering of neoliberal citizenship, understanding how the fuzzy boundaries between public and private produce a militant masculinity and a militant femininity, and critiquing how humanitarian citizenship has replaced rights-based citizenship in a way that most impacts low-income women and those seen as security threats. What I call an advanced neoliberal rearticulation of the public/private divide has consequences for feminists and gendered subjects, as well as for expanded and nonheteronormative notions of family and citizenship. Some critics suggest that neoliberalism reduces the state and abdicates power to private realms.[117] However, feminists interested in transnational and postcolonial analysis have shown that neoliberalism is better understood as a changing and flexible set of practices that produce deeply uneven genders and sexualities across the world.[118] Such insights have led to feminist scholarly debates on terror and terrorism, security, and citizenship under contemporary transnational neoliberalism. Some feminists have argued that the war on terror reveals how "terror" becomes simultaneously a form of regulation, a mode of securitizing populations, and a technology producing gendered subjectivities in hetero- and homonormative ways.[119] However, other feminists suggest that the term provides a useful way to examine particular forms of violence. They resignify the term and use it to examine violence as the purview of the state rather than of nonstate transnational actors and networks. Arguing that "terror" is an appropriate term for the violence to which many bodies, especially those gendered as female, are subjected, they argue that "terror" can be a useful term to describe such subjection.[120] In particular, some feminists argue that violence within the family, and the failure of the state to control male violence, are examples of the terror with which many women live.[121] Yet terms such as "terror" and "terrorism" are too imbued with imperial and racial power to be repurposed for more progressive politics.

Advanced neoliberalism involves both contemporary manifestations of authority as raced, classed, gendered, and sexualized and the protests to such authority. Critiques of such politics require attention to the relation between powerful masculinities and aspirational patriarchies, white racial sovereignty, and forms of authority dispersed over self-improving and self-commoditizing subjects, "private" corporations, and the security state. These entities collaborate with the state to use violence to assert their power over other groups. The advent of digital technologies, of panics over what is seen as public and private security, and of formations in which entrepreneurial and statist individuals are seen as normative citizens means that feminist approaches to citizenship have to address the ways in which neoliberal capital and the security state have stakes in the production of gender, sexuality, and the family. Feminist critique that is antiracist and anti-imperial, and which incorporates postcolonial and transnational theories of gender and sexuality that attend to the specificities of neoliberal empire, remains necessary. While such critique will examine how feminism can have neoliberal versions, it has to provide possibilities for continuing to struggle against forms of masculine authority that are both national and transnational.

This Book

Examining surveillance and humanitarianism as the governmentalization and securitization of US empire's "soft power," this book's chapters relay interdisciplinary approaches that disrupt the academic compartmentalization of state and security analyses. I draw on postcolonial and transnational theory, media studies, and law and society approaches, as well as critical race and gender studies, to understand the complexity of twenty-first-century US neoliberalism. This is not a "media studies" book, though a concern with media and technology appears throughout. As law is a key way the state becomes present to individuals, I examine how law appears more as "state effect" than simply "the state" itself, as that which regulates sovereignty between fuzzily bounded public and private entities. Studies of colonialism provide tools for understanding empire, and my previous research on the British empire and its cultures, as well as continuing interest in South Asia, provides the vantage point from which I trace the transnationalisms, specificities, and differences of US politics. Critical race studies and American studies scholarship enable understanding of sovereignty and empire that is both national and transnational.[122] And the fields in which I have been most engaged, transnational and intersectional gender and cultural studies, provide the interdisciplinary spaces to understand cultural politics and the critical engagements with state and security that are often compartmentalized in fields such as security studies.

I begin the book with a chapter about Hurricane Katrina as revealing ruptures that characterize what I see as the condition of advanced neoliberalism. Here, contestations between sovereignties, militarism, and security lead to the rise of humanitarianism as a solution to the crisis of the neoliberal security state. In the aftermath of the hurricane, private individuals and corporations were brought in to provide welfare and support, but many communities and social movements protested, calling for state action instead. The spectacle of racial injustice provides an opening for a mediated geopolitics, as critiques of the United States and its inability to care for its citizens circulated around the world. In this context, the United States appeared banal rather than exceptional, described as a "third world" nation, and its citizens as "refugees."

My second chapter focuses on the humanitarians who become exceptional US citizens. Such humanitarianism is securitized, as the US government and military incorporates these practices into their imperial arsenal. I examine the subjects of humanitarianism: missionaries, "voluntourists," nonprofit organizations, microlending agencies, and armchair/online donors.

Continuing this thread in the third chapter, I trace the US government's crackdown on Muslim charities in the aftermath of 9/11 and argue that humanitarian citizenship becomes a state security project by producing Muslims as outside such citizenship. Here, I focus on the production of race not only though a historical sedimentation of racialized institutions, but also through expanding modes of neoliberal racialization. In the twenty-first century, evangelical Christian missionaries following a neoliberal theology (what John and Jean Comaroff term "millennial capitalism") collaborate with and become part of the state to become the good humanitarians,[123] turning Muslims into "bad" humanitarians. Under George W. Bush's leadership, the US government put evangelical church leaders in charge of disbursing state funding to their own churches.[124] The separation between church and state disappeared when there was little oversight of these funds and little attention to federal laws requiring accountability and nonpreferential hiring. These processes of selective inclusion of Christians existed alongside the selective exclusion of Muslims from neoliberal citizenship, enabled by a proliferation of legal statutes and policing mechanisms that pervaded so-called public and private entities. Yet this alliance was also provisional, as militarism and imperial war came into conflict with Evangelical missions.

In chapter 4, I turn to the emergence of the "security mom" and "security feminist" as figures of motherhood and female empowerment who attempt the work of state security in the aftermath of 9/11. These figures embody the exceptional individual as one who governmentalizes security in the private realm of the family, leading to a rearticulation of family and gender relations. Motherhood, here, becomes more about surveillance than about other tasks of parenting; the technology industry creates and markets products that enable such surveillance. The security mom and the security feminist thus become figures of power, yet remain conflicted because of their failure to secure the family or gain liberal equality.

In the fifth chapter, I examine the concept of "parental control" technology to show how the technology industry uses moral panics to sell products. Although both state and technology changes suggest that complete security is impossible, I argue that security's impossibility is differently experienced. Privacy is only possible for some families, over others, so these technologies produce their own racial formations differentiating between citizens and Others. As the child becomes rearticulated as a figure to be protected from Internet dangers, it becomes also a "digital native"—one whose generational difference makes it a citizen to be nurtured as well as a neoliberal consumer and a potential threat to parental authority.

In the coda, I bring the themes of the book together to examine the horrific murders at a Sikh temple in Oak Creek, Wisconsin, a killing similar to that which took place in Charleston, South Carolina, some years later. I look at the figure of the exceptional, white, male, Christian citizen—the "shooter"—who polices the nation and embodies the white racial sovereignty that he claims to possess. This figure is contrasted with those nonwhites who are seen as terrorist threats, or those whose possession of guns is seen as a threat. I propose that the transnational connections between white supremacist organizations suggest that these individuals might also be seen as "international" rather than "domestic" terrorists.

I began my career as a postcolonial studies scholar at a time when a critique of colonialism was seen as tendentious. Yet the study of colonialism, whether ongoing or sedimented in everyday life around the world, remains crucial to understanding global conditions. Imperial cultures and projects abound, and become intertwined with national and transnational formations. Contemporary conditions show that colonialism and empire are diverse and ongoing projects that assert the power of certain entities over others in the continued production of inequalities. Global capital, neoliberalism, heteropatriarchies, and powerful masculinities; continuing settler colonialisms; racial/imperial histories; geopolitics between new and old empires; struggles between transnational insurgencies and national states—all of these require us to engage with the present in light of colonial and imperial technologies and histories. Importantly, the heterogeneous protests, insurgencies, and uprisings of the present warrant such analysis.

Feminist approaches and methods coming from studies of race and empire are necessary to understand neoliberalism in the United States. This book, though about the United States, is also a product of postcolonial and transnational theory as it engages with contemporary cultural politics of gender, race, and capitalism. Written from within the United States but with a concern for the politics elsewhere, this book reflects my engagement with where I live, but also with the enormous power of the United States. I write along with many around the world and in the United States who are critiquing neoliberalism and authoritarian power. I write with the hope that my critiques (and those of my fellow scholars) can shift some of the racialized humanitarianisms and the surveillance regimes of our times to goals that are not just about "giving back" (after one has taken so much), bemoaning how America has lost its power or its "American dream," or claiming that one person "can make a difference." Rather, I write with the conviction that we all need to change the policies of the United States as neoliberal empire that affects so many around the world. If there is work to be done, it is to ensure that authoritarian security regimes lose their power, and that feminist antiracist, antisecurity, and anti-imperial projects proliferate.

1. Katrina, American Exceptionalism, and the Security State

On Monday, September 5, 2005, Shailaja Bajpai wrote in the daily New Delhi newspaper *Indian Express*:

> When CNN proclaims "State of Emergency" we expect to see Africa or Asia because that is where states of emergency occur, right? But when it describes . . ."the United States of America," you don't know what to think. Not even after the catastrophic 9/11 did CNN expose the human toll of the attack. . . . When Katrina swept Mississippi and Louisiana off their feet, suddenly everything was altered: we see disorder, chaos, suffering and yes, dead bodies in flooded New Orleans. . . . Everyone the camera encounters cries out tales of woe; each correspondent looks like he's been hit by a minor tsunami. Like 9/11, coverage of Hurricane Katrina has changed the way we perceive America.[1]

In Kenya's *Daily Nation*, Ambrose Murunga similarly wrote, "My first reaction when television images of the survivors of Hurricane Katrina in New Orleans came through the channels was that the producers must have been showing the wrong clip. The images, and even the disproportionately high number of visibly impoverished blacks among the refugees, could easily have been a re-enactment of a scene from the pigeonholed African continent."[2] Another commentator in the same newspaper stated that the United States had shown itself to be an underdeveloped, rather than a developed, nation because it could not shield its population from these natural disasters as could a developed nation.[3] In France, *Le Progress* published, "Katrina has shown that the emperor has no clothes. The world's superpower is powerless when confronted with nature's fury."[4] From Spain, *La Razón* read, "It is clear that the USA's international image is being damaged in a way that it has never known before."[5] In *Business Times Singapore*, there appeared an article that summed it up: "America's eroding credibility: Fallout from Baghdad and New Orleans makes it difficult for Bush administration to mobilize support."[6]

All around the world, there was astonishment at the spectacle of misery unfolding in the United States.[7] Through the "disaster marathon" showing the hurricane's impact across the US Gulf Coast, television viewers around the world were stunned at seeing—perhaps for the first time—reporters covering a major US metropolis as a disaster zone lacking a government that was able to help contain the disaster, or lessen its impact. The media coverage of desperate people, inadequate rescue operations, lack of coordination and communication, and the overwhelming visibility of African American women and children as victims all fueled speculation about racism and US power. Marcin Zaborowski, a Polish commentator wrote, "It is difficult to overestimate the effect the disaster has had on American politics and on America's perception of itself as well as on the role of the US in the world."[8]

Just a year before, images of the Indian Ocean tsunami led to the mobilization of humanitarian aid from many countries. While the Indian Ocean tsunami of 2004 produced images of suffering and destruction in Sri Lanka, India, Thailand, and Indonesia—among other nations—such images belonged to a long history of spectacularized "third world" suffering and of Asians needing US and European support. The Katrina news coverage showed suffering victims in the United States (many of whom were nonwhite women and children), dead bodies floating in the water, people being rescued from houses while others were left behind to die, and survivors without adequate resources. All of these images enabled comparisons to the third world. These comparisons indexed stereotypical images of disasters in Africa or Asia that have long been a staple of US television, radio, and news media. That so many of the Katrina victims were African American women was another connection to the global catastrophe media spectacle, as was the widespread focus on women with children as the primary disaster victims. For instance, reporters regularly called the survivors who were taken to the New Orleans Superdome sports arena "refugees." The term reflected the general perception that what was visible on television was unthinkable in a US context. Audiences were startled to see the spectacle of suffering, so normative and banal in global media coverage of so-called failed or developing states, or the "Third World," depict the United States. The fact that the disaster was in the United States made it different from disasters in other parts of the world, for while there were similarities of death and destruction with other international disasters, what was new was the astonishment of so many across the globe at the lack of government assistance.

Not surprisingly, ninety countries—small and big, poor and prosperous— offered aid to the United States,[9] much of which was not accepted or went unused. Nations rallied to give aid to the United States, even as they used the opportunity to criticize President George W. Bush and his ineffective response. What ensued was a geopolitics of "disaster diplomacy,"[10] as people around the world assessed the US government's poor response and passed judgment on the US government and, especially, the Bush administration. In the public opinion expressed and circulated in UK newspapers, for instance, support and condemnation were both visible. In an article subtitled "But Why Does the World's Richest Nation Need Handouts?," the BBC reported that President Bush stated no aid was needed since "this country is going to rise up and take care of it." But, it was also revealed that Secretary of State Condoleezza Rice had said, contradictorily, "No offers of assistance will be refused."[11] While the ostensible goal of the BBC article was to publicize a call from the British Red Cross seeking help for Katrina's victims, it also provided a window into many UK opinions. The piece included a British Red Cross spokesman saying, "There are broader political questions about the response of the richest country in the world to such a disaster on its own soil. Hopefully they will be addressed in the fullness of time and lessons will be learned." The article concluded by wondering if anyone in Britain was going to help and included comments from its readers that framed the issue in terms of whether or not UK people should help the "richest country in the world." Not surprisingly, there were those who argued that anyone in need should be helped, but the article also included comments such as "to ask other nations for help, and then retaining wealth makes my skin crawl." Another person commented, "I will not be giving to this appeal. The United States is the richest country in the history of the modern world. They should be diverting their wealth into domestic social care programs not into imposing their economic will on the rest of the world. Maybe this is the wake-up call that the people of the US need."

In the United States, many discussions in national newspapers focused on whether the United States could expect aid and support from other countries, particularly because Americans were represented as selflessly rescuing developing countries in international crises. Bradley Jones, in his research on media and Hurricane Katrina, points out that the national image of Americans as global good Samaritans was the framework for third world comparisons. The *New York Times* reported Secretary of State Condoleezza Rice as saying, "We have seen the American people respond generously to help others around the globe during their times of distress. . . . Today we are seeing a similar urgent, warm, and compassionate reaction."[12] Both Rice and the *Times* ignored the pervasive international and national negative commentary on the role of the US government. At the same time, foreign nations' efforts to help were rebuffed by some in the Bush administration, who considered these efforts as an affront to the ability of the United States to help itself.[13] Iran offered help, which was refused because the US State Department said that it came with a condition of lifting the embargo on oil sales.[14] Greece offered free cruise ships to house the many who had lost their homes, but was turned down. Instead, the Department of Homeland Security (DHS) awarded a Florida-based company, Carnival Cruise Lines, a contract of $192 million to provide housing and meals to evacuees, though it was emergency workers who ended up using the ships. CorpWatch, a nongovernmental organization (NGO) that monitors corporate corruption, suggested that the DHS awarded Carnival the contract because Carnival was an important Republican donor. The ships were never used for the purpose for which they were intended.[15] In the hurricane's aftermath, as the General Accounting Office and other governmental agencies and NGOs assessed how foreign aid had been dealt with, many across the political spectrum concluded that the superpower status of the United States got in the way of its ability to help those in need. In their report from 2011 "Accepting Disaster Relief from Other Nations: Lessons from Katrina and the Gulf Oil Spill," the conservative Heritage Foundation concluded that "an unresponsive policy toward foreign offers of aid can also have negative diplomatic consequences, potentially alienating important allies whose assistance the United States needs on other issues." It noted that while by "late February 2006 foreign countries had offered or pledged a total of $854 million in cash and oil," there were embarrassing problems such as the 400,000 UK Ready to Eat (RTE) meals that were refused because they included UK beef, which the US had banned in earlier legislation due to fear of Mad Cow disease.[16]

The global media spectacle surrounding Katrina portrayed the superpower in ways that departed from the normative script of US exceptionalism that has been a part of US culture, media, and politics through the second half of the twentieth century. Occurring in the aftermath of 9/11, and the invasions of Iraq and Afghanistan that proclaimed US military might, and circulated by the power of digital media, Katrina was a shocking transnational spectacle. While many were not astonished by the images of the earthquake in Haiti of 2010, the US war in Iraq of 2003–present or even 9/11, Katrina's images surprised viewers around the globe. The bungling of foreign aid further signaled US governmental incompetence, becoming one more piece of evidence of US similarity to long-standing images of developing and third world states.

Media Geopolitics and State Effect

One reason Katrina's images had such a global impact was transnational media networks, which enabled the technological proliferation of images transmitted instantly through satellites, fiber optic cable, and digital technologies.[17] As a television and photojournalism staple, disaster coverage reporters could not avoid covering what was going on, from the storm to its aftermath, as such stories almost always deliver high ratings and viewer numbers. As Elihu Katz and Tamar Liebes argue, disasters have become ever more important as media events enabled by mobile recording and transmission technologies. Increasingly, such events upstage the broadcasting of ceremonial events, and the state may not be able to ideologically control them.[18] Liebes suggests that we increasingly watch "disaster marathons," rather than the news bulletins of the broadcast television era.[19] Kevin Fox Gotham asserts that Hurricane Katrina coverage is an example of recent changes in the news media spectacle of disasters, in which the characteristic features of entertainment—ephemerality, fragmentation, immediacy, and intense drama—determine the representation of tragic events and catastrophes."[20] In the case of Katrina, these features, with unprecedented speed and circulation, supported an implicit comparison with Asian and African countries, leading to a particular state effect of waning US power.

The framings and narratives accompanying the images also helped to produce the global reception that I narrated at the beginning of this chapter. In a transnational media context, the images revealed that in the United States, neoliberal retrenchment of welfare had produced an impoverished population that did not have the resources to help itself and that the US government would not do what was necessary to assist it. Offers of aid, as well as the context of the Iraq War and the war on terror, added to that perception. The application of developing world catastrophe narratives to New Orleans, an important US tourist destination, caused the images to have widespread effect.

Although disaster marathons do participate in what Naomi Klein has called "disaster capitalism" and opportunities for capital accumulation,[21] there were important moments in which Katrina's effects could not be wholly contained by capital and in fact revealed the contradictions of neoliberalism. Katrina's images became part of a broad international and transnational media whose numerous articulations and decodings could be ascertained neither in advance nor subsequently.[22] Yet, there were some transnational commonalities among reactions to the United States as an exceptional superpower. While US television producers were unwilling to directly challenge the powers of state and capital, a broad array of international media producers criticized American neoliberal policy, the government's inattention to poverty, US racism, and its imperialism. The *Indian Express* quote presented at the beginning of this chapter was one of many such commentaries circulating across transnational media.

To overcome global disaster comparisons, US media makers created discrepancies in their coverage of suffering and death for US citizens. Media scholar Susan Moeller notes that American news organizations treated "American" victims with "more respect" by showing a distance between the viewer and the victims. Television producers did not, according to Moeller, present a large number of dead bodies laid out in rows, or grieving families, preferring to show wide-angle images of the destructive flooding. Media organizations stated they were trying to show "restraint in terms of just good taste," leaving out images of severed and bloated bodies found abandoned in debris, since the newscasts "air at the dinner hour."[23]

Other comparisons of *New York Times* and the *Washington Post* media coverage of Hurricane Katrina in 2005 and the Indian Ocean tsunami in 2004 also revealed such differences.[24] The tsunami images depicted more unattended bodies (often lying uncovered on the ground), had greater focus on damages and relief work and survivors, and showed less interest in local or national political contexts. The latter's erasure in the tsunami is perhaps most telling for the transnational project of empire, in which mention of the work of local politicians and community groups is often erased in favor of reporting that focuses on Western rescue and humanitarian operations.

While US journalists also found ways to question the Bush administration, foreign news media more directly seized the opportunity to critique US news media and what they saw as its failures. As a New Zealand newspaper put it, "not for decades has there been such merciless questioning of the president and his administration by the US media."[25] The same article reported that "never before . . . have US reporters been so emotionally involved in a story to the point of being enraged." The article's author commented that the US media had come to have too cozy a relationship with the government and had become "part of the political establishment," so that television reporters did not have the skills or ability to cover such an event. "Used to reporting on comparatively harmless storms, heroically riding out storms with wind-blown hairdos, they were then confused with the 'Big One.' "[26] The same article quoted a BBC reporter who asked whether Katrina had saved the US media.[27]

A cartoon in the UK newspaper the *Guardian* by cartoonist Steve Bell depicted the international opinion that Katrina was a blow to the US's reputation (fig. 1.1). Bell referenced the storm's aftermath, in which the rescue operation became militarized. In Bell's drawing, the Statue of Liberty lies drowned in the water, as shadowy military figures roam the bridges. In doing so, Bell alluded to the emerging story that local police and the US National Guard had prevented those fleeing flooded neighborhoods from crossing the bridge to middle-class sections of the city.[28]

The US national media was not unaware of international responses and took the opportunity to bring their concerns over the laggardly state response to the public through ventriloquizing the international coverage. The *New York Times* revealed that many Europeans blamed the Bush government for lack of environmental awareness, and for its lack of care for the victims. The *Times* suggested Europeans felt a "dismay . . . mingling with sorrow."[29] It mentioned a BBC report that focused on the "shameful" aspect of "the dark underbelly of [US] life," as white policemen mistreated black residents. It also reported that a French television station interviewed a US specialist who stated that the images "reveal to the world the reality in the Southern states; the poverty of 37 million Americans." The article concluded that the Katrina images "have tended to confirm the worst images of America that prevails in Europe, the vision of a country of staggering inequalities, in-

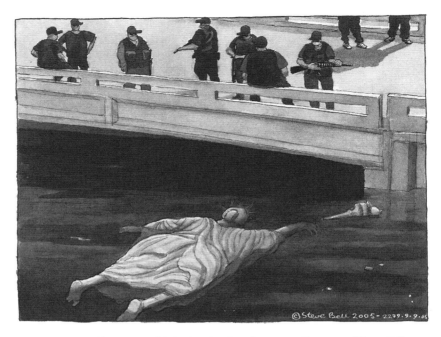

FIG. 1.1. Steve Bell cartoon published in the *Guardian*, 2005. Courtesy of Steve Bell.

difference to the general welfare (especially during the Bush administration), and lacking in what Europeans call 'solidarity.' " The article enabled the *New York Times* to indirectly critique the Bush administration through presenting such opinions from abroad.

Despite this tactic, most journalists could not bring themselves to probe the effects of neoliberal state retrenchment in relation to Katrina, and they blamed nature or poor government response, shying away from identifying the effects of poverty, racism, and lack of infrastructure to shore up the levees. At the same time, they noted that the images reflected poorly on the Bush administration. For example, CBS News reporters Robb Todd and Charles Wolfson stated, "Hurricane Katrina clearly exposed America to being vulnerable to Mother Nature. The fact that parts of the Mississippi Gulf Coast look like Indonesia after the tsunami is inescapable. Less visible is the perception abroad of Washington's handling of the problem. Initial confusion about the government's response and political finger pointing is being watched in foreign capitals. To the extent others see the Bush administration preoccupied with a domestic crisis of the first order, attitudes toward Washington might well affect upcoming foreign policy challenges."[30] At

Salon.com Sidney Blumenthal wrote, "Bush's credibility gap is a geopolitical problem without a geopolitical solution."[31] A *Newsday* author saw Katrina as leading to an "image problem" for the United States.[32] *Foreign Policy*, an established US geopolitics journal that is read by a broad spectrum of political elites, echoed the worry that Katrina had dealt a blow to the United States' image abroad. Daniel W. Drezner, in a short journal comment titled "Post-Katrina US Foreign Policy," quoted Richard Haass from *Slate* about Katrina's "profound foreign policy costs."[33] In Haass's analysis, the Katrina catastrophe showed that the "world's only remaining superpower seemed anything but" and that the government response's disarray allowed opponents to criticize the United States.[34] Haass concluded that the handling of Katrina was a blow to the neoliberal market democracy approaches promoted by Bush: "But the attractiveness of the American model, and the ability of the United States to be an effective advocate for more democratic, capitalist societies, which had already been weakened by the disarray in Iraq, is now weaker still as a result of the disarray at home. It will be more difficult to make the case for free markets and more open societies if the results of such reforms come to be associated with the disorder seen in New Orleans."[35] While Haass seemed critical of neoliberalism, Drezner was more concerned about the image of the United States and its power. In the *Foreign Policy* article, Drezner also quoted conservative commentator Andrew Sullivan's remarks that "what the response to Katrina has done is make the U.S. super-power look a lot less credible, a lot less fearsome, a lot less capable."[36]

Some leftist and centrist US commentators, including E. J. Dionne and Richard Haass, assailed the post-9/11 neoliberal domestic policy of diverting resources away from social programs to fund antiterrorism campaigns. Dionne, a *Washington Post* commentator, suggested "the source of Bush's political success was his claim that he could protect Americans" but that was disproved by "the surging waters of New Orleans."[37] Other reporters and policy commentators pondered whether even right-wing, conservative Bush supporters would question the president's security policies if he were unable to protect Americans. Dionne differentiated between notions of security—national security versus security as welfare of the population—while the Bush administration was intent on substituting state security for protection from the catastrophe. In a later *Foreign Policy* comment on the Bush presidency, Stephen M. Walt lists Katrina as a "blunder":

> It takes a truly spectacular domestic-policy blunder to register as a foreign-policy screw-up, too. Yet Bush's bungled response to Hurricane

Katrina was exactly that. Observers around the world saw this debacle as both a demonstration of waning U.S. competence and a revealing indicator of continued racial inequality, if not outright injustice. (You know you've screwed up when you get offers of relief aid from Venezuela's Hugo Chávez.) Because America's "soft power" depends on other states believing that we know what we are doing and that we stand for laudable ideals, the disaster in New Orleans was yet another self-inflicted blow to America's global image. If the United States cannot take good care of its own citizens, why should anyone think we can "nation-build" in some distant foreign land?[38]

Such commentators emphasized the "spectacular" nature of the catastrophe that became as much a "foreign policy screw-up" as the Iraq fiasco.

While many outside the United States saw Katrina images as revealing how inadequately the United States cared for its population, many US activists, journalists, and scholars saw the New Orleans disaster as a Bush administration failure that reflected poorly on the United States as a superpower and as a purportedly exceptional nation. US media coverage of Katrina, even in very controlled formats such as print and television, showed images of US soldiers patrolling the streets, a lack of government aid, and Federal Emergency Management Agency (FEMA) directors more concerned with their television appearances than with saving lives.

Katrina's media coverage highlighted US racial, gender, and class divides and revealed the complexity of the state, as local Louisiana officials struggled against the military and security apparatus of Bush's global war on terror. This was reflected in the visible racial geography that showed parts of the United States, such as New Orleans, were similar to so-called developing states in their use of development projects, human rights approaches, or military repression. The emergence of this development terminology to describe the United States suggests that the "superpower" was no different from the rest of the "developing world." More recently, Jeffrey Lowe and Todd Shaw have argued that much of the Gulf Coast region needs development and "capacity building" to fulfill the United Nation's 2000 Millennium Goals for ending poverty[39]—a call that is more usually addressed to the so-called developing world. As Paige West argues in her ethnography of Papua New Guinea's recent development projects, "capacity building" generally references the development logic of "accumulation by dispossession" in which a society seen as unable to take care of itself must open itself to private capital.[40] That such terminologies now apply to the United States reveals its fall to unexceptional status and the crisis of representation and power that emerged from Katrina. Lowe and Shaw try to move away from the third world comparison by referencing the post–World War II Marshall Plan rather than UN development programs as an applicable government assistance model. They end their piece by stating that volunteerism is not enough to solve the problems, and greater state intervention on the order of the Marshall Plan is required: "The United States has the resources to insure the security and prosperity of all those along the Gulf Coast, but it is currently lacking the political will to ensure an equitable reconstruction of the region. . . . Now is an opportune time to argue for a national recommitment to rebuilding the Gulf in the interest of those most in need."[41] That the Katrina disaster ranks among the most memorable events of the twenty-first century, only a few years after 9/11, says a great deal about the effects of neoliberal policies and the disastrous impact of the George W. Bush presidency. Even the Heritage Foundation, a conservative Republican-led organization, was concerned enough about these consequences that it compared the Gulf Coast BP oil spill of 2010 with Katrina to prove that President Obama's response to the BP disaster was just as incompetent as Bush's response to Katrina five years earlier. Even for this staunchly Republican organization, Bush's handling of Katrina remains the benchmark of poor management and administrative failure.[42]

I suggest that while images of US sovereign power (as exercised in Iraq, Afghanistan, and Guantánamo Bay) have flashed around the world since 2001, they have not altered perceptions about America, both within and outside the United States, in the ways that images of Katrina did. The Katrina images produced the "state effect" of the US government unable to provide security to its population. This may be because the Katrina images departed from the dominant race and nation ideologies circulated globally by US cinema and media cultures. These dominant images have long depicted the United States as an exceptional superpower and African Americans as perpetrators of violence.[43] In the Katrina images, African Americans were not perpetrators of violence, as a racialized US media tends to suggest, but rather its victims. The Katrina images challenged these visual histories and the power and legitimacy of the US state. They also challenged US state claims about its humanitarian leadership and ability to protect a population. That is, they challenged US "hard" and "soft" power and the state's authoritative moral claims to both wage war and to protect citizens. If the much vaunted superiority of the Western liberal welfare state was, in some part, based on its claim to provide security to its populations and its ability to enact humanitarian rescue, the Katrina images signaled that the US state could not or would not fulfill this task.[44]

The Crisis of the Media Spectacle

In the wake of Katrina, Internet images became geopolitically powerful, pointing out the United States' lack of exceptionalism and expressing popular outrage as the tragedy unfolded. Digital media makers' focus on content—provided by a wide range of observers and commentators, as well as by some local reporters—allowed many who were not powerful authorities to present their commentary and opinions. In addition, Internet-based news media turned out to be more widely used and more accessible for obtaining news than traditional media. Although the US government hoped to suppress images in conventional media, and television and print news presented images in some controlled and normative frames, photographs were visible on numerous websites devoted to hurricane coverage.[45]

Hurricane Katrina was also remarkable for the role played by new media that quickly synthesized political commentary, images, and opinions from around the world. The Internet quickly became the primary way newspaper editors and journalists circulated news,[46] revealing shifts in the political economy of media and rupturing older narratives. Local newspaper websites were swamped with hits because the television news was not functioning, nor were newspapers able to put out print editions. Newspapers set up websites for emergency news, missing person information, and all kinds of emergency help. The city of New Orleans also began to communicate via the web. As Mark Lisheron points out, "At the height of its effectiveness, the website of the New Orleans newspaper, the *Times Picayune*, was getting 30 million hits a day."[47]

Such hypertrophic Internet coverage highlighted the infrastructural failure of communication and coordination between the US state and private organizations. Rescue operations and support coordination could not work, because of communication problems. The BellSouth telephone company had to evacuate its main New Orleans office for fear of violence.[48] There was little connection between FEMA and other government agencies, because of poor decisions made by FEMA director (and Bush appointee) Michael Brown. A US Senate report from 2006 found that key government agencies did not know the levees had failed and had no idea what was happening at the New Orleans Convention Center. The Department of Homeland Security, in particular, did not know what was transpiring and did not seem to understand the dangers.[49] New Orleans mayor Ray Nagin's calls for evacuation did not recognize that low-income families might not have resources for transportation or housing, resulting in the loss of many lives. Police with shotguns prevented evacuating African Americans from moving onto higher ground occupied by wealthier whites. Those who were evacuated to the Convention Center faced a chaotic situation, since there was no infrastructure or provisions to feed all those who were there. The failures of government and the private companies that owned the infrastructure were compounded by the militarization of the rescue and the aftermath.

US producers of both digital and print media covered not only the disaster and its aftermath but also resulting protests against the government. African American leaders, church communities, and politicians were amongst the most visible and vociferous protestors. Many critiqued the racism behind the Bush administration's lackluster response. The *New York Times* reported that Reverend Jesse Jackson, Representative Maxine Waters, and NAACP leaders were visiting affected areas and emergency centers, while Secretary of State Condoleezza Rice was vigorously defending the president.[50] The *Times* article reported that African American leaders were quick to point out the similarity between the devastated region and other places hit with catastrophes. Representative Waters said "she had traveled throughout Africa and never seen anything quite like that scene" (referring to the Convention Center). The *Times* article also quoted Reverend Sharpton objecting to the use of the word "refugees" as he said sharply, "These are not refugees. . . . They are citizens of Louisiana and Mississippi, tax-paying citizens. They are not refugees wandering somewhere looking for charity. They are victims of neglect and a situation they should have never been put in in the first place."

These representations—globally circulating through multiple media—showed not only the anger, horror, and suffering of a community, but also the horror of powerful, white, male journalists as they reflected and directed the reception of the representations. For example, television showed the shocked faces of Anderson Cooper and Brian Williams, who could not believe that they were seeing in the United States what they had reported on as foreign correspondents in Asia and Africa. One NBC television reporter shouted, "This isn't Iraq, this isn't Somalia, this is our home."[51] In *New York Magazine*, Jonathan Van Meter reported on Cooper's coverage of Katrina: "He is a stew of emotion: dejection, regret, sadness, anger. 'I was really affected by the bodies,' he says, his voice cracking. 'I've seen a lot of dead bodies before, and I'm not sure why these dead bodies affected me so much, but I sort of haven't been able to stop thinking about them.'"[52] Cooper's affective coverage resulted in a 400 percent increase in viewership. In particular, Cooper took government officials to task for what he saw, and his shock, tears, and anger resonated with viewers.[53] According to Katherine Fry, television coverage produced a narrative of heroes and villains, with news anchors such as Cooper and Williams as heroes for living in a dangerous and flooded city to provide a story, and government officials as the "bad guys."[54] In his memoir published a couple of years later, Cooper would write about the shock of what he saw in New Orleans: "I never thought I'd see this in America—the dead left out like trash."[55] New Orleans was different from being in Sri Lanka or in Africa, because he felt, in his words, "connected to what's around me, no longer observing. There is no hotel to go back to, isolated from the destruction, as there was in Sri Lanka."[56] But, Cooper also records that seeing government response after Katrina was an emotional experience because he realized that things could fall apart in America, that all the funding for Homeland Security could not help in such a disaster and that "We" cannot "take care of our own. The world can break apart in our own backyard, and when it does many of us will simply fall off." Cooper does not point to which groups of people would "fall off" as he compares the US government with the ineffective governments, such as those of Sri Lanka or Niger, in other disasters he has covered in his career.[57]

Cooper's shock and outrage registered with viewers in the United States, and the comparisons with the tsunami made the United States seem also to be a nation without resources or concern for its own citizens. The location depicted in these images was what distinguished them from other images of catastrophes, and the particular geopolitics of Katrina underscored the horror.[58] The familiarity of war correspondent Anderson Cooper contrasted with the unfamiliar terrain of a major US metropolis. Frank Durham has argued that a "decentered media" emerged in which presence of journalists on the ground was not framed by official interpretations.[59]

Images of Katrina spectacularized the crisis of welfare and of security upon which the West and America had claimed their superiority and asserted their power to rescue people in distant regions of the world. For a short period, the media spectacle became emergent, in Raymond Williams's terms, challenging Guy Debord's idea that media spectacle can only affirm capitalist logics.[60] Neither corporations nor the state could contain Katrina's spectacle.[61] The unstable spectacle could not justify neoliberalism, given that the dispersed and transnational media could not completely control visuality.[62] Rather, the many fragmentary images—the racialized bodies, the immiseration, the US location, the horror and outrage of viewers and journalists—all of these showed a critique, through global comparison and its racial components, that revealed neoliberalism's contradictions in a country that saw itself as an exceptional superpower. Instead of focusing on individual suffering (undercutting any systematic analysis of structural reasons for the suffering), media images showed large numbers of desperate African Americans, particularly women and children. Thus it was possible to become "witnesses to the catastrophe and its injustice" because the images showed something more than "just an anonymous mass without context," as popular media often depicts minorities.[63] At the same time, the rupture provided by the media coverage produced what one scholar calls an "anti-racism of the center."[64] In such antiracism, the professional news media could position itself as objective and could point to the effects of racism and class that it had long ignored. This contrasted with the way the media ignored the later unfolding of a "racist logic of neoliberal capitalism" in Katrina's aftermath, a logic that contributed to racial inequality through the privatization of rescue.[65]

This rupture, however, was incomplete and built on earlier US media histories of gender, race, and class. Television news still framed the news anchors as heroes, repeating the history of Western disaster journalism. Williams's and Cooper's anger and passion enhanced their value for the television public, showing that they were caring, could report on a catastrophe mostly affecting poor African Americans, and were willing to demand that the government assist those groups. The spectacle's rupture was thus incomplete, and fed the context of US empire and racialized nationalism.

Unsurprisingly, then, the spectacle could only be postponed for a brief period because new images took the suffering narrative in a different direction.[66] Victims became divided into heroes and villains as well. For example, Ray Nagin, the African American mayor of New Orleans, told of people murdering and raping women in the Convention Center. Fox News said that "violent gangs are roaming the streets at night, hidden by cover of darkness," and the *Financial Times* said that rapes and murders were rampant while "looters and madmen exchanged fire with weapons they had looted."[67] In New Orleans, the rapid return to black criminality stereotypes showed how quickly the racialized state, police, and paramilitary soldiers brought the images under control.[68] Neoliberalism's contradictions, which had been in full view, disappeared quickly and the critique of neoliberalism that the first Katrina images provided began to fade. The insecurity produced through the counterspectacle of race- and class-based discrimination was erased by a mass-mediated moral panic over allegedly violent and criminal African Americans.[69] As Jordan Camp suggests, "neoliberal racial regimes of security" and mass-mediated discourses of counterinsurgency and security are "expressions of a moral panic that relies on ideological constructions of race and crime. . . . Racial domination pervades discourses of security."[70] Looting and rape stories suggested that there were many who did not deserve rescue. The moral panic of the disaster was therefore contained through normative images of racialized crime.

Managing the Crisis

What became clear in the days after the hurricane was that the crisis of protection, understood by the local population as security for citizens, was quickly turned into a crisis of state security and corporate power. It was not simply governmental incompetence that was on display, but also corporate indifference and malfeasance. Landstar, the Jacksonville, Florida–based federal contractor hired to evacuate people from the New Orleans Superdome, waited eighteen hours to order three hundred buses for evacuation. Landstar was connected closely to the Bush family.[71] The Bush administration awarded the Shaw Group, whose lobbyist was a former FEMA director under Bush, the government contract to provide tarps to cover damaged homes, despite the fact that the company charged three times more than other bidders.[72]

The Bush administration turned a rescue crisis and accusations from within and outside the United States into a project of state security, militarizing the region with policing and military personnel and linking the disaster to the war on terror project. Though Nicholas Mirzoeff suggests that the visuality of "global counterinsurgency" was apparent in the government response, where military commanders used militaristic language to describe their work,[73] there was more than governmental power at work. Private corporations active in Iraq and Afghanistan—such as Halliburton, Kellogg, and Brown and Root—were also awarded large contracts in the affected areas. According to one report, military personnel stated, "This place is going to look like Little Somalia. . . . This will be a combat operation to get the city under control."[74] The reference to Little Somalia is not simply a racialization and militarization of a domestic population, but also reveals the imperial visual history of the catastrophic event, which conflated African Americans with African refugees and a black neighborhood with what is seen as a violent African country.

Stephen Graham reveals that in military journals such as *Army Times*, there was talk of the need to launch "urban combat" operations to oppose "insurgents" who were supposedly fomenting violence.[75] Graham points out that the security offered by the Bush administration was antiterrorist surveillance and reproduced the war on terror discourse that enriched administration cronies while cutting security related to welfare and urban and social needs.[76] Spike Lee's documentary film about Katrina reveals that the government militarized the catastrophe as a response to protests against state withdrawal, a view echoed by many African American and antiwar activists. Lee connected the military presence to the long history of racial protest in which "U.S. troops have routinely been training their weapons on their own citizens."[77] Lee argues that the government response was slowed down because of the background checks they conducted.[78] "Shoot to kill" orders also hampered responses of the search-and-rescue teams, resulting in a greater numbers of deaths.[79]

War on terror ideologies also emerged via the actions and presence of security personnel charged to protect New Orleans. They helped create the city as a war zone. As Dave Eggers writes in *Zeitoun*, police, soldiers, and corrections officers created a military base out of a bus terminal, focusing on state security rather than on rescuing people from the floodwaters. The terminal parking lot became a "vast outdoor prison" with chain-link fence and barbed wire, and was guarded by soldiers with German shepherd dogs and M16 rifles.[80] Along with three friends, Abdulrahman Zeitoun, a Syrian immigrant, was arrested and incarcerated in a secret jail because he was suspected of being a terrorist and of being affiliated with Al Qaeda.[81] Zeitoun had spent the days after the hurricane rescuing people in his neighborhood, but he was incarcerated without any evidence or due process. He was not allowed to make phone calls or ask why he was arrested, though he supposed it was because he was from the Middle East and suspected of being a terrorist. A guard told Zeitoun and the three friends he was arrested with, "You guys are terrorists. You're Taliban." Zeitoun was familiar with the construction business because he owned a house painting company and had worked on ships before coming to the United States. He calculated that the prison must have been built immediately after the hurricane, and the structure suggested that a great deal of funding and labor had been devoted to building it. Instead of working on rescue operations, police, soldiers, and corrections officers had devoted time and effort to building a prison. The prison itself looked to Zeitoun like images of the Guantánamo Bay Naval Base prison, and the guards called it "Angola South" or "Camp Greyhound," implying it was a prison in a war zone outside the United States. Zeitoun was ultimately accused of having stolen property, without any evidence. Police, soldiers, and corrections officers seemed to have built the prison and filled it with people to show that there was looting in the city and that guards and a prison were needed to protect people. But Eggers and Zeitoun suggest that the prison was filled with people picked up from the street, many of whom were innocent, like Zeitoun, but who were nonetheless disciplined with pepper spray, body searches, and SWAT teams looking for drugs. In Zeitoun's case, his interrogators did not imagine that a Middle Eastern or Muslim man could be a rescuer; the only identity possible for him was that of a terrorist. In this militarization of the disaster, the context of the war on terror ensured that Zeitoun was not an exceptional citizen to be praised for his heroism and his support of the community.

Eggers's account reveals the militarization of the response to the catastrophe. This militarization was not just undertaken by soldiers and police, however. The government outsourced relief efforts to private military corporations such as Blackwater and Halliburton, which provided privatized and securitized services. Both companies rose to prominence amid responses to 9/11, when Halliburton's former CEO, Vice President Dick Cheney, helped make war in Iraq. Anthropologist Vincanne Adams's research team heard from informants that armed men "hit the streets of New Orleans in armored cars, patrolling with machine guns" and that their operation resembled "more of a military tactical operation in a war zone than a civilian recovery process in a beloved American city."[82]

Militarization did not stop protests, however. Many critiqued both the use of military in the city and the false reports of stereotypical black criminality that were used to hide what was happening to impoverished communities. The discursive opening provided by the Katrina images and their similarity to narratives of global suffering, as well as the critiques of US neoliberalism, signaled that neoliberalism could rupture. These factors brought back a "movement" politics in which black politicians, clergy, leaders, singers, and filmmakers were particularly vocal. Protestors foregrounded the continued crisis of the imperial superpower spectacularly unable to provide for its own citizens. Katrina signified a return to the hope of the biopolitical welfare state. Some called for liberalism's return, while others demanded security in nonmilitarized forms. Some of those hailing a post–civil rights era also argued that the United States was in a postracial era.[83] Others, however, used this phrase to call for a new state agenda to combat racism.[84] There were also many who intervened in the debate to reveal that the struggle was as much for economic rights as for civil rights.[85] Such calls articulated the continued hope for a politics that could deliver such social justice and rights. Since then, the work of uncovering what went on during and after the hurricane has continued the struggle against neoliberal state policies.

Aftermath: Advanced Neoliberalism, Collaborations, and Protests

Even ten years later, the very mention of Katrina remains a sign of the Bush administration's failures. However, these failures have come to be seen as failures of the state, as Congress and the White House in the Obama administration paid greater attention to FEMA and disaster support, rather than failures of private entities. The failures of corporations and nonprofits to undertake repair and welfare are also emerging, in the work of advocacy and nonprofit organizations such as CorpWatch, and in scholarly analysis that does not make media headlines, especially on the national or transnational stage. While protests emerged right after the hurricane to criticize government response, numerous entities have remained attentive to the aftermath, monitoring the plight of residents unable to return, and trying to understand the complexities of race, gender, age, and class that produced differential exposure to the storm. NGOs such as Save the Children were critical of the temporary housing provided by FEMA, finding that families—especially those led by single women—were further impoverished by the catastrophe. On the other hand, NGOs such as the Red Cross, which received massive donations from across the country, had employees who used donations for their private gain, discriminated against Latinos and Native groups, and failed to follow many of their own policies for tracking and distributing supplies.[86] Many of the trailers provided by FEMA were substandard, and insurance companies refused to accept claims and respond adequately to this problem. The states of Louisiana and Mississippi had to file lawsuits against these companies.[87] Local businesses did not benefit from the disaster while large, politically connected corporations—such as Halliburton, Kellogg, and Brown and Root—received most of the funding. A US House Committee found that billions of dollars had been wasted or mismanaged due to government lack of oversight and diligence, and there was also fraud and corruption in awarding contracts to private companies.[88]

As with development after disaster in other parts of the world, rebuilding in New Orleans has not brought back all residents, nor has it made it more possible for working-class people, especially people of color, to live there. Many former residents remain unable to return, or cannot afford to rent or buy in the rebuilt areas.[89] The US government has not been able to mitigate the hurricane's effects for many New Orleans residents, as "disaster capital-ism" has undermined social welfare and replaced it with private contracts.[90] Charges of entrenched corruption and difficulty of navigating bureaucratic "nightmares" pervade the responses of many who tried to return or rebuild, while volunteer agencies and private corporations became sources of sup-port or assistance.[91] Although activists demanded support from the govern-ment, the government simply subcontracted out the work or collaborated with private businesses and corporations to do it. Thus, the disaster repair work consolidated the power of a connected corporate and state elite. A con-gressional report found that half of all Department of Homeland Security contracts were given without open competition and that most of the $34 billion spent by the DHS was wasted. Of the $20.5 billion allocated to federal agencies for hurricane recovery, only $2.7 billion went to local businesses while the majority of the funding, 73.8 percent, went to large businesses. Neither the Army Corps of Engineers nor the Department of Defense ad-equately monitored the subcontracting work.[92]

Disaster capitalism requires the collaboration between the state, corpora-tions, NGOs and individuals, as well as the active participation of the state in passing its welfare functions on to private enterprises.[93] Numerous religious and nonprofit organizations continue to work in the area. As with the work of all such NGOs in disaster areas, there are many who welcome their contri-butions and many who see them as signs of neoliberal withdrawal from wel-fare.[94] Media images of Katrina linger online, while many of the issues that arose after Katrina—infrastructure problems, impoverished cities, and lack of preparedness for global climate change and its effects—have disappeared from news sites.

Media attention has shifted from those in need to those who are doing hu-manitarian work in the area. Celebrities such as Brad Pitt grab headlines for helping rebuild homes in the area, becoming exceptional citizens coming to the rescue of the city, and supposedly doing the work of the state.[95] Celebri-ties and welfare providers emerged as responsible individuals, as exemplary exceptional citizens, while New Orleans residents were represented as in-sufficiently neoliberal and thus unable to help themselves. The consequence of this neoliberal process, made visible by the disaster response in New Or-leans, is that state sovereignty has become dispersed to corporations, NGOs, and individuals, as these entities become the subcontractors for the state. Importantly, though, none of these entities have provided what is needed for the low-income African American populations who were dispossessed and displaced. Instead, many of those displaced by the hurricane cannot return, while some more connected groups are recipients of the millions of dollars that were sent by US groups and individuals. Although the local women-led, community-based nonprofits that ran after-school programs and did a great deal of community work could not come back, many other women became part of NGO networks or gatekeepers, as Pamela Jenkins argues.[96] Additionally, the churches and religious nonprofits (the "faith community," as it has come to be called) became a key sector that helped low-income residents of the region. These faith-based groups played a large role in providing recovery funding and volunteers.[97] Cedric Johnson argues that the enlisting of community groups in this neoliberal process is best described as "grassroots privatization," because "they advance neoliberalization through empowerment and civic mobilization."[98] Such reconstruction, Johnson argues, reproduces inequalities, benefits the more powerful and connected rather than the disenfranchised, and encourages "participation without power."[99] These are precisely the critiques made of NGOs in other parts of the world.[100]

The visibility of volunteerism is not specific to the United States. In fact, this reliance on volunteerism marks the banality of the neoliberal turn of the United States, rather than its exceptionalism, especially since welfare comes to focus on addressing needs after catastrophic events rather than ongoing support for all inhabitants. This banality reveals how the neoliberal "Western" welfare state is formed against both the "developing/development" state in the Global South and the importance in those regions of organizations that have come to be called NGOs. A neoliberal discourse has come to define the state as inefficient and corrupt, recuperating histories of struggle against colonial and liberal powers. This is the case not only in the Congo or India, for instance, but also in the United States through claims of state disfunctionality and the rising importance of private-sector welfare work. This neoliberalism incorporates an ideology of an inefficient and unwilling government, delegitimizing the state for those who believe it is too powerful, even as the state downplays the predations of privatized capitalism. It comes to provide welfare in conditions of disaster relief, when the state's retrenchment becomes visible and catastrophic. Over recent decades, NGOs, as private entities, have stepped in to provide patchy welfare to populations when the development state has failed to do so. While NGOs have been characterized as more caring, honest, and "grassroots" than states,[101] private corporations are seen as more efficient and productive, unlike the state and its agencies. Furthermore, NGOs—many of them using corporate language and mechanisms—increasingly create new professionals, professions, and work hierarchies based on gender, race, nationality, and religion.[102] Many NGOs offer employment that is not steady and not pensioned, but in some parts of the world it is often the only employment for certain populations, especially middle-class women.[103] NGOs have come to be seen as institutions who mediate the power of the US state and as having what might be called "soft power," which provides the welfare and care that accompanies the "hard power" of its military.

If NGOs have become providers of welfare in many regions of the Global South, however inadequate or intermittent such welfare becomes, those regions in the Global South are understood as failing in their welfare function. When such conditions have become part of the US context, it is important to show US citizens as providing the welfare, rather than simply becoming recipients of relief. Through NGOs and nonprofits, the US state exercises its "soft power," empowering humanitarian individuals and their governmentalization of welfare. In the case of Katrina, private organizations and individuals provided welfare to many affected by the hurricane even as the Bush-led state remained unable and unwilling to help. Those who did step in to help, convinced that their contributions could make a difference, also exercised soft power. What we see in this shift is that instead of an exceptional state, there appear exceptional individuals celebrated for their ability to give donations and to help others. Even so, the scale of private responses has little relation to the needs of displaced communities. Yet media producers and journalists represented these humanitarians as exceptional individuals across a media in which celebrities and wealthy entrepreneurs become visible as leaders helping others.

These representations come in the wake of the US government turning to private welfare to provide support to New Orleans inhabitants while also trying to revitalize FEMA. Many have understood this turn to private, market logics as demonstrating neoliberalism's triumph over liberalism.[104] Yet this turn to private welfare also aligned the United States with the Global South, as in both contexts "state failure" spurred the need for NGOs to pick up the slack. Although media representations showed the US government as in charge, especially in its militarization of New Orleans, the NGO sector was also shown as having a role in "disaster management."[105] Thus, the role of volunteer labor and charity organizations has remained important in debates and narratives of New Orleans' rebuilding.[106]

The events of Hurricane Katrina reveal the crisis of Bush-led advanced neoliberal policies,[107] as well as the resolution of this crisis through a shift in the security state. As I have argued, advanced neoliberalism emerges as governments respond to the crisis created by previous versions of neoliberalism.

Neoliberal policies have become deeply sedimented in political and economic life, but they also create contradictions that enable political subjects to remember, with what Lauren Berlant calls "cruel optimism," the lost promises of liberalism.[108] The US state thus was forced to address its own waning power, produced by media images as state effect, by turning to corporations, individuals, and NGOs to undertake rescue operations and repair the city.

Ten years later, many within and outside the United States condemn the continued immiseration of Gulf Coast residents. For instance, the United Nations has passed judgment on the abandonment of the population during the hurricane. In 2009, the UN's special rapporteur asked the US government to enforce civil rights laws, prevent discrimination by the police, and establish a special commission to examine "the progress and failures in the fight against racism"[109]—recommendations that US politicians ridiculed. In 2006, the Inter-American Commission on Human Rights presented a paper, with contributions from the University of California, Berkeley's School of Law and the Southern Poverty Law Center, in which it argued that international human rights laws had been violated when the US government did not provide adequate help to those in need during the hurricane.[110] The United States Human Rights Network (USHRN), made up of hundreds of US-based NGOs and advocacy organizations, submitted a report to the United Nations Human Rights Committee stating that the US government's actions after Katrina violated the International Covenant on Civil and Political Rights.[111] Similarly, the Institute of Southern Studies' report on Katrina from 2008, subtitled "A Global Human Rights Perspective," stated that the United States had not followed the UN's "Guiding Principles on Internal Displacement."[112] Such condemnation has often been leveled at impoverished nations around the world, but this time it was directed at the United States. Scholars have argued that race, gender, and class violences explain what happened in New Orleans, and Katrina has become a case study of US racial divides as well as an example of the empty promises of equality.[113]

Scholarly attention to the hurricane and its aftermath represents Katrina as an example of the racialized precariousness caused by decades of neoliberalism, a precariousness connected transnationally to the 1970s "structural adjustment" programs mandated by the International Monetary Fund (IMF) in the Global South that most impacted low-income women and families. Scholars also use the event's massive impact to draw attention to the politics of gender, race, and class at work in liberal genealogies, US state failures to extend equality to all citizens, US racism, and the more recent neoliberal retrenchment of state welfare.[114] Scholarly critiques of such policies have been pervasive, but have had little impact on government policies. Shirley Laska argues that "resiliency" and "human rights" might be necessary terms to address the hurricane's preconditions and aftermath—the "poor condition of the people and the community" that led to loss of lives, livelihood, and ability to return.[115] Kevin Fox Gotham suggests that Katrina "articulated submerged fears about risk, safety, and security in an age when the federal government is withdrawing resources for disaster-prevention and relief."[116] Scholars have shown that the lack of resources that prevented many from leaving were caused by decades of neoliberal accumulation of wealth by elites and the gutting of welfare and support for low-income women and people of color.[117] Scholarly research on Katrina has become a large and interdisciplinary enterprise, with numerous special issues of academic journals as well as monographs and essays on the topic.[118] The Social Science Research Council became a supporter and repository of numerous research publications concerning the disaster, all of which contributed to scholarly research on the political, social, and economic issues revealed by the disaster.

For many researching African American communities, the spectacle indicated what has been happening to black communities through decades of neoliberal policies.[119] For instance, Clyde Woods has stated, "The tragedy of New Orleans continues to haunt American notions of equality, governance, knowledge, morality, and progress."[120] Katrina made visible how the US turn to neoliberalism has adversely impacted disenfranchised communities. The racist US state embraced neoliberalism to evade its responsibilities.[121] Michael Ralph argues that Katrina revealed that we are in a "post-civil rights society," which means that, in neoliberalism, one cannot rely on either the state or a charismatic leader representing the community. The promise of liberalism (and even political representation, I would argue) is misplaced.[122] Ralph argues that cultural productions also "reveal how black people of varied stripes now find the prospect of democracy dubious and consequently turn to hustling as a way out of economic and political marginalization."[123] The Katrina images mobilized communities against the long-standing and pervasive racism of US liberalism and validated hustling as a response to catastrophe.

In addition to scholars, artists also expressed outrage at Katrina's handling.[124] The most prominent was director Spike Lee, who made two award-winning documentaries, *When the Levees Broke: A Requiem in Four Acts* (2006) and *If God Is Willing and da Creek Don't Rise* (2010). Lee gathered news footage, images of pre- and post-Katrina New Orleans, and interviews with politicians, activists, flood victims, journalists, musicians, artists, and a host of others to bring to public attention the state's racist ineptitude and the victims' plight.[125] Together, this artistic and scholarly work has shown the Bush administration's ineptitude and carelessness as well as the ways neoliberal policies created vulnerable populations.

Katrina's images brought about widespread critiques of George W. Bush, his presidency, and his politics. "Brownie, you're doing a heck of a job," referring to Bush's praise of FEMA director Michael Brown's handling of the disaster, has become a sardonic cliché referring to a clueless employer with an incompetent employee. People from across the political spectrum use the term "Katrina" to reference a visible and spectacular failure. Katrina continues to resonate in debates about the role of FEMA and the state in helping communities recover from catastrophes. While Katrina indicated that there were incompetent bureaucrats working in the Bush administration, many also argued that a retrenchment of government services, as well as the costs of an unnecessary war, led to the problems. At the same time that the US government, led by the geopolitics of the Bush White House, was trying to project an image of power through its wars in Iraq and Afghanistan, its handling of Katrina revealed the state as inept, bungling, and uncaring. These two representations of the state became symptomatic of the US government as both exceptional superpower and unexceptional failure. This heterogeneous state effect revealed the contradictions of a neoliberalism in which citizens' demands for welfare (which the state could not and would not provide) existed alongside the state's powerful ability to wage war. These two state effects— the exceptional war state and the unexceptional failed state—showed that the project of war had its effects at "home" and that the costs of external wars became visible on the home front.[126]

This chapter has been focused on Katrina and its impact as paradigmatic of those shifts in the state and in US power that I call "advanced liberalism." In this disaster what was visible was not simply state unwillingness, but also its slow, deliberate move toward incompetence that could only to be ameliorated by corporate and private intervention. Advanced neoliberalism is also characterized by protests, visible during and after Katrina, and made transnational by the media spectacle of catastrophe and a failing imperial power. Protests include the research and activism that brought attention to the ways that neoliberalism had come "home" to the United States with a vengeance. Protests about inequality have proliferated since then, and the debates about class and race continue unabated.

In examining neoliberal's impact as exemplified by Katrina, it becomes clear that the waning of imperial power and its logic of security became visible globally through transnational media, leading to the massive outpouring of opinion and commentary from outside the United States. Katrina's geopolitics included condemnation, sympathy, mockery, and concern. This was a geopolitics that constructed state effect; not simply state power but also its lack of power, its violence, and its collaboration and partnership with corporations. Thus, the US state crisis became both a cause and effect of neoliberal retrenchment, played out in endless national and transnational mediascapes to reveal both state power and its ruptures. In the case of Katrina, this crisis was resolved by the private organizations that came to be seen as embodying the virtues of self-helping, American individuals. These organizations simultaneously challenged, supported, and constructed state power as both inefficient and all-powerful through a variety of technologies and power relations. The damage to the US state has remained, even as neoliberal discourses of private efficiency and humanitarian welfare, supported by the state itself, have become powerful. The contradiction for neoliberal states—that such ideologies affect their power and sovereignty—contributes to the difficult balancing act that the US government performs. Such a difficulty can be understood as the process of shifting exceptionalism from the nation-state to the individual and citizen. In this neoliberal ideology, the claim is that what the state will not or cannot accomplish, exceptional American citizens will undertake.

2. American Humanitarian Citizenship

The "Soft" Power of Empire

By the end of the first decade of the twenty-first century, US military advertisements claimed that its military does not simply protect the country but also saves lives the world over. As a television ad from 2009 explained, the US Navy is a "global force for good."[1] The one-minute ad showed images of black and Asian servicemen and servicewomen stating that the navy, like a religious path, is a "calling to serve," a calling to do good. An advertisement from the same period for the US Marines titled, "Towards the Sounds of Chaos," showed images of soldiers moving boxes labeled "AID" into planes and helicopters, taking supplies to Haiti, and working in tsunami-hit areas.[2] According to the *New York Times*, the ad campaign was partly the result of a national online survey conducted by the marketing firm JWT, which revealed that many young adults considered "helping people in need, wherever they may live" to be an important component of good citizenship.[3] Such campaigns downplayed what might have drawn recruits in previous eras: the experience of military brotherhood, the excitement of battle, patriotism, and the desire to protect, or the educational benefits made possible by military service. Instead, these twenty-first-century ads showed the marines bringing help in times of chaos. By claiming the military saves lives around the world, the ads downplayed the lethal violence of American wars.

The growing spread of humanitarianism as part of military and imperial power is shared across many other American institutions. Print, television, and digital news media cover such humanitarian work, focusing on heroic Americans working on global and national crises to save and improve lives. The American humanitarian has emerged as an affective subject who embodies a normative American citizenship produced by both state institutions and private entities. While this subject gains power from a longer history of empire, it is also being written into American history as part of the American "character." For instance, in 2011, Bill Keller of the *New York Times* claimed that Americans have "rediscovered" their "missionary spirit," which "manifests itself in everything from quiet kindness to patronizing advice to armored divisions."[4] He goes on to argue that this "spirit" is "one strong fiber in our national character," which he traces from the Charter of Massachusetts Bay (1629). Although expressing some wariness over military intervention, he suggests that philanthropy is a key part of the American missionary spirit.

Keller is not alone in this view. Indeed, for many Americans, humanitarianism is the soft power of US empire, stretching across numerous public and private institutions as an aspect of national and global citizenship and as part of daily life. As a term, "humanitarianism" references the giver of humanity—the "humanitarian"—rather than the receiver. As such, it is as much about self-making and self-improvement as it is about a world in which such self-making is seen as essential not only to the welfare of Americans but also to those around the world. Humanitarianism thus combines the work of self-help with the work of "helping others" (volunteering is understood to build self-worth and lead to jobs and careers), and through media culture and commodities, people disseminate its narratives and power. This American humanitarian has emerged as an exceptional citizen of the US state.

As I argued in chapter 1, under advanced neoliberal conditions in which inequality has resulted in protests and critiques of state welfare rollbacks, the US nation-state's exceptionalism has now moved to its citizens. Instead of an exceptional nation, there are exceptional citizens, and one way their exceptionalism is produced is through their participation in humanitarianism. The exceptional citizen is a key component of the growing "nonprofit industrial complex," connecting individuals to states and to private enterprises.[5] As inequality has become a political issue, neoliberal and nationalist logics constituted by class, race, and religion are naturalized precisely when Americans (often allied with many other Westerners) feel compelled to rescue others—when they see themselves as uniquely qualified to enact this rescue.[6]

That such subjects are neoliberal is evidenced by the emergence of neologisms such as "social entrepreneur" and "social enterprises" that incorporate the exceptional humanitarian individuals into the market economy. Corporate mechanisms and corporate funding become connected to private and public humanitarian projects through donations, support, volunteerism, and favorable tax advantages. For the elites, it turns philanthropy into a humanitarian project. Although humanitarians see themselves as separate from the state, and indeed as more efficient and caring than the state, they are inseparable from it.[7] Through the merging of public and private institutions, humanitarianism has become a state project supported through government funding for private welfare groups and government encouragement for individuals to participate in humanitarian projects.

American humanitarianism shares in the project of Western humanitarianisms and their imperial histories, but it has its own specificities. It builds upon common histories of "charity," missionary work, and the "civilizing" project enacted in the so-called developing world through war, institutions such as the church and the state, and transnational NGOs. The long history of Western missionary work and humanitarianism legitimizes current "Western" rescuers in distant places.[8] It is mostly American, Christian Westerners who circulate, in transnational news media in particular, as proper humanitarians. While we do see nonwhite and non-Western and non-Christian individuals celebrated as exemplary activists, these brown and black humanitarians from the Global South are more often represented as anomalous citizens of their cultures and countries, unlike US humanitarians whose exceptionalism is represented as normative. Malala Yousafzai, the youngest Nobel Prize winner, is an example of one such anomalous Pakistani celebrated for her support of girls' education in that region and for speaking out against the Taliban.

While these humanitarian endeavors have become part of contemporary consumer and citizen practices in the United States, they are the result of many Western-led international projects begun after World War II. Many of these organizations—including the United Nations (UN), Amnesty International, Oxfam, Doctors without Borders, and Human Rights Watch—have based their advocacy for "the international community" in a new international form of juridical power, derived from human rights or the International Court of Justice.[9] While some have argued that these humanitarian institutions constitute a new global civil society in Habermasian terms, others have seen them as the agents of a new imperialism.[10] Miriam Ticktin argues that humanitarianism constitutes new biopolitical practices and transnational governance.[11] Didier Fassin analyzes humanitarianism through the affective and moral dimension of "humanitarian reason" and the biopolitics of "humanitarian government." He sees both of these as producing inequality, arguing that the term "humanitarianism" became important for French governance and colonialism.[12] Luc Boltanski has suggested that distant suffering produces what he calls a "politics of pity," which can be distinguished from a "politics of justice."[13] He argues that the former compels the viewer of suffering to connect politics with humanitarianism within a genealogy of Christian and French revolutionary subject formation. But Boltanski leaves out colonial and racial histories in his genealogy, which are central to any consideration of European or US practices. His focus lies more in analyzing how suffering plays into politics and presents a problem for the universalization of suffering. Lilie Chouliaraki examines the work done by "humanitarian communication" in media and the emotional repertoires generated by mediated images of suffering that become part of lifestyles and consumption.[14] She has argued for a "post-humanitarian" politics that emerges after compassion fatigue and which connects consumers to immediate and individualized modes of humanitarianism.[15] Chouliaraki's important interventions are helpful to understanding the affective and communicative registers of mediated humanitarianism, and her work suggests that fine-grained analyses are required to examine the vast enterprise of humanitarianism. Despite all these scholarly interventions and continuing research examining the impact and results of the work done by humanitarian NGOs, there remains the widely disseminated commonsense notion that without such work, many more people would suffer. The stubbornness of this perception is not to be discounted, because it is exacerbated and enabled by the same neoliberal retrenchment of state welfare across the globe that has created cultures of protest, and which private or authoritarian capitalism rapidly captures in many regions, including the United States.

While these scholars focus on the global contexts in which humanitarianism as a term circulates, here I examine the term's circulation in the United States to show that humanitarianism has become central to American neoliberal citizenship. The subject claiming this citizenship is normatively middle class, Christian and Western, placing them in the "West" and in America through civilizational, developmental, and human rights discourses. While such a subject is also visible in other parts of the West, it has become pervasive in the United States across numerous institutions.

In this chapter, I focus on US humanitarian soft power as it is enabled through consumption, mobility, and the production of difference and distance. Humanitarianism makes visible inequalities between Americans and others, extending the power of the nation-state while showing both the lethal reach of its military and the limits of military hard power. US humanitarian citizenship is coupled with surveillance, as well as individualizing and racializing sovereignty. In the context of humanitarianism, soft power is mobilized as "the power of the media to cast cultural difference and political struggle in the language of military conflict and war," thereby revealing how war is mediated as a humanitarian project in the twenty-first century.[16] In this mode of citizenship, humanitarian projects animate and utilize what are presumed to be American impulses of kindness, caring, and good citizenship. These projects rely on Americans' perception of themselves as "good" and "generous," giving aid and coming to the rescue of distant others. Andrea Muehlebach has argued that in the case of Italy, neoliberalism has dissolved the difference between the Left and the Right though the articulation of a moral order rather than simply an economic one.[17] Her analysis rings true for the United States as well, as the humanitarian project unites political actors of all stripes. The humanitarian order encompasses a wide range of individuals, groups, and organizations from both the Left and the Right, uniting them within a neoliberal citizenship that brings together militarism and empire.

The power of such humanitarian citizenship is visible when charity and missionary work, long part of religious practices in many cultures, have become incorporated into a common American humanitarianism. The language of humanitarianism unifies and homogenizes nonstate welfare; it works across public and private institutions and creates normative, ethical, and affective forms of belonging to an American empire. These practices and their subjects depend on constructions of race, class, sexuality, religion, and gender but also appear to transcend them through a common humanitarianism.

Humanitarianism enables the continued production of inequality and difference—racial, gendered, and nationalist—that I examine in this chapter. I focus on three mainstream forms of American humanitarianism: "voluntourism" as a new version of mass tourism, adventure travel that calls upon a long imperial history of white masculinity and individuality, and "laptop humanitarianism" as online charity cultures. While focusing on these three formations, I also see them as dependent on affective and imperial projects that are shared across many other institutions that have transformed American citizenship and everyday life. Rather than elaborating on the representational practices that construct the figure of what Cynthia Enloe has called the "global victim,"[18] this chapter focuses on the subjects who are doing the saving and on the visibility and emergence of US humanitarian citizenship.

Cultures of Humanitarian Citizenship

Large-scale US government support for humanitarianism began in 1961 with the Peace Corps and education abroad programs. The government provided direct and indirect state support for these programs to promote goodwill for the United States.[19] Some scholars argue that the United States has been participating in humanitarian imperialism since the Philippine–American war.[20] Mimi Thi Nguyen suggests such a project exists in the context of a US empire that gives the "gift" of refugee status to many who have suffered from US imperial violence.[21] Others have argued that US humanitarianism is a "gift economy" involving both imperial power and a "language of active citizenship."[22] Ann Vogel concludes that the formation of nonprofit foundations in the United States during the 1990s created elite mechanisms for wealth distribution, while humanitarian projects export American understandings of democracy and form notions of what seems "global" for many Americans.[23] Other researchers understand humanitarianism as the product of a sensationalistic mass culture that has existed in the United States since the early twentieth century.[24] This affective and material context of US empire suggests how and why the recent version of humanitarianism became so powerful and so ubiquitous.

It has come to be taken for granted that no entity except the "West" or the "good American" can rescue different and distant others and that those different and distant others are unable to help themselves. Even though distance is a mediated notion—produced through travel, journalism, television, cinema, and photography as well as through representations and practices that emphasize inequality and difference in spatial terms[25]—the ability to use distance to mystify humanitarian actions as always benevolent has become crucial. Moreover, the mark of the good American citizen is an ability to distance oneself from violence by being able to separate deserving victims from undeserving ones, both in the United States and outside of it—as became visible in the humanitarianism that emerged in New Orleans after Hurricane Katrina. Even those who live in physical proximity in cities and neighborhoods can be distanced as undeserving and improper citizens. Many who call themselves humanitarians believe that they can "make a difference" in distant regions, whereas local change is believed to be difficult or downright impossible. Race has been critical in producing such distinctions in US history, as African Americans and Native Americans in the United States become pathologized in segregated regions and neighborhoods. For example, Michael O. Emerson and Christina Smith have argued that white evangelical Christians are unable to see how structures of racial inequality pervade life in the United States.[26] It is not surprising then that so many evangelical missionary projects take place outside of the United States; the presence of strong African American churches and advocacy organizations means that humanitarian racism can be resisted and opposed. The strong protests and media uproar that emerged during and after Katrina, which denounced the racist state and racist NGOs, explain why these mostly white Christian organizations prefer to be humanitarian in distant regions where their activities take place away from the limelight of local or national media and antiracist organizing. Melani McAlister has shown that many faith-based missions are directed overseas in racialized and imperial projects that include missionary tourism, conversion projects, and projects directed at rescuing Christians from Muslims or Hindus.[27]

In addition to producing spatial distance, this humanitarian citizenship erases divisions between public and private, and sutures state and nation. American humanitarian citizenship is transnational and national in that it is constructed against those who are not allowed to be citizens and on behalf of those believed to require Western rescuers. Juridical and policing mechanisms enforce such distinction, as I show in chapter 3. Humanitarianism works through networks of private foundations and public funding, and resources from the state, as well as from groups and individuals. Humanitarian citizenship is governmentalized across many institutions in the United States, including the military, schools and colleges, churches, and community groups, as well as big and small businesses and corporations. Not only does this citizenship rely on private foundations but also on numerous state projects, institutions, and regulations. Importantly, it is also a government project endorsed by both Democrats and Republicans, including Presidents Clinton, George W. Bush, and Obama.[28]

Humanitarian citizenship produces American citizens as normatively Christian and replaces the language and activism of rights with that of charity, reducing demands on the state by citizens, placing low-income citizens at the mercy of the wealthy, and weakening the connections between people and the state. Charity claims to help the needy, but it cannot scale up as much as the state, nor can it replace the safety net that a state should provide. It produces only humanitarians as sovereign subjects rather than the state as sovereign. At the same time, because it works as a mode of citizenship, humanitarianism is also multicultural (allowing participation of many groups) yet racialized as the work of a normative white American. The dominant visual culture of humanitarianism constructs a racial and geopolitical difference between the white American donor and the nonwhite, Global South receiver. It is also gendered, sometimes relying on essentialist representations of masculine (and colonial) adventure and travel, and sometimes evoking sexual difference via the nurturing feminine subject. Although such citizenship is normatively white, becoming American for people of color can also mean becoming humanitarian.

Humanitarianism has become an integral part of the US economy, bringing together corporations, foundations, and individuals. Denis Kennedy points out that "the humanitarian project ... [has] been transformed into a $10 billion a year industry."[29] The humanitarian economy flourishes because consultants, NGOs, and UN agencies (along with a network of wealthy corporations, donors, and states) benefit financially from being mediators of such work. Humanitarianism links corporations, states, and individuals within a corporatized political economy of charity. At its very worst, humanitarianism has emerged as a form of celebrity public relations enabling certain figures and corporations to circulate and accumulate value so that they can sell commodities. Numerous for-profit businesses have come into existence for this purpose. The website Look to the Stars, for instance, lists media celebrities involved in humanitarian work. It gathers information from multiple sources to show how much charitable work is being done by the wealthy and the famous.[30] Charity balls, auctions, parties, and sporting and social events are organized to support NGOs, turning wealthy celebrities into humanitarians.

In many instances, whether actual support is given to humanitarianism targets is debatable, and how much is spent on social events versus actual charity is often a question for organization leaders who believe that there are few other paths to raising "awareness" or funds for their causes. In a trenchant *New York Times* article, John Colapinto provides one example of this political economy of charity, describing the work of Trevor Nielson at the Los Angeles–based Global Philanthropy Group, which works with wealthy individuals and celebrities such as Angelina Jolie and Brad Pitt.[31] Colapinto reveals that for some entrepreneurs such as Nielson, humanitarianism is a new public relations business that rehabilitates reputations and builds star images and brands. Often these entrepreneurs make millions from their wealthy clients, while the philanthropic causes receive a trickle of that money. Colapinto gives the example of one celebrity who promised millions to a youth homeless shelter but ended up just sending T-shirts.

US feminism has also played a role in constituting non-Western women as targets of humanitarian projects, though this project is not solely an American one.[32] In the aftermath of the four UN World Conferences on Women (1975–95), feminist and women's NGOs have come to occupy a large part of development discourse.[33] These organizations are of many kinds and operate at many levels. Many organizations, especially the transnational ones, participate in humanitarian endeavors around the world, working on development projects such as "capacity building" or "microfinance" that focus on women as targets of rescue. Many activists see themselves as doing what the "corrupt," "inefficient," "patriarchal," or "failed" state refuses to do to improve women's lives. In some places, as Sabine Lang has argued, the NGOization of feminism has replaced more movement-oriented projects.[34] This trend, which Sonia Álvarez has called the "NGO 'boom,'" now exists transnationally and in development discourse.[35]

Humanitarianism creates enormous publicity for some causes and mobilizes donations using affect and media. Yet it often does so in ways that contribute to global and national inequality by emphasizing the economic and racial difference between the West and the "developing" world, between rich and poor, and between whites and nonwhites. It justifies unequal accumulation of wealth with the logic that private philanthropy is necessary and that the generosity of the wealthy can ameliorate the structural inequalities created by capitalism and empire. In this way, American humanitarianism hides the violence generated by wars and colonialism, as well as the systems of power that have expanded inequalities throughout the twentieth and twenty-first centuries.

Humanitarian Travel and Tourism

In recent years, increasingly large numbers of Americans have traveled to Africa, Latin America, or Asia to visit slums, poor neighborhoods, and the children or communities to whom they send money. This has produced new itineraries and projects that combine travel with humanitarianism. This "voluntourism" or "socially conscious tourism," as Gada Mahrouse terms it,[36] is promoted by numerous nonprofits such as Global Exchange, and also by companies catering to colleges and university students. College students have become a big market for these organizations, as they hope to gain skills and build resumes. Senior citizens and tourists who are dissatisfied with traditional tourist experiences and are politically aware of global inequalities are also often attracted to such forms of travel.[37] This travel is both religious and secular. Melani McAlister has written about evangelical missionary work that emerged in the 1990s, including evangelical causes to "save" Christians and Christianity around the world.[38] Although historically, religious organizations such as the Mormon Church have created spiritual missions, secular voluntourism has increased dramatically as Americans continue to travel to places they see as different from their home countries to experience racial, cultural, and national difference. For the most part, the paradigmatic voluntourist is white and the country visited is one in the Global South.

Numerous tourist guidebooks provide information to enable such travel. Lonely Planet publishes *Volunteer: A Traveller's Guide to Making a Difference Around the World*, and there are many others including *Volunteer Vacations: Short Term Adventures That Will Benefit You and Others*, which is now in its eleventh edition, and *700 Places to Volunteer before You Die: A Traveler's Guide* by Nola Lee Kelsey.[39] Most of these texts provide guidance in terms of organizations to work for, types of volunteer work, how to choose organizations to work with, and what kinds of "exchange" can be expected. For the most part, the authors use stock phrases such as "making a difference" and "following your passion" to help readers decide where and how to volunteer, and they imply that individuals can overcome all kinds of global differences. These authors deploy a prevailing ideology of peer-to-peer exchange in which power differences between peers cannot be acknowledged. Further, the plethora of volunteer opportunities provides a wide range of consumer choices that are similar to those made by tourists deciding which country to visit for pleasure.

For these authors, volunteers can benefit from "cultural exchange" and "global citizenship," as well as improve their careers and health and "give something back," suggesting that their regular work does not have much social benefit. Some guidebooks, such as *Volunteer Vacations*, claim to be selective in choosing reputable and vetted volunteer opportunities, implying that there are many organizations that are not reputable and revealing the highly competitive market of these organizations that cater to Western volunteers. The guidebook states that it provides "in-depth information about each organization,"[40] though it is not clear who vetted them or how they were vetted, and the "in-depth" information is remarkably sparse. This guide lists organizations by region, type of work, excerpt of mission statement, number of volunteers for the last year, funding sources, costs for volunteers, and skills provided. For the most part, information about who funds the organization is presented in one phrase or sentence, such as "Foundations and Private Donors," even as the book tells us that this information is crucial for volunteers. The guidebook includes organizations that charge travelers nothing to volunteer, as well as those that charge over $3,000, and includes both local and global nonprofit and for-profit organizations.

What all these guidebooks reveal is that voluntourism is a large enterprise, and much of it is based on notions of "making a difference," "person-to-person" relationships, "cultural exchange," and consumer choice. Individual choice and individual experience are central to this tourism. As *Volunteer Vacations* puts it, the reader must "evaluate an organization to see if it is right for me."[41] Although other volunteers' personal vignettes are presented to inform the reader, with most volunteers claiming that their experience changed their lives, the text suggests that readers must choose their own path, or else the "experience" will not work. Because volunteering is a project of self-improvement, such a focus is necessary, and the stories of self-improvement and satisfaction are important features of these texts. All these guidebooks argue that volunteer help is necessary and that volunteers are needed and welcomed everywhere; indeed, oftentimes the funds and work done by voluntourists sustain organizations even as they lead to tensions over different economic and affective needs.[42] The language of "exchange" pervades these texts, suggesting that the notion of reciprocity obviates racial, class, national, or any other difference, and that all regions or organizations benefit from volunteers in excess of the tourist dollars or euros they may bring. Despite this, there is often little evidence of actual exchange that does not benefit the voluntourist. Because these experiences take place within the context of tourism, they often cannot sustain the communities being helped or the organizations orchestrating the tourism.

All of these guidebook authors assume that the volunteer is white and Western, while the regions of need are in the Global South. Although the Lonely Planet guide states that volunteers come from many regions and races, there is only one South Asian voluntourist quoted several times through the book. The photographs and vignettes mostly focus on white volunteers working in the non-West among nonwhite people.

Many of these authors demonstrate awareness of the critique of imperialism and the imperial history of travel. But they propose that imperialism and imperial attitudes can be avoided, suggesting that imperialism is not structural but rather about attitudes and behaviors. In addition, they position humanitarians as working outside the state and without overt state or national support, thus suggesting that voluntourism exists outside of the empire. While these authors identify war as part of an imperial project, they name humanitarianism as benevolence that is outside of militarism. Represented as an exchange between individuals, humanitarianism becomes free of the taint of empire. The authors suggest that the humanitarian and the recipient of aid are equals because they are part of a process of exchange between individuals. The authors of *Volunteer Vacations* state that volunteering can "begin to halt the tide of the nastier effects of globalization and instead promote the benefits of international understanding and cooperation. Through personal, one-on-one exchanges and dialogues, individuals around the world—including people from different communities in the United States—will better understand and appreciate the people in their national and global neighborhoods."[43] The Lonely Planet guidebook, *Volunteer: A Traveller's Guide*, constructs American Others as foreign, a practice that became visible during Katrina.[44] It also asks right at the beginning, "Is International Volunteering the New Colonialism?"[45] It responds that it can be but that volunteers can escape being these "new colonialists" if they have the right attitude. Power and inequality are acknowledged but ignored, since the voluntourist is understood to be sacrificing so much to undertake volunteer work by giving up a comfortable life to live in the Global South. Power is not seen as structural but as an individual avocation. Thus whether or not someone is a colonialist depends on their personal attitude, rather than on the racial/colonial histories or global structures in which they are enmeshed. Through their own attitude, an individual can either become or refuse to become a colonialist: "Whether international volunteering is the new colonialism or not is, in large part, down to the attitudes of you, the volunteer and the organization you go with."[46] Histories of colonialism may influence attitudes toward volunteers, but the volunteer can, by their individual attitude and behavior and by their selection of organization to work with, either become a colonialist if they behave in a condescending manner, or not be a colonialist if they see those other people as teaching them something. It suggests that "if you don't want to be a twenty-first century colonialist, rule out organizations that suggest you'll be 'saving the world' or give a patronizing image of the developing world."[47]

Continuing the emphasis on the individual, the Lonely Planet guide's section on "Why Volunteer?" describes benefits to the traveler/volunteer. The benefits include learning a foreign language, skills "you'll acquire or develop (that) can be used back home in your profession," leadership and communication skills, and "listening and understanding skills," as well as the ability to "develop self-confidence, focus [your] career objectives and show adaptability, self-motivation, and dedication. All of these benefits can kickstart a career and can sometimes be more valuable than undergraduate (or even postgraduate) education."[48] The book quotes one volunteer stating that gratitude and appreciation for the volunteer were also a benefit: "the delight on people's faces when they realize they now have a clean and safe water supply or better school facilities." The same person goes on to list "personal benefits" such as being "exposed to new cultures" as well as physical improvement: this person became "fitter, lost weight, and felt terrific when I came home."[49]

It is telling that none of these guidebooks include narratives from those who have purportedly been helped, or whose lives have allegedly been bettered. The "exchange" seems to be one-way. The language of person-to-person, individual exchange, and individual benefit is thus about a neoliberal and racial approach to the humanitarian's personal growth. Such texts thus become antipolitical, to use James Ferguson's phrase for the development bureaucracies in Lesotho,[50] transforming Americans into development experts.

Greg Mortenson and *Three Cups of Tea*: Media and Pedagogy

American humanitarianism citizenship and its racializing and gendering processes also circulate beyond the tourist industry, particularly in popular culture and media. Information about these projects circulate through books, documentary and feature films, television news and shows, websites, journalism, and artistic practices. These images and practices traverse popular and elite culture, development discourse, state projects, missionary groups, and consumer and military culture. Relying on historically sedimented colonial histories, but recuperated in new digital forms of media and consumption, humanitarianism circulates in media to produce soft power as that combination of sedimented imperial history and subjectivities, powerful masculinities and femininities, global citizenship, and emerging forms of consumer culture.

An excellent example of this kind of American humanitarian in popular culture is the *New York Times* bestseller *Three Cups of Tea: One Man's Mission to Promote Peace... One School at a Time* (2006), which is an account of Greg Mortenson's efforts to establish girls' schools in remote areas of Pakistan and Afghanistan.[51] Mortenson's account has since been attacked as a fabrication and his NGO has lost some of its prominence and power, but the narrative remains powerful because it belongs to a genre of imperial travel writing whose elements are understandable and familiar, widely disseminated, and read. This is the travel narrative genre in which the lone white male traveler ventures into unknown lands for adventure, becomes accepted by the locals as benevolent, and then emerges as a savior of a "native" culture. Since nineteenth-century male figures such as Richard Francis Burton and T. E. Lawrence and female ones such as Isabelle Eberhardt, the continued popularity of this figure enables it to become part of current commodity and consumer cultures, though with some key differences, as I will argue. As narrated in *Three Cups of Tea*, Mortenson is both a throwback to such romantic and unique individuals, as well as a key soft power figure in the contemporary US wars in South Asia. As a "global citizen" and a caring and powerful figure, he embodies American power as benevolent and caring, rather than as lethal and violent. While he originally supported the US war in Afghanistan, believing that it was a step to rebuilding the country, his school-building agenda is designed to win the war on terror through development projects focused on girls' education. In *Three Cups of Tea*, we learn that no one else can make this happen, and that Mortenson has to struggle against Afghan locals and ignorant Americans to reach his goals. The book downplays his connections with the US military as well as the fact that American drone warfare has extensively bombed some of the regions in which he claims to work. Despite the unpopularity of Americans, we are told, Mortenson makes the local Pakistanis and Afghans love and revere him, and can also collaborate with the US military to turn it into an organization that saves lives, as suggested in the advertisements with which I opened this chapter. The book includes a quote from one of the girls, Fatima Batool, who, we are told, was able to attend one of Mortenson's schools after she fled her home because of Pakistan's war with India: "I've heard some people say Americans are bad. . . . But we love Americans. They are the most kind people for us. They are the only ones who cared to help us" (224). Echoing Bill Keller's quote from early in this chapter, one of Mortenson's supporters and donors urges him to share his knowledge of Muslims when he receives hate mail from other Americans: "These horrible hate letters are a mandate for you to get out and tell Americans what you know about Muslims. You represent the goodness and courage that America is all about" (280). Such testimonials to the goodness of Americans may be one reason for the widespread popularity of the book in the United States.

Educational institutions of various kinds presented Mortenson as an exemplary and exceptional individual and role model. Mortenson's account was endorsed by celebrities and journalists, supported by wealthy donors, and championed, importantly, by the US military. It also circulated across tourist and consumer cultures because it showcases how a tourist and mountaineer—the rugged male and white adventurer—could become a humanitarian. David Oliver Relin, who collaborated with Mortenson to write the book, created a narrative that convincingly combines many of the key aspects of adventure travel: race, nationalism, masculinity, tourism, and empire. Relin created Mortenson as the model humanitarian, showing how whiteness, hetero-masculinity, and American individuality could be harnessed for altruistic purposes.

The narrative constructs the hero as masculine and caring, enmeshed in a lonely and brave struggle. Mortenson emerges as the only person doing this work in the Pakistani region near the Karakoram mountain ranges, close to the border with India. The Pakistani state is inefficient and uncaring, locals are patriarchal and religious, and he becomes the lone savior of Pakistani girls, with the help of some heroic sympathetic locals and mercenaries. In the two villages where the narrative tells us he built his first schools, he is the local hero. The mountain climber, whose goal was to ascend the highest peaks in the Himalayas, ends up doing humanitarian work. This book combines adventure and rugged travel experience—Mortenson is not the usual tourist but the heroic mountain climber—with the work of "helping" those presumed to be helpless. Consumption and charity are thus combined in a powerful package. In *Three Cups of Tea*, numerous references to American mountaineering communities and to the travails and difficulties endured by mountain climbers in the area, create a Western and American familiarity with the region. For all the white, American consumers who see themselves as different from regular tourists,[52] who wish to combine volunteer work with travel, and for whom travel to the developing world is imbued with charity, Mortenson is a powerful role model.

In the book's introduction, Relin writes in his own voice, giving an account of Mortenson's popularity in Pakistan. The chapter recuperates imperial travel narratives and positions Mortenson as a heroic adventurer-traveler-savior. Relin tells us that Mortenson is restless and at home in remote regions, personally charismatic, and capable of surviving in a region where few others (he means white Americans) venture. By establishing Mortenson's credibility through some overblown prose, Relin can then claim the narrative's objectivity and truthfulness. Local terms and colorful figures are thrown in to provide authenticity, and the need and deprivation of impoverished locals—especially girls and women—garners sympathy from the reader.

We are told that after a "failed attempt" to climb K2 in Pakistan, the world's second-highest mountain, Mortenson ends up in the village of Korphe with momentous results: "In this impoverished community of mud and stone huts, both Mortenson's life and the lives of Northern Pakistan's children changed course" (2). Even a Pakistani pilot tells Relin that "Greg Mortenson is the most remarkable person I've ever met" (3). Mortenson's wife is quoted saying that "Greg is not one of us" (4). All who know him are "pulled into his orbit" (3). Relin asserts Mortenson's masterful knowledge of the region, stating that everyone "who had had the privilege of watching Greg Mortenson is amazed by how encyclopedically well he has come to know one of the world's most remote regions." His admirers range, we are told, from "former Taliban fighters" to "illiterate high-altitude porters" and "volunteers and admirers from every stratum of Pakistan's society and from all the warring sects of Islam" (3). Later in the narrative, Relin tells us that Mortenson comes to be known as "Dr. Greg" because he is able to use his nursing skills and medications to help poor villagers; he is considered the son of the village elder. He feels, we are told, more at home in this Pakistani village than in the United States.

The book unfolds through an omniscient narrator perspective, beginning with Mortenson's mountain climbing experience that leads him to the village of Korphe, but also establishing his credentials as a global citizen who lived in Tanzania as a child of Lutheran missionaries. Colonial racial logics pervade the text. In describing the local community of Balti people, Relin quotes a paragraph from an Italian mountaineer, Fosco Maraini, who had been to the region in 1958 and had written what the narrator calls a "scholarly treatise on the Balti way of life": "They connive, and complain, and frustrate one to the utmost. And beyond their often-foul odor, they have an unmistakable air of the brigand . . . but . . . you'll learn they serve you faithfully, and they are high-spirited" (21). Such colonial phrases racializing culture and poverty in terms of difference and servility are seamlessly incorporated into this contemporary narrative that proceeds from suspicion to cultural knowledge, following the conventions of many travel narratives. Mortenson's education enables Korphe's residents to move from being odorous to admirable, as Mortenson realizes that "they live with a rare kind of purity" (112). Although the villagers are recognized for the brutal work they do in carrying loads for Western mountaineers, the narrator tells us that they are different from Westerners and more like "the ibex they pursued" in that they work to survive and have little interest in climbing mountains (117).

Despite the fact that Balti people are likened to animals, we learn that Mortenson becomes a native—hunting, eating, and dancing with Balti men:

"Together, the Balti and the big American danced like dervishes and sang of feuding alpine kingdoms, of the savagery of Pathan warriors pouring in from Afghanistan. . . . Korphe's women, accustomed by now to the infidel among them, stood at the edge of the firelight, their faces glowing, as they clapped and sang along with their men" (144). The inhabitants of Korphe are not presented as contemporaries but live in noncoeval time with Mortenson. In light of this "schizogenic temporality," as Johannes Fabian has called the co-lonial denial of coevalness,[53] Mortenson's goal becomes the uplift of women. Consequently, he is narrated as especially attuned to their needs; even before building a school, he builds a bridge that shortens the distance they have to travel to reach the town across the river. Here, he suggests that he is differ-ent from the bureaucratic state that is deaf to the needs of people, especially women, and his humanitarianism is more feminist and thus more modern.

Much like the "exchange" that constructs the voluntourist, Mortenson's "exchange" is the lessons he learns from Korphe elders. Mortenson learns to be patient and realizes that the Baltis are not stupid even though they are uneducated. Haji Ali is quoted as making this last point, and Mortenson then responds by saying that "Haji Ali taught me the most important lesson I've learned in my life" (150), that nothing can be accomplished quickly. Morten-son also learns that it is not "shock and awe" that can end wars, but rather "building relationships" (150). In such "lessons," the text constructs a his-tory of travel as educational, of "primitive" cultures as providing lessons for modern subjects, and of distance producing traditional and slow cultures in comparison to the tourist-traveler's own mobility. Mortenson's mobility comprises a large part of the book as he moves around in the United States raising funds and traveling to Pakistan and later to Afghanistan.

While many sections and phrases in the book recall the language of nineteenth-century Orientalism, other sections reveal Mortenson's imbri-cation in American wars of the twenty-first century. Such sections show Mortenson working to distinguish the good Pakistanis from the bad ones. The Baltis are narrated as good—neglected by the Pakistani government and in danger of losing people and culture to emerging wars with the Taliban. Building schools means saving them from madrassa education that would supposedly turn them into radical Islamists, and this is the project that gains support from many donors in the United States. Building schools for girls thus becomes enmeshed in the work of US empire, winning the war against the Taliban, and working against the Pakistani government. This project is especially highlighted as Mortenson travels to the Pakistani border area of Waziristan, where he sees the Saudi-built madrassa attended by, we are told,

John Walker Lindh. Mortenson describes Waziristan as a "medieval" region, where he is captured and imprisoned for several days, released only after he shows familiarity with the Koran. Jon Krakauer has challenged this claim of being imprisoned by the Taliban, and in doing so, he challenges as well Mortenson's claim of deep knowledge about the region and culture.[54]

As Mortenson moves to working in Afghanistan, the US military agenda of fighting Islamicization and Saudi-funded madrassas takes him to speak to US legislators in Congress. Republican California congresswoman Mary Bono becomes a champion, introducing Mortenson to fellow Republicans as "a real American hero" who is "fighting terror in Pakistan and Afghanistan by building girls' schools" (291). A legislative aide then tells Mortenson that he has never heard anyone give such an account of the region. A general donates to Mortenson's NGO, the Central Asia Institute, and invites him to the Pentagon, where he is offered millions that he rejects. Mortenson is quoted as saying that he would lose credibility in the region if he took money from the US military. Relin describes Mortenson's growing concern for people of the region, as he relinquishes his original support for the US bombings.

In the wake of the book's popularity, and despite Relin's and Mortenson's claims, journalists revealed Mortenson's work with the US military. Stanley A. McChrystal, then chief of staff of the US military, befriended Mortenson, seeing him as an example of the soft power needed by the US military in Afghanistan. In a *New York Times* article, Elisabeth Bumiller reveals some of the connections between Mortenson and the military even as she constructs Mortenson as a heroic and credible figure. Bumiller's article also reveals how Mortenson's humanitarianism was celebrated by journalists and by reputable newspaper such as the *New York Times* without verifying the facts on the ground. In this front-page article, Bumiller reports that "in the frantic last hours" of General Stanley A. McChrystal's command in Afghanistan in 2010, he reached out to "an unlikely corner of his life: the author of the book, *Three Cups of Tea*, Greg Mortenson."[55] We learn that Mortenson came to McChrystal's attention through a soldier's wife who asked her husband, based in Pakistan, to read the book. The husband then recommended the book to McChrystal, who contacted Mortenson. Bumiller goes on to mention that Mortenson was present in meetings between village elders and US military representatives, showing that McChrystal and Mortenson ended up working together. Bumiller states that McChrystal's initial note to Mortenson "reflected his [Mortenson's] broad and deepening relationship with the US military, whose leaders have increasingly turned to Mortenson, once a shaggy mountaineer, to help translate the theory of counterinsurgency to tribal realities on the ground."[56] What is remarkable in this article, which is typical of much coverage of Mortenson since his book was published, is Bumiller's acceptance of both a hypermasculine Mortenson—the "shaggy mountaineer"—and his unverified account. For example, she tells us that Mortenson is "responsible for the construction of more than 130 schools in Afghanistan and Pakistan, mostly for girls" and that he has struggled to undertake this task despite lack of financial resources, even once living out of his car in Berkeley, California.[57] Bumiller did not verify whether the schools were operating or had even been built. In fact, Jon Krakauer and the *60 Minutes* team both investigated Mortenson's claims later and found that Mortenson had either exaggerated or fabricated them.[58] Despite this revelation, Bumiller's article is instructive because it reveals how narratives celebrating American humanitarians circulate. Like many others, the article unquestioningly repeats a narrative of the bravery, deprivation, and sentimentality of the heroic white man who eschews military solutions.

In February 2011, after leaving the military, McChrystal brought Mortenson to speak at Yale University, where McChrystal was teaching a seminar on leadership at the Jackson Institute for Global Affairs. In a YouTube video of that event, McChrystal presents Mortenson as an exemplary leader, and Mortenson speaks of his soft power credentials: He favors "empowerment" rather than war, schools instead of bombs.[59] He emerges as a cosmopolitan who has lived in diverse cultures in Africa and Asia and who speaks many languages, a throwback to the missionaries and colonial adventurers who saw themselves as melding into "native" cultures. He becomes a leader in the necessary cultural work of soft power, which has convinced some anthropologists and cultural experts in the Human Terrain System project to support the war in Afghanistan.[60] Even though Mortenson's *Three Cups of Tea* has since been discredited, there are many books, images, films, and media productions reproducing this humanitarian narrative that take his place and show that others can be better humanitarians.

Mortenson also published a children's version of his project, *Listen to the Wind: The Story of Dr. Greg and Three Cups of Tea* (2009), which became extremely popular as required reading in schools across the country.[61] Another of Mortenson's books, *Stones into Schools: Promoting Peace with Books, Not Bombs, in Afghanistan and Pakistan* (2010), continued this publishing juggernaut, claiming to show how peace in "a volatile region" can be achieved and how, as venerable news anchor Tom Brokaw states on the back cover of the book, "one man can change the world."[62] Images of Mortenson with smiling, hijab-clad girls are visible on the book's cover.

It is no coincidence that *Three Cups of Tea*'s popularity, bolstered by the credibility of journalists such as Tom Brokaw, occurred at the same time as the escalation of American bombing in Pakistan and Afghanistan. Mortenson's long list of speaking engagements at and awards from schools, colleges, and universities attests to the power of imperial travel and its collaboration with humanitarianism. Humanitarianism has become both a job qualification and an essential part of imperial education. American students travel to Africa, Asia, and Latin America to work and intern in NGOs, and many volunteer in their cities and neighborhoods. Humanitarianism has become incorporated into school and college curricula, and into prizes and projects. Some US business schools even teach students how to be discerning philanthropists. Entrance to colleges often depends on evidence of such work, high schools assign seniors community service as a graduation requirement, and businesses have emerged to enable travel for these projects. Some large corporations set aside a day for employees to undertake volunteer work. Celebrities remake their careers by starting charities and foundations and by attending fundraisers. Bill Gates, for example, has been able to use his wealth to address health issues across the developing world. The Bill and Melinda Gates Foundation's budget is larger than the national budget of most of the countries in which it works. The Gates Foundation's efforts to eradicate polio, for example, have recuperated Microsoft Corporation's public relations image as a helpful rather than predatory organization. Through concern about the poor, the world, or more recently for "Africa," "social service" has become central to American power. The US government encourages such work with tax deductions, direct funding of NGOs, and the creation of service corps: AmeriCorps, Senior Corps, and a host of other such programs.

The mystification of distance enables ideas of progress or accountability to remain unclear as narratives about "helping" and "saving" flourish without being verified or contradicted. Often, even reports that contradict the effectiveness of humanitarian actions are ignored,[63] making it difficult to counter the huge apparatus of popular images and knowledges of the efficacy and importance of humanitarian aid. Because these hegemonic knowledges have produced distant others as requiring interventions while celebrating white, Western humanitarians, and saviors, there is little in popular media about the difficulties and challenges of such work, nor are there many challenges to the inequalities created by such work. But humanitarianism flourishes because it is productive in creating narratives of "good Americans" that circulate widely within and outside the United States, producing a supposedly benevolent empire.

Kiva and Online Microlending: The New-Media Humanitarians

While voluntourism has become a new, popular form of travel, humanitarian opportunity also exists online. Greg Mortenson's nonprofit organization, the Central Asia Institute, has a website that allows viewers to scroll through images of schools that the institute claims to have built and donate to a school and region of their choice. Despite this rhetoric of abundant choice, the same photographs are used for several schools, and many have no markers of place or region, making it difficult to verify whether or not such a school actually exists or is currently active. Such images and choices mark the commodification of charity online, offering the ability to anyone with online access to become a humanitarian. Opportunities to become humanitarians flourish online, as donors are asked to give funding as charity or even as loans.

The phenomenon of microcredit and microlending has spawned new forms of armchair humanitarianism that provide the experience of cultural difference and tourism (central to travel to the Global South) from the comfort of home and computer screen. Such digital travel also enables individual and person-to-person connection across racial, national, and cultural difference. Online organizations have emerged to enable microlending with the click of a button, and organizations such as Kiva.org and HandUP.org exemplify some of the ways in which contemporary US humanitarianism relies on neoliberal welfare privatization that is the analog of digital corporate cultures.[64] The microlending model for gift giving is a popular project for those who believe low-income individuals and communities need work rather than welfare. Microfinance is often represented as the new panacea for global poverty, even as critics of the practice have shown its many flaws. For example, microfinance may increase gendered inequality and rural indebtedness, and even intensify the power of patriarchies.[65] It is also based on the assumption that giving aid or state subsidies to people does not improve their lives, and that poor people worldwide would rather have loans and become entrepreneurs. Further, the sporadic and uncertain nature of private charity and privatized microfinance adds greater insecurity and uncertainty to the lives of many who already live on the edge, and it cannot provide the scale of welfare that long-term state support may bring.

Microfinance humanitarianism is now becoming part of a panoply of consumer choices, seamlessly incorporated into everyday culture so that helping
and saving distant others is easier than ever before. It has become a rite of
passage for middle- and upper-class Americans to be involved in charitable
online giving—Christmas, birthday, and even wedding gifts can be a goat
or money given to the women on Kiva, to projects such as Heifer International, or to projects supporting a child in Asia or Africa through one's local
church. Child Fund International produces a catalog with smiling children,
and women holding goats, pigs, cattle, chicken, bicycles, and hand pumps.
Captions in the catalog state: "Help an orphaned girl in India continue her
education" and "Help a child carry homework to school and back." The latter appeal comes with a price tag of thirty-six dollars for "One Backpack
for a Child in Angola." The organization gets three stars out of four from
the charity-vetting organization Charity Watch, suggesting that it is a trusted
organization, though the money might easily buy more than one backpack in
Angola. Charity-vetting organizations such as Charity Watch, Charity Navigator, and Philanthropedia have become powerful, giving donors the ability
to decide online whether to give to an organization or not. Charity Navigator
claims to have 4.7 million unique visitors to their site and has been increasing its online visitors each year, though these visitors may be only a fraction
of those who donate to charity.[66]

Such charity is now also directed within the United States, as state retrenchment on welfare and education has increased domestic needs. Some
online sites enable donations to schools that have lost funding due to state
retrenchment, once again replacing state support with sporadic individual
charity. Sites such as DonorsChoose.org enable donations to school districts
or to individual teachers or projects, thus producing popularity contests that
are detrimental to the morale of many teachers.[67] These sites have become
so normalized as useful and "good" that they let many forget the time when
it was the state's job to provide teachers and schools with what they needed,
diverting attention away from the need to pressure school boards and state
governments to attend to teachers' needs.

Kiva.org is one of several nonprofits that rely on new media to produce
online humanitarians. However, it uses its online and Silicon Valley credentials
to imply it is different from other microfinancing nonprofits, claiming, as
Megan Moodie reveals, that it is more transparent and provides more direct
access and connections between donors and recipients.[68] Kiva encourages
donors to form "lending teams," create online communities, and debate issues. However, the problems of humanitarianism and microfinance remain,

and a decade of microlending seems to have tarnished its image even among policy makers; even so the project continues to proliferate precisely because it has become so entrenched into consumer culture, self-empowerment regimes, and Western humanitarianism. The images and narratives distinguish between domestic and international communities, between American givers and international recipients. With an emphasis on donors choosing whom they want to help from a long list of names, faces, and narratives of those seeking help, the privatization of welfare creates uncertainty for those on the receiving (or nonreceiving) end, turning them into supplicants whose lives continue only at the whim of the unseen, individual donor.

Kiva's website contains images and descriptions of large numbers of people around the world seeking loans for myriad entrepreneurial activities. Unlike Mortenson seeking charitable donations to support his work, Kiva seeks microloans from all those who believe that poor people around the globe need more work rather than welfare or social justice. The website showcases images of brown and black women accompanied by an informational paragraph about each recipient who can be helped if the user "chooses" her. Donors are urged to give small amounts, as low as twenty-five dollars. Kiva thus calls on ordinary people to become global humanitarians. Most Kiva donors are US based, though there are donors across the world. Similar to calls to action on eBay or other retail sites, some of Kiva's loan calls to action add a sense of urgency and opportunity by listing the hours remaining for the donor to contribute. More recently, the credit card and finance company Capital One has donated half a million dollars as a matching loan to expand its partnership with Kiva, in a gesture of corporate humanitarianism.[69]

Kiva's website also contains narratives of would-be entrepreneurs who want loans to start small businesses. Lilie Chouliaraki has described such narratives as a new mode of "post-humanitarian" communication that is incorporated into lifestyle choices and that is distinct from previous humanitarianisms based on grand emotions and representations of suffering.[70] This emphasis on consumption and choice without discourses of suffering are certainly key to online organizations such as Kiva that use commodity and market strategies to "sell" the women and men seeking microloans.[71] However, as I have shown in the case of Greg Mortenson's project, grand narratives of suffering, complete with images of little children, remain powerful in other humanitarian enterprises. Grand narratives of "saving" work alongside humanitarianism as lifestyle choice, but all of these rely on the figures of exceptional Americans who either travel to distant places to rescue or volunteer, or incorporate charitable giving into new forms of individual connection via microlending. US imperialism and war rely on multiple forms of humanitarianism to hail diverse subjects into citizenship through online and armchair participation, travel, and consumption. These modes of consumption and participation rely on narratives of heroism and suffering as well as the power to transform distant others into entrepreneurial and neoliberal subjects through microlending. But, what is also important is that these exceptional Americans are supposed to disdain the state as a source of social welfare, preferring to support someone whom they themselves choose as worthy of support. These exceptional citizens believe they are better able to decide who can get welfare and who cannot, believing that the state is not efficient or reliable, or that it gives welfare to those whom they do not consider worthy of saving. For those on the receiving end, who are often poor, their citizen rights to demand state welfare have been replaced by requests soliciting aid and support, with little surety for getting this support and no long-term prospects for welfare. Those in need then are outside the exceptional citizenship of the humanitarians.

While Kiva's microlending was originally focused on international giving, the post-2008 economic downturn prompted calls to enable microlending within the United States as well. Beginning in 2009, at the urging of Maria Shriver, then the First Lady of California, Kiva.org now includes US recipients who wish to start businesses, though international recipients remain the main borrowers. Kiva partnered with US microcredit organizations ACCION USA and the Opportunity Fund to disburse loans. This change to microlending within the United States created some dissatisfaction among Kiva donors, who wanted the organization to focus on international locales, where they felt the need was more dire and where small sums might go further, reflecting the belief, visible after Katrina, that distant others are more deserving and that local people may be less honest or more intransigent. One lending team, Unhappy Kiva Lenders Group, came together to voice this dissatisfaction. In response, an oppositional team, USA Against Kiva Bigots, was created and has now morphed into USA 4 Equality. In the process, the Unhappy Kiva Lenders Group has disappeared from the Kiva.org home page, indicating that the website is less community driven than it claims to be.[72] As this example shows, Kiva promotes its own policies and monitors participants' interactions to achieve its goals.

An additional source of dissatisfaction among some Kiva lenders was the realization that Kiva did not provide loans directly, as the loans went to intermediaries at distant sites. While the visual technology of Kiva's site provides a great deal of information, there is no way for anyone to know whether the organization's money has actually reached anyone because the funds go to local microlending organizations, and Kiva does not verify whether the funds have actually reached borrowers or improved their lives. There is little information on Kiva's website about the workings and finances of the organizations to whom Kiva provides the loans, and their claim of transparency belies the gulf between the lenders and the borrowers. While Kiva.org does provide a graphic depicting the ways in which the money gets to the recipient, the model does not show us exactly how "field partners" in distant regions find the recipients or give them the funds. Indeed, the visuals of Kiva's site provide pleasures for the donor-viewers in scrolling through the photographs and narratives of borrowers, providing satisfaction for donors that they are helping people in need, while foreclosing any probing questions. The *New York Times'* Nicholas Kristof, who has become well known for supporting neoliberal individualized humanitarianism, tweeted in 2009: "Just made a microloan on www.kiva.org to a Nicaraguan woman. Great therapy: always makes me feel good."[73] Sitting at a computer and sending money to an unknown woman provides Kristof with the ability to improve himself, invoking Nikolas Rose's argument that one of the hallmarks of neoliberalism is the self-improving subject.[74] Such a subject is thus the exceptional citizen with the sovereign ability to give support and life to some and to withdraw it from others.

Kiva remains popular because it enables welfare as consumer choice, allowing viewers to scroll through the names, images, and descriptions of people in need, or to choose whether to give to a male or female, or community. There are quite a few choices—Kiva shows there are so many needy people around the world—even as viewers learn nothing about why and how so many become needy, if their neediness and the US consumer's prosperity are linked, or how and why inequality seems to be increasing across the globe. Megan Moodie has argued that Kiva obfuscates a highly unequal relationship enabled by these networked connections that are assumed to be peer-to-peer, but which are actually organization-to-organization.[75] She further observes that the site, like so many others, provides no information on how and why borrowers (most of them women) become needy. Moodie points out that the most important risk associated with these transactions affects the donors rather than the borrowers. She critiques the belief that such online giving provides a closer connection to the clients, as both Kiva and many journalists claim. For instance, the *Wall Street Journal* reports: "Some of the newer Web-based nonprofits, such as DonorsChoose and Kiva, are attractive because contributors say they allow them to connect directly with their recipients. Donors or lenders can hand over money directly to, respectively, teachers and students in urban public schools or individual entrepreneurs in developing countries, rather than sending a check that ends up with an abstract recipient."[76] This narrative of both digital media and humanitarianism—that digital media can provide the transparency lacking in most corrupt organizations or developing states—utilizes what are seen to be the democratizing aspects of new media. Digital media is assumed to be more direct and more transparent because clients are vetted by the new media organization and because the donor can choose among recipients. These online humanitarian sites rely on the putative closeness and immediacy of the Internet experience and its possibilities for encouraging consumption, even as they also rely on distance to enhance the narrative of need and to mystify the process of welfare and development.

Despite its popularity, Kiva has not been immune to criticism. After complaints from its donor communities, Kiva had to admit that it does not actually have direct connection with borrowers. However, it continues to suggest that technology can one day provide this experience. Premal Shah, one of Kiva's founders, admitted that though legal issues prevent direct peer-to-peer contact, he sees this "disintermediation" happening in the future "when people in the developing world begin using their mobile phones to use credit and make payments."[77] Yet, the problem is not just technology. It is also is that sites such as Kiva imply that the viewer is capable of deciding on the more worthy recipient simply by consuming online images and narratives. Although these images produce entrepreneurial and capitalist subjects that seem to be different from the usual images of the pain and suffering of distant others in the Global South,[78] all of these projects intensify the inequality between donors and borrowers, between generous humanitarians and suffering others. At the very least, those in need are now indebted to new groups and individuals who may or may not continue to support them.

Some critics of microlending have charged that such organizations seem to benefit only distant others. In response, newer organizations have emerged to both give to local people in need and to replace microlending with outright charity. This model combines the crowdfunding approach of Kickstarter with the charity and humanitarian aspect of Kiva. The newer online giving organization HandUP.org focuses on giving to local homeless people in San Francisco. Created in 2013 by Rose Broome and Zac Witte, who sought to connect San Francisco's wealthy tech community with local homeless people in need, it too relies on an individual's decision to give to one of the many needy people described on the website. Once again, there are portraits and narratives of those seeking help, hoping to attract the attention of an online humanitarian. As an article in the *New Yorker* described, "donors can adopt a homeless person through financial contributions, and receive progress reports on how he or she is doing."[79] The *New Yorker* article reported that the founders are hoping to expand the model to other cities. While the project hopes to move people's attention to those living in their own city, it also departs from Kiva's model in that giving is not related to awakening entrepreneurship among the recipients, but to allowing donations for all sorts of reasons, from buying shoes for children to getting furniture or equipment for people's homes. It is thus a more openly charitable enterprise rather than a microlending one. However, HandUp produces charity as the main connection between people dwelling in the same city, and, similar to other private welfare models, it replaced the language of rights or welfare demands with the language of charity and choice, with their attendant uncertainty and short-term, consumer-based attention. At best, it draws attention to local homeless people and their needs (if, indeed, the narratives that accompany recipient photographs are their own), but it also suggests that charity and inequality are now the main modes of relating to fellow citizens.

There is no doubt that humanitarianism, whether online or off, depends on individuals genuinely wishing to help, but it also bolsters the neoliberal idea that states cannot provide for their citizens. In the process, these organizations consolidate the power of the exceptional American humanitarian. They provide images of suffering others that are contrasted with empowered, choice-making rescuers. The latter are visible as the numerous volunteers and humanitarians traveling to the Global South and celebrated as role models or celebrities; or, as Kiva's armchair donors and communities who are described on the website as "Kiva's vibrant community of active and inspiring lenders."[80]

Conclusion

In *Contemporary States of Emergency*, Didier Fassin and Mariella Pandolfi argue that well-meaning individuals who are ethically motivated to humanitarianism share a great deal.[81] For instance, they have in common "the temporality of emergency . . . [they] reject the sovereignty of states in the name of a higher moral order" and "together construct a previously unseen political and moral order in which cynicism and ethics mingled and became indistinguishable."[82] Fassin and Pandolfi argue that what has emerged is a "new international political order" in which "the politics of military intervention are now played out in the name of humanitarian morality."[83]

In the widespread circulation of US humanitarian projects, the "moral order" that Fassin and Pandolfi describe has become domesticated as American through the reiterations and intertextualities of popular media in collaboration with nongovernmental organizations, educational institutions, corporations, state security projects, and sedimented histories of empire. Exceptional American humanitarian citizens claim the sovereign power of rescue and welfare, as well as its opposite: the power to neglect and abandon the others they create. In the process, the moral order remains a form of US soft power, intimately linked to the imperial state; the state does not disappear, since it is also involved in moving the work of welfare to individuals and enables the actions of the humanitarian citizen. Nonstate organizations and individuals are supported by state funding, citizenship privileges, tax rebates, documents, transportation, militarized security, and other forms of implicit and explicit support. While the visual culture of humanitarianism that circulates in the United States constructs public and private divides between the US government and the American citizen, humanitarian visual culture only exists because of collaborations between private and state entities. This visual culture enables American citizens to see themselves as generous in alleviating the suffering of distant others. In the context of ongoing militarizations and an endless war on terror, neoliberal welfare and humanitarianism constitute the soft power of American empire. How such imperial power becomes visible in who can or cannot be the exceptional citizen becomes clear in the contestations and ruptures of missionary projects in the new century, as I show in chapter 3.

3. Muslims, Missionaries, and Humanitarians

In chapter 2, I argued that humanitarianism became a requirement for American exceptional citizenship, embedded, ubiquitous, and visible in numerous institutions—educational, business, religious, and government—during the first decade of the new millennium. I also argued that this humanitarianism built on a history of European colonialism and its production of the male adventurer-turned-humanitarian who testified to the necessity and altruism of imperialism, especially in the context of the US empire's ongoing violence and wars. In the context of advanced neoliberalism, most people in the United States become convinced of the necessity of humanitarianism, and of the goodness of humanitarians, even as the state reduces welfare and the rights of all its inhabitants. In this chapter, I focus on how humanitarianism became incorporated as soft power and essential to the geopolitics of the war on terror during the presidency of George W. Bush. Humanitarianism worked to produce exceptional citizens and their Others in four key ways: first, it produced the United States and its citizens as exceptional Christian humanitarians, especially in contrast with Muslims, whose humanitarianism became suspect as linked to terrorism. Second, the state used the law of exception, as delineated in the work of Carl Schmitt, to deploy legal statutes that were deliberately vague and flexible to criminalize mostly Muslims (along with a few Others) claiming to do humanitarian work; the use of "material support" clauses in US antiterror laws only focused on "foreign" (mostly, Muslim) humanitarians, while white Christian or "domestic" organizations (such as white supremacists) were not targeted by the "material support" law. Third, in the first George W. Bush administration, white Christian evangelicals received sovereign, exceptional status through government support and funding to carry out welfare work that allowed them to remain unaccountable to federal guidelines, with little oversight on hiring, budget, and disposition of government funds. Finally, fourth, what emerged was a geopolitical struggle over who could be humanitarian since numerous countries, religious organizations, and churches carried out missionary work and began to rename it as humanitarian and also carried out humanitarian work that enabled them to hide missionary activities. In global contexts of widespread suspicion of missions and missionaries by those wielding political power, such politics of humanitarianism and missionary proselytizing are sites of struggle between nationalisms, authorities, neoliberal capital, and sovereignties.[1]

In the book *Three Cups of Tea*, when Greg Mortenson travels to Afghanistan to build schools for girls, his efforts gain urgency when he sees the existing schools funded by the Saudi government. Mortenson compares his progress to that of the Saudi government, mentioning despairingly that "it seemed that ten *Wahhabi madrassas* had popped up nearby overnight."[2] He feels that American influence cannot compete with Saudi power in Pakistan and Afghanistan that has provided an education to children based on the Wahhabi version of Sunni Islam supported by the Saudi monarchical state. For Mortenson, such proselytizing is illicit because of "the unlimited supply of cash that *Wahhabi* operatives smuggle into Pakistan, both in suitcases and through the untraceable *hawala* money-transfer system—that has shaped their image among Pakistan's population."[3] Thus, not only is religious education to be deplored but also the method of money transfer, called the *hawala* system, based on verbal contract and honor systems between parties in different sites. Mortenson neglects to mention that such transactions have been going on for centuries across South Asia and the Middle East and were central to histories of trade. Instead, like the US government, he sees hawala funds as threatening because they are outside the corporate banking systems of the West.[4] He notes that one Saudi publication reported in 2000 that the Saudi-based Al Haramain Foundation "had built '1,100 mosques, schools, and Islamic centers' in Pakistan and other Muslim countries, and employed three thousand paid proselytizers in the previous year."[5] While admitting later in the book that not all madrassas fund extremists, Mortenson nevertheless holds them responsible for indoctrinating bright students and teaching them to be misogynistic. "Arab Sheikhs," he says, "were bringing the brightest students back to Saudi Arabia and Kuwait for a decade of indoctrination, then encouraging them to take four wives when they came home and breed like rabbits."[6] Oil wealth, he concludes, "is aimed at Pakistan's most virulent incubator of religious extremism—Wahhabi *madrassas*."[7] Here, concerns about the power of Gulf money are linked to racialized views of Muslim cultures and to criminalizing money transfers that come from histories of trade, which continue to be low-cost ways for immigrants to transfer funds to families across nations and continents.[8] Coauthors Mortenson and David Oliver Relin present this conclusion three-fourths of the way through the book, after readers are confronted with much evidence of Mortenson's bravery, humanitarianism, and expertise on the region. While deploring the effects of Wahhabi schools and preachers, they do not mention other proselytizers in the region, such as Christian groups, or even the effects of his own, American secular presence as another form of "soft" power.

Three Cups of Tea, published in 2006 in the midst of George W. Bush's global war on terror, captured and disseminated popular perceptions about the need for American soft power. Mortenson presents Wahhabi madrassas and the hawala funding networks that seemingly operate outside Western and international banking systems as anti-American. Even though the book mentions the effects of regional wars and state neglect, and recognizes that madrassas are often the only educational institutions in the region, Relin and Mortenson assert that madrassas foment anti-American and radical Islam. They construct the urgency of Mortenson's work through a particular understanding of the war on terror and its alleged cause in Wahhabi Islam proselytizing. In doing so, they erase the longer regional history of anticommunism and Soviet–US wars, International Monetary Fund (IMF) structural adjustment programs, South Asian geopolitics, British partition and colonization, the rise of Wahhabi and non-Wahhabi movements, and US support of Saudi Arabia.

The war on terror context in both South Asia and the Middle East has meant that both so-called secular organizations such as Mortenson's Central

Asia Institute and religious organizations and charities came to exist in different conditions and take on new meanings. The war on terror's modes of differentiation categorize religious organizations as enabling the US's soft power. Further, they position these organizations as extensions of national-religious, rather than sectarian, projects. After 9/11, American power became identified with Protestant Christian right-wing identity under the George W. Bush administration, appearing in the language of a new "crusade" against Islam.[9] This constructed "war" between homogenized notions of Muslims and Christians erased the many divergent sects and groups within these religions as well as many other religious groups existing across Arab and Middle Eastern communities. Realigning American identity and nationalism with Protestant Christianity, Bush also erased the presence of so many Christian denominations as well as other religious communities in the United States. In using such phrases, and giving special status to late twentieth-century right-wing evangelical movements, the Bush administration went on to fund religious organizations in new collaborations between public and private religious agencies. To be sure, Bush did come to change his rhetoric over time, taking back the "crusade" remark, and not all Christian organizations made such antagonistic claims. Yet for some, evangelism took on intensified fervor and the recognition given to such groups by the George W. Bush White House in its first term suggested they were exceptional citizens for the nation in a time of a full-blown war on terror.

I argue in this chapter, however, that for many Christian and Muslim religious organizations both in the United States and the Middle East, neoliberalism and postwar religious movements created similar ways to conceptualize nationalism and religion in terms of a notion of humanitarianism. More traditional versions of religious charity and volunteerism took on new guise as humanitarian projects, aligning them with the humanitarianism I discussed in chapter 2, in order to argue for the legitimacy and necessity of their volunteer work. Yet, in the context of the war on terror, the US government demonized the work of Muslim charities and NGOs while seeing Christian ones as legitimate; indeed, the government constructed Christian humanitarians as exceptional citizens while seeing Muslim ones as potential terrorists. I bring a postcolonial and transnational approach to understanding both Islamic and Christian missionary work in South Asia and the Middle East to critique how US imperialism demonized the former while relying on the latter, in the process rearticulating the meaning of these religious identities, given that Christianity and Islam have long and heterogeneous histories in these regions. Such an approach brings to bear a history of colonialism and

European Christian missions within the modern period in understanding how missionary work participated in imperialism, and also allows us to see the complex relations between colonial governments and missionary organizations.[10] This history, finally, reveals how distinctions between the colonial state and private Christian churches can be, at times, extremely fuzzy.

I examine Muslim and Christian organizations' post-9/11 recuperation of missionary work as a humanitarian project. Such humanitarianism reflects the logic of both modernizing development regimes and neoliberal notions of the entrepreneurial subject and of private welfare as superior to public, even though the public–private division is often unclear. In the twenty-first-century transnational context, with so many missionary projects arising from different nations and communities, the US government and US churches worked hard to valorize Christian humanitarianism as benevolent and Islamic humanitarianism as terroristic, thereby erasing their many commonalities and constructing humanitarianism as a Western and Christian project.

Historians suggest that humanitarianism rests on the idea of a common humanity and a particular ethics of saving by a heroic Western and secular subject. In examining the history of what he calls "the humanitarian narrative" in nineteenth-century Europe, Thomas Laqueur argues that this narrative is marked by a claim of a common bond between those who suffer and those who are helping, as well as by a belief in the necessity of action in helping. He locates this narrative within the rise of eighteenth-century capitalism, rather than of Christianity,[11] though he leaves out the colonialism that undergirded capitalist industrialization. Identification with victims through aestheticized sentiment was important, as I showed in chapter 2 with Mortenson, the US Navy, voluntourists, and digital humanitarians. But as these examples demonstrated, racialized histories of colonialism produced the American belief that only certain groups of people (particularly, white American, Christians) could express that sentiment. In this framework, others cannot be humanitarians, because their goals are seen as nefarious. As discussed in the previous chapter, with the neoliberal withdrawal of states from welfare, especially in the Global South and the United States, humanitarian work became seen by many around the world as one way to address social needs without disturbing the inequality and privileges of dominant Western elites. That many religious missions began to call themselves humanitarians by the end of the twentieth century is noteworthy in this new phase of advanced neoliberal capitalism.

In the United States, the context of what was called the global war on terror allowed the United States government to monitor and block the movements of funds by nonwhite and mostly Islamic, Muslim, and Arab charitable organizations based in South Asia and the Middle East over concerns that these donations were enabling terrorism. In the process, the US government came to view hawala transfers as criminal, even though such transfers of funds had operated for centuries across South Asia and the Middle East, and had also extended into Europe and North America via diasporas from these southern regions. The hawala system is based on individual peer-to-peer money transfers, whereby a person in one country would pay another in the same country, and the latter would instruct their contact in the second country to pay that money to whomever was intended as a recipient. Done without going through banking systems and by forms of trust and relationships, these continue to be used by immigrants, who are impacted when these become criminalized by the American state. Such criminalization contrasted with the lack of such scrutiny over organizations such as Kiva, which also claimed to be doing peer-to-peer connections. In seeking to find how Al Qaeda and other organizations designated as supporting terror were moving their funds, the US government criminalized many Muslim citizens as well as Arab and Muslim-supported or -created NGOs, thus expelling these citizens and groups from becoming humanitarians and exceptional citizens.

Sherene Razack has argued that after 9/11, Muslims were cast out of citizenship in Canada and the United States. Extending her argument, I suggest that they were not simply cast out of citizenship in general, but were specifically expelled from the exceptional citizenship of white, US Christians who claimed humanitarianism and neoliberal charity as normative Christian practices. Under the claim that it was cracking down on "terrorist" funding sources, the US government created laws and criminal cases against Arab and Muslim-sponsored charities, which it almost always called "Islamic charities" to suggest that these were especially linked to radical Islamists, rather than to the more widely accepted notion of zakat and charity that have long existed across the world in Muslim communities. Such charities were then accused of supporting terror.[12] The *Washington Post* reported in 2006 that since 9/11, three Muslim charities in the United States were shut down and over forty were targeted for investigation.[13] New forms of racialized profiling and surveillance were used to cast suspicion on Muslim organizations seeking to transfer zakat funds (those given as part of the duty of all Muslims to the community) to organizations in the Middle East. As one of the seven pillars of Islam, zakat has been important for supporting poor Muslims the world over. Zakat funds are used for giving of alms, feeding the poor, and creating orphanages, as well as supporting refugees, travelers, and migrants.[14]

The US government crackdowns were enabled by security expertise and news media that suggested that zakat funding was merely a cover for terrorism funding.[15] In contrast, white Christian humanitarian organizations went unquestioned and were assumed to be legitimate charities. Christian humanitarian work was supported by state regulations and celebratory media coverage of humanitarians as exceptional Americans, as well as neoliberal ones who brought together religion and capitalism.[16] There are others granted US citizenship status who are excluded from such belonging as Americans, and these unexceptional figures become visible as either criminals or threats to national security.[17] Especially in the George W. Bush administration, the US government explicitly supported Christian faith-based organizations (FBOs) providing welfare, while criminalizing Muslim agencies doing similar work.[18] Such criminalization continued even during the Obama presidency. Through this practice, the liberal doctrine of separation of church and state, and of public and private, has become further muddied, enabling the exceptional charity of Christians. In the process, Muslims' rights to religious expression through zakat was impacted, leading to legal challenges.[19] The fact that many of these challenges did not succeed also means that Muslims had to struggle to participate in the humanitarianism that could make them exceptional neoliberal citizens.

Religion and Charity in the Neoliberal Era

Beginning in the 1970s, neoliberal welfare reforms created opportunities for religious organizations to provide welfare in the wake of retreating state provisions. In this context, many US Protestant churches began operating nationally and transnationally under new logics. Transnational religious activists found opportunities in the Global South in the aftermath of IMF-mandated structural adjustment programs reducing state-sponsored welfare. American evangelical church leaders were particularly aggressive in this regard, emphasizing free market reforms as central to religious "choice," adopting development and human rights language.[20] They were heavily supported by the US government and by many American citizens.[21] These evangelical church leaders aggressively identified and aligned their work with white, American nationalism. Billy Graham's ministry is a good example of such an alignment.

The trajectory of Billy Graham's ministries, including the organization Samaritan's Purse, is an example of the relation between the US state and evangelical organizations through the twentieth and twenty-first centuries. Graham's success reveals the rise of American evangelical missions after World

War II.[22] Although American Pentecostal churches have a longer history of missionary activity,[23] Graham's "crusades" (as Graham called them) exemplified the postwar charismatic preaching and televangelism that reached millions of people both in the United States and outside of it. In his preaching, Graham identified the United States as a Christian nation, and, as one historian suggests, his theology "blurred the boundaries between religious, national, political, and spiritual identities," transforming the "civil religious frame of the Christian nation into an evangelical one."[24] Graham was close to several presidents, including Lyndon Johnson and Richard Nixon. He spouted virulent anticommunism (at one point, he advocated bombing North Vietnam in ways that would have killed a million people) and anti-Semitism, but also supported capitalism and an end to segregation, as well as the work of Reverend Martin Luther King Jr. and Nelson Mandela. He preached his gospel to millions, creating evangelical "world congress" meetings in the 1960s and 1970s. In the 1980s Graham began to train evangelists to work around the world, and the later spread of American evangelical Christianity is partly attributable to this work.

The post-9/11 effects of Graham's preaching are visible in an offshoot of his ministries, the organization Samaritan's Purse. Bob Pierce founded Samaritan's Purse in 1970 and after Pierce's death, the organization was headed by Graham's son, Franklin Graham. In its mission statement, Samaritan's Purse describes itself as both evangelizing and undertaking rescue and development work: "Samaritan's Purse travels the world's highways looking for victims along the way. We are quick to bandage the wounds we see, but like the Samaritan, we don't stop there. In addition to meeting immediate, emergency needs, we help these victims recover and get back on their feet."[25] Operating in many countries around the world, the organization focuses both on spreading Christianity in Africa, Asia, and Latin America as well as on emergency needs and long-term welfare. Development and proselytizing go hand in hand, and much of this proselytizing involves denouncing Islam and converting Muslims. Franklin Graham has called Islam an evil, terrorist religion and has said that Islam has "declared war on the world."[26] In 2003, Samaritan's Purse created controversy when its lobbyists asked the Bush administration to allow it to enter Iraq during the American occupation.[27] The organization has been active in several Muslim countries; for example, one of its missionaries sued the organization when she was kidnapped in Sudan in 2010.[28] Samaritan's Purse has gained global adherents by involving many church members, not simply missionaries who want to travel overseas but also members in projects such as Operation Christmas

Child, which sends gifts, school supplies, and Bible stories all over the world. Rescue, proselytizing, missionary saving, and development work collaborate as the group preaches American Protestant evangelical ideas that combine neoliberal capitalism with individual responsibility, Bible study, and an antiabortion, antigay agenda. Samaritan's Purse shows the blurry line between private and public/state funding under US neoliberalism, especially when the organization disburses US government funding during its rescue operations. In 2001, villagers in El Salvador receiving United States Agency for International Development (USAID) funds via Samaritan's Purse had to participate in prayer meetings, and were given religious tracts and asked to accept Jesus Christ as their savior before they could get help. US officials did express concern when such practices were reported, but noted that the organization met performance goals.[29] Organizations such as Samaritan's Purse are not alone in this work of constructing American Protestant evangelical missions as development and humanitarian projects. World Vision and Christian Care are two other such organizations, among many, and they share Samaritan's postwar American evangelical approach.

Erica Bornstein's research on these organizations' work in Zimbabwe finds also that they blur the language of humanitarianism and development, creating emergent ideologies of Christian development that conjoin spirituality and capitalism. Protestant evangelical organizations were present in Zimbabwe before independence (1980) as relief organizations and continued their presence after independence, undertaking more welfare work as neoliberal structural adjustment became institutionalized. Such organizations, Bornstein argues, mediated discontent but were unable to correct burgeoning inequality.[30]

In recent decades, World Vision has promoted the agenda of gender equality as a path to development, one that has been promoted by many feminist NGOs. It does so by focusing on preventing sex-selective abortions, child marriage, and gender-based violence. World Vision's website is full of images of young girls, similar to Mortenson's book cover, so that it relies on notions of innocence and the deployment of figures of children, especially girls, as proper targets of humanitarian work. Such images are designed to attract donors and missionaries.[31] In a shift away from missionary goals, the organization began to engage with major development projects that came to focus on women as catalysts and harbingers of development, a focus visible also in the United Nations Development Fund's Millennial Development Goals.[32] In doing so, they continued to claim, as colonial regimes have done for centuries, that Westerners are more open to women's empowerment than are other cultures and communities. In such cases, humanitarian work for women's empowerment becomes the sign of the progressive exceptional citizen.

The twenty-first century marked an increase in Christian missionary activity, expanding American humanitarian citizenship as a new form of exceptional, Christian, imperial sovereignty.[33] Christian evangelical missions (fundamentalist, Pentecostal, and others) became part of the American state and US geopolitics. In the process, the practices of these missions and missionaries shifted. Ju Hui Judy Han finds that in the new century, South Korean and American Protestant evangelical missions to China and Africa incorporated secular notions of humanitarianism and development into their religious arguments. These missionaries began viewing themselves as compassionate donors and humanitarians, undertaking mission work under the new guise of humanitarianism. In the process, they furthered global inequalities, as I detailed in chapter 2.[34] Some reject the term "missionary" for the term "volunteer" in attempting to downplay the evangelical goals of their organizations.[35]

Evangelical missions to Muslim countries have continued though shifting Middle East politics have altered these projects, as the missions are now shorter and fuse voluntarism, tourism, and evangelism,[36] thus incorporating evangelism into the Greg Mortenson–like projects of "saving" brown women and girls. Development NGOs often have religious affiliations, and conversion and welfare work in tandem.[37] For example, George W. Bush's funding for HIV/AIDS in Africa involved funding faith-based organizations that promoted abstinence to prevent the spread of the disease.[38] In Muslim central Asia, in a more West-friendly country such as Kyrgyzstan, US evangelical groups have created a powerful network of missionaries who work through development projects. As anthropologist Mathijs Pelkmans demonstrates, "by connecting fleeting humanitarian efforts with the long-term residence of missions teams" these missionaries are able "to integrate local communities in a network that spans from the rural heartlands of Missouri to the mountains of Kyrgyzstan." Pelkmans also notes that these missionaries often hide their proselytizing by calling themselves "volunteers" or development or aid workers, using notions of "freedom of choice," "open societies," and "democracy" to promote their efforts. For example, the evangelical Christian missionary organization Frontiers, which focuses on proselytizing to Muslims, teaches its members to hide their missionary identities and instead act like aid workers or language teachers.[39] In some countries, conservative American Christians have come under fire for spreading discrimination and violence against LGBT people,[40] as well as for forcing conversions in exchange for development.

Since the 1970s, Islamic religious revival movements have not been far behind Christian evangelical ones in gaining supporters and donations and, much like Christian movements, have taken advantage of new technologies and neoliberal inequalities. What Mona Atia calls "pious neoliberalism" has drawn millions into the *dawa* ("volunteer") movements in the Arab and Muslim countries of the Middle East. Dawa movements conjoin charity and economy, public practices, and Islamic norms, and they build on traditional practices of doing good deeds through private actions within a public sphere.[41] In the case of Egypt, as Atia relates, while zakat donations helped poor people in some ways, the Egyptian zakat committee was unable to enact distributive justice. In the late twentieth century, some zakat committees began seeing zakat, traditionally a right for the needy (orphans, widows, education, medical support), as more useful in enabling microenterprise and development. Such zakat committees connected microenterprise and development to religious precepts—mirroring the neoliberal work of organizations such as Samaritan's Purse and World Vision. This produced what Atia calls "faith-based development." During and after the Hosni Mubarak regime (1981–2011), Egyptian zakat committees increasingly used zakat funds not just to support the poor but also to give them religious lessons and produce entrepreneurial subjects.

Islamic charities sponsored by Saudi Arabia and other Persian Gulf states have also been active in charitable and humanitarian projects that are tied to religious teaching. For example, Saudi Arabia began heavily funding Islamic NGOs in many parts of the world, since that nation had benefited hugely from the same oil crisis that had bankrupted many countries of the Global South and led to structural adjustment programs. In his book on famine in Africa, Alex de Waal analyzes the Islamic NGOs operating in Sudan since the 1970s, showing they played increasingly active roles in the Sudanese government in the 1990s.[42] Gulf states also funded religious schools during this period, and Islamic NGOs worked with Muslim and non-Muslim governments in many regions.[43]

In the context of the twenty-first-century global war on terror, as well as increased Palestinian displacement and dispassion, zakat has become increasingly criminalized in the United States, particularly zakat from diasporic Muslim communities. Much of the criminalization stemmed from accusations that US-based Muslim charity organizations had contributed to Hamas, which the US government designated as a terrorist organization.

However, as Jonathan Benthall points out, such accusations are largely unsubstantiated. Benthall's fieldwork in the West Bank town of Nablus found little evidence of this alleged relationship between zakat funds and Hamas, finding instead that the needs of impoverished and displaced Palestinians has led to zakat donations from much of the Middle East, most of which is directed toward medical and educational support, as well as toward needy families and orphans.[44] In the context of the war on terror, Muslim organizations, whether supported by Islamic states or Muslim individuals, have generated greater suspicion from the US government because they are perceived as more radical and as racially Other to secular and religious European or American Christian organizations. Muslim organizations have also generated greater suspicion because they are new players in the Western-style development projects that have previously been funded by those supposedly secular and religious European and American institutions.[45] One result of these missionary geo-conflicts is that in the United States, Euro-American organizations can claim exceptionalism while Muslim organizations doing similar work are criminalized.

Since 2001, as the war on terror has shaped US national security concerns, crackdowns on Muslim charities have come at the same time as expansion of funding for evangelical US Christian organizations. During the Bush presidency, this close relationship between evangelical Christian organizations and George W. Bush led to charges of religious discrimination and financial abuses by evangelicals, as well as several constitutional challenges.[46] In this context, the US government began to use antiterror laws to surveil and regulate financial transfers across national boundaries, with the result that transnational development agencies avoided working with Muslim organizations, since they could been seen as linked to terror groups.[47] Muslim charities were seen as partners of terrorists, while Christian charities— especially conservative evangelical Christian organizations—gained federal and state funds for missions and welfare work. The Bush administration also poured funding into projects empowering so-called "moderate" Muslims, intent on gaining some legitimacy in Muslim communities and nations. But the results of these endeavors were limited, since few in the Bush administration could agree on whom or what to target as threats, or the chief reasons for growing anti-Americanism.[48] Despite this, Bush tripled the USAID budget after 9/11, with more than half of those funds heading to Muslim-majority countries.[49] Evangelical Christian organizations benefited from these changes in US funding policies. Under the George W. Bush presidency, US Christian evangelical missions were major grantees of USAID, pushing neoliberal agendas that include free market capitalism, individual agency, and limited government.[50]

In this twenty-first-century neoliberal context, it has become difficult to separate religious from humanitarian organizations (which can be religious or secular and from any political stripe) both in the United States and the Middle East because all such organizations claim to be doing humanitarian or development work, and states have come to sponsor religious organizations even in what is seen as the secular West. Humanitarian organizations are hardly apolitical, given both the long history of European colonialism and the more recent geopolitics of exceptional American soft power.

Expanding State Welfare Funding by Faith-Based Organizations

In the last decades of the twentieth century, the United States empowered US Christian missionary projects by incorporating religion into welfare, with the goal of reducing state-provided welfare. While federal funds had gone to religious organizations for decades before this, though under the condition that funding for religious work would not be state funded and had to be kept separate from welfare work, in the 1990s it became possible for faith-based organizations (FBOS) to receive federal and state funds even while professing religious practices during their welfare work. These changes began with President Bill Clinton's welfare reform, the Personal Responsibility and Work Opportunity Reconciliation Act of 1996, which created a charitable choice provision allowing community organizations and churches, which were clearly religious organizations for the most part, to obtain government funds for welfare programs.[51] Faith-based organizations were encouraged to compete with secular organizations for government grants under the logic that they had previously been discriminated against, though they were not to use the government money for direct funding of religious activities. During debates over the bill, several scholars and experts argued that FBOS were essential because the state could not hope to provide the services necessary.[52] While the provision was partly also a political strategy by Democrats and Republicans to garner the votes of religious conservatives, it came under criticism during the Bush administration for enabling employment discrimination on grounds of religious affiliation.[53] It was also criticized for violating the constitutionally mandated separation of church and state.[54]

President George W. Bush, a conservative Christian (Episcopalian), established the White House Office of Faith-Based and Community Initiatives (OFBCI) in January 2001.[55] Five centers in the Departments of Education,

Health and Human Services, Housing and Urban Development, and Justice and Labor were created to audit and eliminate obstacles to providing government funding to FBOS. The OFBCI's goal was to reduce state responsibility for welfare, a practice that Bush had begun as governor of Texas. Throughout his presidency, Bush issued executive orders that replicated what he had done in Texas as governor and which aimed to increase and expedite the participation of FBOS in government agencies. The Bush administration also encouraged private giving through a variety of tax deductions and the removal of federal impediments. It sought to expand the work of those who saw themselves as "social entrepreneurs," combining market solutions and humanitarianism to provide welfare, both in the United States and globally.

In his remarks about the OFBCI's founding, entitled "Rallying the Armies of Compassion,"[56] Bush emphasized that while government "has a solemn responsibility to help meet the needs of poor Americans and distressed neighborhoods," it does not have "a monopoly on compassion." He described "civic, social, charitable, and religious groups" as "quiet heroes" and compared their putative success to the "failed formula of towering distant bureaucracies that too often prize process over performance." "Americans," he stated, "are a deeply compassionate people and will not tolerate indifference towards the poor." While he conceded that government "cannot be replaced by charities," he suggested that "it can and should welcome them as partners." In his plan, "neighborhood-based caregivers" have to replace "traditional social programs (that) are often too bureaucratic, inflexible, and impersonal." He positioned nonprofits as valiant, "outmanned and outflanked" underdogs that have been "neglected or excluded" and now need a "level playing field" and a "seat at the table." He claimed that they use "care and compassion," helping in "ways that government cannot," and are "lonely outposts of energy, service and vision" and "precious resources, great gifts of American society."

While the OFBCI project seemed to open the doors for all religious organizations to collaborate with the government, it was designed politically to incorporate Christian conservatives as key members of White House staff and thus keep Bush's political base intact. In practice, the OFBCI distinguished between trustworthy FBOS (Christian, preferably white, conservative, and evangelical) and duplicitous FBOS (Muslim). Bush's courting of Christian conservatives involved incorporating well-known Christian conservative activists into the White House, with the blessing and support of a broad army of activists excited that they were going to be able to expand the ambit of the charitable choice provision into Christian conservatism.

R. Marie Griffith and Melani McAlister report that Andrew Natsios, a former vice president of World Vision, was brought in to head USAID in 2001; in 2005, World Vision became the second-largest recipient of USAID funds for work overseas.[57] Natsios became controversial for his racial biases about Africa and Africans, once saying that Africans could not be given antiretroviral drugs because they lacked "a concept of time" and that there were no roads or doctors on the continent.[58]

Christian conservatives also had particular goals for their organizations. As Christian conservative activist David Kuo recollects, these conservative activists wanted "real" FBOs to get federal funding, but they also wanted to circumvent federal nondiscrimination laws put in place by the Civil Rights Act of 1964.[59] The Christian conservatives wanted, according to Kuo, "religious groups receiving federal funds [to have] an unfettered right to hire and fire people based not only on their professed religion but also on whether they lived according to the 'rules' of their religion."[60] Republicans such as Tom Delay and Dennis Hastert wanted the law to allow FBOs to discriminate on the basis of not just religion, but "practices." Specifically, they wanted FBOs to be allowed to purge LGBT people from their organizations and to discriminate with impunity, revealing how state power endowed such persons and organizations with sovereignty, making them exceptional citizens operating under the law of exception. The transfer of sovereignty to these citizens thus takes place through the participation of the state, breaking down, in many instances, the divisions between what is public and private.

While some Christian conservatives such as Kuo professed a "compassionate conservative" approach, clearly that was quickly forgotten both in courting votes and in supporting prominent Christian conservatives, as well as in the provision's implementation. While fiscally conservative Republicans were more interested in "tax cuts, business growth, [and] a strong military,"[61] the FBO legislation was clearly meant to draw more socially conservative and evangelical voters to the Bush White House. The strong presence of Rick Warren, Chuck Colson, and other evangelicals in the policy's drafting, as well as in the many conferences created by the White House about the OFBCI, all suggested a strong evangelical Christian project that was decidedly antiabortion, anti-LGBT, and very white.

Although the OFBCI's Compassion Capital Fund was supposed to disburse major funding to small groups previously ineligible for federal funding, most of the funding initially went to Christian conservative groups. According to David Kuo, who served as the OFBCI's deputy director under John Dilulio in the Bush years, such discrimination was not seen as deliberate but rather as the result of the fact that evangelical Christians constituted the faith-based policy world around the White House. The review board that distributed funds to selected organizations, those that were "politically friendly to the administration,"[62] was made up of mostly white, Christian conservatives. One reviewer later disclosed that she had given non-Christian groups zero points on their applications. As she related to Kuo, "when I saw one of those non-Christian groups in the set I was reviewing, I just stopped looking at them and gave them a zero."[63] Many other reviewers did the same, thinking that the project's goal was to help specific Christian groups. While activists such as Kuo claimed their goal was to convince socially conservative African Americans and Latinos to join the Republican Party on the basis of shared anti-LGBT and antiabortion politics, such groups often did not get funding while the heavily white Christian conservative insiders did.

For the most part, larger, older, and more savvy FBOs obtained greater government funds than smaller and newer organizations,[64] and the wall between public and private was broken down for these organizations. In the context of faith-based initiative implementation at the state level, one research study found that these new policies were more likely to be implemented in states where evangelical movements were strong, and were used to strengthen these movements while further weakening the church/state separation,[65] thereby turning FBOs personnel into exceptional citizens. Such practices brought evangelical Christians into bureaucracies by creating faith-based "liaison" positions, thus promoting one religious denomination over another and "legitimizing religious actors as political actors."[66] These changes created a greater role for religion in the public sphere, but there is little evidence that these organizations were able to significantly improve social services.[67] Importantly, in states where the faith-based liaisons were African Americans, FBOs received fewer resources than in states where liaisons were white evangelical Christians.[68]

Until 2004, most OFBCI funding went to Christian groups, raising constitutional questions over government funding for organizations that discriminate in hiring on the basis of religion.[69] Critics argued that these organizations did not abide by federal nondiscrimination regulations governing beneficiaries and hiring requirements. In a report from 2006, the General Accounting Office (GAO) found that FBOs regularly violated the rule that federal funds could not be used for "inherently religious activities."[70] This report came as a response to questions from Congressmen George Miller (D-CA) and Pete Stark (D-CA), who asked GAO to investigate whether the new laws provided more or better welfare than the state, whether constitutional safeguards were in place, and whether grant-review procedures were fair to all organizations.[71] No doubt, this was in response to the Christian conservative presence in the White House, which, by the end of the first term of President George W. Bush, had fallen somewhat out of favor with the White House, especially with the rising power of Vice President Dick Cheney.

The GAO report highlighted just how much these evangelical groups had operated as exceptional, citizen groups, being endowed with the sovereign power of the exception, since they used federal funding with little oversight and no accountability to federal guidelines. In its response to Miller and Stark, the GAO found that grant reviewers stated that the review process was fair because it did not ask organizations to identify whether they were FBOs. Between 2002 and 2005, federal agencies gave over $500 million to encourage FBO participation.[72] The GAO report also noted that few agencies included information on safeguards for federal compliance with nondiscrimination and the prohibition of using federal funds for "inherently religious activities." One agency even told GAO that one program it funded was exempt from such prohibition. The GAO found that "the scope of the exception was unclear" and that some organizations violated the law by undertaking explicitly religious activities (such as praying) during federally funded work.[73] The GAO also stated that it was unable to find data to answer whether FBOs received funding advantages over secular organizations, first because it was unable to figure out how an FBO was defined (the report mentioned this limitation several times), and second because such publicly available data did not exist. In addition to these concerns, the GAO reported that in 2005 the five centers established in federal agencies spent most of the funds dedicated to expanding FBO and community participation on staff salaries and benefits. Some funding even went to intermediary organizations intended to help expand FBO participation.

Clearly, there were multiple problems with the OFBCI project, raising questions about discrimination. The GAO report also revealed that government agencies did not collect credible data in the standardized way, which would have allowed proper analysis of the effectiveness of the new provisions. The GAO report showed that some parts of government were unwilling to go along with the mandates of other government agencies or the White House, and it thus challenged the exceptionalism of evangelical groups. It is clear that the exceptional status given to this particular group came under attack from within the government itself, as their sovereignty led them to see themselves as outside the law, eliciting protest and critique from other bureaucracies, denominations, and groups.

Outside research replicated these findings and even went further. One researcher has stated that there is little evidence to show that FBOs are more effective than state programs in providing welfare,[74] and there have also been questions raised about the training and knowledge of service providers, especially around discriminatory hiring practices. The American Civil Liberties Union (ACLU), in particular, challenged the constitutionality of the charitable choice provision on the grounds that it violated the separation of church and state. In a statement from March 12, 2003, the ACLU stated: "We need to protect individual religious freedom, including the freedom to receive social services without feeling forced to adopt religious beliefs with which one may disagree. Explicit protections must be put in place that prohibit religious coercion in the provision of social services. Taxpayer-funded programs must respect the private choices of all Americans to worship as they see fit."[75] Mark Chaves argues that the charitable choice provision was flawed because it was based on the misguided assumptions that FBOs had been previously discriminated against during federal-funding procedures, that FBOs were doing a great deal of welfare, and that they were better at doing it.[76]

In summary, during George W. Bush's first term, increasing state support was given to evangelical Christian organizations, though this discrepancy did not last beyond the first term. Such state actions enabled the White House to build political support by creating one white Christian group as having an especially favored status as exceptional Americans and, indeed, endowing them with sovereignty that enabled them to function as exception to the law.

Excluding Muslims from Humanitarian Citizenship

State surveillance and racial harassment of Muslims, Arabs, and South Asians, so overt and punitive after 9/11, was a contrast to the exceptionalism accorded to evangelical Christians.[77] In examining how such a broad net of suspicion and criminalization was cast across so many Muslim groups, many scholars compellingly argued for the salience of race as an analytical framework. David Goldberg's theorization of the "racial state" has also been a critical contribution to this debate, as he considers how racialization is central to all modern states,[78] and there is a long history of the United States as a racial state from its founding moments. Yet, in examining more recent state practices, Sherene Razack argues that Muslims have become a "race" in Canada and the United States alongside nonwhite immigrants and First Nations groups because they have been "cast out" of citizenship as targets of policing and constructed as different from a white "civilized' community.[79] The surveillance and security state has incorporated race into its logic of rule. In examining the global emergence of the security state, Paul Amar suggests that new global "racial, caste, and ethnic" distinctions have emerged, and "new missions of policing" require recognition of their "embeddedness within racial, ethnic and/or caste orders."[80] For Amar, recent iterations of "race" and "ethnicity" are a global effect of policing and security formations that have commonalities across national divides. Legal scholar Asli Ü. Bâli argues that the preventive detention of Muslim and Middle East immigrants in the United States after 9/11 suggests that Bush's war on terror included a war on particular immigrant groups, revealing the connections between the eighteenth-, nineteenth-, and twentieth-century US history of discrimination against racialized immigrant groups and the new twenty-first-century politics of terror.[81]

Within this longer history, there emerged new forms of discrimination against such groups that worked alongside older forms of criminalization through surveillance and detention. This new form was to use the American security state to construct Muslims and Arabs as criminal and therefore not exceptional Americans by criminalizing their humanitarian work. It is now well known that these groups were subject to a great deal of harassment, from unauthorized surveillance and detention, demonization in media and in politics, defacement and attacks on houses of worship, and violence against individuals who "looked Muslim," as well as deportation and secret rendition to prisons outside the country. Brought to bear were all technologies of state and nonstate sovereign power to work outside the Constitution and to violate the rights of these citizens.[82] The state also began to carry out monitoring and surveillance of Muslim NGOs and charitable organizations through their money transfers; Wadie Said argues that the ban on providing "material support" to a designated foreign terrorist organization (FTO) is "by the government's reckoning, the most important statute employed in terrorism prosecutions."[83] This ban emerged within Section 2339B of the Antiterrorism and Effective Death Penalty Act of 1996 and criminalized any "material support" of organizations designated as an FTO to prevent charity becoming a pretext for supporting terrorism.[84] Section 2339B's definition of an FTO refers to the Immigration and Nationality Act, Section 219, through which the secretary of state has to designate an organization as an FTO. It enjoined financial organizations to report the existence of any funds linked to an FTO, with the threat of penalties if this reporting was not done. It also allowed the attorney general to proactively initiate civil action, stating:

"Whenever it appears to the Secretary or the Attorney General that any person is engaged in, or is about to engage in, any act that constitutes, or would constitute, a violation of this section, the Attorney General may initiate civil action in a district court of the United States to enjoin such violation."[85] In addition, using the International Emergency Economic Powers Act of 1977, Bush issued Executive Order 13224, enjoining the Office of Foreign Assets Control, part of the Department of Treasury, to block the assets of any organization if it determined the organization was linked to a terrorist threat to the United States.

The result of such laws was that giving to American Muslim charities declined by 40 percent after 9/11. The ACLU report *Blocking Faith, Freezing Charity* argues that a "climate of fear" intimidated Muslims and prevented them from religious practices, including giving zakat.[86] Anthropologist Erica Caple James finds that antiterrorism financing laws had "reportedly chilled" Muslim-to-Muslim philanthropy.[87] The decline in giving came as a result of the government advising donors to heavily scrutinize their charities through "anti-terrorist financing procedures."[88] The government linked many of these charitable associations to transnational finance networks that were said to be funding "specially designated terrorist organizations," and these activities were heavily surveilled by the US government. In particular, Muslim charities were and continue to be seen as terrorist-related groups under both 2339A, which targeted material support for particular designated offences, and 2339B, which focused on support of FTOs. In reviewing cases under the material support statute that took place between 2001 and 2007, Sam Adelsberg, Freya Pitts, and Sirine Shebaya found that one-third involved support to Al Qaeda, with two other major organizations being Hamas or FARC (the Colombian cartel). This constitutes a substantial number of prosecutions of Muslim or Arab organizations.[89] They point out that the fear of prosecutions has also impacted many other aid organizations.

The government's surveillance of Muslim Americans slowed zakat donations and required many private businesses and religious organizations to share information with the state. As one legal scholar reveals, "the government subjected mosques to surveillance, wiretapped phones, fingerprinted and registered more than eighty thousand Arab and non-national residents," and issued "well over one hundred thousand secret warrantless demands, known as national security letters, to financial institutions, telecommunications companies, and other businesses to obtain data on unknowing targeted individuals."[90] Electronic fund transfers and emails became, and continue to be, particularly subject to government surveillance.

While both the definition of what counts as "terrorism" and the question of how organizations become identified as being FTOs or as supporting terror or FTOs are vague and imprecise and often generate legal controversy,[91] the "material support" clause led to harassment and persecution for many Arabs and Muslims and their organizations. Significantly, domestic terrorists such as neo-Nazis and other armed white militias believed to have only domestic networks, were left out under statutes 2339A and 2339B because it focused only on foreign-connected organizations. As legal scholar James Ward points out, "inexplicably, the statutes make no mention of funding to terrorists without any international connections," revealing the statutes' purpose of prosecuting US residents and citizens with international connections.[92]

The Global Nonprofit Information Network has traced how US government investigations, as well as its antiterror laws, affected charities working in the Muslim world and those run by Muslims. Government actions and surveillance troubled many non-Muslim organizations and all banks and financing businesses because they were left with the burden of showing that funds were not linked to FTOs or any acts of terror. These organizations sought guidance from the government to create "safe harbor" provisions, arguing that one problem with the US Treasury Department's Anti-Terrorist Financing Guidelines was that they require nonprofits to take on the "burden of government-style investigation on charitable organization and convey no presumption of innocence even if the Guidelines are followed to the letter."[93] There were other legal concerns as well. Legal scholar Eric Sandberg-Zakian argues that designating an entity a "specially designated terrorist organization" under the International Emergency Economic Powers Act violated the Fifth and Sixth Amendments to the US Constitution because such designation occurs without a trial even though it becomes a "criminal punishment."[94] He argues that the groups become so designated by bureaucratic process that expels them from the rights given to others. In addition, it is often extremely difficult to get off the list, once an organization becomes designated as supporting an FTO.

The "material support" statute has raised First Amendment issues, as some argue it violates the right to religious freedom and civil liberties.[95] According to Michael Freedman, the law hindered Muslim religious practices, which is unconstitutional, without helping the government prevent terrorism.[96] As one legal scholar puts it, "because Islamic law mandates that members give alms, known as zakat . . . the giving of money to groups that represent their objectives to be humanitarian complicated Western efforts to prevent the flow of fund to Islamic groups that both help people and engage in violence."[97] As a result, the material support clause and the designation of groups as aiding terrorism have faced challenges in the courts, which ask how funding political and humanitarian work can be criminalized.[98] US courts have ruled that, indeed, such humanitarian or political giving can be criminalized and that "even 'humanitarian money'—that is, funds intended for benevolent purposes—simply cannot go to foreign groups that engage in political violence."[99] In some cases, says one scholar, "court decisions left the impression that, despite the requisite 'should have known' statutory intent, even innocent donors can be persecuted for supporting terrorism."[100] Such decisions reveal how Muslim humanitarianism cannot be seen as the work of exceptional citizens, but may be always under suspicion as threatening to state security. In contrast, many other so-called international organizations have not been scrutinized or even prosecuted as have Muslim organizations.

For instance, in 2006, the Treasury Department froze the assets of Kind-Hearts, an Ohio-based organization, without instituting criminal proceedings or even designating the organization an FTO. The Treasury Department did not give the organization this designation until four years after their assets were frozen. It seized all of its assets, including paper documents and computers, leaving the organization unable to continue. Under the Patriot Act, the government did not have to provide evidence to justify the seizure. KindHearts sued, with the help of the ACLU, to have the government-seized documents returned. The district judge overseeing the suit agreed that the organization's Sixth Amendment right, "impairment of the right to counsel," was violated if the government did not turn over copies of the documents to KindHearts' counsel. The government had to allow defending counsel copies of paper documents but still did not provide copies of electronic files. The judge stated that the paper documents were insignificant because the electronic data was more significant to the government's case, declaring, "given the government's underlying contention that KindHearts was a money funnel for overseas terrorists, its records of its electronic communication are of especial importance and potential pertinence."[101] The government refused to provide any evidence that KindHearts was sending funds to Hamas. Instead, government lawyers stated that KindHearts fundraisers and officials rendered the organization suspect because the individual officials had allegedly "coordinated with Hamas leaders and made contributions to Hamas-affiliated Holy Land Foundation for Relief and Development and the al-Qaida affiliated Global Relief Organization."[102] In 2009, the ACLU won the case, blocking the government from designating KindHearts a "specially designated global terrorist," that is, an FTO designated as such by the secretary of state without further judicial review. However, the court did not return the organization's seized assets.

Even as the US government views electronic communications and transfers as particularly suspicious, it criminalizes Muslim individuals in particular. Here, it is not the mediated regulation of money or the surveillance of money transfers that finds criminal activity, but rather the profiling of Muslim individuals. Experts state that funding surveillance has not yielded much in the way of results and has allowed the FBI to target US citizens and to expand surveillance over more and more groups and populations.[103] In the process, banking corporations raise fees for customers on the grounds that they have to add onerous regulation costs to their expenses, and they complain about the heavy burden of such regulation.

While many prosecutions of zakat-giving organizations have not been successful, the US government has won some significant cases with the help of the Patriot Act's "material support" clause and problematic trial practices. The government was able to use the "material support" charge as the lead count in eight convictions out of 162 total federal prosecutions; however, out of 108 material support prosecutions, just nine resulted in convictions and several resulted in hung juries, some of which were later turned into convictions.[104] For example, in 2007, charges against the Holy Land Foundation for Relief and Development tried in Dallas resulted in a hung jury. However, in 2008, the Holy Land Foundation was convicted on charges including money laundering, tax fraud, and supporting terrorism, while about three hundred other organizations and individuals were named as "unindicted co-conspirators" so that they could be named in the trial without charging them of crimes.[105] The "material support" clause and the designation of groups as sponsoring or aiding terrorism, despite their vague and contested nature, were used to show that Muslims and Arabs could not be exceptional citizens.

Legal and State Logics

One legal scholar states that post-9/11, the US government closed down some of these "American Islamic charities" with "speed and efficiency."[106] This new crackdown on Muslim organizations was made possible by George W. Bush's executive order targeting humanitarian organizations, which was a divergence from previous government policy.[107] In media coverage of the trials, however, few journalists mentioned the humanitarian or welfare work done by Muslims or zakat organizations in the United States. In contrast to their lauding of individual white humanitarians such as Mortenson, who are constructed as exceptional, Muslim humanitarian activity was viewed with suspicion. As discussed in chapter 2, this selective criminalization of humanitarian work is visible in Dave Eggers's account of the Muslim man detained in New Orleans after Hurricane Katrina on suspicion of terrorism while he was rescuing people trapped in their homes.[108] After 9/11, Muslim organizations have increasingly found it difficult to even get a bank to work with them, and without a reputable bank they face difficulty in transferring funds to organizations they support.[109]

Since 2001, most US courts have upheld these examples of charity asset freezing, despite numerous constitutional challenges.[110] In the process, Muslim humanitarian work becomes criminal activity precisely because money is seen to be fungible; humanitarian funding, the US courts ruled, can also be aiding terrorism. It is believed that the "[specially designated foreign terrorist organizations] that accept contributions for a school or hospital can funnel those resources to instrumentalities of violence, or free up resources for violent goals."[111] In this framework, even refugee camps can be used for planning violence.[112] The clause has been upheld in *Holder v. Humanitarian Law Project* (2010), which examined whether the Humanitarian Law Project would be allowed to help Kurdish and Tamil movements with human rights and humanitarian issues without being designated as helping terrorism. After a decade of litigation, in 2010 the US Supreme Court upheld the material support clause, citing Congress's declaration that "foreign organizations that engage in terrorist activity are so tainted by their criminal conduct that any contributions to such as organization facilitates that conduct." The decision goes on to state that "support frees up other resources within the organization that may be put to violent ends. It . . . helps lend legitimacy to foreign terrorist groups."[113] The implication of this decision is that such organizations are false humanitarians, using charity to recruit and retain followers. As such, Muslim organization are implicitly defined as different from non-Muslim, white American organizations, which are believed to be the true humanitarians and exceptional American subjects.[114]

In the wake of the Patriot Act, legal scholars and finance experts began to worry that donor-advised funds (DAFS), many of which had been created by finance corporations such as Fidelity and Vanguard, were being used to channel funds to terrorist organizations. One scholar suggested that "terror-free DAFS" be created to enable "open and legitimate charitable giving by well-intentioned Muslim-Americans [that] could send an unambiguous message that such people are not radical extremists, they neither espouse nor support terrorism, and they desire to contribute to U.S. national security."[115] Despite this intent, the very concept of a DAF that has to be scrutinized and made "terror-free" may end up replicating the same problems of antiterrorism legislation. That is, no matter how much organizations may try to avoid funding a terrorist organization, it is not clear on what grounds a group may become designated as a terrorist group. Organizations are continually added to or removed from the State Department lists of terror organizations so that there is no surety that once an organization is believed to be in the clear, it will remain so in the future.

Some of the accusations against Muslim organizations come from "experts" such as Matthew Levitt, a former State Department official who has stated that "terrorist groups systematically conceal their activities behind charitable, social and political fronts."[116] Jonathan Benthall, an anthropologist who has done extensive fieldwork with zakat organizations in the West Bank, has refuted Levitt's argument, finding no evidence of such subterfuge, even though Israeli state policies have pushed Palestinians to even more desperate living conditions that then compel them to rely on zakat support from around the region.[117] Other government "experts" argue that because money is fungible, financial assistance does not need to be directly linked to a "terrorist act" and that there is a "functional link between nonviolent programs and violent acts" allowing groups to recruit and retain membership.[118] The US Supreme Court has ruled that "providing material support to a foreign terrorist organization—even seemingly benign support—bolsters the terrorist activities of that organization."[119] The important assumption here is that non-Muslim (and often Christian), white, normatively "American" humanitarian organizations are not supporting violence, unlike Muslim organizations. As I showed earlier, the deceptive practices of evangelical Christians, who disguise missionary work as development or aid work, are examples of how humanitarianism can be used as a cover for proselytizing. But such missionaries also claim to undertake development projects in the process, revealing that such white Christian and non-Muslim humanitarian organizations provide welfare in some of the same ways as do the Muslim ones.

In an article titled "Charity Considered as a Terrorist Tool," legal scholar Norman Silber writes that "terrorists and their sympathizers may have been using one of America's greatest strengths—its tradition of philanthropy—to undermine national peace and security."[120] Silber claims that the Bush administration suspected "several Muslim groups operating in the United States" of "being fronts for terrorists committed to violent activities here and abroad."[121] He calls for new controls on chartering nonprofits and for donor-advised funds to better investigate the organizations receiving funding since the "vulnerability of donor-advised funds to potential abuse is significant."[122] He discloses that even though one organization, the Quranic Literacy Institute, had its assets frozen by the US government in 1998, two years later Fidelity, the US finance corporation, gave them funds. Although there is little evidence in Silber's article that any of these donor-advised funds were giving to groups that the US government managed to successfully charge as providing material support for terrorism, the generalized claim of possible terrorist infiltration informs the article as well as much of the other post-9/11 writing on donor-advised funds.

Becoming Humanitarians

Despite US government surveillance and criminalization of US Muslim organizations, many who work in these organizations see themselves as humanitarians working in humanitarian organizations. Some even reject the Muslim zakat framing of their work, instead claiming to be nonreligious humanitarians. Historian Sally Howell reveals that one organization, the Al-Mabarrat Charitable Organization, which was established in 2000 by Lebanese Americans to support orphanages in Lebanon not associated with Hezbollah, was raided by the FBI, which froze its assets and harassed its members. The organization leader rejected the claim that they were a religious organization. Rather, he said, "We are a humanitarian organization. We have no religious or political affiliation." This rejection of religious affiliation and affirmation of humanitarianism are repeated on Al-Mabarrat's website.[123] Perhaps organization leaders see humanitarianism as less suspect than religious charity, as the former term is supposedly more secular. Calling themselves humanitarians might also align organizers with normative US citizens, rather than with those constructed as outsiders or aliens,[124] though it is unclear whether such claims might work to prevent surveillance or even the "material support" charge.

The uncertainty and vagueness of the "material support" clause, along with regulations established by the International Emergency Economic Powers Act, have created a great deal of anxiety for many nonprofit organizations. Organizations providing consultation and support to nonprofits spent a great deal of time trying to make sure that their clients could steer clear of the clause's perils, since the government's terrorist watch list constantly changes. There have been attempts by humanitarian umbrella organizations, religious groups, and the government to create some means for Muslims to carry on with zakat duties, but these attempts reveal the extra burden carried by Muslim organizations. And in the end, there are no guarantees that organizations can escape surveillance or persecution. The *New York Times* reports that "Muslim groups struggled for years to persuade the Treasury Department to produce some kind of seal of approval for legitimate charities that adhered strictly to humanitarian work."[125] Erica James's research shows that groups in Michigan turned to "risk-based" philanthropy and charity in an attempt to work with "best practices" and avoid governmental harassment and scrutiny.[126] The American Charities for Palestine had to sign an agreement with USAID to make donations only to vetted educational and health organizations.[127] Muslim Advocates, a legal network based in San Francisco, teamed up with the Better Business Bureau to "improve the fiscal management and administration of American Muslim charitable organizations."[128] According to the Muslim Advocates staff attorney, they aimed to "restore donors' confidence in charitable organizations that support Muslim causes" by demonstrating that they meet "the highest standards of legal compliance, financial accountability, and good governance."[129]

In 2005, the Treasury Department issued a "best practices" report as "voluntary" guidelines for charitable organizations.[130] The report begins with the concern that humanitarian and charity organizations are vulnerable to becoming conduits for inadvertently enabling transfer of funding to terrorist groups. The report lists all the organizations on US, United Nations, and other countries' terrorist watch lists so that "terror financing" can be avoided. It warns that its guidelines are only suggestions and that each organization must exercise due diligence to avoid supporting terrorist groups. It insists that there is considerable risk that charitable organizations will support terrorism and provides, within a footnote, a list of publications and evidence for the statement.[131] This "voluntary" and "best practices" approach is directed toward all kinds of charities, not just Muslim ones.[132] In 2010, the Treasury Department amended some of the guidelines in response to some critiques, but they vigorously refuted two specific critiques: one, that the risk was overstated, and two, that the guidelines were burdensome.[133]

Techno-War and "Terror" Financing

Armand Mattelart argues that the war on terror was enabled by collaborations within "the entire information and technology complex."[134] Concepts such as "network-centric" warfare and cyberwar by shadowy government agencies and private corporations exist alongside nontechnological and much more "traditional" mechanisms such as federal antiterror laws that popularize surveillance and secrecy technologies. Racist and Orientalist ideologies combine in the twenty-first century with current technologies to create new entities to be surveilled and feared. The "terror network" concept so loved by security experts,[135] which has a vast political economy, has emerged with the help of media makers circulating criminality narratives through powerful organizations that provide credibility and content. The images of "terrorists" are made visible across media of various kinds, including digital databases, television news, crime shows, cinema, and even flash cards that are issued by government officials to identify "terrorists."

Internet and communication technologies have enabled global inequality at new scales and speeds, and new cyberwars are aimed at blocking the movement of information that enables transfers of people, goods, and weapons. David Murakami Wood and Stephen Graham argue that such technologies are "configured to add friction, barriers, or logistical costs to the mobility and everyday lives of those deemed by dominant states or service providers to be risky, unprofitable, or undeserving of mobility."[136] Organizations such as Kiva, which I described in chapter 2, may be able to move funds relatively quickly, depending on destination country, unlike those organizations suspected of terrorism. Kiva then comes to be an exceptional citizen, whose claims of transparency seem to function without government regulation of terror financing, and which can become an example of American humanitarian generosity. While Kiva's transfer of funds across national boundaries is assumed to be transparent and seamless, with donors believing that microlending organizations are more honest than more traditional NGOs, the movement of funds by organizations marked as Muslim are assumed to be suspect, and heavily scrutinized. In this war on terror framework, money transfers based on personal connections, such as hawala transfers, are the most suspect because unlike multinational bank transfers, they exist outside state regulation and surveillance and outside the financial cybernetworks of the global banking system. Because of suspicions of terrorism, even reputable nonprofits may come under surveillance by the US government, the UN, or other counties around the world if they are run by Muslims. No Kiva-like honesty or transparency is assumed for the funding flows of these organizations.

The US exceptionalized discourse of "foreign terror networks" is constructed around fears that informal personal mobility and networks may escape the scrutiny of authorities. For instance, one former Justice Department official writes, "even as sanctions, regimes, and blocking actions have been expanded internationally with increasing cooperation and technical savvy, they do not fully reach the most crucial regions . . . the current regulation of informal value transfer systems (IVTS, i.e., hawala transfers) and alternative funding models lack the sophistication necessary to penetrate these havens." He goes on to argue for more public and private aid to "render vulnerable populations more resilient to terror groups."[137]

Tracking the networks of so-called "terror" groups has included surveillance and mapping of the finance networks of many organizations around the world. Since 9/11, the US government has required banks to monitor, save, and report information on customers and transactions. Technology companies sell millions of dollars of software products to allow banks to comply with such regulations, even as there is debate as to whether such technology is required or effective. Companies such as World Check have databases, according to an article in the *Economist*, that offer "banks and governments profiles of more than 300,000 people who may present a 'heightened risk' to financial institutions."[138] Some security experts argue that terrorists do not need all this funding to operate, while others argue that these regulations have prevented terror attacks in the United States. The *Economist* also points out that few terrorists have been caught because of fund transfer surveillance, that money laundering and other fraud continues, and that most terrorist attacks required very little money to carry out.[139] The banking industry, however, did not escape charges of culpability, since they settled charges filed by the US government for helping transfer funds that were linked to Iran.[140] Arab Bank was also charged in a similar suit for aiding Hamas and lost, based partly on testimony by a witness who had headed the Israeli military's Palestinian affairs division, which given the long history of the conflict in Palestine, might have been driven by a political agenda. In addition, in 2014, the relatives of US military killed in the Iraq War filed a lawsuit against major European banks, charging that they had helped move funds between Iran and those attacking US military in Iraq.

Armand Mattelart suggests that further evidence of the collaboration between public and private entities is clear in the US Treasury Department monitoring of global funding flows.[141] The CIA's Terrorist Finance Tracking Program works with the collaboration of the Society for Worldwide Interbank Financial Telecommunication (SWIFT), a Belgium-based organization that enables the transnational functioning of banks.[142] National security agencies collaborate with technology organizations and corporations to track the movements of funding through transnational organizations such as SWIFT, whose acronym suggests that European finance organizations are conduits for speedy fund transfers. However, the organization also collaborates with governments in the search of "terror networks." Thus, the technology that allows financial mobility may, in collaboration with international and national policing agencies, become an obstacle, a checkpoint, or a policing mechanism for some organizations and some groups.

During the Barack Obama presidency, government-sponsored humanitarianism was further expanded, and the Bush FBO initiative was modified. Obama modified Bush's Office of Faith-Based Initiatives,[143] and he established the Faith-Based and Neighborhood Partnerships Office with the goals of reducing abortion, promoting better fathering, and increasing interfaith dialogue. The Serve America Act of 2009 expanded the number of AmeriCorps participants from 75,000 to 250,000. It included incentives for Senior Corps, as well as school-based funding for "service learning" (i.e., unpaid volunteer work by students). The White House Office of Social Entrepreneurship was created with $50 million dedicated to nonprofit growth and innovation. In his remarks at the twentieth anniversary of the Points of Light Institute in 2009, President Barack Obama sent a message about the importance of volunteer service: "In the end, service binds us to each other and to our community and to our country in a way that nothing else can."[144] President Obama, too, favors neoliberal notions of humanitarianism and volunteerism as he reveals through his view of "service." In his remarks at the twentieth anniversary of the Points of Light Institute held at Texas A&M University, Obama recognized the importance of the collaboration between former presidents Clinton and George H. W. Bush to raise money for Asian countries after the Indian Ocean tsunami and then after Hurricane Katrina in 2005. The combination of neoliberalism with nationalism and empire are visible in this collaboration between Democrats and Republicans. Here, we see the bipartisan use of the language of American exceptionalism as linked to humanitarianism, and indeed, as beyond politics.[145]

As he spoke to students at Texas A&M, Obama recognized that "service" is needed: "that service isn't separate from our national priorities, or secondary to our national priorities—it's integral to achieving our national priorities." He announced that because of the need for everyone to do such "service," he had signed the Edward M. Kennedy Serve America Act and expanded AmeriCorps and Senior Corps, which "gave people a change to give back" as well as created hundreds of partnerships with organizations, nonprofits, foundations, and corporations. Although Obama did mention that government is important, he asked people to do "service" rather than advocacy or fight for rights. This neoliberal politics is not surprising, nor is his continuation of some war on terror surveillance programs. Despite his repudiation of the term "war on terror," he did not stop its surveillance projects, including the surveillance of Muslim charities, persons, and organizations.

Ultimately, given that the United States is a majority Christian country, the Welfare Reform Act's Charitable Choice provision of 1996, which is still the law of the land, cannot but end up expanding and favoring the majority religion. Even President Obama's review board for these funds included a majority of people affiliated with Christian organizations, though it also had a smattering of Jewish organization–affiliated people, one South Asian organization–affiliated person, and one Muslim organization–affiliated person. Under the Obama administration, US government sponsorship of private religious humanitarianism may not have heavily favored Christian conservatives and evangelical groups as much as it did under the first George W. Bush administration, but it still seemed to favor Christian organizations as constituting exceptional citizens, those who are endowed with the sovereign right to give welfare to those they wish, to take on the task of saving the security state, and to support the soft power of the empire through their humanitarianism. Yet, simply being humanitarians is not enough to save the empire. Indeed, as I will show in later chapters, private exceptional individuals also share the tasks of surveillance and security.

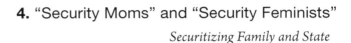

4. "Security Moms" and "Security Feminists"

Securitizing Family and State

As feminism has become disseminated across the global landscape through the twentieth century, it has become heterogeneous, diffuse, and diverse. Feminisms have become entangled with states, nations, transnationalisms, religion, class, race, caste, and sexuality, among numerous social movements. Feminisms have also emerged in conservative, liberal, and radical versions in the US context, producing social movements, identities, and subjects as well as many contestations over political affiliation and terminologies. What has been called "imperial feminism" has a long European history that has come to be shared in the United States through attachments to whiteness and empire.[1] Many feminists in the United States provided consent to a war based on the Orientalist idea of "saving" Muslim women, a project that came to include mostly white women and some others as well. Others saw themselves as allies of government and supported the war, demanding more security—for state and family—from the government. In the process, a particular American imperial feminism altered what it means to be an American woman or feminist: to claim equality, empowerment and alliance with a state and nation. This process was not, however, without contradictions over normative ideas of motherhood, femininity, and sexuality.

Within the United States and across the globe, feminisms are diverse, contested, and conflicted. The twenty-first-century global war on terror has highlighted this diversity. Some who call themselves feminists collaborate with constructions of the normative white citizen or the white, Christian, heterosexual mother—a struggle that I examine in this chapter. Meanwhile, others struggle against racial feminine and feminist norms: for instance, women of color, intersectional, antiracist, or anti-imperial feminists, and antiwar feminists, as well as many who do not want to call themselves feminists because of its association with whiteness, race, and empire. Some joined antiwar movements, distraught by the death of soldier sons and daughters,[2] while others joined the military, seeking jobs and wages. Yet others became patriotic after 9/11. Some feminists are concerned with empowering women or enabling their equality and parity with powerful males, while others focus on opposing racism and imperialism from within the United States. Despite these differences, all feminists and feminine subjects were affected by neoliberal policies and imperial wars, as all were recruited into the militarization and securitization of everyday life. For instance, the ubiquity of warnings posted in all public spaces in the United States that "if you see something, say something" enabled an extra vigilance on the part of everyone to be alert concerning the presence of nonwhite and "Muslim-looking" persons, and reporting these Others became a duty for some.[3]

This context of an ongoing and endless war on terror, as well as the impact of decades of neoliberal policies that have come to naturalize self-improving and self-protecting subjects working as individuals to save not just the nation but the security state, produced three subjects that I focus on in this chapter: the security feminist (a specifically feminist subject empowered by the state); the security mom (a female, not necessarily feminist, subject but with some aspects of US feminism); and the national security mom (mom and feminist), who combines the work of protecting the national security state and the American family while struggling for empowerment and against gendered discrimination in her workplace. These are different but linked figures of exceptional citizenship. They are different in the locations where they are found (the home and/or the workplace) and in their goals (keeping safe the American family or the American security state). Yet, they share similar investments in US empire; they are exceptional US citizens working to save and protect the American security state. They are also linked through a notion of female empowerment as an important state and imperial project, one justifying US military intervention.

The security feminist appears as a liberal, white, and patriotic feminist working for the state and military. The security mom appears as a conservative, white, and patriotic supporter of state security and the heterosexual, white family. They both build on a long history of US women's participation in imperial expansion, tying nationalist and military projects along with the state security, to women's advancement and security in the home and nation.[4] For instance, after 9/11, First Lady Laura Bush, along with many American women from both political parties as well as some feminist organizations, supported the bombing of Afghanistan as a way to save Afghan women and girls from the Taliban.[5] This was a project of "saving brown women from brown men," as Gayatri Spivak and others have made clear.[6] It tapped into long-standing European and US imperial projects and extended them into the twenty-first-century war on terror.[7] Participation in this project of rescue produces the female exceptional American citizen, securitizing feminism and saving the security state. Yet, even the sovereignty of this female figure is not secure given the context of the continued production of insecurity by the state, corporations, and neoliberal policies that reduce welfare and individualize adversity, as well as the gendered and raced inequalities embedded in US culture that privilege dominant white masculinity. The security state uses this feminism and feminized work while not according it the powerful sovereignty that it gives other exceptional subjects. Thus, the security mom and security feminist come to be insecure and often tragic figures.

The security feminist and the security mom are twinned figures in the twenty-first-century US neoliberal empire, offering both liberal and conservative, "hard power" and "soft power" ways that women can uphold, enable, and belong to the empire.[8] Yet, both figures also reveal how the security they seek for family and nation is increasingly impossible. Like US empire itself in this period, the security feminist and security mom become increasingly anxious and insecure. As a mode of power generated by the state and its political economy, insecurity creates subjects and institutions of racial empire, such as the feminist and the mother. Still, differently raced mothers and feminists come to have quite divergent sorts of insecurities, as some come to support the security state and some are targeted by it.[9] Insecurity is also a gendered project, as forms of sexual, economic, social, and psychological violence produce subjects who work unceasingly as exceptional citizens to protect themselves, their families, the state, and nation.[10] In this chapter, the figures I examine emerge through the intersectionalities and contradictions of twenty-first-century security and surveillance in two intertwined institutions: the American family and American counterterrorism. The security mom is a conservative female feminist and exceptional citizen who embraces whiteness and fears nonwhite and foreign Others as threats to the heterosexual family. The security feminist is a female counterinsurgency expert whose empowerment and claim to liberal equality are dependent upon her participation in the global war on terror and the security state. The figure of the security mom recuperates histories of racialized fears of brown and black males entering the white home and nation, and also recalls the presences of women in peace movements. Meanwhile, the security feminist builds on histories of militarized femininity and feminist struggles for equality and parity in the military. The long history of US surveillance of African Americans, as well as the history of women supporting the US empire and white nation,[11] ground the logic of security that asserts itself through these twinned figures.

After decades of neoliberal state retrenchment and economic policies benefiting the wealthy, security has come to have both affective and material consequences. The insecurity of jobs and livelihoods has increased alongside the security state's militarization and endless wars. In this milieu, security and fear are prevailing structures of feeling experienced differently depending on gender, race, religion, and class. Emergent moral panics, fears of terrorists, discourses of child predators, and concerns regarding sexual violence have accompanied a period of financial instability leading to the financial crash of 2008 and growing awareness of widening economic disparities.[12] Such fears produced a powerful conservative movement, while they also created struggles for equality and social justice. The National Security Administration's (NSA) continued surveillance of all people—not just Muslims or noncitizens—meant that fear of government, terrorists, immigrants, men of color, LGBT people, and many others became part of the fabric of everyday, ordinary life.[13]

The logic of vigilantism, enjoined by the ubiquity of the phrase "if you see something, say something" that governmentalized the war on terror, has securitized the domestic sphere of home and nation. Since the eighteenth century, the family has historically and affectively been considered a secure space in Western liberal thought, a "haven from a heartless world." Social contract theory suggested the separation of public and private realms, which gave the home its sacredness. However, as feminists have argued, this construction of home didn't protect women but rather protected the heterosexual family and white male privilege. As Carole Pateman and Charles Mills reveal, the social contract is a sexual-racial contract empowering white males to rule the private sphere and keep it sacred.[14] As these feminist critiques of home as the site of violence and power have shown, the idea of home is rife with contradictions including desires for protection, the violence of protection, a haven as well as imprisonment and enclosure, normative ideas of property, family, and citizenship as well as constraints on neoliberal ideas of human potential.[15]

Building on this complex history, the project of securitizing the home and the family in the twenty-first century harnesses powerful surveillance technologies and a particular version of female empowerment concerned with breaking the "glass ceiling" in order to save the security state. To be sure, security feminism is not the only social movement that has become militarized and securitized with the rise of the US security state, and women are not the only subjects incorporated into it. Immigrants, people of color, and LGBT people all have been hailed as participants through the projects of "diversifying" the military and government agencies. Yet these two female figures, the security mom and the security feminist, the one protecting the home and the other protecting the security state, are important in their attempts to maintain the division between public and private even while transgressing the boundaries of civilian and military, home and work, domestic and international. Their work in securitizing the security state makes them exceptional citizens, even as their sovereignty is more insecure than that of their male counterparts.

Motherhood, Neoliberalism, and the Security State

The combination of social, sexual, and economic insecurity emerges from decades of neoliberal policies that have now become naturalized, producing tensions and contradictions, as well as desires for a more militarized state. While this book focuses on the United States, neoliberal policies were implemented by leaders of the UK and the United States, Margaret Thatcher and Ronald Reagan, respectively, in both countries starting in the 1980s. These policies created new sorts of moral panics that deflected public attention from institutional changes that reduced public welfare and increased private corporate power. In an insightful essay concerning the moral panics regarding child predators and media representations of child sexual abuse that emerged in the UK in the 1990s after Prime Ministers Margaret Thatcher and Tony Blair had promoted neoliberalist domestic policies, Vicki Bell argues that representations of child abuse and sexual predators produced the mothers as vigilantes and abusers as monsters, but also challenged neoliberal policies. Such mediations, argues Bell, diverted attention away from ongoing concerns over government security and legitimation.[16] Mothers demanded the whereabouts of those accused of being pedophiles, and Bell argues that this challenged the political rationalities of neoliberal government: "Neoliberal government runs smoothly only if parents can trust that the state is indeed providing both a basic level of general security and trustworthy information by which to make their risk assessments."[17] She argues that because the state was unable to provide information that would enable mothers to "fulfill their roles as rational risk assessing parents," the media stepped in, reaffirming the state as rational and the mothers as emotional and nonrational.[18]

Bell's essay is useful for analyzing the limits and crisis of twenty-first-century neoliberal security.[19] There are links between what was happening in the United States and the UK, but also some divergences. Although Bell describes the UK, neoliberal policies of welfare retrenchment and the global war on terror in both countries led to an emergent network of state security and surveillance technologies stretching across state agencies, corporations, and powerful individuals. The UK had already been a heavily surveilled society, but new forms of surveillance against a different set of bodies emerged through moral panics in both places. In the United States, the American family was a key part of this project. The project of state security sutured parental concerns about family security to government concerns about state security, incorporating parents—and mothers in particular—into the security state. Securitizing motherhood in the form of the security mom naturalized state security as intrinsic to normative motherhood, rather than providing contradictions to the neoliberal or security apparatus.[20]

As this chapter will show, the US security state claims to secure the family by producing normative and exceptional citizens, but in the process it also produces precariousness and insecurity for most of its inhabitants. For the most part, such a protection project is used for the security of the heterosexual, middle-class family (normatively seen as white), though sometimes queerness is also scripted into these security concerns.[21] In the convergence of numerous fears created by social movements and the neoliberal security state—which are enhanced, commoditized, and circulated by multiple media—the security mom, in this first decade of the twenty-first century, became powerful by assuming the militancy of an anxious and fearful nation. Needing to secure the family from multiple social, economic, and political threats, such a mother became a product and a consumer of media security and surveillance projects. In the context of the war on terror, the security mom feared "terrorists" and "aliens" while she surveilled her nation and home. The security mom embodied both the assertion of authority and the anxieties of the end of the century and its new wars, and was a key vehicle and target of neoliberal power, becoming an exceptional citizen in the process. Similarly, the security feminist, increasingly either a single woman or a single mother, became visible as the counterinsurgency and counterterrorism expert. Her empowerment as a security expert and as a woman became conjoined. Working in government and military to carry out surveillance to save her state, she was also neoliberal in her belief in individual striving to succeed and to gain equality with her male counterparts. Yet such success, and its focus on the struggling individual, often produced the security feminist as a lonely and tragic figure. It was against this female figure that the masculinist state asserted its gendered power to suggest that such striving was necessary "soft power" but also unfeminine or queer.

The Rise of the Security Mom

Security moms, birthed from twenty-first-century wars and neoliberal economic reforms, emerged into public view during the US presidential election of 2004,[22] building on what was earlier called the "soccer mom," enabling women to self-identify as powerful, and politicized guardians of the (mostly, white and middle-class) home. The outpouring of concern for the American nation, support for wars, and victories for political candidates claiming to be strong on security made the security mom normative and part of the security economy thereby producing profits for private enterprises in militarization, policing, and incarceration industries.

In a *USA Today* article published on August 20, 2004, conservative columnist Michelle Malkin published a manifesto introducing the security mom to the nation.[23] In this manifesto, Malkin explains that she owns a gun, is a voter, is married to a fellow conservative, and has two children. Malkin's website explains that she is also Asian American, a Christian, and calls herself a Generation X'er,[24] suggesting that women of all races could become security moms. As she states: "Nothing matters to me right now than the safety of my home and the survival of my homeland. . . . I am a citizen of the United States, not the United Nations."[25] Since 9/11, she writes, she had begun to monitor everyone around her: "I have studied the faces on the FBI's most-wanted-terrorists list. When I ride the train, I watch for suspicious packages in empty seats. When I am on the highways, I pay attention to larger trucks and tankers. I make my husband take his cellphone with him everywhere. . . . We have educated our 4-year-old daughter about Osama bin Laden and Saddam Hussein. She knows there are bad men in the world trying to kill Americans everywhere. This isn't living in fear. This is living with reality. We drive defensively. Now, we must live defensively too."[26] Malkin quotes a conservative activist, Kay R. Daly, a security mom of two in Northern Virginia, who has said, "Hell hath no fury like a momma protecting her babies." The two figures that Malkin states she fears most are "Islamic terrorists" and "criminal illegal aliens"—both figures of nonwhite males infiltrating the American nation—though she mentions that she also keeps a watchful eye on truckers and her husband. Although clearly a Republican commentator in the media, she claims she would vote for whoever provides the most security: "Do they have what it takes to keep suicide bombers off our shores and out of our malls?"[27] Malkin ended her manifesto thusly: "To paraphrase the Iron Lady, Margaret Thatcher: Gentlemen: this is no time to go warm and fuzzy. Security moms will never forget that toddlers and schoolchildren were incinerated in the hijacked planes. . . . As they (the terrorists) plot our death and destruction, these enemies will not be won over by either hair sprayed liberalism or bleeding-heart conservatism."[28] There is much to take apart, here. At the very least, this article in a mainstream newspaper, *USA Today*, constructs American children as requiring a pedagogy of "terror."[29] It ventriloquizes Margaret Thatcher—one of the chief architects of neoliberalism—as having a strong security vision and articulates a version of US nationalism,[30] in which home is joined to homeland, and motherhood involves protecting the state and/as family. While such a discourse of home as homeland is often found in other periods and regions, the US context of the war on terror enabled this version of the mother for whom state, national, and family security were merged. The security mom figure is not just a mother who sacrifices her children to state security, nor is she a subject of the state by sole virtue of her reproductive labor. Rather, she sees the security of home, state, and nation as coconstitutive, requiring the actions and vigilance of private individuals who are members of the heteronormative, American family. Within the family, the mother is tasked with upholding this security project through violent surveillance and a pedagogy of the war on terror.

Malkin's conjoining of neoliberalism and security harnesses gendered essentialisms to resolve several contradictions in conservative, neoliberal ideologies. These contradictions are visible in her designation of liberals as "hair sprayed" and conservatives as "bleeding hearts," deliberately transposing political ideologies and perhaps ridiculing any remnants of George W.

Bush's "compassionate conservatism" (and displacing Margaret Thatcher's famous hair-sprayed style onto a liberal motherhood) for a 2004 election-year spin. Security is to trump all other considerations, even the concern for privacy and protection from the government that formed much libertarian and conservative thought. The economic rationales against government spending and deficit reduction, which are part of the rhetoric of conservatism, are to be left aside in claiming the necessity of a vast security apparatus. Malkin reprised a national motherhood, willing to send its young people to war—though determined to keep her own husband and children close to her and under her surveillance.

As of the writing of this book, more than a decade after this *USA Today* article, Malkin's security mom manifesto remains posted on her website. This website is active, celebrating mothers (for instance, one mother who lost her son in 9/11, and another who lost her son to drug war on the US-Mexican border).[31] The site continues the project of her manifesto of 2004, but with condemnation of the Obama administration for not providing security even though there have been few incidents of terrorism by any Islamic groups in the United States. On her website in 2016, Malkin says that there are many women like her who remain concerned with national security. These women have become "warbloggers," she says, with "intense passion and dispassionate analysis," and they have had to "take homeland defense in their own hands."[32] By championing these bloggers, Malkin implies that neither President Obama nor the US government can be trusted to provide security—despite the fact that over a trillion dollars have been spent on homeland security over the decade since 9/11.[33] While she claims security moms are concerned about the "war on terror," Malkin says they are also concerned about the threats caused by "illegal aliens," because the borders (by which she means the Mexican border, for the most part) have not been secured, allowing jobs to leave and "illegal aliens" to enter. She argues that even the "GOP elite gravely underestimate the wrath we security moms feel toward Washington's fatal addiction to 'cheap labor' and 'cheap votes' at the expense of secure borders."[34] Malkin sutures global and national economic precariousness through a populist and racialized anti-immigration and Islamophobic politics that casts immigrants as dangerous Others, disguising the predations of economic and political elites and solidifying white racial sovereignty. Malkin's politics and her website reveal her political shifts and continuities between the early 2000 and 2016, as the logic of the security state and of anti-immigrant racism comes into conflict with the global aspects of neoliberal capital, though not with the neoliberal project of welfare retrenchment nor the individualization of security.

In the period of Jim Crow, white women's safety was used to justify the lynching or imprisonment of black men.[35] In the twenty-first-century war on terror, middle-class women's safety is used to justify the detention of Muslim men, the widespread incarceration of people of color, and the surveillance of everyone.[36] New modes of online data gathering have led to "predictive analytics," which government agencies use to increase policing and surveillance, create "no-fly lists," ramp up detention, implement renditions, and deport migrants.[37] Malkin's discourse of proper motherhood, starting in 2004, attempts to erase racial difference through participation in surveillance. Thus, she states that she practices "surveillance" on her husband for his safety, never letting him leave without a phone. Her paranoia coincides with the widespread belief that all children now, especially teenagers, must have a phone so that they can be reached at every moment to make sure that they are safe, a project whose racialized dimensions I explore in chapter 5. The injunctions posted all over public spaces in most cities and towns, asking people to "say something if you see something," has governmentalized security as a task for all citizens who can become exceptional by protecting the security state. It is not just public space that must be surveilled but also the domestic. According to this security framework, even the heterosexual family must be under surveillance since in Malkin's imaginary, it is under attack from gays, lesbians, feminists, immigrants, black men, and Muslims. Malkin continues to use safety and security discourse to justify surveillance, constructing the family as threatened and surveillance technologies as tools for the empowerment of the mother.

Malkin was a frequent commentator on Fox News for some time, and published opinion columns in several newspapers.[38] A Filipino American, she started her conservative career opposing affirmative action policies while a student at Oberlin College, and later married a fellow student, who is a white man and a conservative. She was, and continues to be, particularly useful to the Republican Party as an Asian American woman who espouses an anti-immigration, prowar, and antigovernment ideology, and can be used to show that right-wing conservatism has nonwhite members too. Malkin inhabits the position of the token nonwhite, who can rise within the political media since there aren't that many Asian Americans who would profess such allegiance to anti-immigration politics. The Republican Party uses her as an alibi to deflect critiques of their racism, while prominence given to her by

Fox News and Republicans gives her a platform. Her books, published by a conservative press, establish her credentials as a conservative advocate for a strong military, hard power, surveillance, and anti-immigration policies. She has, for instance, argued (against all evidence to the contrary) that the internment of Japanese Americans was appropriate because of their supposed loyalty to the Japanese emperor, and that the racial profiling of Arab Americans is justified.[39] She is also evidence of the minority of Asian American immigrants who are socially conservative and who understand themselves as model Americans who need to protect America against newer immigrants.[40] There are Asian Americans who profess strong conservatism, based on a variety of reasons, both political, religious, and historical. Some arrive in the United States with upper-class and conservative beliefs, and comprise transnational elites who have incorporated neoliberal ideals against welfare and a desire to participate in American capitalism. Others come with military backgrounds and histories in their countries of departure that push them toward strong support for the security state, though some of these groups might oppose anti-immigration and racist politics. Yet, others profess patriotism in face of the "forever foreign" status given to Asian Americans over their two-century presence in the United States. There is also racism against African Americans and Islamophobia among Asians and Asian Americans in both the Asian continent and in the United States, as well as a strong support for a security state. Such a complex politics among Asian Americans—emerging from diverse histories, ethnicities, and transnational allegiances—suggest that Malkin's racial identity and political beliefs are not remarkable, and enable her to become valuable as a media figure, adding an image of "diversity" to the Republican Party. She becomes useful for disavowing the whiteness of American racial sovereignty and for consolidating the project of racialized violence, even as she gains prominence among conservatives in the process, and shares the power and privilege of association with whiteness.

In response to Malkin's security mom manifesto of 2004, many liberal commentators asked whether the security mom was in fact "real." For instance, columnist Ellen Goodman responded to Malkin by claiming that the security mom was an urban legend rather than a new demographic (though Goodman also stated that women are inherently concerned about security),[41] perhaps missing the point that Malkin was constructing an identity that would hail many women. In her article "The Myth of 'Security Moms,'" Goodman writes: "I'm not denying women's concerns about security. Whether it's domestic violence or crime in the streets or terrorism after 9/11, women are more likely to worry that they or theirs are vulnerable." Goodman protests

Malkin's conservatism and militarism, though she too comes to see protection and security as central to motherhood. For Goodman, too, women have an intrinsic desire for security. In her account, all women need protection from "terrorism" and "violent crime," but she also includes "healthcare security, retirement security, and economic security" as women's needs. Like Malkin, Goodman (who identifies as a liberal) connects the term "security" to a naturalized and essentialized definition of women. While Malkin uses the term "security mom" to designate women as mothers seeking to protect their innocent children, Goodman allies herself with the 1990s UN internationalist human security paradigm that recuperated the term "security" to change its focus on particular nationalisms and states.[42] This "human security" paradigm was used to move away from state security as the project for American women, suggesting that a less warlike project would be liberal protection of all persons. Although Malkin and Goodman seem to be politically at odds, they both understand women to have an essential relation to security as protection. Although Malkin's nationalism and Goodman's internationalism set them apart and Malkin's security mom relies on nationalist feminist discourses as its condition of possibility, both assume a feminist project that essentializes gender, suggesting a woman's natural role is as a mother who protects her children.

The security mom is both a political and media demographic who emerged in the early 2000s, but she is also a subject of the security state who embodies the insecurity produced by the neoliberal securitization of everyday life. In 2003, Karen Tumulty and Viveca Novak wrote in a *Time* magazine article that the security mom was created out of anxiety following 9/11, because women felt more vulnerable and became more protective of their families, wanting more defense spending and state security. Tumulty and Novak attributed these anxieties solely to 9/11, rather than to decades-long decline in the economic health of working- and middle-class families, to black concerns about police and state violence, and the emerging notion of new threats for post–Cold War militarism, as well as the many racial projects that reduced welfare benefits for nonelite and nonwhite populations.[43] Given this framing, it is not surprising that security moms appeared again in the US presidential election of 2012, when right-wing groups struggling for electoral gains against the Democrats and Barack Obama's candidacy asserted a white racial sovereignty based on anti-immigration views, social conservatism, oligarchic masculine power, and corporate hegemony. News media stated that the security mom was back and visible through polling in states such as Florida and Ohio.[44]

Perhaps it can be said that the security mom never went away, because conservative politics relied on proliferating threats to the American family from LGBT politics, feminists, immigrants, Muslims, black groups, as well as terrorists. The protection of this family is not a new phenomenon, though, within the modern state, the family has long been a site of struggle for individuals, the nation, the state, bureaucracies,[45] and, more recently, a variety of private entities including corporations and NGOs. In the US neoliberal context—in which social conservatism, white racial sovereignty, and imperial projects are intertwined—these diverse entities have stakes in defining the normative family. Conservatives mobilize citizenship and consumption through racialized and heteronormative discourses about the "traditional" family needing special protection. At the same time, neoliberal elites use the term "class war" to deflect critiques of economic inequality and the massive concentration of wealth within a tiny group of people and corporations.[46] Both state and federal governments rely on corporations for surveillance, adding to insecurities emerging from changing ideas of privacy, fuzzy public/private divides, and new collaborations between states and private transnational capital. Combined with new media technologies, the project of surveillance encompasses all kinds of social relations, including the family. In this context, US motherhood is constructed through media and its technologies in ways that link it to security and surveillance. Cindi Katz suggests that in the privatized state, such as the twenty-first-century neoliberal security state, parents become spies, doing the work of the shrunken neoliberal state that cannot provide a social wage. Instead, she reveals, "All the state does is monitor."[47] Katz describes how within the context of twenty-first-century war, the US government relies on individuals and groups to participate in surveillance and how parenting turns into surveillance. Yet the state is not as enervated as she suggests, because it actively enables such surveillance, even by devolving sovereignty to and collaborating with particular individuals and corporations. Although the US state has lost its ability (and willingness) to embody power in the form of providing welfare, it seeks to be powerful through collaboration with private entities—not only with the family but also transnational corporations and with security moms and security feminists who then become exceptional citizens.

In this context, the security mom's genealogies include white racial libertarianism, American antigovernment and hyperindividual beliefs, and a long history of anticommunism and social conservatism.[48] Yet she has some aspects of the liberal humanitarianism that I discussed in chapter 2: liberals who believe that private individuals and nonprofit organizations can better provide social welfare because the state is inefficient and ineffective and that Americans are exceptional citizens who are able to save the nation, the state, and the world. While not all humanitarians share the virulent antigovernmentalism of the conservative security mom, many have come to see neoliberalism as the new normal while they decry the corruption and power of elites. Both humanitarians and social conservatives support private welfare, sharing some opposition to government surveillance (depending on who is being surveilled), and they both believe in American exceptionalism and empire. Many across political divides now consider surveillance necessary to both the state and the family, which, as I argue in the following chapter, unites public and private domains in new ways. The neoliberal security state provides opportunities for collaboration across political differences through the securitization and militarization of motherhood in the form of the security mom. It also provides such opportunities through the securitization and militarization of feminism in the figure of the security feminist.

The Rise of the Security Feminist

Although there has been important work on the relation between empire, women, and domesticity, the emergence of security feminism comes in the aftermath of long struggles for equality and parity in many institutions in the United States, including the military, corporations, and education. Security feminism reveals this struggle as well as a devotion to the security state, and it is the security feminist's loyalty to the latter and desire to work for it that brings up contradictions and marks the complexities of those who inhabit such a feminism. Such a feminism's contradictions have been difficult to resolve, as I will show in the rest of this chapter.

The relationship between empire and domestic ideologies has a long history in the United States,[49] showing indeed that domesticity and imperialism have always been interconnected. As I've demonstrated, neoliberalism produces the security mom as one kind of exceptional citizen. Another exceptional citizen produced in this context is the security feminist, who has ties to the US military and counterterrorism agencies. The US military utilizes women and mothers as officers, soldiers, and contractors, producing both the subjects and agents of militarized security through their participation in combat as well as their support for military power.[50] Similarly, US government agencies utilize women and mothers as spies and counterterrorism experts, many of whom move over into these civilian jobs after their military careers. The generalized anxiety caused by the war on terror's public and private security enterprise, as well as widespread economic insecurity, leads many women to seek jobs in the military and intelligence agencies that can offer some stability. Occupying these positions, along with the military's need for diversity and patriotic subjects, produces emergent security feminisms.

Security feminists have become increasingly visible in popular media especially in the aftermath of 9/11, as figures both heroic and tragic. Valerie Plame, for instance, became famous as a Central Intelligence Agency (CIA) operative whose name was disclosed by a member of the Bush administration in retaliation for her husband's opposition to the Iraq War, so that she could no longer continue in her position. In popular culture, such figures have become more and more common, as women are often now represented as heroic soldiers of the nation, even as gendered inequality and insecurities suffuse those representations. The series *Covert Affairs* ran from 2010 to 2015 on the USA Network, with the main character, Annie Walker, as a CIA agent. In contrast to the centrality of motherhood in representations of the security mom, security feminist characters such as Annie Walker (played by Piper Perabo), Carrie Mathison (played by Claire Danes) of the Showtime award-winning series *Homeland* (2011–present), and Maya (played by Jessica Chastain) of the Oscar-winning film *Zero Dark Thirty* (2012) are most often single women, obsessed and haunted by their responsibility to secure the nation. Carrie Mathison is a character with bipolar disorder and though suffering emotional difficulty and breakdowns, she is able to obsessively focus on deflecting terror attacks, ordering drone bombings and sleeping with the enemy, while being critical of the CIA bureaucracy. Along with the focus on this character's mental illness, the series also suggests the power of a female character able to break with the institution she works with and follow her own obsession with counterinsurgency work. As James Castonguay has argued, the series may be critical of the effects of the war on terror, but it upholds the power of what he calls "the democratic security state" to carry out surveillance and counterinsurgency. Castonguay argues that the series is invested in creating an insecure empire that ends up copying its enemy, in the style of Cold War cinema's "paranoid style."[51] Advertisements for this series use Orientalist representations to contrast Carrie's whiteness and visibility against veiled nonwhite women, suggesting a long European colonial narrative of the whiteness of the powerful Western woman contrasted with her hidden, mysterious, and threatening Other.

Zero Dark Thirty's Maya brought attention to the role of women in the CIA, largely because of the film's notoriety and its depiction of the effectiveness of torture; this question of effectiveness became a matter of debate and disclosure by the government.[52] Numerous journalists covered these concerns in the wake of the film's release and attempted to describe the "real" women in the CIA who had inspired the film. In the process, these intelligence analysts and agents came to be celebrated as strong women and as feminists who were able to break the glass ceiling in the security and military industries—though such praise was not unalloyed with gendered assumptions about women's essential nature and proper behavior. Women did work in US and UK security forces and intelligence services during the Second World War.[53] However, this recent war on terror harnesses contemporary feminist politics to show these women as heroic subjects *and* as victims of neglect, discrimination, or inequality,[54] as well as deviant gendered subjects. Their exceptional feminism is depicted as securing the state, even as there is disapproval of the women's behavior and media commentary about such deviance and misogyny resulting in pain and anxiety. Their reconciliation with motherhood and the heteronormative American family is itself insecure.

Many women in the counterterrorism services and industry have come to deplore these popular culture representations. Some of these women have turned to writing their own books to claim that such contradictions are simply fictional. Reporters have also taken up their cause. In a *New York Times* article from 2015 titled "Good Riddance, Carrie Mathison," columnist Maureen Dowd writes that Mathison's "real-life counterparts" in the CIA "can't wait for her to clean out her desk."[55] According to Dowd, the "C.I.A. sisterhood is fed up with the flock of fictional C.I.A. women in movies and TV who guzzle alcohol as they bed hop and drone drop, acting crazed and emotional, sleeping with terrorists and seducing assets." She quotes one such "real-life" agent, Gina Bennett, describing her as "a slender, thoughtful mother of five who has been an analyst in the Counterterrorism Center for 25 years" and who "first began sounding the alarm about Osama bin Laden back in 1993." Dowd goes on to report that another agent, Sandra Grimes, "a perky 69-year-old blonde who helped unmask her C.I.A. colleague Aldrich Ames," dislikes the TV and film characters who look like models wearing clothes their real-life counterparts could not afford. Dowd reveals that Bennett and her cohorts claim that they are better agents than their male colleagues and not as dysfunctional as their fictional counterparts. According to Dowd, the women say that they have much to offer because women are good "puzzle-solvers" and are more rational because they trust their "gut less." Dowd quotes Kali Caldwell, an African American woman, who tells Dowd that senior military officials are surprised at her presence in the CIA, not only because of her gender but also because of her race. Having established the diversity of this group of real-life counterterrorism security feminists, Dowd argues that they have made gains for diversity at the CIA. There is a daycare center at Langley, the CIA offers flex time, and the agency even went to recruit at an LGBT conference in Miami.

Notwithstanding these strides, Dowd also includes comments from her interviewees about the difficulties of combining the work of being wife, mother, and counterterrorism expert. Bennett tells Dowd that family and security are difficult to reconcile, and she had to create a "wall" between her family and the horrors she saw at work where she was faced with "people who are trying to kill lots of people in horrendous, painful ways." Although her marriage broke down, she calls herself "Elastigirl," both mom and superhero. She tells Dowd, women like her are at the "top of their game." Dowd reports Bennett saying, "I'm right up there with the big dogs. Girls, c'mon. Leave the saving the world to men? I don't think so."

Despite her key role in security industries, the security feminist herself feels insecure and reveals an insecure form of feminism. This feminism combines arguments for gender equity and the language of empowerment with stress produced by the proximity to foreign threats and counterterrorism work. The security feminist's career leads her to attempt to wall off work from home, even though it seems to have interrupted her marriage and infiltrated the home. Security feminism, consequently, seems rife with difficulties, as Dowd's article reveals. Dowd and her interviewees demonstrate and disavow the violence of war, conjugate "bed hop" with "drone drop," and offer the animated character of Elastigirl (white girl power) as real inspiration. Family, job insecurity, multiculturalism, inclusion, and violence are comingled in this articulation of popular feminism and empire. Security feminism's version of motherhood suggests that while there is need for a "wall" between the foreign and the domestic, between the horrors outside and the children within, there cannot be such a wall. Counterterrorism requires the belief that foreign agents will enter the domestic space, as much as terrorism work cannot but enter and affect their own homes and families. The horrors of the war on terror that infiltrate the home become productive, however, since they empower women to be effective counterterror agents and security feminists.

Dowd's column, which purports to show the power of the "real" women in counterterrorism, inadvertently reveals the anxieties of security feminism. The division between public and private—the wall that Bennett describes—becomes a futile attempt to separate imperial war from the family, the domestic from the foreign, and heterosexual marriage from the insecurities of neoliberal gendered inequalities. Walls, as Wendy Brown argues, are being created all over the world by twenty-first-century security states, indexing popular desires to keep the unmanageable results of neoliberal globalization at bay.[56] Yet these do not prevent the traffic between public and private; the walls simply spectacularize the desire for an impossible sovereignty. The walls stand for a desire for sovereignty based on territoriality, but also reveal a white feminism hoping to claim sovereignty by aligning with state security (as are other neoliberal security subjects I have been examining thus far in this book). Yet in Dowd's column, for these security feminists, the failed desire for the wall subtends the American family, as it does this version of female empowerment and equity feminism. The search for security, consequently, is aporetic and vexed. Security feminism is empowered but fractured, powerful but traumatized, as it cannot secure the heteronormative, white, American family.

As with Dowd's media coverage of real-life counterterrorism experts, popular media similarly produces an empowered and anxious feminist who fails to resolve the contradictions of security feminism. In director Kathryn Bigelow's film *Zero Dark Thirty* (2012), the main character Maya is a strong woman, conventionally attractive because she is white and thin, but also obsessive, nervous, and unhappy. Her devotion to counterterrorism is made visible when Maya is able to observe brutal interrogations and remain focused on the hunt for Osama bin Laden. She is represented as an Ayn Rand–like feminized version of the American hero figure found in numerous Hollywood films, whose masculinity is exceptional and autonomous, and who flouts his superiors, his organization, and its rules in order to achieve his goals; bureaucracy and the state are impediments to his progress and achievements. Maya is the normatively white, blonde American female version of this type, showing the triumph of the individual and his or her work to secure the state,[57] despite the obstacles of a bureaucracy determined to thwart her quest. The film's dark colors and the lighting used to depict the South Asian setting accentuate her whiteness,[58] even as her friendship with another woman, Jessica, at the military base, suggests queer possibilities that come to have no future. Timothy Melley has argued that the film denies the asymmetries of American power by depicting it as a quest of one individual, Maya. At the same time as it gestures toward the violence of the security state in torture scenes,[59] it resolves any potential threat by focusing on the heroine's struggle for recognition within the CIA. Maya embodies the exceptional neoliberal citizen—the security feminist—who will save the state and American power, because the state is characterized as nurturing an inept bureaucracy.

Maya is able to participate as an equally competent American operative in the male-dominated world of the CIA, and this equality requires her to use violence, torture, and single-minded devotion to her goal. Her whiteness and Americanness stand out among the many burqa-clad women (and men hiding as women) in the film. The Pakistani women are stereotypically represented as dark, veiled, unfree figures who serve to highlight Maya's white, American empowerment. Her friendship with Jessica also gestures to a homonationalism that is to be contrasted with South Asian culture.

Despite her success, however, Maya does not have the male American hero's triumphant power, since the film depicts the personal cost of her devotion to state security. Her only affection and joy seem to come from her connection with another woman, Jessica, who, in a conventional turn within Hollywood's depiction of lesbian tragedy, seems to be more interested in the men she meets, and whose death Maya is unable to prevent. Although Maya-as-security-feminist shares much with the security mom, including her support of violence and her concern for state security, she diverges from the security mom through her renunciation of family, sex, and all relationships with men. She sees other men as obstacles to her path, or as instruments of violence who are to be used to take out enemies. In addition, her friendship and desire for Jessica also have no future. In dislodging a purely heteronormative narrative by combining security feminist and female friendship stories that cannot acknowledge desire or sexuality, Bigelow depicts Maya's only friendship as being with another woman, though this female bond becomes a source of sorrow: Jessica is killed, recalling a long history of the tragic lesbian in Hollywood cinema.[60]

In *Zero Dark Thirty*, both femininity and feminism emerge as central to the protection of the security state through the killing of bin Laden, but it is a feminism based on binary gender and which struggles to remain exceptional and white. As a female counterterrorism expert, Maya leaves the task of killing to the men, telling the all-male US Navy SEAL team tasked with killing bin Laden, "Kill him for me." The film distinguishes Maya from these men by contrasting their camaraderie and masculinity with Maya's loneliness and femininity. The value of maternal and familial ties is made evident by their very absence; once the mission is accomplished, Maya cries as she leaves for home, bereft by her lost relationships, the death of Jessica, and the sacrifices she has made for state security. Femininity is also at the center of the film's most important traumatic scene, when Jessica—who is depicted as Maya's opposite in being feminine, social, and, thus, vulnerable—is killed by a suicide bomber.[61] White femininity is a source of power and pain, of success in counterterrorism but also leading to tragedy, insecurity, and unfulfilled desires. As film commentator Larry Gross puts it, "Maya is quite simply one of the loneliest, most solitary characters ever to serve as the protagonist of an American studio film."[62] Gross ignores the long history of similar masculine characters in numerous Hollywood productions. For Gross, male protagonists are allowed to be lonely, while female protagonists, especially those not heteronormative, are damaged by such loneliness.

Several scholars have asked whether Maya is an example of feminism or of a postfeminism that considers feminism as either redundant or passé in the United States and within the new century. Some commentators have seen Maya as a feminist.[63] Others consider her a product of an antifeminist or postfeminist culture.[64] Some argue she is postfeminist because despite her portrayal as the equal of men, the film does "little to aid the cause of feminism."[65] For one scholar, Maya's neoliberal postfeminism resonates with audiences of many political stripes because "it tethers together several taken-for-granted clusters of appealing nationalistic tropes—the notion of fighting just wars, the neoliberal notion of benefiting from hard individual labor, the profit that comes from unswerving dedication to country," and a celebration of American exceptionalism.[66] Although these commentaries are insightful examinations of the film's contradictions, they homogenize feminism as a singular project of white women and American power.

In contrast to those claiming Maya as an antifeminist or postfeminist, other commentators described her as explicitly feminist. One popular commentator claiming Maya's feminist credentials is Peter Bergen, CNN's national security analyst and author of the book *Manhunt: The Ten-Year Search for bin Laden*.[67] Bergen was an advisor on the film, and explains in his article from 2012 "A Feminist Film Epic and the Real Women of the CIA" that *Zero Dark Thirty*'s Maya could be based on a woman at the CIA who was also single-mindedly focused on finding bin Laden.[68] Bergen argues that this woman embodied the CIA's progress toward gender equality. Bergen quotes a retired CIA operative, who says that when he started in the agency "there were to my knowledge four senior operation officers who were females, and they had to be the toughest SOBs in the universe to survive. And the rest of the women were treated as sexual toys."[69] Over time, Bergen reports, the CIA appointed many more women, some of whom did counterterrorism work, especially in the unit focusing on bin Laden. One woman, according to Bergen, was Jennifer Matthews, a CIA officer who worked on the Pakistan-Afghanistan border. According to Bergen, Matthews "provides something of a model" for the character of Jessica in the film. Matthews graduated from a small Christian college in Ohio and started to follow bin Laden's activities in the mid-1990s, but, unlike Maya, she married and had three children. Bergen states that she "knew Islamic history cold, and how al Qaeda believed it fit into that history, which made her a formidable interrogator of al Qaeda detainees, some of whom found the fact that she was a well-informed female particularly disconcerting."[70] Matthews died in Afghanistan after an Al Qaeda operative, whom the CIA was trying to attract, detonated a bomb killing Matthews and several other CIA officers.

In a *Washington Post* article from 2012, Greg Miller explains that the woman on whom Maya is based was seen as "prickly" by the CIA, was not promoted for her work in the search for bin Laden, and hence felt slighted by the agency.[71] At the time of the film's release, many news reports questioned why women in the CIA were not promoted and suggested that gender discrimination was an ongoing problem at the agency. Former CIA agent Valerie Plame suggested that women were particularly suited to the CIA because they are more attentive to facts, are "more attuned," and can "read body language better"—adding that "sometimes the subtleties are more important."[72] In a PBS television interview with Charlie Rose, director Kathryn Bigelow, one of the few powerful and Oscar-winning female directors in Hollywood, similarly commented on women's special qualifications for intelligence services.[73] Such commentaries argued powerfully for the feminist inclinations of the filmmaker, and the film as a feminist project representing some of the problems and progress faced by women in the intelligence services and, importantly, by security feminists hoping to be exceptional citizens saving the security state.

The disclosure in 2014 of CIA torture reports by the US Senate Intelligence Committee, led by another powerful woman, Senator Dianne Feinstein, later revealed that another counterterrorism CIA agent, Alfreda Frances Bikowsky, might also have been an inspiration for Maya.[74] Bikowsky has now become associated with CIA torture. Many have vilified her participation in torture as violation of the Geneva Conventions and also as unproductive because it could not even be justified on the grounds of producing intelligence.[75] In examining how torture came to be normalized as standard procedure during the Iraq invasion, some journalists were indignant about the torture, while others sensationalized the fact that a woman, implicitly against her essential nature, could authorize torture. Bikowsky has also been discredited as being incompetent at her job because she failed in warning about 9/11 even though she had been on the Al Qaeda investigation since 2000. In her book from 2008, *The Dark Side: The Inside Story of How The War on Terror Turned into a War on American Ideals, New Yorker* staff writer Jane Mayer described Bikowsky as "hard-driving" and "overzealous,"[76] and especially excited to be present at Khalid Sheikh Mohammed's interrogation. Mayer reports one CIA colleague saying that Bikowsky "thought it was cool to be in the room" when Sheikh Mohammed was being water-boarded, and she was reprimanded and reminded that the torture "was not supposed to be entertainment."[77] Mayer describes Bikowsky as the "hard-driving, redheaded former Soviet analyst who had been in the Bin Laden Unit . . . who was reviled by some male colleagues for what they regarded as her aggression."[78] As these descriptions show, the CIA's aggressive war-corporate network included both essentialized notions of gender and nods to diversity, in the process of vilifying the security feminist. Mayer's book suggests that Bikowsky was both promoted and disliked and that her pursuit of bin Laden and willingness to watch torture were seen as aberrant both to her gender and to the CIA. It is surprising that Mayer pays little attention to the gendered dimension of scapegoating Bikowsky for what seems a widespread practice of torture by the CIA, one that reportedly was condoned by the highest powers in the Bush White House. Mayer's book reveals also the CIA's essentialized notions of gender and of Muslim cultures that were used in the torture of detainees. For instance, she reports that Mohammed was "questioned by an unusual number of female handlers, perhaps as an additional humiliation," and another prisoner was subjected to the sounds of "hysterical screams that he was told was his wife being tortured."[79] Security feminism is thus useful to save the security state, asserting sovereignty and exceptionalism in claiming American empire and its power over life, death, and the suspension of international laws. Yet security feminism across media platforms is both celebrated and reviled.

National Security Mom: Bringing Together Security Feminist and Security Mom

In his news article from 2012 about the Bigelow film, Peter Bergen mentions another woman in the CIA, Gina Bennett, who might also have been a model for the movie's feminist figures. While Maureen Dowd presents Bennett in her article from 2012 as primarily a counterterrorism expert, Bennett was also a writer at the time of Dowd's interview, having published in 2008 a book titled *National Security Mom: Why Going "Soft" Will Make America Strong.* Bennett is not a security mom in the vein of the politically and socially conservative Michelle Malkin, or the aggressive security feminists of film and print media. Instead, she sees herself as an advocate of what she calls "soft power"; in contrast to military invasion, she claims a different version of counterterrorism that she has learned from being both a mom and a security expert. In *National Security Mom*, she presents herself as reconciling national and family security in ways that differentiate her from security moms such as Michelle Malkin or the Maya-like heroic security feminists in film and television.[80] If Malkin and Maya are belligerent and rely on violence and militarism to achieve their goals, their exceptionalism lies in their being able to accept violence and war and thus take on the task of the state. Bennett, however, seeks a soft power maternalism for protecting the security state, arguing that hard power may not be the best road to defeating terrorism. *National Security Mom* combines normative notions of motherhood (the security mom) and the superachieving counterterrorism woman (the security feminist) to domesticate the CIA. Through analogizing the work of the CIA and the work of parenting, Bennett securitizes motherhood and the family, depicting the mother/spy as exceptional citizen working to secure the nation through her maternal power and prowess.

Bennett's authority and expertise come from having worked in the US State Department's Bureau of Intelligence and Research. On her cover, Bennett alleges her book is based on twenty years of experience working for the CIA. Bennett's expertise is stated in the claim that she was the main author of the now-declassified *Trends in Global Terrorism: Implications for the US* report from 2006, which warned that decentralized and diffuse groups of Muslim jihadists continued to be a threat to the United States and Europe even after many years of counterterrorist war.[81] Her book is presented as sharing much of what she has learned about counterterrorism, which she suggests are lessons learned also from her experiences in parenting. The book's website states that it offers "the basics of current terrorism trends and national security policymaking from a parent's perspective."[82] In the book, Bennett eschews the kind of security feminist approach represented by Maya in *Zero Dark Thirty*, criticizing women who "try to out-tough-talk men to avoid being considered soft."[83] She insists that "understanding the suffering of people is not being 'soft' on terrorism" but is instead "a critical step towards figuring out how to diminish the influence of terrorists."[84] Bennett appeared on *The Oprah Winfrey Show* during a segment devoted to "superwomen," and the CIA mentioned this media appearance on its website.[85]

Like Malkin's security mom, Bennett's national security mom analogizes family and nation-state, claiming that governing a family is similar to governing a nation-state. In doing so, she places the heterosexual, middle-class, white family at the center of the US state and identifies its members as normative citizens. Yet, it is clear that her normative claims are difficult to sustain, as Bennett's later divorce—mentioned in the interview of 2012 with Maureen Dowd—makes visible. Even as Bennett's belief that the world can be understood through good parenting could, on the one hand, be seen as more positive than the usual demonization of the Other, it infantilizes the world and its myriad peoples. Her comment to Maureen Dowd in 2012 that women make better counterterrorism experts because they can outthink their male colleagues is tempered by a claim in her book from 2008 that being a good mother and wife make her a good agent. Her family analogy flattens the pluralism and heterogeneity of the nation-state, and indeed, of the world, portraying multiple forms of difference as phases of growth to be outgrown in the making of a country or nation.

Bennett's folksy tone in *National Security Mom* is meant to resonate with a maternal audience interested in national security; counterinsurgency becomes akin to mothering in this bizarre juxtaposition. Chapters in the book include "Redefining National Security: A Parent's Perspective," "Scrapbooking is a Requirement," "What We Teach our Kids Is Good Advice for America," "If You Make the Mess, Clean it Up," "The Strength of a Nation Derives from the Integrity of the Home," and "The Hand that Rocks the Cradle is the Hand that Rules the World." Using homespun sayings to provide parenting and counterterrorism advice, Bennett suggests it is not military power but "values" taught at home that make "America strong and secure."[86] She believes there are similarities between parenting and counterterrorism. For instance, she argues, if intruders destroy a house, they cannot destroy a family because its values and relationship hold it together.[87] Cleaning a house becomes similar to cleaning up the mess in Iraq, and in both cases, the result may not be perfect. Although children may use different ways to clean up their rooms, working according to their personalities and inclinations, such a cleanup will not be perfect or long lasting.

The more serious message of the book is the rationale for endless war. Like parenting, the struggle for security must always continue. Bennett avers that it is not possible for counterterrorism work to remove all terrorist threats, and she advocates a maternal approach to global problems. She argues that the main question is what is tolerable and acceptable, rather than what can be completely cleaned up. Similarly, she cautions that terrorism cannot be eradicated and that there will always be terrorists, thus justifying a war without end. Because of this, she warns, it is better to learn how to live with some risk and threat, much as good parents teach their children to survive dangers. Knowing about threats is helpful, and understanding motivations, underlying reasons, and the role of political actors can help, but complete security is not possible. Parenting and national security are aligned. The values of democracy, Bennett believes, will secure the United States. Like the struggle to maintain the American family, the struggle to maintain the security state as exceptional continues.[88] Bennett's security mom thus expresses the devotion to security visible in Malkin's conservative politics, but it is tempered by her experience as a counterterrorist security feminist.

After its release in 2008, the CIA reported that Bennett's book had been featured on the *Oprah Winfrey Show* during a tribute to "superwomen," revealing the book's credibility through a hugely popular television show that caters to many groups of American women.[89] Oprah presented the book to daytime, mostly female audiences, but the book also circulated among more specialized and scholarly audiences as well. In a presentation in March 2009 about the book at the Woodrow Wilson Center for Public Policy in Washington, DC, Bennett appeared intent on forging a security approach by which Americans could retain their global power through values, maternalism, and knowledge.[90] She presented herself as able to see the flaws of American policies just as a mother might see the flaws of her child, while still being a good parent: "I prefer to accept that American policies have had bad results in some places rather than sticking my head in the sand. I do not believe a war of attrition can defeat terrorism; I believe it demonstrates more character to allow people whose beliefs you reject have their say; it takes more integrity to admit you've made mistakes; and it takes far more courage to refuse to change in the face of a threat. I'm a mother and that is the strength I know." In this presentation, as in her book, Bennett depicts terrorism as a problem that can be managed by mothers, because they understand the world in the same way they understand their children. Mothers all are different, according to Bennett, and have different motivations, as do children. In cautioning that all terrorism cannot be prevented, Bennett constructs herself as the proxy of the security state that promises only partial security, working in the realm of culture and information, rather than with "harder" tools. At the same time, she also presents herself as an entrepreneur in the counterterrorism business, busily engaged in surveillance and security as projects of pedagogy for all. This produces a world in which enemies of the United States proliferate, and "American" values become the purview of the heteronormative family. While Bennett, the national security mom, might disagree with Malkin, the security mom, and Maya, the security feminist, over waging war as an effective tool of counterterrorism, like Malkin, Bennett upholds the normative heterosexual, white American family as the locus of American exceptionalism—even as this family cannot be sustained because of the demands of war. This exceptionalism and the insecure yet normative family are the founding assumptions of her work, such that her care and sympathy toward non-American Others stem from her role of global parent and global police. This is a soft power approach to the endless war on terror, one more akin to Greg Mortenson than to Michelle Malkin.

What is visible in the construction of all three of these exceptional citizens—the security mom, the security feminist, and the national security mom—is that counterterrorism and the security state cannot ensure complete security of the normative family and nation. Gender impacts how sovereign these subjects can be. In the context of an advanced neoliberalism that engenders protests and ruptures, these contradictions become visible in the media narratives I have described. Consequently, security moms and security feminists remain tragic, or afraid to be taken seriously. What results is the counterterrorism expert trying to hold her roles as wife, mother, Elastigirl, and spy, or the lonely Maya weeping as she returns to the United States. The white-identified American woman claims to save the world or to have better intelligence, even as wars seem unending and unwinnable. What is apparent in the twenty-first-century United States, then, is the limits of security, even for those exceptional subjects who securitize the family at the expense of welfare and social security.

5. Digital Natives

Threats, Technologies, Markets

On her website *Digital Security Mom*, Bernadette Murray writes that she created the site "to empower parents with the ability to protect their families online."[1] She relates that she began the site when she found photographs of her son posted on Facebook, apparently without his permission. As an information technology project manager, she believes that sharing her experience and expertise can help other parents protect their children's privacy and security. Murray joins many parents who, with the advent of digital and social media, have become concerned about their children's online safety. These safety concerns reveal the imperative for security moms to protect their children in the face of new media technologies as well as the impossibility of security in a context where multiple entities benefit from producing insecurity. Insecurity has a political economy, one that is considered an economy of information, but that information comes to have several forms: as *intelligence* for the security state, as a *commodity* for Internet and media companies to collect and sell, and as *personal information* for families to ensure the security of children.

Murray's concerns and hopes are reflected in scholarly research on children's online safety as well as in popular advice for parents, which have appeared in numerous books, articles, and websites. These texts reflect a powerful rhetoric of moral panic about sexuality and safety on the Internet, which is allied with broader concerns about state surveillance resulting from fears about terrorism and the war on terror. Much of this insecurity is generated by the widespread belief, shared by the public as well as technology and parenting experts, that Internet and communication technologies have created a generational divide between children who think and behave differently from their parents because they have grown up in the digital age.

This chapter is concerned with the production and consumption of the idea of the "digital native," the notion of children in the digital age being different from their parents, and the ways that this notion of generational difference is integrated into the economy and the regulation of information. The figure of the digital native reveals the relationship among digital communication technologies, proper parenting, the normative white, heterosexual American family, and the making of exceptional citizens in the context of the security state. In the first decade of the twenty-first century, children became, as Caren Kaplan, Erik Loyer, and Ezra Claytan Daniels have revealed, the "precision targets" of these technologies.[2] Gary Marx and Valerie Steeves suggest that to both complement and counter such precision targeting, parenting came to include surveillance.[3] This chapter focuses on the construction of the child as the instrument and target of security state surveillance, specifically the child as the digital native. I argue that the construction of the digital native as an exceptional security state citizen is of critical concern to a number of institutions and individuals. These include experts who provide parenting advice about media use, state agencies that create laws protecting children and corporations while also using corporations to surveil customers, and corporations that participate in the political economy of insecurity to gather personal information to sell to other businesses. All of these entities create the American digital native as an exceptional citizen: a white, "native" and middle-class consumer and informant, who is both feared and celebrated as the subject needed to save the security state, but also a subject in need of protection from their own dangerous desires.

As Marx and Steeves point out, parents are now expected to surveil; the American family is securitized in the twenty-first century as a project of surveillance, connecting militarism to family and gender. This securitization reveals itself in both the figure of the digital security mom and the popular belief in a "digital divide" between children and parents. Parenting and education experts suggest that though parents are insecure about their knowledge of new technology compared to their children, they must both enable children to work and play on the Internet while also protecting them from its dangers. How to nurture children—and *which* children is the issue here—to become "exceptional citizens" of the neoliberal security state becomes the project of proper parenting. At the same time as the Internet is viewed as essential to education and to the future,[4] panics arise about the safety and protection of the child. This concern for children's online safety has produced state and familial insecurities that I trace in this chapter.

In chapter 4, I suggested that motherhood has become an object of control and a technology of the security state. The confluence of antiterrorism practices, existing social divisions, emerging social media, economic inequality, and wars in the Middle East all contributed to the making of the insecure security mom. In the United States, motherhood not only governmentalizes the security state but also articulates and recuperates its anxious desires for security and surveillance. The concern around surveillance is critical to creating what is seen as the private sphere of the normative, white, liberal family, even as notions of privacy have been altered in relation to the long history of race, class, and sexuality, the advent of state/corporate surveillance and data collection, and the needs and desires of consumers. In the twenty-first century, the ruptures of the liberal state are also more visible, as the security state became the dominant state form in the United States. The confluence of militarism and neoliberalism altered notions of the private and public sphere such that the critique of the liberal idea of separation between public and private, made by feminists and critical race studies scholars,[5] became recuperated through decades of neoliberal policies as an outmoded liberal ideal. It, then, was incorporated across a range of political projects, both progressive and conservative. The insecurities resulting from such changes were often represented in popular media as a consequence of the Internet and new media, rather than to a host of other economic or political causes. These fears produced a new invented past for the white heterosexual American family, a past in which American children roamed freely and safely across urban and rural spaces. This imagined past was reserved for the white family, since the period of post–Cold War prosperity benefited white families more than those who were engaged in struggles for civil rights or whose lives were circumscribed by the violence of the state. This imagined past was contrasted to a fearful present, though forgotten was how such a past was only possible for white and middle-class Americans—and perhaps only for some decades after the Cold War since, by the 1970s, inequality had begun to rise.[6]

The pervasive twenty-first-century technologization of surveillance enabled by Internet economies, advanced neoliberalism, and empire created fears around security and insecurity that has helped construct what is seen as proper American parenting and the normative American child. As economic and social insecurity became endemic through neoliberal state policies and practices, making boundaries visibly contingent, flexible, and fuzzy, the struggles to remain liberal and to separate the public from the private, the family from the state, and the corporation from the state became more difficult. How to keep this family secure in the terms of normative, neoliberal citizenship became a difficult question.[7] The emergence of Internet and new media came to be seen as the cause of these anxieties, in ways that we recognize from the history of technology, when every new technology receives blame for sociopolitical changes and social anxieties.

While every new technology has produced these fears, Internet and media technologies instrumentalized them, especially regarding the safety of children, in order to sell more technology products and to gather consumer information. By the end of the twentieth century, and the emergence of what came to be called the "information society," Internet companies were gathering data from millions of customers, as were governments. Moreover, with the advent of closed circuit televisions (CCTVs) and webcams, anyone could carry out surveillance. Gary Marx called this new form of social life "surveillance society,"[8] characterized by the ways that digital information could be gathered by anyone able to purchase the tools. Such tools became easily available for all kinds of projects that enabled discrimination based on social ideologies and biases.[9] Surveillance became part of everyday activities in places such as North America, where a vast array of tools for monitoring children, neighbors, friends, intimate partners, consumers, citizens, and noncitizens proliferated, putting into crisis older notions of privacy and the idea of the private sphere. The digital surveillance regime of the US government became powerful into the new century, and it gathered information from digital media companies, making it even more difficult for any individual to control their information.

Such surveillance and data gathering and selling were not unopposed. Some argued that if corporations gathered data on ordinary people, these people should have access and knowledge about what was collected.[10] The leaks of National Security Agency (NSA) data gathering by Edward Snowden showed that all citizens, and not just Muslim Americans or nonwhites, were being surveilled by the state in tandem with telecommunication companies. Digital technology surveillance tools suggested the impossibilities of and desires for security, leading to a now constant search for better and more effective security products. The desires for the privacy of the American family, while aligned with the security state, also came into conflict with the state and technology companies seeking to extract private and personal information from consumers. In addition, the production of the "American family" as white, heteronormative, and middle class—despite all demographic evidence to the contrary—continued apace with racialized language of dangers from new media technologies. Many whites expressed anxieties over online dangers, echoing other white fears about immigrants and nonwhites as dangerous and foreign others infiltrating the white home and nation. Consequently, in the first few decades of the twenty-first century, how to remain "exceptional" as a citizen and nation, and how to create such citizens within the American family, became struggles against changing inequalities and new populations, as well as racial/imperial and geopolitical fears.

Securitizing the Family, Racialized Surveillance, and the War on Terror

Global concepts of privacy have shifted considerably in recent decades as states now have the capacity and desire to use digital technologies to surveil their populations in new ways. Governments increasingly desire this because the Westphalian state is now threatened by all sorts of insurrections, particularity what is now called "terrorism." In their desire for control and information, nation-state governments construct data profiles of figures of threat and danger from the masses of digital footprints gathered by corporations.[11] Transnational collaborations in the pervasive hunt for "terrorists" have enabled states to amass authoritarian power over many groups across the globe; for example, Muslims along with many brown and black Others, are being criminalized across Europe and North America, racialized in ways that recall the targeting of communities within American imperial history. Other groups become targets as well: Kurds in Turkey, Christians and Muslims in India, Shi'a Muslims in the UAE, and political dissidents everywhere. The long colonial history of racialized criminalization in Europe and North America endures in the digital age, where struggles over data privacy and data collection now define the reach of the security state. Even the advent of "predictive analytics," in which some groups are profiled as having the capacity and intent to commit criminal acts, relies on racial and colonial logics.[12] The predictive analytics used in making the profile of a putative criminal or terrorist is based on data collecting and constructing—itself an ideological activity—and on mining for correlation rather than causation, so that the profile itself is presumed to imply intent.[13] For black youth this profile, gained through policing that now includes mining social media, has led to further surveillance and incarceration. The New York Police Department (NYPD), for instance, has already tried to incarcerate one African American youth on conspiracy charges by looking at online social networks such as Facebook.[14]

The historical effects of racial, colonial, and Orientalist stereotypes have long been used to suggest that some groups are more dangerous than others. Predictive analytics have primarily relied on ideologies of group identity rather than individual behavior to judge criminal intent, as suggested by the widespread net cast on immigrant communities after 9/11.[15] The security state and corporations intent on creating consumers and markets collaborate to gather information that constructs, justifies, and enables such analytics.[16] In 2002, the FBI as well as the New York City Police began to carry out surveillance on Muslim mosques and neighborhoods. Some of this surveillance involved using demographic information to "map" neighborhoods and carry out video surveillance and tracking of individuals, as well as using digital technologies to gather information and to monitor activities of individuals. It also included recruiting community members who were asked to spy on friends and family and to surf websites connected with their networks in order to report their findings to the FBI.[17] In carrying out such surveillance on their own communities, these informants were offered the difficult choice of supporting the security state and becoming exceptional citizens who further the work of empire and capital, or being seen as aliens and threats to the nation. Yet, for many Muslim Americans, such choices are foreclosed; their religion and race mean that they cannot become exceptional citizens, but instead are stigmatized within communities and also by the police who seek their help. Many carry out this work to protect themselves or to aspire to good citizenship, but this aspiration is difficult to fulfill.

If surveillance includes the work of antiterrorism, as the FBI and other police claim, it is also the case that media and Internet corporations gather information about consumers. With the leaks about government surveillance by Edward Snowden, struggles between such corporations and the government over the control and disclosure of US citizens' personal data show the extent to which such data is both commodity and intelligence. It is a commodity when Internet and media corporations can gather and sell consumer information to enable the production, advertising, and marketing of consumer goods.[18] It is intelligence when it is gathered and used by governments and the security state. Such surveillance, which is extensive and encompasses many groups, creates widespread concerns about privacy and the desire to control personal information.[19]

When parents participate in the task of monitoring their children, they are also sharing information about these children with the technology industry, thereby naturalizing the family as the agent and product of surveillance. With technology tools, parents believe they can keep their children safe by surveilling their online and offline movements; thus, governmentalized surveillance and security are not just produced through the idea of mothering and parenting, but also through a mediated rearticulation of family relations *as* relations of surveillance. In this framework, the normative family is one that surveils children and wherein children surveil each other, while the dysfunctional family is one unable or unwilling to surveil.[20] If constant monitoring of children is the norm, those who could not or would not carry out such monitoring—like those families who, based on class or race, have to work several jobs and do not have the time or resources to monitor—can then be seen as dysfunctional. In this securitization of the "private" family sphere, middle-class children are constructed as digital natives, characterized by their proficiency with new technology and their purported inability to distinguish between life online and offline, as well as their constant connectivity. The concept of the digital native, of course, relegates to the margins all those who are unable to afford the new gadgets or the connectivities that they require.

Surveillance by nonwhites, noncitizens,[21] or Muslim youth often leads to terrorism charges, while surveillance of these groups by whites, citizens, and Christians flourish—as the latter are emboldened by the state's injunction "if you see something, say something." Moral panics about the dangers of the Internet are linked to the capabilities of digital technologies to transform social relations, especially relations between parents and children when parents feel that children are more knowledgeable about the Internet and computer hardware. At the same time, these technologies construct the normative family as one that uses technology to protect children from new dangers, new identities, and new modes of profit making.[22] While national security mom Gina Bennett analogizes parenting and counterterrorism (as I argue in chapter 4), the digital security mom suggests that parents must use surveillance technology products to guide children along productive paths to enhance their education via Internet access and to keep them from becoming either perpetrators of violence or victims of cyberbullying and sexual predators. Rather than fighting Internet surveillance, both the state and individual families encourage regulating it, though such regulation has been weak in controlling corporations and the state.[23] In sum, the state's interest in surveillance and in gathering information on citizens and Others have trumped all other interests, including those of individuals. As neoliberalism became naturalized, individuals have assumed the work of surveillance as well as the blame for insecurity, if it failed as all such products do.

As Internet technologies flourished in the last decades of the twentieth century, numerous companies have emerged to sell surveillance and security software and hardware. Gary Marx and Valerie Steeves reveal that surveillance and "related communication are offered as tools of responsible parenting and convenience" and that tracking—"online and offline—is presented as an essential part of effective and loving parenting" as well as effective family relations.[24] Not only are middle-class children surveilled by innumerable technologies from conception on, with fetal and baby monitoring taken for granted as responsible parenting, but gadgets and toys that encourage spying and sharing personal information also teach them to surveil themselves and others.[25] National security mom Gina Bennett (whom I discuss in chapter 4) participated in the project of governmentalizing security, enlisting children in the project, so that they could grow up wanting to be spies and counterterrorism experts.[26] In this context, parenting includes constant surveillance, and those parents who cannot or will not maintain constant surveillance over their children are now blamed for their poor parenting. Thus, those parents—especially those not white and middle class, who work at multiple jobs, or who cannot access surveillance technology—are constructed as delinquent.

It is not that technology is responsible for these renewed moral panics, or even for the surveillance and securitization that I discuss in this chapter. Gill Valentine and Sarah Holloway suggest that properties of technology are "not inherent but emerge in practice."[27] I would argue that these properties also are part of the design. Technology is shaped by the needs and desires of capital and, in the case of the Internet and with the advent of email, by military research.[28] Torin Monahan suggests that "technologies shape social practices in non-neutral ways . . . encouraging certain uses or interactions and discouraging others" while enabling social and historical inequalities.[29] New technologies recuperate old fears and shift human relations precisely because corporations and people endow technologies with specific properties. Twenty-first-century surveillance responsibilities emerge from the properties attributed to new technologies as well as from political, social, and economic contexts and histories of gender, sexuality, empire, and capitalism.

It is not just the state that benefits from the insecurity and surveillance of the family. Companies that collect and commodify personal data also benefit. These companies constitute the other "private" entities (along with the family and individual citizens) charged with being exceptional citizens, by sharing surveillance and information with the state. In the contexts of the security state, new media, and concerns over American empire, sovereignty has become split between three sometimes competing realms: the family, the security state, and corporations. Concerned with safety and privacy, the US Congress created laws regulating the gathering of information by businesses, though in ways that were weak and often ineffectual. Most important, collaborations between states and corporations for surveillance purposes resulted in flexible and fuzzy boundaries between what is public and what is private. Furthermore, the heterogeneity of the security state has meant that some state agencies allow self-regulation and some promise weak regulation, while others collaborate with businesses to surveil their citizens. The citizen is figured in all of these contexts as both consumer and informant. Corporate sovereignty comes into tension with individual and family sovereignty, a struggle between two realms of private power that the state regulates by according certain corporations, individuals, and families their liberal rights while denying them to others.

Not all children have benefited from state protections. While black and brown youth continue to be seen as criminal threats to community and state because of their race, the concerns regarding children and new media focus on online safety and the necessity for education, thus endowing these children (and particularly middle-class and upper-class ones) with a futurity denied to children of color left to the carceral state. While the surveillance of the white, middle-class child is articulated through the need for protection from outsiders, "aliens," and strangers, as well as from the harmful effects of pornography available in visual media, there is also a pervasive fear that children themselves are dangerous.[30] One reason given is because they are assumed to be easily corrupted by external forces outside the home and the heteronormative family, as digital security mom Bernadette Murray reveals. Children are seen as unable to understand why such privacy is important.[31] Some of these attitudes may be attributed to a long history of childrearing in the West based on Christian ideas of original sin.[32] The fear of children's sexuality has been a driving force in much of Western social and cultural politics.[33] The history of every new technology reveals these fears, especially with regard to fears of girls' sexuality.[34] While some parents fear new technologies would bring new dangerous influences into the home, others view these as enabling children's latent dangerous tendencies. Importantly, what lurks in this familial discourse is the fear that children are not what parents believe them to be. These coconstituting fears, antagonisms, and desires for protection are part of the war that was waged within the rapidly changing "American family," a war with religious, political, and topical overtones referencing Christian, imperial, and domestic politics—which include the "war on crime," the "war on drugs," and the "war on terror."

The Digital Native

The construction of the child as a digital native brings histories of race, gender, and empire into the advanced neoliberalism of the twenty-first century, as ideas of racial and gendered differences are used to claim that public education is inadequate and needs technology experts as well as private technologies to improve it. Education and technology expert Marc Prensky coined the term "digital natives" in 2001 to name what he saw as differences between the generation growing up with new technologies and older generations whom he called "digital immigrants."[35] In his widely read and circulated article "Digital Natives, Digital Immigrants," Prensky argues that students in the Internet age "think and process information fundamentally differently from their predecessors" and that growing up with digital technologies has caused their brains to develop differently.[36] According to Prensky, "our students' brains have physically changed" from those of previous generations. Although he partially qualifies this declaration, questioning "whether or not this is literally true," he goes on undeterred to assert that "we can say with certainty that their thinking patterns have changed."[37] In another article titled "Do They Really *Think* Differently?" Prensky claims that evidence from neurobiology and psychology bolsters his claim that because all brains are malleable, children's brains must have changed under the impact of computers.[38] This unproven connection then becomes the basis of his expertise and his ability to sell educational technology products.

He asserts assumptions about generational differences while making technologically determinist claims, many of which have been disproved by researchers,[39] but what is noteworthy about Prensky is how his description of the culture of new technologies and media expressed essentialist notions of gender, race, and migration. For Prensky, the "native" is the child of the

Internet, a normative figure who is gendered male, while the immigrant is the older, analog subject living in the historical past as well as in another anachronistic country. The foreignness and otherness of the digital immigrant—that she is not a citizen, much less an exceptional citizen—are clear. Prensky states that such immigrants need to assimilate into the new world, and their older knowledges are of little use for this new generation of "natives." In these two articles, Prensky argues that the generation coming of age with computers is fundamentally different in the ways their brains learn and process information. Consequently, they need different educational products, such as video games and other new teaching methods. He advocates not only advice and consulting for schools, parents, and educators but also new educational products that capitalize on these ideas of newness and brain malleability.

In using these metaphors, and relying on notions of generational difference, Prensky ignores the fact that many of these technologies were made and invented by actual immigrants who have contributed to the making of Silicon Valley, for instance. Moreover, his claims regarding Internet usage based on generational difference homogenize and Americanize the existing diversity of national and global users and producers. In the process, the argument simplifies terms such as "native" and "immigrant" as it constructs an exceptional citizen supposedly born of new technology. Prensky ignores racial, class, and gender differences within generations, and uses a racially charged language of nativism that erases American history of Native Americans as natives and white European Americans as immigrants. By ignoring these specificities, Prensky makes American contexts into universal ones and the white, male, middle-class, computer-owning, and video-game-playing American child into the normative citizen.

In using the language of native versus immigrant, Prensky calls upon a number of racialized assumptions about migration and belonging that emerge from the history of US racial formations. First of all, he suggests that immigrants are neither pedagogically adept nor intelligible, because of their strange accents and speaking styles. For example, he states that in schools, "Digital Immigrant instructors, who speak an outdated language . . . are struggling to teach a population that speaks an entirely new language."[40] To this generation, school "feels pretty much as if we've brought in a population of heavily accented, unintelligible foreigners to lecture them," such that students "often can't understand what the immigrants are saying."[41] Prensky's claim draws on a long history of racism against immigrants, particularly Asians, who are often discriminated against for their accents. Jane Hill has argued that such statements produce a "white public space,"[42] through monitoring the speech of immigrants; Prensky certainly whitens Internet technology production and consumption. Legal scholar Mari Matsuda has argued that such "accent discrimination" hides a host of other forms of discrimination based on race and that injunctions to enforce American accents are a form of domination used particularly against Asians.[43] Within this US racial history, Asians and Asian Americans are viewed as always foreigners, thus having precarious links to national belonging and citizenship.[44] Prensky's formulation expels Asian Americans from American belonging and from the possibility of becoming exceptional citizens.

It is not simply that these digital immigrants are accented foreigners that Prensky finds to be a problem but also that, according to him, they lack the skills needed to be part of the workforce of the future. While digital natives receive information fast, and can "parallel process and multi-task," he argues, "digital immigrants typically have little appreciation for these new skills that the Natives have acquired and perfected through years of interaction and practice." Digital natives, he claims, have "little patience for lectures, step-by-step logic, and 'tell-test' instruction."[45] The digital immigrants thus have to change—to move forward—because "it is highly unlikely the digital natives will go backwards."[46] That Prensky is implying many non-English-speaking immigrants as the context for this argument—particularly Asians, Africans, Latinos, and Middle Easterners—is clear not simply in this language of migration to America as moving forward in time and space, but also when he argues that digital immigrants can learn the new language from their children, echoing the racialized assumption that immigrant children are more adept at learning English than their parents. It is not surprising then that Prensky goes on to argue that "smart adult immigrants accept that they don't know about their new world and take advantage of their kids to help them learn and integrate. Not-so-smart (or not-so-flexible) immigrants spend most of their time grousing about how good things were in the 'old country.' "[47] For Prensky, the immigrant can be "smart" only when she realizes her ignorance about the "new world" and valorizes life in the United States over that of the country from which she emigrated.

While Prensky's digital native is constructed as a nonimmigrant American, this figure is also constructed as male. His criticism of school teachers becomes gendered when taking into account the fact that a majority of K–12 teachers are women. Prensky reveals this assumption in an example of one way in which the educational software his company offers is more relevant to this new generation. He mentions that when some professors came to his company with a new computer-aided design to be used by engineers, they were faced with resistance from users. Prensky and his marketers had the "brilliant idea" to make the software into a first-person shooter game because the users of the CAD software were "almost exclusively male engineers between 20 and 30."[48] This game, called "The Monkey Wrench," Prensky recalls, became "phenomenally successful" among digital natives, such as "engineering students around the world." Once again, by referring to a group gendered in a particular way, in this case engineering students as males who would be attracted to a shooter game, Prensky suggests that these digital natives are male even as he pushes his generational argument to suggest that these professors behave like immigrants. Prensky also insinuates that even the "professors" found the game difficult, while digital natives had no problems with it, saying that though it was "easy for my digital native staff to invent it (the game), it was more difficult to apply for use by professors, though eventually they were able to have the 'mind-shift' needed to use it."[49] Although Prensky does not explicitly use the phrase "digital immigrants" to describe these professors as he does with the K–12 teachers, he does imply that even these—presumably male professors—are unable to understand the digital natives who are comfortable with shooter games.

While professors are shown as close to being digital immigrants, Prensky's greatest scorn is for the K–12 teachers, whom he does see as digital immigrants: "It's just dumb (and lazy) of educators—not to mention ineffective— to presume that (despite their traditions) the digital immigrant way is the only way to teach," he states, concluding that "if the digital immigrant educators really want to reach digital natives—i.e., all their students—they will have to change. It's high time for them to stop their grousing, and as the Nike motto of the digital native generation says, 'Just do it.' "[50] Here, Prensky's target is not only the racialized and gendered figure of the teacher who has an unintelligible accent, but also the teacher he considers "lazy," "dumb," unwilling to change, "grousing," following "traditions," and thus unsuccessful at teaching. According to Prensky, these teachers need to follow the Nike motto, "just do it." He excoriates "immigrant educators" for not being more corporate and consumerist. Students and teachers should thus become consumers, following advertising slogans in their classrooms and learning to be market driven. Since Prensky is also in the business of selling technology to educators, his use of corporate slogans reveals attempts to make the classroom more neoliberal, with teachers and children becoming more entrepreneurial.

Prensky's descriptions of teachers are part of a broader attack on education and teachers (and their unions) that is led by technology companies and educational NGOs. Many leaders of these companies and NGOs claim that public schools and teachers are inefficient and have failed, that new technologies can provide better education, and that technology companies better understand effective teaching and learning. Such technology companies and technology NGOs have done much to undermine existing school systems through representations of teachers as incompetent and lazy, and schools as not accountable or efficient.[51] These attacks are gendered in particular ways, as the teaching profession is predominantly female. As such, attacks on teachers by so-called experts such as Prensky are implicitly condemning digital immigrants as feminized and failed neoliberal subjects. In contrast, the masculine digital native is understood as more successful and efficient. These neoliberal attacks on teaching have changed attitudes toward public school teachers, who now are constantly monitored and surveilled, are hired and fired more frequently, and have less independence to develop new pedagogies in the classroom. Classroom audits and tracking metrics have become the norm, and even the Obama administration made neoliberal arguments about education through its policies on testing and on education being necessary for jobs, ignoring how important education might be for a host of other creative careers as well as for learning and citizenship. Consequently, Prensky seems to sell his educational products and services—through his company Games2Train—by attacking teachers with a racialized and gendered language of educational technology expertise and citizenship. In using the logic of technology as the secret to better education, and digital games as teaching tools, he offers educational products that promise to be more effective in the classroom. By retraining digital immigrants to be better teachers, his goal is to turn digital natives into exceptional citizens.

Digital Security Mom: Educating the Digital Immigrant

For technology industry producers, the digital native is an exceptional neoliberal citizen (hence also entrepreneurial and productive), and the pedagogy required for his learning requires more and better technology products. Because Prensky's digital immigrant is ignorant, she—as teacher and as parent—is also a target for educational technology products. Through these products, Prensky suggests, she can become a proper pedagogue. In constructing the digital native as a child, Prensky suggests that the child is more knowledgeable than "immigrant" parents and teachers. Such an implication has produced its own insecurities and moral panics, especially for parents. Teaching parents to overcome their ignorance has become a lucrative industry, with a variety of experts, how-to books, magazines, websites, and products promising better parenting through better social media and digital knowledge.

By the end of the first decade of the twenty-first century, these parenting fears produced the aforementioned digital security mom Bernadette Murray, whose concern for her son led to a blog offering her expertise about parenting digital natives. Much of her advice focuses on how to use "parental control" software, providing "digital immigrant" parents with basic information about computers, cell phones, and their security features. She also recommends particular security products. Along with information about Facebook scams, how to limit screen time, and how to address Internet bullying, her blog features requests she has received to speak at schools and offers to try out or recommend new software. In her pedagogy directed at parents, Murray reiterates Prensky's concept of a dangerous digital divide between children and parents. That these security concerns point to divergent futures for different populations is made visible in Murray's use of terms such as "curfew," her warnings about undesirable "infiltration" into the home, and her argument that "playing outside" is a desirable alternative to time spent online. These recommendations ignore the context of many students of color who have curfews (implicit or explicit, across many cities) or students who are immigrants, often seen as threats to the nation, and for whom it is too dangerous to play outside.

In a September 11, 2013, post, Murray reports on a new app that puts a child's phone in "curfew mode," preventing Internet access. As Murray reports, not long after the Internet connection on her son's phone was activated, the " 'time wasters' began infiltrating the home," meaning that her son was not just using his phone to stay connected to her and complete schoolwork, but also using it to access other websites. She states:

> I soon realized it was far more difficult[:] taking away the phone also meant taking away the ability to communicate with my son and track his whereabouts via Find my iPhone.
>
> Now I use AppCertain to put his phone in "curfew mode" whenever I need a little parental help encouraging the use of other non-phone activities like homework, playing outside, doing chores, and the like.[52]

Murray's post reveals the normative idea that a parent, a mother in particular, must make sure her child is able to use the Internet for education and safety; surveillance is productive because it enables homework or chores. She must know the whereabouts of her son at every moment and needs to circumvent any chance of her child escaping this surveillance. If her child wants to remove his connection to his mother, this desire is viewed as a danger, though she absolves her child from blame. Murray suggests that it is not her child who is responsible for this resistance but outside "time wasters" who are "infiltrating" the home. Proper parenting means helping her child eliminate any online activity that is not about schoolwork or family work. Voicing nostalgia for the practice of "playing outside," Murray shows how much she, as a parent, is both a digital native and a digital immigrant. Murray, the mother, must step in like the state to enforce an online "curfew" for her son if he does not agree to her surveillance or answer the phone when his mother calls. Murray does not tell us much about the companies that created or marketed the AppCertain product, whether it is reputable or not, or if there are any problems with the product itself.[53]

On her website, Murray does not mention the regular curfews for youth of color enforced in some US cities. Nor does she mention the economic insecurity, food insecurity, and deportations that separate families and prevent children from "playing outside." Nor is she concerned with preventing the US government from surveilling families in the war on terror, or keeping young African American children safe from violent police, gun-toting citizens, and vigilantes policing the nation. Murray includes no reviews of apps for parents of these children and few ways to produce security or privacy for low-income or nonwhite children, let alone digital maps helping them find safety. "Time wasters" are the threat here, as they take white, middle-class children away from the development of their bodies and minds toward exceptional neoliberal citizenship. The threat is from outside elements, foreclosing any recognition of children's agency by turning them into victims. Yet, this child is to be feared, as he could be an activist, a protestor, a hacker, or plotting violence;[54] Murray's child cannot be trusted to be left alone online and needs his parents to be always on the alert.

Murray's recommendations for security technology products are designed to empower parents to better surveil their children. Surveillance apps to monitor children keep alive the belief that technology will solve all problems, that technological improvements will continue to provide greater security, and also, paradoxically, that parents have to be constantly on alert in surveilling their children because the technology cannot work by itself. Proper surveillance by parents will turn the digital native into the exceptional citizen, who will use the capacities of the Internet for the security of the family and the state rather than for threatening this security.[55] On her digital security mom website, Murray constructs the child as the digital native who is an exceptional citizen but may also be the Other; anyone designated a native might be an intimate insider as well as a threat, and so must be kept protected from her own desires as much as from external threats.

Digital Natives and Gendered Dangers

There is a large popular literature about protecting children, especially girls, from online dangers.[56] Many fears also concern children's access to each other beyond parental control, so that interactions between teens, for example, are now more securitized with various sorts of tracking and monitoring devices. "Parental control" is a term that refers both to the Internet-filtering software that comes installed on many computers, as well as to a parenting style derived from security concerns (such as those exhibited by the security moms I examined in chapter 4). Although researchers have debunked popular beliefs regarding online dangers as common to a history of new and old media,[57] the insecurities and anxieties raised by digital technologies have created new parenting projects.

Some researchers suggest that the panic over outside threats is partly the result of American beliefs that the Internet is too transnational, diverse, and large; thus, they have little control over it or ability to understand it.[58] Others, such as Prensky, argue that because digital technology has created digital "natives," who have more advanced knowledge of the technology than do their parents, it has created a reversal of parent-child roles that make some parents very fearful.[59] This argument relies on some of the same generational logics expressed by Prensky. Given the remarkable variances in dangers to youth of different communities, it is notable that much of the popular anxiety over Internet dangers does not concern the safety or security of youths of color, who are most in danger of being targets of violence. Few books or websites focus on Internet dangers for African American children, for instance.[60] Rather, much of the focus is on a child undisturbed by racial violence, whose description represents middle-class, white, male children as digital natives in need of protection.

When it comes to girls, however, it is mostly in relation to sexuality that these online dangers are articulated, though, even here, class differences matter. For instance, while the Internet may allow many parents under Megan's Law to identify where "sexual offenders" reside, and thus presumably to move away from those areas, it offers few options for those not financially able to relocate. Similar to older anxieties over TV, radio, and other communication technologies, anxieties over new media reflect a fear of strangers with regard to sexual assaults, "sexting," online stalking, sharing of "private" information (such as addresses and phone numbers), and bullying. Media experts warn parents about sexual predators lurking on websites and luring girls to meet them outside the home.[61] Parents are warned not to let their children give away personal information online or identify themselves in ways that might lead these predators to them. Few media experts warn of the threats to children from police or vigilantes, even though children of color are routinely securitized as carceral subjects both online and off.[62]

In response to these insecurities, technology companies have marketed additional parental control tools for cell phone as well as computer users. Some of these technologies are direct transfers of military technologies.[63] Others are the result of software professionals and developers moving from government surveillance jobs to the private sector.[64] Such software enables parents to control their children,[65] as I have argued here; it also intensifies unequal gendered relationships within the heteronormative family that are already hierarchically organized by gender and differentiated by race.[66] Research suggests that girls are dealt with more authoritatively than boys, and teenagers are given more freedom than younger children.[67] The language of sexual dangers is significant in creating such gendered and sexualized inequalities.[68] Yet these dangers are often overblown. One set of researchers discovered that about 15 percent of students in the study were involved in behaviors that they called "risky," such as sharing information with strangers or sexting. However, this group of students had other risk factors,[69] so it was not the technology that was responsible for endangering these children. Another study found that those with authoritarian parenting styles used the filtering software the most, and focused on restricting access for younger teens rather than older ones.[70]

The marketing of parental surveillance software replicates the digital native/digital immigrant generational and racial divide by suggesting, first, that mothers and parents lack the knowledge of technology necessary to fully control and surveil, and second, that children—particularly boys—know more than parents when it comes to computers. Because of this, such software marketing has pitted parents against children: "we" parents against "them" children. For instance, in 2001, F-Secure, a security software company, addressed parents/consumers by stating in their advertisement that "today's youngsters" are "the first generation of digital natives," and though they may understand the Internet better than their parents, "we cannot remain passive observers." Thus, although the Internet is a "magic playground . . . just a couple of clicks away the Internet is also pornography, child exploitation, gambling, hate messages, bomb-making, and extreme violence." F-Secure warns parents, "we really need to know what they are doing online." The company assumes parents are ignorant about Internet usage, telling them what instant-messaging acronyms mean and emphasizing that children live in a separate world and speak a separate language.[71] In this framing, children are at once both natives and unknown others, to be nurtured but also to be feared.

The production of fear in the context of endless violence sells these products. A survey done in 2010 by Care.com, a company providing caregivers to families, stated that "nearly one in three (30%) parents of children 12–17 years old fear bullying and cyberbullying over kidnapping, domestic terrorism, car accidents, suicide, or any other incident."[72] While the editorial suggests that good parents protect their children from these dangers, and offers advice for doing so, it deliberately leaves out terrorism or police as a lesser fear too; and domestic terrorism, often associated with white males, is not as feared as cyberbullying. Relatedly, in 2012, the company Verify Anybody launched a Facebook application, "Friend Verifier," that claimed to be able to check out Facebook "friends" to see if they have criminal or sexual offender histories.[73] Many parents are concerned about their children's "risky behavior" on the Internet, especially regarding sexual predators and online strangers.[74] One study revealed that about 30 percent of parents are present while their child is on the web, while others relied on parental control software; more than half looked at their children's search histories.[75] These studies did not take race or class into account. Although it is not clear if the surveyed parents' responses aligned with their practices, marketing assumes that parents believe this surveillance is necessary.

The proliferation of parental surveillance software and hardware reflects fears about the future of the heteronormative American family. *Sky Mall*, a catalogue found in the seat pockets of many US airplanes through 2015, recently featured an advertisement for Brick House Security (fig. 5.1).[76]

These advertisements, particularly for the camera to record your bed to "see who is there when you are not," articulates the militarization of the family, fears of its demise, and its surveillance. Unfaithful partners and unruly children can all be controlled by the distant eye of a person who can afford the hardware, software, and monthly subscription fee. Parents can place a GPS tracking device in a backpack or in a car, or send car speed alerts if a driver exceeds speeding limits.

These products suggest that the American family needs surveillance to make its members into exceptional citizens, since, without such surveillance, the digital native could become a danger to family and state. On the one hand, digital media expertise and the ability to surveil are presumed necessary skills for the exceptional citizen. On the other hand, these same skills are presented as creating duplicitous children who lead secret lives by hiding their true activities, feelings, and interests from their parents. The fear engendered by such children is visible in an advertisement from PC World Magazine (fig. 5.2).

This image resonates with horror film representations of the child as well as the fear and pleasure that they engender. The software advertised, Spector Pro, suggests that the child, a young girl, is adept at hiding herself and can take on a mask that hides the "real" person.[77] The ad states that in 2010 Spector Pro was awarded the Mom's Choice Award, for ensuring children's safety while allowing them to "make smarter, safer decisions online." The combination of security and children's development is an ideal rhetorical package for managing the risk of going online, turning the child from threat to one who can be tutored through the software. In the image from the ad, what hides behind white femininity becomes the threat. The ad thus echoes fears of dangerous Others infiltrating the country by hiding behind masks of whiteness, while threatening Americans with terror. The iconography also recalls the dangers of presuming epidermal whiteness as an index of safety in the context of the war on terror. For instance, it echoes concerns that led to the racialization of Arabs, preventing them from being absorbed into whiteness. According to the terms of the US Census Bureau policy of 2014, Arabs now belong to a group called "Middle Eastern or North African" (MENA) after being legally categorized as white for over seventy years.[78] Before that period, Arabs were more likely to be designated as eligible for citizenship if they were Christians rather than Muslims,[79] suggesting that religion was critical for assigning racial identities. The new census term MENA emerges as a nonwhite identity because of the way that it conflates region with religion, assuming that all those from the Middle East and North Africa are Muslims and therefore a threat to America. The threat posed by the child who can change identities online then is compounded by racial fears of those appearing to be white, as well as gendered fears. The necessity of the Internet and its fearful effects work together so that surveillance becomes a commodified way to alert the family to the threat of Others to the nation, and to incorporate the family into the project of surveillance.[80]

The participation of corporations in constructions of childhood has a long history in consumer and media culture.[81] Digital technologies replicate some of these older representations and add newer technological monsters. Parental control technology has a joint policing/protecting function that emphasizes insecurity and nurture. In this context, products abound

FIG. 5.1. Brick House Security advertisement, *SkyMall* magazine, fall 2010.

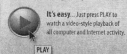

FIG. 5.2. Specter Pro advertisement, PC *World Magazine*, December 2010.

with names such as Net Nanny, eBlaster, Spector Pro, Win Spy, IamBig-Brother, PCTattletale, PC Pandora, McAfee Family Protection, Qustodio, uknowkids, SocialShield, Nearparent, MinorMonitor, PhoneSheriff, BeSecure, Safeeyes, AVG Family Safety, and WebWatcher. The marketing language used to sell these products is similar to that of Spector Pro, warning parents to be afraid of children roaming online, asking parents to monitor computer usage, and warning them to protect their children from being preyed upon by adults or bullies.

Software developers have created several different mechanisms for these parental control products, though these are constantly changing in the quest for more failure-proof technologies. In general, parental control software works by blocking particular URLs on a list in the repository, identifying and blocking banned words or images. Such software records screen captures, images reached, sites visited, and chat and instant message (IM) histories, as well as keystrokes. Software can monitor mobile phone usage as well so that information on the location of phones, photographs taken and uploaded, IM conversations and emails, and websites visited can all be scrutinized. Another parental control technology is time control software that regulates the time a child user can spend on games, chat, or social networking sites. Such software not only records information but also sends alerts to parents. One software product, KidsWatch, monitors for "inappropriate websites," gives "predator alerts," and provides time-management tools, suggesting that children need to be surveilled in order to protect them and to become productive.[82] To meet the challenges of cloud computing and increased mobile technology use, these companies now offer greater capacity to surveil mobile bodies and dynamic monitoring of a rapidly changing Internet landscape. Security companies provide monitoring of mobile phone locations, sending alerts to parents if the phone moves beyond a virtual "fence."

Marketing materials for the software Net Nanny also provide both surveillance and monitoring for time management. Net Nanny asks parents to gather information on each child so they can create different controls for each child. By giving the child's mobile phone information to the company, parents can supposedly carry out remote management via Internet connections, allowing useful activities (such as schoolwork) while preventing harmful ones. According to its website, the product allows children to use the Internet to do their homework but not anything parents may not like. It states: "Net Nanny allows in the good, and keeps out the bad. Your family can use the Internet as a resource for homework and fun without fear of accidental exposure to undesirable material, or encounters with dangerous individuals."[83] Net Nanny makers suggest that children are innocent and unaware of the dangers that face them—contrary to some research that tells us that those doing the "sexting" might be quite aware of what they are doing and may be doing so deliberately.[84] Offering an Entertainment Software Ratings Board (ESRB) rating choice, as well as a "safe harbor" provision (which I elaborate on later in this chapter), the company can claim that it is more responsible than others. Although ESRB sounds like a government agency, it is an agency created by software companies to self-regulate so that government regulation can be prevented. It rates video games based on content, maintains a code of ethics, and certifies that companies are following laws on privacy for children.[85]

Such parental control products, however, often create more insecurity than security, since they are designed with the recognition that many children can bypass the control. Although the software promises "parental control," some manufacturers believe that mothers and parents are inept at or ignorant of technology. Any Google search for information on parental control software brings up websites with discussions on why these products might not work and why manufacturer claims are often overstated and misleading. In an article from 2009, for instance, Davey Winder points out that these controls can be bypassed by teens "who are savvy enough if they know about multiprotocol IM clients or web-based clients."[86] Winder reports that "the new blocking methods encourage the child to find creative ways around the restrictions." He goes on to say that "the majority of parents we spoke to were blissfully ignorant that their children might be bypassing the parental controls" and that a "frightening number, for example, didn't know that they handed over the keys to the padlock by letting their children log in to their PC's administrative account." Winder asserts that some parents leave kids to set up the computer, enabling them to control the administrative settings, because parents are "pretty bad at using hard-to-guess passwords as well."[87] Winder explains that kids can bypass time limits by resetting the system clock, and can easily find information on Google explaining how to hack the parental control software. According to the children that Winder interviewed, Google images showed them how to reach porn using a proxy server, while others used mobile phones to chat and do sexting. Perhaps most worrying for parents, according to Winder, was the revelation that if all else fails and the monitoring software is too good, teenagers can turn to Linux Distro.[88] Distro here refers to Linux's free and open-source operating systems and software that enable applications, also open source, but which can be accessed outside of the commercial operating systems installed on most computers (Microsoft Windows, Apple OS X, or the like).

Many articles in both parenting and computing magazines on this topic conclude that parents need to be online and that the most important issue is "trust." "If your children can't come to you when they run into trouble online, there's no software in the world that's going to solve your problems," says Winder.[89] But it is also possible that many parents are unable to continually monitor their children online. One study revealed that teens reported much less monitoring than reported by their parents, showing that parents are often unable to carry out all the monitoring they wish to do.[90] They might set up the software and not pay it any more attention, or look at it sporadically. While parental control technology requires continual attention, its demanding temporality is often not sustainable for longer periods, especially by parents with few computers in the home or other pressures in their lives. Thus, software companies can shift blame onto parents if complete control of children is not possible, thereby maintaining the rhetoric of successful technology and failed parenting (rather than the reverse). Such a shift in blame produces parents' insecurity and continued pressure on them to surveil their children's behavior. Motherhood and parenting in the United States are thus not simply governmentalizing the security state but also articulating and recuperating fears engendered by the desire for surveillance, precisely because parents cannot carry out the surveillance.

Such insecurity is useful, nevertheless. Many of these parental control products have goals other than simply selling surveillance, since these companies also gather personal information that they can sell to third parties. (In 2016, the government passed laws regulating such sales, but these promise to be short-lived and overturned in the Trump era.) Parents' and children's interaction with these technologies result in commodified information; information about users' habits, desires, and behaviors online is quite valuable. As the subject producing this commodity, the family gains new value in the digital economy. Moral panics, allied with protection and desire for information and communication technologies (ICTs), create economic value because they commodify information.

Some scholars call this collection and analysis of data "dataveillance," which is the by-product of biopolitics. Lynn Wrennall provides the example of the UK's "contact point" database for government health services, which holds the personal health data of eleven million children. She argues that "child protection" services consequently become an apparatus for the making of virtual children.[91] Wrennall suggests that such databases construct child-subjects rather than simply replicating an "offline" reality. As with other media, such databases and technologies are altering family relations.

The digital security mom is thus not simply a figure of fear and security in the context of the war on terror that produces the child as an exceptional citizen. Rather, she emerges as an agent providing information to another contemporary figure that is also private and exceptional: the corporation.

Protecting and Regulating Corporations and Families

As the US government surveils its citizens through collaborations with media and Internet firms—and as parents demand children's online protection— the state has responded by devolving sovereignty to private corporations and other businesses, attempting to simultaneously control their power to surveil consumers and enable information gathering for surveillance purposes. Many businesses have also resisted state control over information. Corporations and other companies have a long history of gathering consumer information. Electronic and digital media have scaled up this practice immensely and produced digital information as commodity in a context where information, especially digital information, is valued by a number of entities. This struggle over privacy and security is part of what Elizabeth Losh calls "virtualpolitik," the new-media-influenced version of *realpolitik* in which the state's main connection with new media is its surveillance use.[92] Insecurity, expressed by a variety of entities and governmentalized across the public, produces the opportunity to gather and sell information as a commodity. State regulation treads a fine line between enabling corporations to make profits and gather information, and protecting individuals and families. Despite these trends, the ideological battle over freedom and rights largely remains between the state and the individual, rather than between the three entities actually involved: the state, businesses as the private sector, and individuals and families as other private entities.

The rise of surveillance regimes enabled by the war on terror suggests that regulation in the new century involves a struggle over sovereignty between corporations, individuals, and state bureaucracies, with individuals on the losing end. The NSA-operative-turned-whistleblower Edward Snowden revealed that the US state gathers extensive telephone data as well as audio and visual information via the PRISM program from media companies including Microsoft, Apple, Facebook, Skype, and YouTube. This government program is able to monitor the emails and online data of most Americans.[93] The PRISM program was launched in 2007 after Congress passed the Protect America Act of 2007 and the amendment in 2008 to the Foreign Intelligence Surveillance Act of 1978 (FISA), which protected corporations from liability if they shared their data with the government. After the Snowden leak, these companies proclaimed they had no knowledge of PRISM, though many viewed this denial as part of the laws that enabled data gathering and surveillance.[94] That such companies had to distance themselves from the state reveals fears concerning the negative impact of such disclosures to customers. As the government passed laws requiring companies to share data with the state, it also passed laws to provide some protection from data gathering even while needing companies to carry out data collecting that the state could mine. State bureaucracies collaborated with the corporate sector while also attempting to regulate it; these shifting state concerns and priorities dictate how much it collaborates with corporations. The security state trades regulation for information, sharing the work of security by forcing corporations to disclose information about citizens and others, but also enabling information gathering by passing weak data-collecting regulations. Such weak regulations are not always antagonistic for business since the state is concerned with collaborating with and enhancing (rather than restricting) the private sector, leading to a struggle of sovereignties between corporations and individuals, rather than between corporations and the state. Although it creates weak regulations, the state is neoliberal and focused on militarism and security rather than the welfare of citizens. Moreover, the state has devolved some of its sovereignty to corporations for the purposes of surveillance and militarization.

Despite individuals' complaints about companies gathering and selling their online information, and state agencies' concern about the increasing predations of businesses buying and selling private data, there has not been much interest in protecting most individuals from the corporate collection of personal data. The US Congress has passed legislation protecting children rather than adult citizens. In 1998 the Federal Trade Commission (FTC) produced a report, *Privacy Online: A Report to Congress*, which revealed that online sites collected information from children without seeking permission or disclosing their practices, and shared that information with third parties.[95] Information security at the time was lax, and images and personal information easily circulated on bulletin boards and chat rooms.[96] The report made the case for legislation protecting children and consumers (not citizens) from the growing online market, though it is important to note that it did not mention protecting individuals and minorities from police or national security projects. The survey included in the report found very low levels of parental consent and control sought by online sites, "in sharp contrast to parents' preferences."[97] Also, the FTC asked Congress for legislation to prevent what it saw as "unfairness inherent in collecting certain personal information from children online and transferring it to third parties without obtaining prior parental consent."[98] The FTC reported it did not have the authority to require sites to obtain such consent, and that though it had tried a three-year self-regulation initiative, it found such self-regulation was ineffective and un-enforceable. The FTC asked Congress to enact legislation to compel all commercial websites engaged in information collecting from children to obtain parental consent.

Both congressional Republicans and Democrats introduced bills, some protecting individuals from corporations and some from the government and law enforcement, but few laws came out of these attempts.[99] Such desires for legislation brought to the forefront anxieties and insecurities around liberal ideas of privacy produced by capital's need for more commodities in the form of personal information gathered from individuals and families. In addition, the state was itself interested in gathering data and personal information from Internet communication corporations, reconstituting notions of privacy and security for purposes of antiterror surveillance while collaborating with private enterprises through what Michael Birnhack and Niva Elkin-Koren call an "invisible handshake."[100] However, anxious to encourage online businesses as well as to support parental authority, one of the agencies of the state, the FTC, seemed to be moving uneasily between, on the one hand, demands of businesses and families and, on the other, competing sovereignties of state, capital, and individuals. Because the FTC consists of five commissioners who are appointed by the president and confirmed by the Senate, with three allowed from one party and two from the other, their regulatory work can change with administrations and be conflicted as well. In addition, agencies take on different roles, some actively promoting surveillance and some enjoined, as the FTC, to regulate it, so that these contradictory roles come to play into both the militarizing data and enabling mostly lax protections.

In the first five years of FTC data privacy regulation, from 1993 to 1998, it favored self-regulation, believing that the free market would ensure companies did not share personal data.[101] Finding that this did not happen, the FTC started to establish principles for self-regulation and turned to Congress for legislation.[102] In 1998, Congress passed the Child Online Privacy Protection Act (COPPA), requiring parental "opt in" consent before websites can collect information from children under thirteen years old.[103] Under this law, which became enforceable in 2000, online companies are required to get verifiable parental consent before gathering and selling personal information from children under thirteen. They also must post privacy policies online and protect the information gathered from children. They are prohibited from requiring children to give information as a requirement for participation on the Internet, such as for playing games online. In 2001, the FTC—the agency charged with preventing unfair or deceptive business practices—subsequently set guidelines to ensure legal compliance, including a "safe harbor" provision if companies followed software industry–approved guidelines.[104] Congress also created a COPPA commission, which issued suggestions that some legal scholars have considered more effective than the current legislation, but these suggestions were also designed so as not to restrict corporations and businesses. These suggestions included more public awareness, funding of better filtering software, and a greater focus on enabling voluntary self-regulation by Internet service and content providers.[105]

Prior to COPPA, the Communications Decency Act (CDA) of 1996, created after moral panics around online pornography, attempted to restrict children's access to sexually explicit materials on the web. This attempt was invalidated by the Supreme Court, however, which ruled that it violated the First Amendment.[106] The Court suggested several alternatives to the CDA, one of them being to provide some tolerance for parental choice, thereby giving parents "choice" even when few might know exactly what information was being collected, who was doing the collecting, or who was buying that information. The language of "choice" often leaves out the fact that consumers have limited knowledge about the products they purchase and that companies may not disclose key information about products to consumers. Despite its shortcomings, the CDA gave some parents a sense of control over their children's use of the Internet or social media.

COPPA included a "safe harbor" provision that allowed companies to self-regulate if their plans to follow the guidelines of the act could be approved by the FTC.[107] With the creation of "safe harbor," a variety of industries—from entertainment to technology to toys—could protect themselves if they kept to their regulatory guidelines, such as not buying or selling personal information from children. For instance, the FTC allowed one such agency—the Entertainment Software Rating Board (ESRB)—as a "safe harbor" program under the terms of COPPA.[108] The Entertainment Software Association also created its own "safe harbor" program in 2001, which was approved by the FTC to monitor game sites directed at children. Several other "safe harbor" applications have been approved after the act of 2000 and its amendments in 2012.

When COPPA was passed, legal scholars were concerned that it would be unable to protect children, given that its parental consent requirement was unlikely to be followed by parents every time a child logged onto a site. Further, once parental consent was given, the site operator could then do whatever they wished with the information gathered.[109] Joseph Zavaletta argues the law was designed to protect "web site operators from liability," especially through the "safe harbor" designation, and that individuals would face a very high burden of proof to be able to claim negligence if the website operator showed they had complied with the COPPA rule.[110] The FTC issued another report in 2000 on the topic of online privacy, noting that companies were collecting an enormous amount of information and that regulation was not sufficient even though it was the least-intrusive solution. Despite this finding, the FTC also stated that given that the companies were most technologically able to implement change, it made sense to have them develop tools to regulate themselves.[111]

The results of new laws about children's privacy have not been encouraging. Legal scholar Danielle Garber argues that although the FTC has been successful in getting companies to comply, parental vigilance is still required.[112] Others have refuted Garber's claim by concluding that in the age of social networking, the FTC's efforts have been ineffective, COPPA does not seek consent in any meaningful way, and creating thirteen years as a cutoff date leaves out the protection of other adolescents.[113] That continuation of data gathering means that regulations are weak or inadequate—"safe harbor" provisions actually weaken the law by creating possibilities for self-regulation. I argue that this weakness ultimately benefits the security state.

Although the FTC has prosecuted companies for not complying with COPPA,[114] it is still the case that media and Internet companies, and not only those marketing to minors, do not have a good record of ensuring consumer privacy. For example, one company, TRUSTe, became a "safe harbor" organization and thereafter launched its Children's Privacy Seal Program, but was found to be twice as likely to share personal information as companies without such a seal.[115] In 2000, the FTC settled the first lawsuit under COPPA with Toysmart.com,[116] and in 2004, the FTC settled a claim with the music company UMG Recordings over its collection of personal information from children below the age of thirteen. One of UMG's websites had specifically targeted young children, and did not obtain parental consent.

In 2001, the FTC gathered fines totaling $175,000 from six online companies, a miniscule amount given the size of the industry.[117] In 2009, the Electronic Privacy Information Center (EPIC), a nonprofit, brought a complaint to the FTC against a parental control software company, EchoMetrix, which was selling data collected from parents to third parties. EPIC stated in its complaint that the company used "unfair and deceptive trade practices by representing that the software protects children online while simultaneously collecting and disclosing information about children's online activities."[118] EchoMetrix settled the case by paying a $100,000 fine and agreeing to discontinue third-party information sharing. Many companies evaded the law by not designating themselves as targeting children under thirteen as consumers, and many complained that the costs of obtaining parental consent were too high. In 2011, the FTC evaluated its rule and found that it had not kept up with technology, especially mobile technology, geolocation, facial recognition, images, voices, and social networking. However, FTC leaders testified before Congress that it had been effective in enforcement, undertaking seventeen enforcement actions and getting more than $6.2 million in civil penalties.[119] That sum is small compared to the size of the industry. Given that the existing regulations were not as effective as they should be, in 2013 Congress added new regulations to COPPA to address the emergence of mobile and new social media technologies that were not covered previously. Definitions of personal information that cannot be collected without parental consent from children below thirteen include geolocation information, addresses, photos, cell phone identifiers, and audio and video files, as well as "persistent identifiers" (i.e., information gathered by cookies).[120] In addition, Congress provided more ways to obtain parental consent, streamlined the parental notification requirements, and made online service providers liable if they collected personal information from third parties.[121] It also asked the FTC to provide periodic reports on the "safe harbor" programs.

Many scholars argue that COPPA is ineffective for several reasons and that even recent regulatory changes do not make much difference to information gathering and selling. For instance, digital media researchers danah boyd, Urs Gasser, and John Palfrey testified to the US Senate that COPPA was ineffective because youth can lie about their age, companies can trick consumers into giving permission, uninvolved parents can remain so despite the need for consent, and, in some cases, children might need to contact sites if they need help or to communicate.[122] For instance, parental abuse can be a concern, especially for youth who are queer, transgender, or are seen to be a "problem." Boyd, Gasser, and Palfrey reported that some parents resented being told how to parent, and others supported their children in lying about their age. They recommended that the government amend COPPA to actually limit data-sharing or selling or how minors can be targeted. They suggested that the law should facilitate information deletion by request and let everyone know "when their data is being shared and with whom."[123] Other scholars argue that in the age of Facebook, there should be clearer information about the extent of information gathering done by companies and clearer language on websites that educates and informs consumers, including teenagers.[124] What seems clear is that in the United States, businesses often get away with violating the privacy of families and children, enabled by the necessities of education and learning as well as all sorts of activities facilitated by digital tools, such as state surveillance. The security mom and digital security mom's racialized fears and moral panics as well as the war on terror become the instruments used by marketers to produce insecurity.

The Obama administration showed concern for the data privacy anxieties of individuals, even as it ratcheted up programs such as Safe Communities to collect data for border control and antiterrorism uses.[125] In doing so, it implicitly supported the privacy rights of some individuals over those seen as threats to the nation, who were therefore excluded from exceptional citizenship. It also refused to protect the rights of all individuals against those corporations wanting to gather information to sell as commodities. In contrast, European courts and governments have mobilized on this front and individuals in the United States benefit from the data privacy collaborations between the EU and the United States. In 2014, the White House recognized that there remained many concerns by individuals regarding data privacy, and it laid out these issues in a report entitled *Big Data: Seizing Opportunities, Preserving Values*. Visible in the document is the importance given to enabling business and the economy. The document states that the "United States has long been a leader in protecting individual privacy while supporting an environment of innovation and economic prosperity."[126] It nods to Fourth Amendment rights, governmental transparency and efficiency, security of data, giving consumers control over their data, and biases in profiling, though it seems unclear if such concerns can translate into action, given the needs of the security state to surveil and collect information. A previous document on privacy policies, *Consumer Data Privacy in a Networked World: A Framework for Protecting Privacy and Promoting Innovation in the Global Digital World* (2012), proposed a Consumer Privacy Bill of Rights that would cover the privacy needs of all those not covered by existing laws, though it did not examine how the existing laws fall short of ensuring privacy.[127]

State and Law: Redefining Privacy and the Family

In promising security while collecting personal data from the Internet, businesses and the state intensify the ideology of the security/privacy exchange: the idea that one can only get security by giving up privacy.[128] In doing so, the political economy of insecurity is left out in this equation. On the one hand, the state and corporations are interested in collecting information that is deemed personal and on the other hand, they sell privacy and control. Here they do not replace liberal ideals of individual sovereignty with neo-liberal ideas of consumer as commodity, but rather deny the sovereignty of individuals while ensuring the sovereignty of corporations and businesses. The narrative of privacy produces a trade-off between individual privacy and state security that is used to justify state surveillance. It is apparent that public and private as concepts are being recuperated in shifting ways producing sovereign subjects pitted against each other. Corporations often defend their inability to grant consumers any sovereignty and blame the state for demanding information about individuals, while the state protects individual sovereignty with one hand—albeit that of some citizens—and takes it away with the other.

In this rearticulation of privacy and sovereignty, children have become private in new ways, as have parents, and mothers more specifically. Most of the "experts" working on children's Internet security suggest that a good parent (often a good mother) is one who can raise her children in privacy, one who can prevent her children from sharing private information on the Internet even while using it for educational and recreational purposes. Yet these experts also state that such privacy is never possible. Moreover, given a historical fear of children's sexuality and secrecy, children's digital native abilities turn them into strange Others, particularly children who are African American, Muslim, or Latino. Parental control, as technology and ideology, turns the "real" offline child—one that is assumed to be white and middle class—into one that exists "online" in spaces and virtual locations hidden from parents, thus materializing the digital profile. At the same time that information and data from parents and children become a material commodity that can be collected and sold by media and data-gathering corporations, the "real" child is also the one who must be hidden away from public scrutiny. The uses and capabilities of digital technologies as they are created by media corporations produce distinctions between online and offline, and muddy those distinctions as well. The suggestion, then, is either that the "offline" is real or, through insecurity, that the "online" is the secret real child who can hide from parents. As Beth Coleman and Clay Shirky argue, there is no virtual or real anymore, but simply configurations that mesh these together.[129]

Some scholars argue that legislation such as COPPA has completely left the question of children's privacy and autonomy in the hands of parents by assuming that children and parents have the same interests. Such laws, these scholars argue, have protected the *family's* privacy rather than that of the child.[130] Moreover, such legislation assumes parents have choices, as consumers. Yet such choices are not meaningful in the absence of widespread knowledge of corporate and state surveillance. Furthermore, parents' own gathering of web search histories, use of GPS software, and general use of parental control software have not emerged as an issue of children's privacy. This is because the "child" remains, once again, in this new technology as with earlier technologies, a consumer and a source of information as well as a product of surveillance, security, and privacy. Even those "children" who do not themselves participate in the Internet and social media have such an existence, produced by statisticians, demographers, NGOs, and development agencies of various kinds.

Inequality within the home and the production of patriarchal and heteronormative family norms continue with other sorts of legislations that assume that the home and family constitute a private domain. Often the private domain of the heteronormative and patriarchal family is even expanded, though such a private sphere is not accorded to families who are not white, Christian, or middle class. For instance, the "Stand Your Ground" laws in many states, which allow killing others in self-defense, evolved from the "castle doctrine" allowing persons, that is, white males, to defend themselves at home. Property and personhood based on race or class, of course, define who has ever had a "castle" to be protected. As of 2016, these laws were present in twenty-three other states, replacing the notion of self-defense only of one's home to self-defense anywhere that a person presumes they are under fear of death, creating "innumerable castles," as one legal scholar puts it.[131]

Meanings of privacy are historically specific. In the United States challenges over gender, race, and sexuality have created a broad area of privacy struggles in terms of individual autonomy and sovereignty, the lack of which can lead to both vulnerability and harm.[132] Definitions of privacy have changed from the now century-old Samuel D. Warren and Louis D. Brandeis's definition of privacy as the "right to be let alone,"[133] created in an era of privileged white patriarchal authority over a private sphere of the family. *Griswold v. Connecticut* (1965) introduced the penumbra idea, and *Katz v. United States* (1967) introduced the standard of "reasonable expectation of privacy."

The issue of data privacy has emerged from contestations between liberal ideals of the patriarchal private sphere, the privacy accorded and denied to citizens as sexual and racial subjects, corporations' right to market and gather consumer information as a matter of their free speech, and fears regarding data privacy and state surveillance. Edward Snowden's revelations concerning the surveillance of Americans and numerous others have also shifted definitions of individual privacy to include debates about an individual, corporate, or state control over personal digital data. Some of these revelations suggest how little support there is of liberal privacy rights for Muslims and immigrants deemed to be possible terrorists. Some scholars argue that struggles over control of personal data, as captured by corporations tracking individuals, have emerged as legal and technological problems,[134] in which the sovereignty of some individuals has been replaced by the sovereignty of data as a commodity that has exchanged value for private corporations.

What have emerged out of these struggles are limited and evolving notions of privacy, as well as its impossibility, available only to a select few. "Information privacy" has become particularly important. Legal scholar Danielle Garber defines information privacy as "control by an individual over data generated during Internet transactions that is either personally identifiable to that individual or which may be merged with other data to become personally identifiable to her."[135] Garber points out that privacy does not imply "total nondisclosure" but rather "selective disclosure."[136] But who does the "selection" is not clear in Garber's analysis, nor is it clear which individuals can have control over their personal data, since many companies track information without user knowledge, and the security state tries to gather as much information as it can about everyone. Privacy as control over personal information has become an important issue, particularly as Internet companies deal with laws outside the United States and with countries with very different historical contexts of privacy. The specter of terrorism has effectively constrained any control of private information by individuals. Some scholars argue that privacy has now been lost. Mark Andrejevic argues that we now have a "digital enclosure," which he describes as the "creation of an interactive realm wherein every action and transaction generates information about itself."[137] It is now well known that the digital enclosure is designed to produce data as commodity since digital media companies struggle over divergent legal interpretations of privacy in the United States and EU, for instance. Despite these concerns, the digital enclosure in a carceral state as a racial concept remains to be critiqued.

The American right to privacy, embedded in the history of race, sexuality, and power, has always been partial—possible for some groups but not for others. Privacy in terms of individual sovereignty remains an important liberal project for some, but it also provides a basis of exclusion for many who are deemed Other or too dangerous to be accorded this right. Both neoliberal and liberal discussions of privacy produce a white, middle-class, normative individual and family and erase the many others without this right. Even the call by children's advocates to balance children's privacy against their right to "protection, nurture, and care" or to consider children's rights as a "relational individual right" that balances the rights of individual and family,[138] may not take into consideration the fact that this balancing act remains a privilege foreclosed for racialized and sexual minorities.

"Antiterror" legislations such as the Patriot Act have enabled greater government surveillance of religious and racial minorities with fewer restrictions from the courts. In the context of the war on terror, many Americans accept the idea that national security requires giving up any right to privacy in general,[139] and data privacy in particular. More recently, with the Snowden revelations, some of this indifference has changed, and over time the Obama administration paid more attention to privacy protections because of uproars over corporate data breaches, leading some to argue for a "second wave" of privacy protections.[140] Although the government does pay attention to outcries against privacy breaches from companies or by certain state agencies, such attention seems to not abate welfare reductions or securitization, which have both become characteristic of the security state. Anil Kalhan argues that the expansion of immigration enforcement in the war on terror, along with new digital tools, constitutes an "emerging surveillance regime" or a "surveillance state" in which "automated immigration policing contributes to a broader transformation in kind that renders immigration status visible, accessible, and salient in more legal and social domains than ever before, and subject to routine monitoring and screening by a wide range of public and private actors."[141] Kalhan argues that new programs that are digitally connected and automated have enabled law enforcement at state, local, and federal levels to all become involved in policing immigrants—more so than was possible in previous projects. Yet, this practice has also led to function creep and errors. The result of such automated systems, then, is fear of loss of control over personal information for many, even for privileged groups. It is clear that privacy produces fearful exceptional citizens differentially concerned for loss of sovereignty, and a struggle over corporate sovereignty. Even before 9/11 or twenty-first-century immigration debates, the logic of the racialized security state meant that children (and adults) came under surveillance in ever more areas of social life, though in different ways and by different programs and projects. In many US cities, teenagers are subject to curfews that ban them from being on the street after 11:00 PM or midnight.[142] Schools have metal detectors, police, and "zero-tolerance" drug policies, as well as mandatory drug tests and searches—all of which are enforced in draconian ways on children of color. Thus, children in inner-city schools suffer much more invasive surveillance than do white children in more affluent schools districts.[143] Military recruiters and police officers in schools with more children of color have greater power over and access to these students, thereby acclimatizing them to an early connection with the military and criminal justice system and producing a system of "sorting" children along "lines of race, class, and gender."[144] Such sorting is especially a characteristic of neoliberal policies that provide surveillance systems to schools when they may not have proper furniture, books, or teachers.[145]

But the ideology of the assumed trade-off between privacy and security produced by parental control technologies suggests also a double bind: to be an exceptional citizen is to be transparent and have "nothing to hide," unlike a "terrorist" or "undocumented worker"; at the same time, to be an exceptional citizen is to claim the right to give up privacy.[146] For many children of color or low-income, immigrant, and Muslim families, having nothing to hide does not mean safety—the impossible desire intensifies racial difference thereby marking such subjects as outside exceptional, neoliberal citizenship. This pressure to be secret, then, sorts good mothers from bad and good parents from bad ones on the basis of older sedimented ideologies of race, gender, sexuality, and religion. It sorts on the basis of race, for instance, when African American women are deemed unable to provide security, when African American children are seen as "gang members," when "welfare moms" are denied state support, or when Latinos are assumed to be undocumented and "illegal." These figures then become pathologized as aberrant and dysfunctional parents and children, the mothers as unable to provide security, and the children as unworthy of it. Such dysfunctional parents and children can then be blamed for producing insecurity because they embody it.

Governmentalizing Terror and Surveillance: A Case Study

In the aftermath of the Boston Marathon bombings, Reddit user Chris Ryves created a thread to crowdsource information about the perpetrators of the bombing and enable the community of Redditors to provide ongoing and real-time breaking news about the event. As an image of the bomber surfaced, another Reddit user claimed to have found a match in a photograph of a missing teenager, Sunil Tripathi. Sunil was a South Asian college student who had been missing and whose parents were circulating his images on social media to locate him.

As the *New York Times* later reported, abusive and angry threats and messages began to appear on the Facebook page that had been set up to find Sunil.[147] His family called the FBI, which told them that Sunil was not a suspect, but they removed the Facebook page fearing that if Sunil found the abusive messages, he might harm himself. Some on Reddit saw this removal as further evidence that Sunil was the bomber, and this suspicion was heavily circulated on the network. It was also circulated by many so-called reputable journalists such as Luke Russert, on sites such as *BuzzFeed*, and across Twitter. A *Slate* article reported that even a *New York Times* reporter helped circulate the rumor, as did *Politico*. Sunil's parents' and sister's cell phones were inundated with abusive messages, many of which were Islamophobic, compounding their grief and worry at Sunil's disappearance.

In another case of racial profiling after the Boston bombing, two young Moroccan students, one who was seventeen, were wrongly identified by the *New York Post* as suspects with their images placed on the cover of the newspaper.[148] These two students went to watch the marathon but had left before the bombing. It is not clear how the *Post* found their photograph and why it placed it on its cover with the caption "Bag Men," though it is obvious that racial profiling played a role. Redditors also circulated the Moroccan students' image as possible suspects.[149]

Ultimately, the second bomber was identified by the police as Dzhokhar Tsarnaev, a Kyrgyzstani American teenager and brother of Tamerlan Tsarnaev, who was the main bomber and who died in a shootout with police. There was much soul searching on Reddit and other social media networks; Reddit's general manager, Erik Martin, apologized to Sunil's parents. The Redditor who had started the thread quit the site in April 2013, protesting that it was not a threat of lawsuits that made him close the thread and stating that users should consider Reddit a place for rumors rather than news.[150]

At the same time, Reddit received a massive publicity boost, with huge increases in traffic to the social network. According to the Pew Research Center, 6 percent of online adults (presumably from the United States) are Reddit users, with young white males as "especially likely" to use the network.[151] It is known for being "content agnostic" and for embracing both anarchic and libertarian tendencies, a pairing that makes libertarian ideas seem progressive. Erik Martin saw the Sunil Tripathi incident as a natural outcome of social media. As he told the *New York Times*, "The loss of personal privacy is an inherent issue to the Internet as a whole. . . . If you go out in public, you should expect that your photo is going to be taken somewhere by either the traffic cameras on the street or by some creepy-ass guy who takes your photo when you're not looking. Twitter has a creep factor, Facebook has a creep factor, but nobody ever really talks about that. They only talk about those things when they show up on Reddit. In reality, it's everywhere."[152] His colleague Alex Angel added, "I just don't understand why the blame was put on us and not on the outlets that did shoddy reporting. Reddit is just a bunch of normal people who are basically chattering. Major news sources put out the bad information without any verification, but we got all the blame. No one but Reddit was really held responsible."[153]

In sum, neither Reddit nor the more traditional news media outlets took responsibility for the circulation of content that was harmful to a family, and in particular, to a family that was nonwhite, immigrant, and South Asian, a family subjected to hate calls and unwanted media publicity in the midst of their grief and worry.[154] Redditors used blurry images to become armchair detectives, circulating information that cast suspicion on young South Asian and Middle Eastern young men as terrorists. While many Redditors hide their identities online, there is little popular interest in keeping others' privacy. As much as Reddit's powerful owners claim that privacy should not be expected in the Internet age, the network itself allows pseudonyms and anonymous postings. Its ability to make information viral is also dangerous, especially since widespread social ideologies tend to circulate rapidly, and Reddit is known for having some nasty sub-Reddits. Thus, it was not surprising that in a *New York Times* interview, Sunil's sister, Sangeeta, thoughtfully told the reporter, "One thing we've been struck by is how porous the space is between social media, the media, and law enforcement."[155] Such porosity means that the users of Reddit and other such media networks have a greater power to circulate their ideas than before with more limited media, ensuring that powerful groups become even more powerful.[156]

In a perceptive essay on how gender gets encoded into websites, Erin Maher writes that "while Reddit's voting algorithm itself may not discriminate, other aspects of the site's infrastructure and the way users interact with it and each other allow many opportunities for prejudice to impact a user's experience."[157] Reddit's notion of popularity and anonymity, she points out, has two problems. First, it allows the posts and will of a few "admins" to masquerade as the will of many users, since most users do not even sign onto Reddit and there are far fewer admins than users of the site. Second, because the site precludes any possibility of identification, the user then becomes by "default, a white, straight, cisgender man," relegating to the margins all those who don't identify as such.[158] Along with this default identity come racist and sexist jokes, which are very popular on the site. Maher writes that the Sunil Tripathi Reddit posts show that the site is unable to separate truth from fiction. This point became evident in subsequent news when, after the posting of Sunil's images, two Redditors were moved to travel to Boston to be part of the manhunt.[159] Maher's analysis that Reddit and Redditors lack any sense of accountability is echoed in Martin's defensiveness in the *New York Times* article, when he claimed that Reddit was itself a victim for accepting blame for what other sites also publicized.

Sunil Tripathi, Trayvon Martin, and other youth of color are often constructed as dangerous because their race, gender, or ethnicity has already placed them outside normative masculine citizenship.[160] The dubious link between South Asian or Moroccan suspects and the Boston bombing was made on a social media network in which a group of mostly white men, judging by the majority of Redditers, collectively took on the task of the police, surveilling the web for a match, helping the police not just with "tips" but by becoming detective-vigilantes themselves. In addition, there was little accountability for the harassment of the Tripathi family, though the families of the two young Moroccan men made suspects by the *New York Post* filed defamation lawsuits. Reddit's platform empowered already powerful communities to police the web, circulating racialized notions of South Asian and Muslim males as terrorists,[161] and revealing a collaboration between private corporations, media, and the police, as Sangeeta Tripathi observed. Sangeeta's remark about "porosity" signals the concern about loss of privacy, liberal or neoliberal, leading those who are nonwhite and non-Christian to fear such circulating power as well as the aggrandizement of powerful collaborations. This has enabled the use of predictive analytics for the purposes of data mining to seek out so-called terrorists.[162] In this context, it is important to know not only the corporations and commodities being created but also the parameters of the "data" being collected and the "profiles" being sought through such technologies.

All parents and families experience insecurity, though for very different reasons and with very different concerns and scales. The insecurities of white, middle-class parents come not from the police, the state, or racialized subordination but from their belief that new technologies make their children into victims of external predators, or into digital natives who threaten their parental authority. Family sovereignty is at stake, as well as white, middle-class parents' authority to keep their family private. For nonwhite and poor parents, privacy has never been a right that they could fight for. Ultimately, privacy remains a project of racialized power as well as a source of insecurity. The implication of individual agency in "giving up" privacy for security then is that privacy enables the uneven sovereignty of citizenship and the sovereignty of corporations enabled by the racial and patriarchal security state in the collaborations and tensions of empire under advanced neoliberalism.

CODA. The "Shooter"

I end this book with a final example of an exceptional US citizen: the "shooter," a subject with the sovereign's exceptional power to use violence. The shooter has long been a figure in US history and its gun culture, but has come to new public attention and media spectacle in recent years as the angry, white, Christian man who sees himself as dispossessed from his rightful place of power in the nation and exerting the sovereignty given to him by virtue of his gender and race. He hopes to save the imperial, security state through gun violence.[1] This figure has come to be associated with the mass shootings that are now commonplace in the United States, where numerous people are killed with high-caliber guns. Not called a killer, murderer, or criminal, this perpetrator is called a "shooter," and he is an exceptional US citizen who belongs to the past and a future of the racial, imperial security state. Though he may be antigovernment, often against any internationalism, seeing government as an illicit power over the freedom of white power, he works to save the security state, in which he finds the power of white supremacy. He recuperates the history of eighteenth- and nineteenth-century Manifest Destiny as well as affective power of twentieth- and twenty-first-century "first-person shooter" video games. The shooter combines an old genealogy of national independence, slavery, and settler colonialism, with a newer genealogy of neoliberal capital, media, and security.[2]

The American shooter and his culture are unparalleled across liberal democratic nations and thus exceptional—not because they are superior, but because few other countries (other than those in the midst of wars) allow their inhabitants to amass weapons as occurs in the United States. As the *Washington Post* describes, US gun culture is different in scale from any other. It has the highest rates of gun ownership, with an average of about nine guns for every ten Americans.[3] The ability to amass arsenals is combined with a lack of regulation over the numbers of guns that almost any person can purchase; consumers are able to purchase almost any kind of weapons, and many of these are high capacity because they are civilian versions of military-style weapons.[4] This link between weapons available for public consumption—or destruction—and military arsenals kept in homes is an example of the ways in which security and the state's exceptional right to kill is given to some citizens and to those who see these weapons as a private and public right, as militia but also as a right of private citizens. They gather weapons, but some of these collectors also carry out shootings in public spaces to display their sovereignty. This sovereignty of particular citizens is protected by regulations and law so that one protected group, white males, has the right to possess weapons and to kill Others.

Amassing arsenals of weapons within homes not just produces the private militia, who are believed protected by the Second Amendment, but also militarizes the home through the production of a patriarchy. As Jennifer Carlson has argued, gun culture in the United States has produced a "sovereign subject" who is to be distinguished from the citizen as a subject of rights, but who performs sovereign power that is shaped and enabled by the state.[5] I consider this subject possessing the sovereign right to become the patriarch, to control those in the home through an implicit or explicit threat of violence, and to have the sovereign right to claim the power to protect or kill within the home, but also outside of it. The privilege of whiteness endows these rights to one group of males, and they proclaim this privilege—often with spectacular acts of violence—against those who see the empire as waning or their rights as contested.

Yet, the racial claims of such sovereign subjects are also linked to their ability to possess guns because the possession of guns by noncitizens or by nonwhites leads to their dispossession of sovereignty—often their deaths—and the claims of sovereignty by the state and white sovereign subjects over them. Gun possession by black males, for instance, becomes a threat to the security state, and black men can be killed or their guns can be taken away by police, while gun possession by white males is protected and remains a right under the Constitution; racial difference operates through law, policing, and the entitlement to citizenship rights. Such a sovereignty is not new, but has newer insecurities and targets in the new century. Similarly, gun possession by other nonwhite groups can lead them to easily become targets of the state.

The numbers of gun deaths in the United States are striking. The CDC calculated 350 deaths of US citizens from terrorism between 2001 and 2013 compared to 406,496 killed in the United States by gun violence during that period.[6] The FBI counted 172 instances of mass killings between 2008 and 2011.[7] These numbers do not include injuries caused by these weapons. White male violence has been responsible for many massacres, though there are a few outliers. In addition, police killings are almost always the work of white males who use their weaponry to kill people of color. White males responsible for these massacres include Timothy McVeigh's bombing of the Oklahoma City Murray Building in 1995, which killed 168 people and left several hundred injured; Eric Harris and Dylan Klebold's killings at Columbine High School in 1999, with 12 killed and 21 injured; James Eagan Holt's massacre in Aurora, Colorado, in 2012 that killed 12 people and injured 70; Christian evangelist Robert Dear's killing of three people at a Planned Parenthood clinic in Colorado in 2015; Adam Lanza's massacre at Sandy Hook Elementary School in Newtown, Connecticut, in which 20 children and 6 others were killed; Steven Kazmierczak's killings at Northern Illinois University in 2008 in which 5 people were murdered and 21 injured. Killings at a church in Charleston and a Sikh temple in Milwaukee (which I discuss below) are important examples as well of killings by white men, some of whom clearly belong to or were followers of neo-Nazi groups. Many other incidents take place, often not even making it to the national news, but are mentioned in local reporting. These mass shootings do not include most other murders committed by guns, many of which are perpetrated on family or community members.

In contemporary media, the term "shooter" appears in specific contexts, particularly in relation to "mass shootings." It may, though not always, refer to the many men who kill their intimate partners on a regular basis in the long, violent history of heterosexuality and patriarchal, heteronormative masculinity. Journalists do not usually use the term to refer to those African American men in impoverished neighborhoods who are instead stereotyped as perpetrators of violence and made victims of the carceral state; the lax regulations of gun ownerships impacts these African American communities, as well as Latinx and Native communities the most, revealing how little the state cares about the deaths of nonwhite Americans. For the most part, journalists and media producers use the term "shooter" for white, American men, reserving the term "terrorist" for those who carry out the same type of violence but who happen to be Muslims.[8] Sometimes journalists use the term "gunman," but most of the time "shooter" is preferred.[9] Both terms, "shooter" and "gunman," are important to examine in understanding how these violent men come to be described in this way rather than a host of other ways. Further, they reveal what work is done by such terms that euphemistically disavow the violence of the exceptional citizen's sovereignty.

These terms are productive in several ways. They hide the excessive violence that is perpetrated through guns and their lethal and injurious consequences by muddying the divide between sport or play, and killing. They mark religious/racial/national difference, suggesting that the "shooter" is a domestic, white male Christian, while "terrorist" is a Muslim male influenced by non-Christian religious or political movements that have origins outside the United States. Other people of color with guns have also been seen as a threat to the state. These terms construct these killings as part of a historical narrative of the making of the exceptional nation, thereby endowing some of these perpetrators with a sovereignty that is shared with the US security state. To be sure, there are some exceptions to this usage of the terms "shooter" or "gunman"; however, most of media coverage follows the convention I describe.[10]

This conventional usage does not go unchallenged, and there are widespread calls for greater regulation and licensing of guns. While movements such as Black Lives Matter have been active in addressing the violence of police and policing that has long targeted African Americans, organizations such as the Southern Poverty Law Center have worked hard to oppose and disable white supremacist organizations. In the context of the war on terror, protests have also emerged over the inordinate attachment of the term "terrorist" to Muslim bodies, charging this usage with racial bias and Islamophobia. Because the term "terrorist" is notoriously vague and ambiguous, scholars have questioned the use of the term in the current context.[11] Activists working to prevent domestic and family violence have also asked that intimate partners (most often males) who kill or stalk their (mostly female) partners should also be called terrorists, coining the term "intimate terrorism" to describe the threat and violence emanating from such killings.[12] Some activists have begun to ask that all incidents of white racial violence be called terrorism.[13] Scholarly research has corroborated this demand. Aaron Winter points out, for instance, that despite stereotypes of Muslims as terrorists, the perpetrators of terrorism in recent decades have largely been members of white militia groups. Winter argues that the focus on Muslims as terrorists then covers up this history of white supremacy.[14] Even President Obama mentioned that gun killings far and away surpass any deaths from what is conventionally known as terrorism.[15]

That such violence continues and is enabled by a variety of laws as well as activism by many gun-rights groups and supported by numerous right-wing politicians means that the shooter is an exceptional citizen as well as a subject of white racism, nation, empire, and a lethal heteromasculinity, one whose sovereign right to kill is enabled by the US security state. Many politicians downplay the violence of the white supremacist groups, seeing terrorist threats as coming only from foreign, "Jihadist" groups.[16] Racism against African Americans belongs to a long history of the United States, but racism against Muslims is not distinct from that history, since black Muslims have long been the target of US government and white violence, and the surveillance and stereotyping of Muslims began before 9/11. Building on this longer history, the fears of twenty-first-century American empire's waning as well as the loss of white supremacy and white patriarchy have produced new racisms and racial identities, which legal scholars Muneer Ahmad and Leti Volpp suggest bring together racism against African Americans, Orientalism, Islamophobia, and the exclusion of immigrants and Asians from citizenship.[17] As I argue in this book, it also produces the violence of the exercise of sovereignty by white, Christian males who wish to save the imperial security state.

The Shooter and the Terrorist

The killing in Oak Creek, Wisconsin, in 2012 of five people and a policeman in a Sikh temple by Wade Michael Smith and the killing in 2015 of nine people in the Emanuel African Methodist Episcopal Church in Charleston, South Carolina, by Dylann Roof were, sadly, not the most lethal in US history.[18] The massacres at Columbine, Virginia Tech, and Sandy Hook all had more fatalities and injuries. But Oak Creek and Charleston were different in that nonwhite religious worshipers were targeted in private places of worship. The white supremacist "shooters"' attacks on churches and gurdwaras

(Sikh temples) targeted places that are understood to be "private" under the liberal right of free association, as well as the freedom of religion sanctioned by the First Amendment and the "equal protection" clause of the Fourteenth Amendment.[19] What these supremacists targeted was the right of these groups to be citizens, to be endowed with the right of freedom of worship that was accorded to white Christians. Consequently, the importance and resonance of these incidents were somewhat different from the public locations of other mass shootings such as the public school in Newtown or the movie theater at Aurora. Such violence reveals the right to sovereignty and citizenship of powerful groups who can take away such rights of those seen as nonwhite religious minorities. Despite this attack on the rights of these minority groups, politicians downplay the violence of the white supremacist groups, seeing terrorist threats as coming only from foreign, "Jihadist" groups.[20] Neo-Nazi groups that have transnational connections to similar groups in Europe, for instance, are seldom seen in the lens of transnational terrorism that is the label given to any Muslim who carries out similar acts. What this disavowal suggests is that the security state will not protect the rights of minorities and that liberal rights remain as disjunctive and discriminating as they have long been in United States and other imperial histories. White men are always seen as belonging to the nation, and their connections to international organizations is often ignored.

In both of these killings in Milwaukee and Charleston, the shooter emerged as an exceptional citizen, one whose violence was derived from the sovereignty endowed to white males. For the victims of these killings, and for many others who have to live with this violence and its threat in public spaces—especially with laws enabling "open carry"—these horrific and seemingly random murders produce insecurity and fear. This fear comes from the knowledge that the US government is unwilling and also unable to completely surveil the numerous white males who belong to neo-Nazi groups; it thus seems unable to address the violence of white sovereignty or work to protect others from such violence, especially if compared to the massive mobilization of surveillance, preemptive detentions, and killings of those Muslims seen as terrorists. Instead, it has allowed sovereignty to be in the hands of private individuals, such as neo-Nazis, and has also enabled the proliferation of corporate private prison systems, racist police, and private militia.

In the Charleston shootings, the distinction between terrorist and shooter became a point of public debate. The FBI had to decide whether to term the killings as "domestic terrorism" or a hate crime, eventually deciding on the latter. That these terms, "terrorism" and "hate crime," are often pitted against each other means that racism and white sovereignty—often associated with hate crimes—is made to be distinct from terrorism. Director of the FBI James Comey explained why he did not believe Charleston was an act of terrorism, saying, "Terrorism is an act done or threatened to in order to try to influence a public body or the citizenry, so it's more of a political act and then, again, based on what I know so far, I don't see it as a political act."[21] This argument refused to acknowledge the inherently political nature of this racial violence, designed to prevent nonwhite groups from access to their right to worship and to private assembly.

Definitions of terrorism are not clear or stable across national and international law, and even US federal law splits the term into "domestic" and "international" versions.[22] As the ACLU summarizes, according to the USA Patriot Act, signed into law by George W. Bush in 2001: "A person engages in domestic terrorism if they do an act 'dangerous to human life' that is a violation of the criminal laws of a state or the United States, if the act appears to be intended to: (i) intimidate or coerce a civilian population; (ii) influence the policy of a government by intimidation or coercion; or (iii) to affect the conduct of a government by mass destruction, assassination, or kidnapping. Additionally, the acts have to occur primarily within the territorial jurisdiction of the United States and if they do not, may be regarded as international terrorism."[23] Despite the fact that this definition of "domestic terrorism" can be used to describe white supremacist massacres in Charleston and Oak Creek, police and prosecutors were reluctant, as was Comey, to use the term, calling these "hate crimes" instead. It was not surprising that some commentators challenged Comey's decision, arguing that Roof's act was indeed domestic terrorism as it was designed to threaten a community and culture.

Consequently, maintaining the distinction between the shooter and the terrorist is not always easy for the US government, given public protests and outpourings of anger at lax gun laws as well as right-wing, conservative politics that support white racial sovereignty. Such protests were visible also after the Orlando massacre of Latinx queers in June 2016. Public protest that the killer, Omar Mateen, targeted LGBT persons and Latinx ones in particular, clashed with police and FBI claims that he was anti-American and working in sympathy with extremist groups in the Middle East.[24] Although Mateen had little contact with Al Qaeda or ISIS, he was seen as a terrorist because he was a Muslim, and because he did claim that he was aligned with radical groups in the Middle East. However, the media also designated the massacre as terrorist violence and as a foreign threat, in the absence of any evidence that Mateen was at all connected to groups in the Middle East or South Asia that are associated with radical Islam. Mateen's father called his son's massacre a terrorist act, eager to dissociate himself from his son's politics.[25] The police called it "domestic terrorism" though, as Juan Cole pointed out, Mateen's motivations did not fit the definition of domestic terrorism because he did not seem to have the political motives that the term requires.[26] Media opinion, such as that by Stephen Donnan in *The Huffington Post*—using a more intersectional analysis combining race, sexuality, and gender—claimed Mateen was motivated by "homophobic terrorism," noting the extent of the violence perpetrated against LGBT communities more generally.[27] Even this more intersectional approach associated homophobia with terrorism and thus with something that was not to be seen as American. Donnan hopes that the charge of terrorism might properly address the fearfulness and violence caused by homophobia, since Mateen was also targeting trans bodies.

Such outsourcing and pinkwashing of homophobia then also left out the complexity of race and sexuality: that most of the victims were young people of color and many were trans people of color.[28] By placing Mateen into the category of "terrorist," his homophobia could become a "foreign" and supposedly Muslim bias, relying on stereotypes of Muslim cultures as homophobic. Claims of American national protection and progress could then be made through "pinkwashing," the idea that the United States is a country that protects LGBT persons and that Muslim and other non-European and American countries are intolerant.[29] That Mateen had been born and brought up in the United States, had seldom expressed any religious sentiment, and was considered by those who knew him a disturbed and unstable young man could then be forgotten if the term "terrorist" were applied to him. Further, his questioning earlier by the FBI in connection with terrorism and subsequent release simply became evidence of the inadequacy of the FBI to find terrorists and the need to redefine the term "terrorist," beyond those networked to ISIS, to include "lone wolf" Muslims who acted in allegiance with ISIS. While it was only the "shooter" who had been understood to be acting as the "lone wolf" and the terrorist was always the figure of collective Muslims, now the Muslim terrorist was also regarded as acting alone. Keeping the link between Muslims and terrorism, the *New York Times* called Mateen "a lone terrorist" rather than addressing the problem of the category itself.[30] Even Mateen's father called him a terrorist while having no clue why Mateen had done such a horrendous act; becoming the "good Muslim" here meant that Mateen's father had to condemn his son.

Yet, Mateen was also like many other workers, especially those in the security industries, whose militarism and violence were harnessed for profit. His violence might not have been unusual at all. He had worked as a security guard at a private security firm, G4S, even though he was unstable and talked about hating many groups of people including blacks, women, Jews, and lesbians, as well as threatening to kill people.[31] G4S is a British-based global corporation that offers security services, including personnel and security systems, all over the world and works in Israel to run jails, checkpoints, and interrogation centers.[32] That he was able to work there for six years makes clear how much a toxic masculinity made up of anti-Semitism, racism, homophobia, and misogyny may have been normalized at his workplace. Yet, such a militarized masculinity could not be called American and could then only be terrorism because Mateen was a Muslim.

Gun Ownership and American Identity

The common practice of differentiating the "shooter" from the "terrorist" and naming some (white, nonimmigrant) violent criminals as shooters constructs the violent, male, white heterosexual individual as an exceptional citizen. There are several ways in which the term "shooter" produces the exceptional citizen. First, it places this figure in the historical genealogy of the making of the American nation, specifically the long history of settler colonialism, Manifest Destiny, and westward expansion. Second, it produces him as a sovereign citizen by claiming the role of the military through the power of owning military-grade weapons as well as through interpretations of the Second Amendment of the US Constitution that suggest he is part of a militia in protection of the nation. In this configuration, the costs of gun violence (not limited to monetary costs) become normalized, acceptable, ordinary, and unremarkable. Third, it makes him an individual with a particular history of loss, family, and alienation or mental illness, in contrast to the terrorist whose motivations are never individualized and are attributed solely to a collective religious or cultural identity. Fourth, the shooter is linked to the subject of new media through the pedagogy of the video game—an extension of the subjects I discussed in the previous chapter. The shooter embodies the technologized masculinity of the gamer, particularly the masculinity represented in what are called first-person shooter games that have links to military training and to technologized futures of youth who affectively learn to be soldiers and citizens through playing these games.[33] Finally, because this subject is an American citizen and belongs to a racial majority, no pre-vention, predictive analytics, or profiling are used by the state to prevent their violence—no mobilization of Homeland Security need occur. To be sure, there have been efforts by the FBI and groups such as the Southern Poverty Law Center to identify white supremacist groups, with some impor-tant successes in incarcerating leaders in the movement. Yet, most of these violent men are not surveilled, because of the unclear boundary between extreme and ordinary racism in a country suffused with racial violence. The violence of white groups is seldom seen as a problem of a culture or group and its paranoid desire for weaponry. Instead, it is normalized in a variety of different ways, as individual psychological illnesses, as normal and expected expressions of rage at the loss of white entitlement, or as forms of endemic and naturalized intimate partner and sexual violence. In recent decades, white militia movements have become more lethal, becoming not only antigovernment but also anti-immigrant and explicitly racist.[34]

As a product of a history of American white settler masculinity, the shooter's sovereignty as an American citizen is supported by numerous right-wing, pro-gun, and neo-Nazi organizations; the United States has long been a culture in which exceptional citizens feel free to use violence to exert power over others. Carl Schmitt's notion of the state as having the sovereign right of violence through suspension of law enables us to account for the long history of racial violence in the United States through a white racial sovereignty in which in-dependence and statehood were produced through militias and settlers.[35] In the making of the nation, sovereignty was dispersed to slave owners, settlers, and white persons who had the right to use violence over nonwhites to cre-ate the nation. Sovereignty was thus part of the right to be an exceptional citizen and to carry and amass weapons in this long history. From the militias of the wars of American independence to the anti-immigrant militias of the late twentieth and twenty-first centuries, guns have been part of US settler colonialism. Advocates of nineteenth-century westward expansion as well as Civil War politicians exacerbated and celebrated gun cultures.[36] In the process, they produced mythologies of white masculinity related to guns.[37] Police became armed in the middle of the nineteenth century, and labor pro-tests were met with lethal police violence.[38] Shooting with guns became a sport, especially in regions in the northeast, where guns were being manu-factured; shooting has remained a sport, with many shooting ranges where almost anyone can participate and video games that include battles, war, and a plethora of weapons.[39] Although it cannot be said that all those playing such video games or going to shooting galleries are ideologically unified or belong to neo-Nazi organizations, the ubiquity and conjoining of pleasure and violence produce subjects who naturalize violence as sport.

Along with the ability of white men and women to collect and use guns, gun possession by black Americans has long been an area of struggle. Leaders of the National Rifle Association (NRA), the main progun organization that has a great deal of influence on Congress, claim that gun control laws are racist because such laws prevented blacks from fighting back, yet the NRA was created to prevent African Americans from having guns,[40] and now it has no response to the carnage caused by guns in communities of color. If the "slave codes" in colonial America forbade slaves from owning guns, voting, or gathering after the Civil War, Black Codes in the South were vagrancy laws used to constrain African Americans' labor mobility through criminalization and forbade them from owning guns.[41] Over a hundred years later, fear of the Black Panthers and their display of guns at the state capitol in Sacramento, California, led then-governor Ronald Reagan to advocate for gun control in the state, even though he was a member of the NRA and advocated against gun control.[42] African American gun ownership has long been seen as a threat, as Adam Winkler argues, from the beginning of the United States to the present day.[43] In the context of what Michelle Alexander calls the "new Jim Crow," the excuse of searching for gun possession is often the reason police give for stopping black Americans on the street, for their imprisonment, or for killing them, while white Americans claim their constitutional right to carry and often assert this right openly without similar repercussions.[44]

This long history helps explain the numerous states and laws that normalize the behavior of those whites who amass guns, including powerful assault weapons that are similar to or copies of those used by military. These arsenals become part of ordinary American life and the home, taken as simply part of "American culture." In such a context, gun ownership becomes part of exceptional American citizenship, enabling male control over the home and the public space. Numerous federal and state laws allow people to carry guns.[45] Often these laws allow carrying openly in public spaces.[46] Normalizing possession of such lethal weaponry, Congress banned the Centers for Disease Control from researching gun violence,[47] and enacted laws protecting gun manufacturers from liability due to the harmful and lethal use of their products. One recent example of this impunity is the Protection of Lawful Commerce in Arms Act, signed into law by George W. Bush in 2005,[48] in the midst of his war on terror and invasions of Iraq and Afghanistan. The federal assault weapons ban of 1994 expired in 2004, and Congress has since refused to pass a new ban. As I have argued in previous chapters, weak regulations enable private sovereignties to flourish.

Although mass shootings have led to more focus on background checks, there are numerous loopholes, and much information falls through the cracks between bureaucracies. For instance, Dylann Roof, the Charleston mass murderer, was able to buy a gun, even though he had a felony drug conviction, because the clerk was unable to reach a police officer who could verify Roof's record within the mandatory three-day waiting period. According to the Gekas amendment to the federal background checks required by the Brady Bill, if a gun dealer does not hear back from the police within three days, he can sell a gun to the customer.[49] Because this particular dealer did not hear back, he sold the gun to Roof—with disastrous consequences. Even if the customer goes on to murder people, as Roof did, the gun dealer faces no penalties.[50]

The remarkable sanctioning and normalization of gun ownerships and deaths enable pervasive violence and insecurity. The US government does little to prevent this violence, focusing instead on external foreign agents as alleged terrorists. Such a notion of "foreign" threat is masculinist and patriarchal because it gives immunity to violence and power in the home, the domestic space. Feminist activists have pointed out that violence is more likely to come from within the home/nation rather than from outside, pointing to the numbers of women killed in their homes by their intimate partners.[51] Yet, the NRA and gun manufacturers oppose any attempt to regulate guns, even in the face of the horrific killings in 2012 of children at Sandy Hook Elementary School in Newtown, Connecticut. Although gun deaths have led many to advocate for stronger background checks on gun purchasers, the power of the gun lobby as well as collaborations between gun manufacturers, gun rights groups, and many Republican politicians and statehouses reveal that white American men's desire to amass firearms remains formidable and unchallenged. Although the majority of Americans have come to support background checks (though with loopholes, such as the one enabling Dylann Roof to purchase weapons), and the number of US households with guns has been decreasing since the 1970s, the numbers of deaths and injuries remain astonishingly high. By some surveys, gun ownership has fallen from 50 percent of households having guns in 1970 to 35 percent in the 2010s. Yet the number of guns collected has gone up,[52] suggesting that fewer people buy guns but those who do, buy several. Mass shootings have also increased.[53] Although statistics about gun deaths are alarming, even more alarming— and often forgotten by those advocating gun regulation—are the statistics on those injured by violence. In 2013, guns killed approximately 30,000 people in the United States, and about 20,000 of those were killed by suicide (mostly youth). Others killed include those in minority communities, women murdered by intimate partners, and those killed by gun accidents.[54] What is not mentioned are the 100,000 people injured by guns each year who are kept alive by modern medicine—many of whom would not have survived without such medical intervention, and who need enormous resources to heal and to live with disabilities. Scott Martelle, writing in *The Los Angeles Times*, calculated that the monetary costs of gun violence in 2012 was $229 billion a year, a sum that includes medical, legal, prison, and lost wage costs.[55] What cannot be monetized and is even more tragic are the loss of loved ones, family, and friends, and the injuries to communities and neighborhoods. The fear caused by private armories is not to be underestimated. Moreover, the effect of this economy globally is considerable. American guns wreak havoc around the world, arming other security states, which spend vast sums on military;[56] the costs of that violence are incalculable—or perhaps, a calculation few might want to make even in neoliberal times when monetary value is assigned to almost every part of life. Neoliberalism's contradictions in this case mean that calculation and risk assessments are abrogated in the face of the sovereignty of white, Christian, American masculinity.

Discrepant Consequences

Many right-wing politicians suggest that the only response to massacres is prayer,[57] but what is meant here is prayer by white Christians, since mass shootings have targeted those seen as religious Others. Although many of the perpetrators are given long prison sentences or even the death penalty, some are killed and some kill themselves during these massacres. Despite the individual punishments, the exceptionalism of the figure of the shooter is visible in the shooter's contrast with the terrorist. In the aftermath of massacres deemed "terrorism," large populations and groups are surveilled, imprisoned, and deported, and billions of dollars of weaponry and militarization are used by the state. In contrast, in the wake of shootings by white men, there are no public warnings about white supremacy, no billboards or subway signs asking people to "say something" if you see white supremacy.

It is striking that given the massive homeland security infrastructure that is in place to prevent terrorism, most gun regulations seem impossible to enact by Congress. Nonwhite populations and religious groups are preemptively detained, but not white Christian males. Such detention is considered an infringement on the rights of citizens, not a mode of preventing violence (though I am not advocating such detentions of anyone). There is little done about white men collecting more and more guns; the racial violence by the state and its police means that nonwhites are much more likely to be killed, detained, or harassed if they do the same. Because of the pervasiveness of racism across the country, many of those white men fade into being "ordinary" citizens, and their numbers and powers mean that surveillance and profiling does not happen to the extent that it can for nonwhite groups. In general, policing and the carceral system reveal these differences, the violence of which has led to the Black Lives Matter movement and numerous protests by activists. As a powerful majority that controls the state and its powers of violence, white males are not subject to stereotyping as a group in the same way as are nonwhites; they are also recognized as individuals rather than groups. Their connections with transnational neo-Nazi organizations can also escape scrutiny, as happened with Dylann Roof as well as Wade Michael Page, the killer in the Milwaukee Sikh temple massacre. As such, they are not considered worthy of surveillance by government security agencies, though there is some monitoring by the FBI.[58] There is no "material support" statute allowing any connection with "terrorist" groups to be seen as a criminal offense (as I revealed in chapter 3) similar to that which criminalizes Muslims. Connections with and support of transnational white supremacist organizations are not grounds for searches or surveillance. For instance, the Southern Poverty Law Center, which has done outstanding work in tracking white militias and racial violence perpetrated by them, saw the Wisconsin killer, Wade Michael Page, as simply one of thousands. They had tracked him, and he had come to their attention because of his affiliations with neo-Nazi rock bands. Mark Potok, SPLC spokesman, said to the *New York Times*, "We were not looking at this guy as anything special until today. *He was one of thousands.* We were just keeping an eye on him."[59]

What happened in the Sikh temple in Oak Creek, Wisconsin, where Wade Michael Page gunned down six people with a high-capacity assault weapon, was then the work of an ordinary man, "one of thousands." Yet Page was affiliated with a large, networked, transnational neo-Nazi movement. Dylann Roof, the neo-Nazi perpetrator of the Charleston massacre, was similarly not under any kind of surveillance. A week before the murders, he was even stopped by police, who found a part of an assault weapon in his car along with several gun magazines capable of killing many people in seconds, but he was let go because "a crime wasn't committed."[60] It was only after the murders that his Facebook page was surveilled, showing his allegiance to neo-

Nazi organizations and his racist ideas. Roof's treatment by police reveals how differently the law operates for white men; there is little doubt that the FBI would have operated very differently had he been Muslim or black. For Roof, there was no preemptive detention, no suspicions caused by the presence of an assault weapon and its magazine, probably because such weapons are all too common among white males and they are seen as a constitutional right.

The Problem of Hate Crimes Designations

Designating the massacres committed by white men as hate crimes is not a clear-cut solution to white racial sovereignty and its violence. Jelani Cobb, writing in the *New Yorker*, took issue with calling the Charleston massacre a hate crime, connecting it to a long history of murders committed by the Ku Klux Klan, and stating that the murders instead fit the legal definition of domestic terrorism.[61] In the case of the Milwaukee massacre, on the other hand, many Sikh groups successfully lobbied for calling it a hate crime to signal that Sikhs were often targets of racial discrimination and hate within a longer racial history. They did so because it was a struggle to get prosecutions under hate crime statutes for killers of Sikhs. Designation of an act of violence as a hate crime can be difficult if an individual is not seen as belonging to a particular class or group that is subject to prejudice. For example, it wasn't until 2009 that federal hate crime law covered violence based on sexual orientation and gender identity. While there are federal statutes against hate crimes, many states do not have such statutes. In the case of the Charleston massacre, Dylann Roof was charged with a federal hate crime because South Carolina does not have a hate crime statute. Having a state statute would have made it easier to charge Roof and to add more penalties. That the state does not have such a statute is also a result of racism. Activists in the state, such as the head of the state's NAACP chapter, Lonnie Randolph Jr., said that white supremacy is behind the lack of hate crime statutes in the state, arguing that "this is the state that taught America how to hate."[62]

But the hate crime statute also individualizes the crime, holding a person rather than a group responsible. Each of these white, male shooters is then understood as having a personality disorder, mental illness, or dysfunctional personal history. Such individualizing, as Katy Pal Sian argues, "exceptionalizes racism" as the behavior of "one particular racist rather than the problem of an embedded societal racism."[63] Within the hate crime framework, the Charleston massacre becomes the work of a disturbed individual, rather than one with racist sympathies that were encouraged by a host of individuals and institutions within and outside the United States, including the military.[64] Wade Michael Page was both a neo-Nazi and an army veteran, and this mixture of institutional and group identities requires us to consider both the American state and a long history of imperial violence as key factors in his violence. Page's background illustrates US military violence in terms of racial violence, colonialism, and empire. Dylann Roof had links to neo-Nazi organizations, and his website was filled with evidence of racism, white supremacy language, and photographs as well as a racist manifesto. His website was discovered, after the massacre, not by FBI or by police, but by a blogger.[65] What seems clear is that the American state does not represent white terrorism as a coherent and concerted project, or as a "rogue" transnational network, as it does other militant groups such as Al Qaeda. Yet, as Neel Ahuja argues, these groups are transnational, linked, and networked.[66]

Many commentators have argued that the shootings at Oak Creek were misdirected—that Page believed Sikhs were Muslims.[67] Such claims sometimes emerge from Muslim groups sensitive to continued Islamophobia, discrimination, and persecution in the United States and also from other South Asians who narrate, even in diaspora, the long history of the Indian subcontinent and the violence of Partition that divided Sikhs from Muslims.[68] There is also continued discrimination in India against Muslims, fueled by the Partition of 1947 and, more recently, by powerful, right-wing Hindu nationalism. Such histories are also transnational in their ongoing production of cultural and religious identities; these transnational identities prevent some in these immigrant communities from working together across national and religious divides. Recent Hindu nationalism in India has had an impact on diasporas, creating divisions between communities based on religion and separating Hindus, Sikhs, and Muslims (especially first-generation ones) even if they all come from the same region or nation. When Sikhs insist they were not the intended targets, they invoke a mode of survival, a mode of Islamophobia, and a willful forgetting of the fact that whereas in the 1980s Sikhs were seen as terrorist and militants in India, now Indian Muslims bear the brunt of such surveillance—a transnational Islamophobia that has emerged over the last decade.[69]

The claim that Sikhs were killed in a case of "mistaken identity" does not account for the fact that the targets of white terror are not one particular, religious community but a diverse group of brown and black people—a vaguely defined group of targets who "look Muslim,"[70] and who are all accused of taking the nation away from whites. White Americans have long targeted violence against African Americans, Asian Americans, Latinos, Jews, and Native Americans.[71] More recently, they have targeted LGBT people, especially LGBT people of color. Although African Americans have long been the target of white lethal violence—from slavery and Jim Crow to the wars on crime and drugs—South Asians (including Sikhs), Arabs, and Muslims have similarly endured over a century of such violence, but have emerged more visibly as targets of white lethal violence since 9/11.[72] Sikhs and Muslims have been killed as a result.[73] Muslim individuals and groups have been surveilled, targeted, and incarcerated; Latinx families are being separated by deportations, and the impoverishment of Native Americans continues, as does violence against African American communities. Attacks on Muslims are connected also to a long colonial history of Orientalism and geopolitics of the so-called Middle East.[74] The history is also a racial one, given how black Muslims have been treated in the United States.[75]

Gamers, Violence, and Masculinity

With the advent of digital technologies, the shooter's ludic history moves from shooting galleries to virtual environments of war and battle. Now the exceptional citizen is trained to be a soldier through online games. The advent of the "first-person shooter" video game is also part of the genealogy of the shooter, masking violence as a game. The US Army in 2002 released its own virtual platform, America's Army.[76] Designed as a first-person shooter game and recruiting tool, it allows anyone to play military games as well as learn about weapons, tactics, practice shooting, or military careers.[77] Although this game reveals the close connections between such games and the military, numerous other games have been created and the genre is tremendously popular and profitable. Many game companies market the games by citing a close connection with the military and the transfer of technology from military to consumer products.[78] In 2012, for instance, the *Atlantic* reported that *Call of Duty: Black Ops II* and *Medal of Honor: Warfighter* had some of the highest first-day sales of any games. They are set in places such as Somalia, Pakistan, Yemen, Bosnia, Philippines; they combine rationalizations of war with realistic details of location and military tactics that seem to have come from classified military information.[79] War is in distant places, against brown and black people, and thus these games share some key American ideologies of empire. With the popularity of such games across many communities, the ability to enact the violence of the exceptional citizen becomes available, albeit virtually and transnationally, to more than just white American males.

Global players share the ability to be perpetrators of this violence, even as consumers and audiences, popularizing through pleasure and play the work of empire and its white sovereignty. Jennifer Terry has argued that the proliferation of combat videos on YouTube that seem to be taken from both the US military (and mostly by white males in the military) and other groups incorporate "visual codes" that are shared with first-person shooter games so that combat becomes domesticated into everyday life.[80]

In general, those who identify as "gamers" tend to be masculine, anti-women, and antifeminist.[81] Most of those who spend long hours playing such games do not call themselves gamers or have violent tendencies—and clearly games do not represent reality.[82] However, there is a link between heteromasculinity, expressions of misogyny, and such games.[83] First-person shooter games, as researchers have found, are not about lonely individuals but rather about participating in gaming communities and about making connections and relationships with other gamers.[84] Yet such communities are male-centered and homosocial, and often become misogynistic, expressing hate and violence toward women.[85] This tendency became evident with the rise of what was called "GamerGate" in 2014, when media critic Anita Sarkeesian and game developers Brianna Wu and Zoë Quinn were targeted by gamers for creating games for women and for critiquing sexism in the gaming industry. They became recipients of hate-filled messages and threats of sexual violence and death, compelling them to go into hiding.[86] Much of this assault was conducted over Twitter using the hashtag #GamerGate. One of these gamers, whose name was not made public by police or press, promised to carry out "the deadliest school shooting in American history" if Sarkeesian was allowed to give a lecture at Utah State University.[87] Although the gaming industry promised to do more about diversity, it has proven difficult for companies to change their profit-making habits, suggesting that sexism in the culture is hardwired into these games and the business models of the industry. Nor does it seem to be possible to stop this kind of online threat and violence. Amanda Hess has noted that laws are often inadequate for the purpose, and the FBI has other priorities, seeing child porn and celebrity stalking as more important.[88] Gamer communities have become online spaces for expressions of sexual violence that can silence, harass, and frighten many players. Male power is expressed as violent and threatening, but also as contained by the game, and thus online rather than "real." Despite these claims, such power does not remain contained in virtual worlds and communities. First-person shooter games normalize this violence, producing online fraternities that become part of everyday life. The misogynistic violence expressed by these gamers is not just part of these new forms of entertainment, since such entertainment has longer histories. "First-person shooter" games have "real" counterparts in the "shooting galleries" that allow people to use any kind of weaponry in target practice for sport.

Neither male violence nor white supremacy is new, as they emerge from long histories of settler colonialism and slavery in the United States. Histories of racism, neoliberal insecurities, and dispersed state sovereignties create violent insecurities for white, Christian men, many of whom perceive themselves as victimized by a long list of groups as well as national and global threats. Interpretations of the Second Amendment that enable gun ownership are both a sign of a state that is unable to control these groups, a sign of tacit state support of white, Christian, and American heteromasculinity and the dispersal of sovereignty to this group. Despite the virulence and prevalence of neo-Nazis, no elected representative in Congress has suggested denying these groups the ability to buy guns if they belong to these groups in the same way that gun control advocates are trying to prevent those listed on what are called "no-fly" or "terrorist lists" from being able to make such purchases. Indeed, if there were any discussion about denying gun ownership to those listed in the FBI's list as belonging to neo-Nazi groups, it would certainly raise the question of their constitutional rights. Given that neo-Nazi organizations are transnationally connected organizations advocating violence, murder, and race war, one might argue for greater concern over their ability to connect, communicate, and arm their followers.[89] Such concerns for constitutional rights, however, do not trouble congressional leaders who, after the Orlando massacre in June 2016, are now seeking to take guns away from those on "terror lists," though these individuals may not have committed any crimes. As sovereignty is dispersed under neoliberalism, and as histories of race and empire continue to subtend citizenship, both militarism (in the form of the shooter or the spy) and humanitarianism (in the form of the NGO worker or the humanitarian) keep alive US exceptionalism through the work of the exceptional citizen.

Introduction

1. My thanks to Srimati Basu for bringing the Tennessee sign to my attention.

2. Jennifer Musto, *Control and Protect: Collaboration, Carceral Protection, and Domestic Sex Trafficking in the United States*, repr. ed. (Oakland: University of California Press, 2016).

3. Patrick Wolfe, *Traces of History: Elementary Structures of Race* (London: Verso, 2016).

4. Timothy Mitchell, "The Limits of the State: Beyond Statist Approaches and Their Critics," *American Political Science Review* 85, no. 1 (1991): 77–96; see also Simon Hallsworth and John Lea, "Emerging Contours of the Security State," *Theoretical Criminology* 15, no. 2 (2011): 141–57.

5. My work focuses on both the "unease" that seems to pervade social life in many sites and the desire for security as both a desire for the "private" (through a sense of public/private divide) that recuperates home, nation, territory, and for difference in the making of citizenship and community. The proliferation of theories of insecurity, precariousness, unease, and disposability, though having disparate genealogies, suggest a broader thematic that has emerged in many scholarly works. See, for instance, Judith Butler, *Precarious Life: The Powers of Mourning and Violence* (London: Verso, 2006); Didier Bigo, "Globalized (in)Security: The Field and the Ban-Opticon," accessed July 18, 2016, http://www.people.fas.harvard.edu/~ces/conferences/muslims/Bigo.pdf; Didier Bigo, "Security and Immigration: Towards a Governmentality of Unease," *Alternatives: Global, Local, Political* 27 (2002): 63–92; Didier Bigo and Anastassia Tsoukala, eds., *Terror, Insecurity and Liberty: Illiberal Practices of Liberal Regimes after 9/11* (New York: Routledge, 2008).

6. Barry Buzan, Ole Wæver, and Jaap de Wilde, *Security: A New Framework for Analysis* (Boulder, CO: Lynne Rienner, 1997).

7. One of the most important ethnographies of neoliberalism was carried out by Faye Harrison, who showed how neoliberal policies changed the lives of individuals

and altered their communities: Faye Harrison, "The Gendered Politics and Violence of Structural Adjustment," in *Situated Lives: Gender and Culture in Everyday Life*, ed. Louise Lamphere, Helena Ragoné, and Patricia Zavella, 451–68 (New York: Routledge, 1997). Also see, for instance, Butler, *Precarious Life*; Bigo, "Globalized (in)Security"; Bigo, "Security and Immigration"; Bigo and Tsoukala, *Terror, Insecurity and Liberty*.

8. Nikolas Rose, *Governing the Soul: The Shaping of the Private Self*, 2nd ed. (London: Free Association Books, 1999).

9. David Harvey, *A Brief History of Neoliberalism* (Oxford: Oxford University Press, 2005), 2.

10. Nikolas Rose, "Governing 'Advanced' Liberal Democracies," in *Foucault and Political Reason: Liberalism, Neo-Liberalism, and Rationalities of Government*, ed. Andrew Barry, Thomas Osborne, and Nikolas Rose, 37–64 (Chicago: University of Chicago Press, 1996).

11. Harvey, *A Brief History of Neoliberalism*; Michael Hardt and Antonio Negri, *Empire* (Cambridge, MA: Harvard University Press, 2000); Ravi K. Roy, Arthur T. Denzau, and Thomas D. Willett, *Neoliberalism: National and Regional Experiments with Global Ideas* (New York: Routledge, 2006).

12. Jean Comaroff and John L. Comaroff, eds., *Millennial Capitalism and the Culture of Neoliberalism* (Durham, NC: Duke University Press, 2001). Another example: Indian neoliberalism demands efficiency, transparency, and development within a history of discourses of corruption of state bureaucracies that have foundations in the colonial state.

13. Cheryl I. Harris, "Whiteness as Property," *Harvard Law Review* 106, no. 8 (1993): 1707–91. Harris's understanding of property and privilege and passing remains a cogent analysis of the relation between race and class, as does David Roediger's on how groups not seen as white in the early twentieth century become whites. New white groups (Eastern Europeans and those from the former Soviet states) have joined the existing immigrant groups who became white over the twentieth century. Jewish groups remain both white yet targets of anti-Semitism.

14. Paul Amar, *The Security Archipelago: Human-Security States, Sexuality Politics, and the End of Neoliberalism* (Durham, NC: Duke University Press, 2013). Amar argues that militarized authority has replaced neoliberalism.

15. Rose, "Governing 'Advanced' Liberal Democracies," 37–64.

16. Nick Maclellan, "From Fiji to Fallujah: The War in Iraq and the Privatisation of Pacific Security," *Pacific Journalism Review* 12, no. 2 (September 2006): 47–65, accessed October 2, 2016, http://search.informit.com.au/documentSummary;dn =265314284958675;res=IELNZC; Peter W. Singer, "The Private Military Industry and Iraq: What We Have Learned and Where to Next?," policy paper (Geneva: Geneva Centre for the Democratic Control of Armed Forces, 2004), accessed October 2, 2016, http://www.jstor.org/discover/10.2307/20034280?uid=3739576&uid=2&uid=4&uid =3739256&sid=21103985333101; Kjell Bjork and Richard Jones, "Overcoming Dilemmas Created by the 21st Century Mercenaries: Conceptualising the Use of Private Security Companies in Iraq," *Third World Quarterly* 26, nos. 4–5 (2005): 777–96, doi:10.1080/01436590500128014; Kateri Carmola, *Private Security Contractors and New Wars: Risk, Law, and Ethics* (New York: Routledge, 2010).

17. Joshua Barkan, *Corporate Sovereignty: Law and Government under Capitalism* (Minneapolis: University of Minnesota Press, 2013).

18. Amy Kaplan, *The Anarchy of Empire in the Making of U.S. Culture* (Cambridge, MA: Harvard University Press, 2005), 164–70; Alfred W. McCoy, *Policing America's Empire: The United States, the Philippines, and the Rise of the Surveillance State* (Madison: University of Wisconsin Press, 2009).

19. Thomas Piketty, *Capital in the Twenty-First Century* (Cambridge, MA: Belknap Press, 2014).

20. William Julius Wilson, *When Work Disappears: The World of the New Urban Poor* (New York: Vintage, 1997).

21. Ray Kiely, *Empire in the Age of Globalisation: US Hegemony and Neo-Liberal Disorder* (London: Pluto, 2005).

22. Zbigniew Brzezinski, *Strategic Vision: America and the Crisis of Global Power* (New York: Basic Books, 2012).

23. Vivian Jabri, *War and the Transformation of Global Politics* (New York: Palgrave Macmillan, 2007).

24. Lisa Lowe, *The Intimacies of Four Continents* (Durham, NC: Duke University Press, 2015).

25. Jean Comaroff and John L. Comaroff. *Theory from the South: Or, How Euro-America Is Evolving toward Africa* (Boulder, CO: Routledge, 2011).

26. India's Terrorism and Detention Act, which was a response to an insurgency in Punjab, India, can be seen as a precursor of the antiterror laws in different parts of the world, including the United States.

27. Comaroff and Comaroff, *Theory from the South*.

28. Achille Mbembe, *On the Postcolony* (Berkeley: University of California Press, 2001).

29. Amy Kaplan, "'Left Alone with America': The Absence of Empire in the Study of American Culture," in *Cultures of United States Imperialism*, ed. Amy Kaplan and Donald E. Pease, 3–21 (Durham, NC: Duke University Press, 1993).

30. Kaplan, "'Left Alone with America.'"

31. Jasbir K. Puar, *Terrorist Assemblages: Homonationalism in Queer Times* (Durham, NC: Duke University Press Books, 2007).

32. Puar, *Terrorist Assemblages*.

33. Inderpal Grewal, *Transnational America: Feminisms, Diasporas, Neoliberalisms* (Durham NC: Duke University Press, 2005), 198.

34. See, for instance, Newt Gingrich, *A Nation Like No Other: Why American Exceptionalism Matters* (Washington, DC: New York: Regnery, 2011).

35. Donald E. Pease, *The New American Exceptionalism* (Minneapolis: University of Minnesota Press, 2009).

36. See, for instance, Mimi Thi Nguyen, *The Gift of Freedom: War, Debt, and Other Refugee Passages* (Durham, NC: Duke University Press, 2012); Chandan Reddy, *Freedom with Violence: Race, Sexuality, and the US State* (Durham, NC: Duke University Press, 2011).

37. Seymour Martin Lipset, *American Exceptionalism: A Double-Edged Sword* (New York: W. W. Norton and Company, 1997).

38. David Bromwich, "It's Time to Rethink American Exceptionalism," *Nation*, October 24, 2014, accessed December 7, 2015, http://www.thenation.com/article/its -time-rethink-american-exceptionalism. One is not sure why this "rethinking" did not take place a long time ago, perhaps when the United States supported dictatorships in various regions of the world.

39. Didier Fassin and Mariella Pandolfi, eds., *Contemporary States of Emergency: The Politics of Military and Humanitarian Interventions* (New York: Zone Books, 2013).

40. Charlie Savage, "F.B.I. Casts Wide Net under Relaxed Rules for Terror Inquiries, Data Show," *New York Times*, March 26, 2011, sec. U.S., A19; James Risen and Laura Poitras, "N.S.A. Collecting Millions of Faces from Web Images," *New York Times*, May 31, 2014, accessed May 17, 2017, http://www.nytimes.com/2014/06/01/us/nsa-collecting -millions-of-faces-from-web-images.html; James Glanz, Jeff Larson, and Andrew W. Leh- ren, "Spy Agencies Tap Data Streaming from Phone Apps," *New York Times*, January 27, 2014, accessed July 6, 2016, http://www.nytimes.com/2014/01/28/world/spy-agencies -scour-phone-apps-for-personal-data.html; Savage, "F.B.I. Casts Wide Net."

41. Kirstie Ball and Frank Webster, eds., *The Intensification of Surveillance: Crime, Ter- rorism and Warfare in the Information Age* (London: Pluto, 2003); Deborah A. Ramirez, Jennifer Hoopes, and Tara Lai Quinlan, "Defining Racial Profiling in a Post–September 11 World," *American Criminal Law Review* 40 (2003): 1195; Junaid Rana, *Terrifying Muslims: Race and Labor in the South Asian Diaspora* (Durham, NC: Duke University Press, 2011); Maya Rhodan, "New Federal Racial Profiling Guidelines Worry Civil Rights Groups," *Time*, December 8, 2014, accessed December 7, 2015, http://time.com/3623851/justice -department- racial-profiling-muslims-sikhs-aclu; Sherene Razack, *Casting Out: The Eviction of Muslims from Western Law and Politics* (Toronto: University of Toronto Press, 2008); Dorothy Roberts, "Collateral Consequences, Genetic Surveillance, and the New Biopolitics of Race," *Howard Law Journal* 54 (2011): 567; Sunera Thobani, "Racial Violence and the Politics of National Belonging: The Wisconsin Shootings, Is- lamophobia and the War on Terrorized Bodies," *Sikh Formations* 8, no. 3 (December 1, 2012): 281–86, doi:10.1080/17448727.2012.752681; Moustafa Bayoumi, *How Does It Feel to Be a Problem? Being Young and Arab in America* (New York: Penguin Books, 2008).

42. Natasha Singer, "You for Sale: A Data Giant Is Mapping, and Sharing, the Con- sumer Genome," *New York Times*, June 17, 2012, BU1, 6.

43. Philip N. Howard, John N. Carr, and Tema J. Milstein, "Digital Technology and the Market for Political Surveillance," *Surveillance and Society* 3, no. 1 (2005): 59–73.

44. Victoria Bernal and Inderpal Grewal, "Introduction," in *Theorizing NGOs: States, Feminisms, and Neoliberalism*, 1–18 (Durham, NC: Duke University Press, 2014).

45. Singer, "The Private Military Industry and Iraq"; Carmola, *Private Security Con- tractors and New Wars*.

46. Karen Engle, "Constructing Good Aliens and Good Citizens: Legitimizing the War on Teror(ism)," *University of Colorado Law Review* 75, no. 1 (winter 2004): 59–114.

47. Thomas Blom Hansen and Finn Stepputat, "Introduction," in *Sovereign Bodies: Citizens, Migrants, and States in the Postcolonial World*, ed. Thomas Blom Hansen and Finn Stepputat, 1–38 (Princeton, NJ: Princeton University Press, 2005).

48. Michael Denning, "Wageless Life," *New Left Review* 2, no. 66 (2010): 79–97.

49. Wolfe, *Traces of History*.

50. Joseph Nye also argues that neoliberalism is waning. Nye sees US military power as strong but US economic power as no longer paramount, which requires "soft power" through public diplomacy and "co-optive power" in which the US government compels other states to realign their priorities with those of the United States. Joseph S. Nye, "Public Diplomacy and Soft Power," *Annals of the American Academy of Political and Social Science* 616, no. 1 (March 1, 2008): 94–109.

51. This literature is far-ranging, going from visual and material culture, to representation, to a historical account of US Cold War history, to knowledge production. Out of this vast literature, some interesting texts include: Charles Geisler, Gayatri Menon, and Shelley Feldman, eds., *Accumulating Insecurity: Violence and Dispossession in the Making of Everyday Life* (London: University of Georgia Press, 2011); John Martino, *War/Play: Video Games and the Militarization of Society* (New York: Peter Lang, 2015); Gretchen Heefner, *The Missile Next Door: The Minuteman in the American Heartland* (Cambridge, MA: Harvard University Press, 2012); Laura McEnaney, *Civil Defense Begins at Home* (Princeton, NJ: Princeton University Press, 2000); Nicole I. Torres, *Walls of Indifference: Immigration and the Militarization of the US-Mexico Border*, repr. ed. (Boulder, CO: Routledge, 2016); Joy Rohde, *Armed with Expertise: The Militarization of American Social Research during the Cold War* (Ithaca, NY: Cornell University Press, 2013); Musto, *Control and Protect*; Marie Gottschalk, *Caught: The Prison State and the Lockdown of American Politics*, rev. ed. (Princeton, NJ: Princeton University Press, 2016).

52. Marie Gottschalk, "Democracy and the Carceral State in America," *Annals of the American Academy of Political and Social Science* 651, no. 1 (January 1, 2014): 288–95, doi:10.1177/0002716213503787.

53. By now there is a considerable literature on this topic. See David Lyon, *The Electronic Eye: The Rise of Surveillance Society* (Minneapolis: University of Minnesota Press, 1994); David Lyon, *Identifying Citizens: ID Cards as Surveillance* (Cambridge: Polity, 2009); Mark Andrejevic, *iSpy: Surveillance and Power in the Interactive Era* (Lawrence: University Press of Kansas, 2007); William G. Staples, *Everyday Surveillance: Vigilance and Visibility in Postmodern Life*, 2nd ed. (Lanham, MD: Rowman and Littlefield, 2013); Torin Monahan, *Surveillance in the Time of Insecurity* (New Brunswick, NJ: Rutgers University Press, 2010); Tom Engelhardt, *Shadow Government: Surveillance, Secret Wars, and a Global Security State in a Single-Superpower World* (Chicago: Haymarket Books, 2014); Will Thomas DeVries, "Protecting Privacy in the Digital Age," *Berkeley Technology Law Journal* 18, no. 1 (January 2003): 283–311.

54. Muneer Ahmad, "Homeland Insecurities: Racial Violence the Day after September 11," *Social Text* 20, no. 3 (2002): 101–15; Michael Sorkin, ed., *Indefensible Space: The Architecture of the National Insecurity State* (New York: Routledge, 2008).

55. Armand Mattelart, *The Globalization of Surveillance*, trans. Susan Taponier and James A. Cohen (Cambridge: Polity, 2010), 139.

56. Michael Dillon, "Network Society, Network-Centric Warfare and the State of Emergency," *Theory, Culture and Society* 19, no. 4 (August 1, 2002): 71–79, doi:10.1177/02 63276402019004005.

57. Puar, *Terrorist Assemblages*; Rana, *Terrifying Muslims*; Razack, *Casting Out*.

58. Caren Kaplan, Erik Loyer, and Ezra Claytan Daniels, "Precision Targets: GPS and the Militarization of Everyday Life," *Canadian Journal of Communication* 38, no. 3 (September 16, 2013): 397–420, http://cjc-online.ca/index.php/journal/article /view/2655.

59. Stuart Hall, Chas Critcher, Tony Jefferson, John Clarke, and Brian Roberts, *Policing the Crisis: Mugging, the State, and Law and Order* (London: Macmillan, 1978).

60. Razack, *Casting Out*.

61. Grewal, *Transnational America*.

62. Ananya Roy, Genevieve Negrón-Gonzales, Kweku Opoku-Agyemang, and Clare Talwalker, *Encountering Poverty: Thinking and Acting in an Unequal World* (Oakland: University of California Press, 2016).

63. Thomas L. Ilgen, ed., *Reconfigured Sovereignty: Multi-Layered Governance in the Global Age* (Aldershot, England: Ashgate, 2003).

64. Thomas L. Ilgen, "Introduction," in *Reconfigured Sovereignty: Multi-Layered Governance in the Global Age*, ed. Thomas L. Ilgen (Aldershot, England: Ashgate, 2003), 3. See also in the same volume Ilgen, "Reconfigured Sovereignty in the Age of Globalization," 6–35.

65. Aihwa Ong, *Flexible Citizenship: The Cultural Logics of Transnationality* (Durham, NC: Duke University Press, 1999).

66. Brenda Chalfin, *Neoliberal Frontiers: An Ethnography of Sovereignty in West Africa* (Chicago: University of Chicago Press, 2010); Aihwa Ong, "Powers of Sovereignty: State, People, Wealth, Life," *Focaal—Journal of Global and Historical Anthropology* 64 (2012): 24–35.

67. Hansen and Stepputat, "Introduction."

68. Hansen and Stepputat, "Introduction," 20.

69. Achille Mbembe, "The Banality of Power and the Aesthetics of Vulgarity in the Postcolony," *Public Culture* 4, no. 2 (1992): 1–30.

70. Hansen and Stepputat, "Introduction," 29.

71. Saskia Sassen, *Losing Control? Sovereignty in an Age of Globalization* (New York: Columbia University Press, 1996).

72. Anwar Sheikh, "Who Pays for Welfare in the Welfare State? A Multicountry Study," *Social Research* 70, no. 2 (2003): 531–50. Sheikh's study shows, interestingly, that US workers paid for their own welfare throughout the 1980s!

73. Amar, *The Security Archipelago*.

74. Jan Nederveen Pieterse, "Neoliberal Empire," *Theory, Culture and Society* 21, no. 3 (2004): 119–40.

75. Harvey, *A Brief History of Neoliberalism*.

76. Hall et al., *Policing the Crisis*.

77. Kuan-Hsing Chen and David Morley, eds., *Stuart Hall: Critical Dialogues in Cultural Studies* (London: Routledge, 1996).

78. Iris Marion Young, "The Logic of Masculinist Protection: Reflection on the Current Security State," *Signs: Journal of Women in Culture and Society* 29, no. 1 (2003): 2.

79. Young, "The Logic of Masculinist Protection," 4.

80. Colin Gordon, "Governmental Rationality: An Introduction," in *The Foucault Effect: Studies in Governmentality*, ed. Graham Burchell, Colin Gordon, and Peter Miller, 1–52 (Chicago: University of Chicago Press, 1991).

81. Thomas Biebricher and Frieder Vogelmann, "Governmentality and State Theory: Reinventing the Reinvented Wheel?," *Theory and Event* 15, no. 3 (2012), http://muse.jhu.edu/journals/theory_and_event/v015/15.3.biebricher.html. Quotation from Michel Foucault, *Security, Territory, Population: Lectures at the Collège de France*, ed. Michel Senellart (New York: Palgrave Macmillan, 2009), 247.

82. Miguel de Larrinaga and Marc G. Doucet, eds., *Security and Global Governmentality: Globalization, Governance and the State* (New York: Routledge, 2010).

83. Puar, *Terrorist Assemblages*.

84. Hugh Gusterson and Catherine Besteman, eds., *The Insecure American: How We Got Here and What We Should Do about It* (Berkeley: University of California Press, 2009).

85. Jennifer Terry, "Significant Injury: War, Medicine, and Empire in Claudia's Case," *WSQ: Women's Studies Quarterly* 37, no. 1 (2009): 200–225.

86. Buzan, Wæver, and de Wilde, *Security*.

87. Thomas Blom Hansen and Finn Stepputat, eds., *Sovereign Bodies: Citizens, Migrants, and States in the Postcolonial World* (Princeton, NJ: Princeton University Press, 2005).

88. Nye, "Public Diplomacy and Soft Power."

89. Bigo, "Globalized (in)Security."

90. Monika Barthwal-Datta, *Understanding Security Practices in South Asia: Securitization Theory and the Role of Non-State Actors* (New York: Routledge, 2012).

91. Buzan, Wæver, and de Wilde, *Security*.

92. Amar, *The Security Archipelago*.

93. Mark Duffield, *Global Governance and the New Wars: The Merging of Development and Security*, 2nd new ed. (New York: Zed Books, 2014).

94. Laleh Khalili, *Time in the Shadows: Confinement in Counterinsurgencies* (Stanford, CA: Stanford University Press, 2012).

95. David Campbell, "The Biopolitics of Security: Oil, Empire, and the Sports Utility Vehicle," *American Quarterly*, 57, no. 3 (2005): 943–72.

96. David Campbell, *Writing Security: United States Foreign Policy and the Politics of Identity* (Minneapolis: University of Minnesota Press, 1992).

97. Saskia Sassen, "Toward a Sociology of Information Technology," *Current Sociology* 50, no. 3 (2002): 382.

98. Giovanna Borradori, *Philosophy in a Time of Terror: Dialogues with Jürgen Habermas and Jacques Derrida*, new ed. (Chicago: University of Chicago Press, 2004), 86.

99. Borradori, *Philosophy in a Time of Terror*, 86.

100. Kayuza Bialasiewicz, David Campbell, Stuart Elden, Stephen Graham, Alex Jeffrey, and Alison J. Williams, "Performing Security: The Imaginative Geographies of Current US Strategy," *Political Geography* 26 (2007): 405–22.

101. Stuart Hall, "Encoding/Decoding," in *Culture, Media, Language: Working Papers in Cultural Studies*, 128–38 (London: Hutchinson, 1973).

102. Jodi Dean, *Democracy and Other Neoliberal Fantasies: Communicative Capitalism and Left Politics* (Durham NC: Duke University Press, 2009).

103. Daniel Trottier and Christian Fuchs, eds. *Social Media, Politics and the State: Protests, Revolutions, Riots, Crime and Policing in the Age of Facebook, Twitter and YouTube* (New York: Routledge, 2014); José Marichal, *Facebook Democracy: The Architecture of Disclosure and the Threat to Public Life* (New York: Routledge, 2016).

104. David Lyon, *Surveillance Society: Monitoring Everyday Life* (Buckingham, England: Open University Press, 2001), 119.

105. Greg Elmer, "Panopticon-Discipline-Control," in *Routledge Handbook of Surveillance Studies*, ed. David Lyon, Kristen Ball, and Kevin D. Iaggerty (Oxon, England: Routledge, 2012), 27.

106. David Lyon, *Theorizing Surveillance: The Panopticon and Beyond* (Devon, England: Willan, 2006), 276. See also Greg Elmer, *Profiling Machines: Mapping the Personal Information Economy* (Cambridge, MA: MIT Press, 2003).

107. Lila Abu-Lughod, "Do Muslim Women Really Need Saving? Anthropological Reflections on Cultural Relativism and Its Others," *American Anthropologist* 104, no. 3 (2002): 783–90; Carrie Rentschler and Carol A. Stabile, "States of Insecurity and the Gendered Politics of Fear," *NWSA Journal* 17, no. 3 (2005): vii–xxv; Cynthia Enloe, *Maneuvers: The International Politics of Militarizing Women's Lives* (Berkeley: University of California Press, 2000). See also Janet Halley, *Split Decisions: How and Why to Take a Break from Feminism* (Princeton, NJ: Princeton University Press, 2008). While Halley makes a strong argument about the formation of "governance feminism," it is difficult to believe that one can "take a break" from feminism simply because it has become powerful in some ways, since there are numerous other forms of feminism that Halley does not consider, which are not powerful. There is a certain privilege to choosing between what one can stick with and what one can discard. Additionally, many social movements have unprogressive aspects to them, and few can avoid conflicts or contradictions.

108. Postcolonial feminist interventions into this discourse have not made much headway in popular culture, even after three decades of academic research.

109. The tradition of feminism that connects women to pacifism and patriarchy to war is visible even before the second wave. Virginia Woolf in *Three Guineas* (London: Hogarth Press, 1986, c. 1938) makes this connection and argues for pacifism. Feminists from Betty Freidan to Vandana Shiva have continued in this tradition.

110. Claudia Koonz, *Mothers in the Fatherland: Women, the Family and Nazi Politics* (New York: St. Martin's, 1987); Patricia Jeffery and Amrita Basu, eds., *Appropriating Gender: Women's Activism and Politicized Religion in South Asia* (New York: Routledge, 1998); Kathleen M. Blee, *Women of the Klan: Racism and Gender in the 1920s* (Berkeley: University of California Press, 2008); Antoinette Burton, *Burdens of History: British Feminists, Indian Women, and Imperial Culture, 1865–1915* (Chapel Hill: University of North Carolina Press, 1994).

111. Kristin Bumiller, *In an Abusive State: How Neoliberalism Appropriated the Feminist Movement against Sexual Violence* (Durham, NC: Duke University Press, 2008).

112. Laura Sjoberg, *Gendering Global Conflict: Toward a Feminist Theory of War* (New York: Columbia University Press, 2013).

113. Young, "The Logic of Masculinist Protection."

114. Aihwa Ong, *Neoliberalism as Exception: Mutations in Citizenship and Sovereignty* (Durham, NC: Duke University Press, 2006).

115. Carole Pateman, *The Sexual Contract* (Stanford, CA: Stanford University Press, 1988).

116. In Citizens United v. Federal Election Commission, 558 US 310 (2010), the US Supreme Court declared that corporations have a right to "free speech" because citizens do. In this case, there is little distinction between corporations and citizens.

117. See, for instance, Harvey, *A Brief History of Neoliberalism*.

118. Ong, *Neoliberalism as Exception*.

119. Puar, *Terrorist Assemblages*.

120. Ann Tickner, "You Just Don't Understand: Troubled Engagements between Feminists and IR Theorists," *International Studies Quarterly* 41, no. 4 (1997): 611–32.

121. Michael P. Johnson, "Patriarchal Terrorism and Common Couple Violence: Two Forms of Violence against Women," *Journal of Marriage and Family* 57, no. 2 (May 1995): 283–94.

122. A very short list out of a large field: Hazel V. Carby, *Cultures in Babylon: Black Britain and African America* (London: Verso Books, 1999); Nguyen, *The Gift of Freedom*; Reddy, *Freedom with Violence*; Amy Kaplan and Donald E. Pease, eds., *Cultures of United States Imperialism* (Durham, NC: Duke University Press, 1994); Sherene Razack, Malinda Smith, and Sunera Thobani, eds., *States of Race: Critical Race Feminism for the 21st Century* (Toronto: Between the Lines, 2010).

123. Jean Comaroff and John L. Comaroff, "Millennial Capitalism: First Thoughts on a Second Coming," in Comaroff and Comaroff, eds., *Millennial Capitalism*, 1–56.

124. David Kuo, *Tempting Faith: An Inside Story of Political Seduction* (New York: Free Press, 2007).

1. Katrina and the Security State

1. Shailaja Bajpai, "Apocalypse Now," *Indian Express*, September 5, 2005, accessed April 23, 2012, http://archive.indianexpress.com/oldStory/77565/.

2. Ambrose Murunga, in *Daily Nation*, excerpted in "Press Dismay at Katrina Chaos," BBC, September 3, 2005, accessed December 8, 2015, http://news.bbc.co.uk/2/hi/americas/4211320.stm.

3. Philip Ochieng, "Katrina and the Poverty of Development," *Daily Nation*, September 11, 2005, accessed May 23, 2016, http://www.nation.co.ke/oped/-/1192/81058/-/we8vorz/-/index.html.

4. Excerpted in "Press Dismay at Katrina Chaos," BBC, September 3, 2005, accessed December 8, 2015, http://news.bbc.co.uk/2/hi/americas/4211320.stm.

5. Ochieng, "Katrina and the Poverty of Development."

6. Leon Hadar, "America's Eroding Credibility: Fallout from Baghdad and New Orleans Makes It Difficult for Bush Administration to Mobilise Support," *Business Times Singapore*, September 14, 2005, sec. Views and Opinions.

7. For an interesting compendium, see Shawn Powers, "The Aftermath of Katrina: An Update of Media Coverage, International Reactions, and Public Diplomacy," USC Center on Public Diplomacy, September 20, 2005, accessed March 30, 2017, https:// uscpublicdiplomacy.org/pdin_monitor_article/aftermath-katrina-update-media -coverage-international-reactions-and-public.

8. Marcin Zaborowski, "Iraq, Katrina and US Foreign Policy: Implications for the EU," European Union Institute for Security Studies, n.d., accessed April 23, 2012. http:// www.iss.europa.eu/uploads/media/analy111.pdf.

9. Associated Press, "90 Nations Offer Aid to Help U.S. with Katrina," September 7, 2005, accessed December 8, 2015, http://www.nbcnews.com/id/9231819/ns/us_news -katrina_the_long_road_back/t/nations-offer-aid-help-us-katrina/.

10. Daan Van der Linde, *The Politics of Disaster: A Study into Post-Katrina International Aid*, November 2008, accessed December 8, 2015, http://www.disasterdiplomacy.org /pb/vanderlinde2008.pdf.

11. "Why Does the US Need Our Money?," BBC, September 6, 2005, accessed December 8, 2015, http://news.bbc.co.uk/2/hi/uk_news/magazine/4215336.stm.

12. Juan Forero and Steven R. Weisman, "U.S. Allies, and Others, Send Offers of Assistance," *New York Times*, September 4, 2005, accessed March 31, 2017, http://www .nytimes.com/2005/09/04/international/americas/04offers.html; quoted in Bradley A. Jones, "Hurricane Katrina, the Politics of Pity, and the News Media" (PhD diss., University of Michigan, 2011), accessed March 30, 2017, https://deepblue.lib.umich.edu /bitstream/handle/2027.42/89727/braajone_1.pdf%3Bsequence=1.

13. Jones, "Hurricane Katrina, the Politics of Pity, and the News Media," 134.

14. Van der Linde, *Politics of Disaster*, 9.

15. Rita J. King, "Big, Easy Money: Disaster Profiteering on the American Gulf Coast," *CorpWatch*, August 15, 2006, accessed December 8, 2016, http://www.corpwatch .org/article.php?id=14004: 5.

16. Jena McNeill, James Jay Carafano, Matt A. Mayer, and Richard Weitz, "Accepting Disaster Relief from Other Nations: Lessons from Katrina and the Gulf Oil Spill," Heritage Foundation, February 2011, accessed October 24, 2014, http://www.heritage .org/research/reports/2011/02/accepting-disaster-relief-from-other-nations-lessons -from-katrina-and-the-gulf-oil-spill.

17. A Nielson and Sony Electronics study found that of the news coverage from the last fifty years, that which had the biggest impact was the 9/11 coverage and the Hurricane Katrina coverage. Courtney Garcia, "September 11 Attacks, Katrina Top List of Memorable TV Moments," *Reuters*, July 11, 2012, accessed December 8, 2015, http://www.reuters.com/article/2012/07/11/entertainment-us-memorablemoments -idUSBRE86A0EG20120711.

18. Elihu Katz and Tamar Liebes, "No More Peace!," in *Media Events in a Global Age*, ed. Nick Couldry, Andreas Hepp, and Friedrich Krotz, 32–42 (New York: Routledge, 2009).

19. Tamar Liebes, "Television's Disaster Marathons: A Danger to Democratic Processes?," in *Media, Ritual and Identity*, ed. James Curran and Tamar Liebes, 71–86 (New York: Routledge, 2002).

20. Kevin Fox Gotham, "Critical Theory and Katrina: Disaster, Spectacle and Immanent Critique," *City: Analysis of Urban Trends, Culture, Theory, Policy, Action* 11, no. 1 (2007): 81–99.

21. Naomi Klein, *The Shock Doctrine: The Rise of Disaster Capitalism* (New York: Metropolitan, 2007).

22. Stuart Hall, "The Television Discourse: Encoding and Decoding," *Education and Culture* 25 (1974): 8–14.

23. David Zurawik, "TV Accords More Respect to Victims in U.S.," *Baltimore Sun*, September 3, 2005, accessed March 30, 2017, http://articles.baltimoresun.com/2005-09 -03/news/0509030074_1_tsunami-grief-natural-disasters.

24. Porismita Borah, "Comparing Visual Framing in Newspapers: Hurricane Katrina versus Tsunami," *Newspaper Research Journal* 30, no. 1 (2009): 50–57.

25. "'Katrinagate' Fury Spreads to US Media," TVNZ, September 6, 2005, accessed March 30, 2017, http://www.news24.com/World/Archives/HurricaneWatch /Katrinagate-fury-spreads-20050906.

26. "'Katrinagate' Fury Spreads to US Media."

27. "'Katrinagate' Fury Spreads to US Media."

28. Steve Bell, *Guardian*, 2008, accessed March 30, 2017, http://www.theguardian .com/cartoons/stevebell/0,7371,1566268,00.html. See also Klaus Dodds, "Steve Bell's Eye: Cartoons, Geopolitics and the Visualization of the 'War on Terror,'" *Security Dialogue* 38, no. 2 (2007): 157–77.

29. Richard Bernstein, "The View from Abroad," *New York Times*, September 4, 2005, accessed December 8, 2015, http://www.nytimes.com/2005/09/04/weekinreview /04bern.html.

30. Robb Todd and Charles Wolfson, "Katrina's Impact on Foreign Policy," CBS News, September 9, 2005, accessed December 8, 2015, http://www.cbsnews.com/2100-18568 _162-830306.html.

31. Sidney Blumenthal, "Breach of a Myth," *Salon*, September 15, 2005, accessed December 8, 2015, http://www.salon.com/2005/09/15/bush_myth.

32. "Polishing the U.S. Image," *Newsday*, September 10, 2005, accessed December 8, 2015, http://www.newsday.com/opinion/polishing-the-u-s-image-1.694159.

33. Daniel W. Drezner, "Post-Katrina American Foreign Policy," *Foreign Policy Blogs*, September 10, 2005, accessed December 8, 2015, http://drezner.foreignpolicy.com /posts/2005/09/09/post_katrina_american_foreign_policy.

34. Drezner, "Post-Katrina American Foreign Policy."

35. Richard Haass, "Storm Warning: How the Flood Compromises U.S. Foreign Policy," *Slate*, September 9, 2005, accessed December 8, 2015, http://www.slate.com /articles/news_and_politics/foreigners/2005/09/storm_warning.html.

36. Drezner, "Post-Katrina American Foreign Policy."

37. E. J. Dionne, "End of the Bush Era," *Washington Post*, September 13, 2005, accessed December 8, 2015, http://www.washingtonpost.com/wp- dyn/content/article/2005 /09/12/AR2005091201433.html.

38. Stephen M. Walt, "Delusion Points," *Foreign Policy*, November 8, 2010, accessed December 8, 2015, http://www.foreignpolicy.com/articles/2010/11/08/delusion_points.

39. Jeffrey S. Lowe and Todd C. Shaw, "After Katrina: Racial Regimes and Human Development Barriers in the Gulf Coast Region," *American Quarterly* 61, no. 3 (2009): 803–27.

40. Paige West, *Rhetoric and Inequality in Papua New Guinea* (New York: Columbia University Press, 2016), 65.

41. Lowe and Shaw, "After Katrina," 823.

42. McNeill et al., "Accepting Disaster Relief."

43. See Herman Gray, *Watching Race: Television and the Struggle for Blackness* (Minneapolis: University of Minnesota Press, 2004).

44. The Indian government did send aid to the United States, giving monetary support as well as a shipment of blankets.

45. Michael Dear, "Remembering Katrina but Please, No Photos of Dead People," *Space and Culture* 9, no. 1 (2006): 89–91.

46. Mark Lisheron, "The Ties That Bind," *American Journalism Review*, August/September 2006, accessed March 30, 2017, http://ajrarchive.org/Article.asp?id=4163.

47. Lisheron, "The Ties That Bind."

48. United States Senate, *Special Report of the Committee on Homeland Security and Governmental Affairs: Hurricane Katrina: A Nation Still Unprepared* (Washington, DC: United States Senate, 2006), accessed March 30, 2017, https://www.gpo.gov/fdsys/pkg/CRPT-109srpt322/pdf/CRPT-109srpt322.pdf.

49. United States Senate, *Special Report of the Committee on Homeland Security and Governmental Affairs*.

50. John M. Broder, "Amid Criticism of Federal Efforts, Charges of Racism Are Lodged," *New York Times*, September 5, 2005, accessed December 8, 2015, http://www.nytimes.com/2005/09/05/national/nationalspecial/05race.html.

51. " 'Katrinagate' Fury Spreads to US Media."

52. Jonathan Van Meter, "Unanchored," *New York Magazine*, September 19, 2005, accessed December 8, 2015, http://nymag.com/nymetro/news/features/14301.

53. Van Meter, "Unanchored."

54. Katherine Fry, "Television News Hero for New Orleans, Hero for the Nation," *Space and Culture* 9, no. 1 (2006): 83–85.

55. Anderson Cooper, *Dispatches from the Edge: A Memoir of War, Disasters, and Survival* (New York: HarperCollins, 2007), 138.

56. Cooper, *Dispatches from the Edge*, 168.

57. Cooper, *Dispatches from the Edge*, 141–42.

58. Susan Sontag's *Regarding the Pain of Others* (New York: Macmillan, 2003) is useful here for understanding why these images jolted the government to action and why this had a lasting effect on the Bush presidency. Sontag argues also that the globalizing of suffering, as in the photographs of Sebastian Salgado, enervates action because of the vast problems they suggest. But that might be precisely because of the nature of globalization, rather than simply the vastness of the issue. Sontag seems to duck the issue of US empire.

59. Frank Durham, "Media Ritual in Catastrophic Time: The Populist Turn in Television Coverage of Hurricane Katrina," *Journalism* 9, no. 1 (2008): 95–116.

60. Raymond Williams, *Marxism and Literature* (Oxford: Oxford University Press, 1978), 121–27; Guy Debord, *Society of the Spectacle* (Detroit: Black and Red, 2000).

61. Gotham, "Critical Theory and Katrina."

62. See Caren Kaplan, "Desert Wars: Virilio and the Limits of 'Genuine Knowledge,'" in *Virilio and Visual Culture*, ed. John Armitage and Ryan Bishop, 69–85 (Edinburgh: Edinburgh University Press, 2013), for a brilliant critique of Virilio's argument about visual technologies and ideological control.

63. E. Ann Kaplan, "Global Trauma and Public Feelings: Viewing Images of Catastrophe," *Consumption, Markets and Culture* 11, no. 1 (2008): 3–24.

64. Jones, "Hurricane Katrina, the Politics of Pity, and the News Media."

65. Jones, "Hurricane Katrina, the Politics of Pity, and the News Media," 24.

66. It is thus in opposition to the brief openings of Katrina's visual cultures that director Spike Lee's documentary *When the Levees Broke* was created. Lee commented, "I had a great responsibility to bear witness. . . . I knew that stories would get misconstrued. I was there to try to tell the truth as best as I could." Quoted in Ernest Callenbach, "*When the Levees Broke: A Requiem in Four Acts*," *Film Quarterly* 60, no. 2 (2006): 4–10.

67. United States Senate, *Special Report*, 325. Fox News quote reported in Susannah Rosenblatt and James Rainey, "Katrina Takes a Toll on Truth, News Accuracy," *Los Angeles Times*, September 27, 2005, accessed April 23, 2012, http://articles.latimes.com /2005/sep/27/nation/na-rumors27. Guy Dinmore, "City of Rape, Rumour and Recrimination," *Financial Times*, September 5, 2005, accessed April 17, 2017, http://www.ft .com/cms/s/0/06483632-1daa-11da-b40b-00000e2511c8.html?ft_site=falcon&desktop =true#axzz4eWeNZFdK.

68. Lauren Barsky, Joseph Trainor, and Manuel Torres, *Disaster Realities in the Aftermath of Hurricane Katrina: Revisiting the Looting Myth*, Quick Response Report (Boulder: National Hazards Center, University of Colorado at Boulder, 2006), accessed March 30, 2017, http://udspace.udel.edu/handle/19716/2367.

69. Linda Robertson, "How Shall We Remember New Orleans? Comparing News Coverage of Post-Katrina New Orleans and the 2008 Midwest Floods," in *The Neoliberal Deluge: Hurricane Katrina, Late Capitalism, and the Remaking of New Orleans*, ed. Cedric Johnson, 269–99 (Minneapolis: University of Minnesota Press, 2011).

70. Jordan T. Camp, "'We Know This Place': Neoliberal Racial Regimes and the Katrina Circumstance," *American Quarterly* 61, no. 3 (2009): 693–717.

71. Chris Kromm and Sue Sturgis, "Hurricane Katrina and the Guiding Principles on Internal Displacement: A Global Human Rights Perspective on a National Disaster," *Southern Exposure*, 36, no. 1 (January 2008), http://www.brookings.edu/~/media /events/2008/1/14%20disasters/0114_isskatrina.pdf.: 20.

72. Gordon Russell and James Varney, "From Blue Tarps to Debris Removal, Layers of Contractors Drive Up the Cost of Recovery, Critics Say," *NOLA.com/The Times-Picayune*, August 3, 2015, accessed May 28, 2016, http://www.nola.com/katrina/index .ssf/2005/12/from_blue_tarps_to_debris_remo.html.

73. Nicholas Mirzoeff, "War Is Culture: Global Counterinsurgency, Visuality, and the Petraeus Doctrine," *PMLA* 124, no. 5 (October 1, 2009): 1737–46, doi:10.1632/pmla .2009.124.5.1737.

74. Havidán Rodríguez and Russell Dynes, "Finding and Framing Katrina: The Social Construction of Disaster," Understanding Katrina, Social Science Research Council, June 11, 2006, accessed December 8, 2015, http://understandingkatrina.ssrc .org/Dynes_Rodriguez.

75. Stephen Graham, "'Homeland' Insecurities? Katrina and the Politics of 'Security' in Metropolitan America," Space and Culture 9, no. 1 (2006): 63–67.

76. Graham, "'Homeland' Insecurities?"

77. Spike Lee, When the Levees Broke: A Requiem in Four Acts, documentary film, HBO Studios, 2006.

78. Lee, When the Levees Broke.

79. Kathleen Tierney, "Foreshadowing Katrina: Recent Sociological Contributions to Vulnerability Science," Contemporary Sociology 35, no. 3 (2006): 207–12.

80. Dave Eggers, Zeitoun, repr. ed. (New York: Vintage, 2010), 218.

81. Eggers, Zeitoun.

82. Vincanne Adams, Markets of Sorrow, Labors of Faith: New Orleans in the Wake of Katrina (Durham, NC: Duke University Press, 2013), 31.

83. Dinesh D'Souza, The End of Racism (New York: Free Press, 1995).

84. Eduardo Bonilla-Silva, White Supremacy and Racism in the Post–Civil Rights Era (Boulder, CO: Lynn Rienner, 2001).

85. Clarence Taylor, "Hurricane Katrina and the Myth of the Post–Civil Rights Era," Journal of Urban History 35, no. 5 (2009): 640–55.

86. Kromm and Sturgis, "Hurricane Katrina and the Guiding Principles on Internal Displacement," 22.

87. Kromm and Sturgis, "Hurricane Katrina and the Guiding Principles on Internal Displacement," 16.

88. United States House of Representatives, Committee on Government Reform— Minority Staff, Special Investigations Division, Waste, Fraud, and Abuse in Hurricane Katrina Contracts (Washington, DC: United States House of Representatives, August 2006), https://www.hsdl.org/?view&did=466563.

89. Vincanne Adams, Taslim Van Hattum, and Diana English, "Chronic Disaster Syndrome: Displacement, Disaster Capitalism, and the Eviction of the Poor from New Orleans," American Ethnologist 36, no. 4 (2009): 615–36.

90. Adams, Hattum, and English, "Chronic Disaster Syndrome."

91. Adams, Hattum, and English "Chronic Disaster Syndrome." I find these discourses quite important as they are reported in this essay, though these are not the focus of the essay itself.

92. United States Government Accountability Office, Disaster Recovery: Federal Contracting in the Aftermath of Hurricanes Katrina and Rita, Testimony before the United States Senate Committee on Small Business and Entrepreneurship (Washington, DC: United States Government Accountability Office, September 15, 2011), http://www.gao .gov/assets/130/126954.pdf.

93. Klein, The Shock Doctrine. Klein argues that neoliberal governments use disasters to create economic clean slates, which can then be re-created as neoliberal economies. I am not sure that governments have such total ideologies or ideological control, but

rather that neoliberalism's contradictions are visible every now and then, and do have lasting effects.

94. John Arena, *Driven from New Orleans: How Nonprofits Betray Public Housing and Promote Privatization* (Minneapolis: University of Minnesota Press, 2012). See also Cedric Johnson, ed., *The Neoliberal Deluge: Hurricane Katrina, Late Capitalism, and the Remaking of New Orleans* (Minneapolis: University of Minnesota Press, 2011).

95. On Pitt's Make It Right Foundation, see Cedric Johnson, "Charming Accommodations: Progressive Urbanism Meets Privatization in Brad Pitt's Make It Right Foundation," in Johnson, ed., *The Neoliberal Deluge*, 187–224.

96. Pamela Jenkins, "Gender and the Landscape of Community Work before and after Katrina," in *The Women of Katrina: How Gender, Race and Class Matter in an American Disaster*, ed. Emmanuel David and Elaine Enarson, 169–78 (Nashville: Vanderbilt University Press, 2011).

97. Lowe and Shaw, "After Katrina."

98. Cedric Johnson, "Introduction," in Johnson, ed., *The Neoliberal Deluge*, xxxii.

99. Johnson, "Introduction," xxxiii.

100. Victoria Bernal and Inderpal Grewal, "Feminisms and the NGO Form," in *Theorizing NGOs: States, Feminisms, and Neoliberalism*, ed. Victoria Bernal and Inderpal Grewal, 301–10 (Durham, NC: Duke University Press, 2014).

101. The literature that takes this view is vast; from federal and state government publications to activist work and scholarly writing, it has grown enormously. See, for instance, Julie Fisher, *Nongovernments: NGOs and the Political Development of the Third World* (West Hartford, CT: Kumarian, 1998); William F. Fisher, "Doing Good? The Politics and Antipolitics of NGO Practices," *Annual Review of Anthropology* (1997): 439–64; Julie Hearn, "African NGOs: The New Compradors?," *Development and Change* 38, no. 6 (2007): 1095–110; Sangeeta Kamat, "The Privatization of Public Interest: Theorizing NGO Discourse in a Neoliberal Era," *Review of International Political Economy* 11, no. 1 (2004): 155–76.

102. Bernal and Grewal, "Feminisms and the NGO Form."

103. Bernal and Grewal, "Feminisms and the NGO Form."

104. Adams, *Markets of Sorrow, Labors of Faith.*

105. Days after the hurricane, Oxfam, an NGO based in the UK, dispatched a team of emergency experts to New Orleans, and the *New York Times* reported that it was the first time that Oxfam had sent such a team to the United States.

106. Jeffry M. Diefendorf, "Reconstructing Devastated Cities: Europe after World War II and New Orleans after Katrina," *Journal of Urban Design* 14, no. 3 (2009): 377–97.

107. A few of the most cited sources include David Harvey, *A Brief History of Neoliberalism* (Oxford: Oxford University Press, 2007); Wendy Larner, "Neo-Liberalism: Policy, Ideology, Governmentality," *Studies in Political Economy* 63 (2000): 5–25, http://spe.library.utoronto.ca/index.php/spe/article/viewArticle/6724; Aihwa Ong, *Neoliberalism as Exception: Mutations in Citizenship and Sovereignty* (Durham, NC: Duke University Press, 2006); Nikolas Rose, "Community, Citizenship, and the Third Way," *American Behavior Scientist* 43, no. 9 (2000): 1395–411; Manfred B. Steger and Ravi K. Roy, *Neoliberalism: A Very Short Introduction* (Oxford: Oxford University Press, 2010).

108. Lauren Berlant, *Cruel Optimism* (Durham, NC: Duke University Press, 2011).

109. United Nations Human Rights Council, *Racism, Racial Discrimination, Xenophobia and Related Forms of Intolerance, Addendum: Mission to the United States of America, Report of the Special Rapporteur on Contemporary Forms of Racism, Racial Discrimination, Xenophobia and Related Intolerance, Doudou Diène* (Geneva: United Nations Human Rights Council, April 28, 2009), http://www2.ohchr.org/english/bodies/hrcouncil/docs/11session/A.HRC.11.36.Add.3.pdf.

110. The Inter-American Commission of Human Rights General Situation Hearing on Natural Disaster and Human Rights, *When Disaster Strikes: A Human Rights Analysis of the 2005 Gulf Coast Hurricanes* (Berkeley, CA: International Human Rights Clinic, Boalt Hall School of Law, March 6, 2006), https://www.academia.edu/10149179/When_Disaster_Strikes_A_Human_Rights_Analysis_of_the_2005_Gulf_Coast_Hurricanes_Submitted_to_the_Inter-American_Commission_of_Human_Rights.

111. Monique Harden, Nathalie Walker, and Kali Akuno, "Racial Discrimination and Ethnic Cleansing in the United States in the Aftermath of Hurricane Katrina: A Report to the United Nations' Committee for the Elimination of Racial Discrimination," Advocates for Environmental Human Rights and Peoples' Hurricane Relief Fund, accessed May 28, 2016, http://www.ushrnetwork.org/sites/ushrnetwork.org/files/cerd2008hurricanekatrinaracialdiscriminationandethniccleansingintheunitedstates.pdf.

112. Kromm and Sturgis, "Hurricane Katrina and the Guiding Principles on Internal Displacement."

113. Michael Eric Dyson, *Come Hell or High Water: Hurricane Katrina and the Color of Disaster* (New York: Civitas, 2006); Henry A. Giroux, "Reading Hurricane Katrina: Race, Class, and the Biopolitics of Disposability," *College Literature* 33, no. 3 (2006): 171–96; Lowe and Shaw, "After Katrina"; Wahneema Lubiano, "Race, Class, and the Politics of Death: Critical Responses to Hurricane Katrina," *Transforming Anthropology* 14, no. 1 (2006): 31–34; David Roediger, "The Retreat from Race and Class," *Monthly Review* 58, no. 3 (2006), https://monthlyreview.org/2006/07/01/the-retreat-from-race-and-class.

114. Scholarly coverage of the disaster has been voluminous, testifying to the impact and outrage it generated. The Social Science Research Council, for instance, has created a bibliography of Katrina, called the Katrina Research Hub, that is available on its website: http://katrinaresearchhub.ssrc.org/KatrinaBibliography.pdf/view, accessed July 15, 2013. It also established a task force on the topic. The SSRC bibliography, however, concerns social science research and does not include interdisciplinary, humanities, or science research, which is also considerable.

115. Shirley Laska, "The 'Mother of All Rorschach's': Katrina Recovery in New Orleans," *Sociological Inquiry* 78, no. 4 (2008): 580–91.

116. Gotham, "Critical Theory and Katrina." See also many outstanding analyses produced by scholars through support by the SSRC: http://understandingkatrina.ssrc.org.

117. Jacquelyn Litt, Althea Skinner, and Kelley Robinson, "The Katrina Difference: African American Women's Networks and Poverty in New Orleans after Katrina," in *The Women of Katrina: How Gender, Race and Class Matter in an American Disaster*, ed. Emmanuel David and Elaine Enarson, 130–41 (Nashville: Vanderbilt University Press, 2011).

118. I have cited many of these in this chapter, though many more are available.

119. Johnson, *The Neoliberal Deluge*; Arena, *Driven from New Orleans*.

120. Clyde Woods, "*Les Miserables* of New Orleans: Trap Economics and the Asset Stripping Blues, Part 1," *American Quarterly* 61, no. 3 (2009): 769–96.

121. See for instance, Camp, "We Know This Place."

122. Michael Ralph, "'It's Hard Out Here for a Pimp . . . with . . . a Whole Lot of Bitches Jumpin' Ship': Navigating Black Politics in the Wake of Katrina," *Public Culture* 21, no. 2 (2009): 343–76.

123. Ralph, "'It's Hard Out Here for a Pimp,'" 351.

124. Social Science Research Council, "Understanding Katrina: Perspectives from the Social Sciences," accessed April 7, 2017, http://understandingkatrina.ssrc.org.

125. Lee, *When the Levees Broke*; Spike Lee, *If God Is Willing and Da Creek Don't Rise*, documentary film, HBO, 2010.

126. The BP oil spill has its Katrina shadow too, showing the extent of Katrina's impact on public perception of the state. See Helene Cooper, "Shadow of Hurricane Katrina Hangs over Obama after Spill," *New York Times*, April 30, 2010, accessed December 8, 2015, http://www.nytimes.com/2010/05/01/us/politics/01obama.html; Richard Wolf, "Obama Goes to La. to Address Oil Spill," *USA Today*, April 4, 2010, accessed December 8, 2015, http://usatoday30.usatoday.com/news/nation/2010–05–02 -obama-spill_N.htm.

2. American Humanitarian Citizenship

1. US Navy, "About the Navy," Navy.com, n.d., accessed July 10, 2013, http://www .navy.com/about/gffg.html.

2. James Dao, "Ad Campaign for Marines Cites Chaos as a Selling Point," *New York Times*, March 9, 2012, sec. US, accessed January 4, 2016, http://www.nytimes.com/2012 /03/10/us/marines-marketing-campaign-uses-chaos-as-a-selling-point.html.

3. Pauline Jelinek, "New Ads Pitch Marine Corps' Kinder, Gentler Side," *Washington Times*, March 8, 2012, accessed January 4, 2016, http://www.washingtontimes.com/news /2012/mar/8/new-ads-pitch-marine-corps-kinder-gentler-side/.

4. Bill Keller, "The Return of America's Missionary Impulse," *New York Times*, April 15, 2011, accessed January 4, 2016, http://www.nytimes.com/2011/04/17/magazine /mag-17Lede-t.html.

5. Incite! Women of Color Against Violence, *The Revolution Will Not Be Funded: Beyond the Non-Profit Industrial Complex* (Cambridge, MA: South End Press, 2009).

6. Vincanne Adams, *Markets of Sorrow, Labors of Faith: New Orleans in the Wake of Katrina* (Durham, NC: Duke University Press, 2013).

7. Victoria Bernal and Inderpal Grewal, "Introduction," in *Theorizing NGOs: States, Feminisms, and Neoliberalism*, 1–18 (Durham, NC: Duke University Press, 2014).

8. Craig Calhoun, "The Idea of Emergency: Humanitarian Action and Global (Humanitarian) Order," in *Contemporary States of Emergency: The Politics of Military and Humanitarian Interventions*, ed. Didier Fassin and Mariella Pandolfi, 29–58 (Cambridge: Zone Books, 2013).

9. Kamari Maxine Clarke, *Fictions of Justice: The ICC and the Challenge of Legal Pluralism in Sub-Saharan Africa* (Cambridge: Cambridge University Press, 2009).

10. Sangeeta Kamat, *Development Hegemony: NGOs and the State in India* (New York: Oxford University Press, 2002).

11. Miriam Ticktin, "Where Ethics and Politics Meet," *American Ethnologist* 33, no. 1 (2006): 33–49.

12. Didier Fassin, *Humanitarian Reason: A Moral History of the Present* (Berkeley: University of California Press, 2012).

13. Luc Boltanski, *Distant Suffering: Morality, Media and Politics* (Cambridge: Cambridge University Press, 1999).

14. Lilie Chouliaraki, "Post-Humanitarianism: Humanitarian Communication beyond a Politics of Pity," *International Journal of Cultural Studies* 13, no. 2 (2010): 107–26.

15. Chouliaraki, "Post-Humanitarianism."

16. Lilie Chouliaraki, "Introduction: The Soft Power of War," in *The Soft Power of War*, ed. Lilie Chouliaraki (Philadelphia: John Benjamins, 2007), 8, http://site.ebrary.com /id/10176615.

17. Andrea Muehlebach, "Complexio Oppositorum: Notes on the Left in Neoliberal Italy," *Public Culture* 21, no. 3 (2009): 495–515.

18. Cynthia Enloe, *Bananas, Beaches and Bases: Making Feminist Sense of International Politics*, 2nd ed. (Berkeley: University of California Press, 2000), 15.

19. Talya Zemach-Bersin, "Imperial Pedagogies: Education for American Globalism, 1898–1950" (PhD diss., Yale University, 2015).

20. Kenton J. Clymer, "Humanitarian Imperialism: David Prescott Barrows and the White Man's Burden in the Philippines," *Pacific Historical Review* 45, no. 4 (1976): 495–517.

21. Mimi Thi Nguyen, *The Gift of Freedom: War, Debt, and Other Refugee Passages* (Durham, NC: Duke University Press, 2012).

22. Ann Vogel, "Who's Making Global Civil Society: Philanthropy and US Empire in World Society," *British Journal of Sociology* 57, no. 4 (2006): 635–55.

23. Vogel, "Who's Making Global Civil Society."

24. Nikolas Rose and Kevin Rozario, " 'Delicious Horrors': Mass Culture, the Red Cross, and the Appeal of Modern American Humanitarianism," *American Quarterly* 55, no. 3 (2003): 417–55.

25. Henri Lefebvre, *The Production of Space*, trans. Donald Nicholson-Smith (Oxford: Blackwell, 1992); Johannes Fabian, *Time and the Other: How Anthropology Makes Its Object*, 2nd ed. (New York: Columbia University Press, 2002).

26. Michael O. Emerson and Christina Smith, *Divided by Faith: Evangelical Religion and the Problem of Race in America* (Oxford: Oxford University Press, 2000).

27. Melani McAlister, "What Is Your Heart For? Affect and Internationalism in the Evangelical Public Sphere," *American Literary History* 20, no. 4 (2008): 870–95; Melanie McAlister, "Guess Who's Coming for Dinner: American Missionaries, the Problem of Racism, and Decolonization in the Congo," *OAH Magazine of History* 26 (2012): 33–37.

28. Bill Clinton, *Giving: How Each of Us Can Change the World* (New York: Random House, 2007).

29. Denis Kennedy, "Selling the Distant Other: Humanitarianism and Imagery. Ethical Dilemmas of Humanitarian Action," *Journal of Humanitarian Assistance*, February 28, 2009, http://sites.tufts.edu/jha/archives/411.

30. "Celebrity Charities: Facts and Daily News," Look to the Stars, n.d., accessed July 10, 2013, https://www.looktothestars.org/.

31. John Colapinto, "Looking Good," *New Yorker*, March 26, 2012, accessed January 4, 2016, http://www.newyorker.com/reporting/2012/03/26/120326fa_fact_colapinto.

32. Karen Engle, " 'Calling in the Troops': The Uneasy Relationship among Women's Rights, Human Rights, and Humanitarian Intervention," *Harvard Human Rights Journal* 20 (2007): 189–226.

33. Arturo Escobar, *Encountering Development: The Making and Unmaking of the Third World* (Princeton, NJ: Princeton University Press, 2011).

34. Sabine Lang, "The NGOization of Feminism," in *Transitions, Environments, Translations: Feminisms in Contemporary Politics*, ed. Cora Kaplan, Debra Keates, and Joan Wallach Scott, 101–20 (New York: Routledge, 1997).

35. Sonia E. Álvarez, "Advocating Feminism: The Latin American Feminist NGO 'Boom,' " *International Feminist Journal of Politics* 1, no. 2 (1999): 181–209.

36. Gada Mahrouse, "Feel Good Tourism: An Ethical Option for Socially-Conscious Westerners?," *ACME: An International E-Journal for Critical Geographies* 15, no. 3 (2011): 372–91, acme-journal.org/index.php/acme/article/view/903.

37. Mahrouse, "Feel Good Tourism."

38. McAlister, "What Is Your Heart For?"

39. Nola Lee Kelsey, *700 Places to Volunteer before You Die: A Traveler's Guide* (Hot Springs, SD: Dog's Eye View Media, 2010); Bill McMillon, Doug Cutchins, and Anne Geissinger, *Volunteer Vacations: Short-Term Adventures That Will Benefit You and Others*, 11th ed. (Chicago: Chicago Review Press, 2012); Charlotte Hindle, Rachel Collinson, Mike Richard, Korina Miller, Sarah Wintle, and Nate Cavalieri, *Volunteer: A Traveller's Guide to Making a Difference around the World*, 3rd ed.(Melbourne, Australia: Lonely Planet, 2013).

40. McMillon, Cutchins, and Geissinger, *Volunteer Vacations*, xx.

41. McMillon, Cutchins, and Geissinger,, *Volunteer Vacations*, xxi.

42. Aviva Sinervo, "Connections and Disillusion: The Moral Economy of Volunteer Tourism in Cusco, Peru," *Childhoods Today* 5, no. 2 (2011): 1–23, www.childhoodstoday.org/download.php?id=66.

43. McMillon, Cutchins, and Geissinger, *Volunteer Vacations*, xvi.

44. My thanks to Cathy Hannabach for pointing to this implication of the quote.

45. Hindle et al., *Volunteer: A Traveller's Guide*, 10.

46. Hindle et al., *Volunteer: A Traveller's Guide*, 10.

47. Hindle et al., *Volunteer: A Traveller's Guide*, 10.

48. Hindle et al., *Volunteer: A Traveller's Guide*, 10.

49. Hindle et al., *Volunteer: A Traveller's Guide*, 9.

50. James Ferguson, *The Anti-Politics Machine: Development, Depoliticization, and Bureaucratic Power in Lesotho* (Minneapolis: University of Minnesota Press, 1994).

51. Greg Mortenson and David Oliver Relin, *Three Cups of Tea* (New York: Penguin, 2006). Subsequent references to this edition appear in parentheses in the text. Multiple

editions of the book have been published, and there was also a website promoting the book and humanitarian endeavors: http://www.threecupsoftea.com. The site has since been taken down.

52. Caren Kaplan, *Questions of Travel: Postmodern Discourses of Displacement* (Durham, NC: Duke University Press, 1996).

53. Fabian, *Time and the Other*.

54. Jon Krakauer, *Three Cups of Deceit: How Greg Mortenson, Humanitarian Hero, Lost His Way* (New York: Anchor, 2011).

55. Elisabeth Bumiller, "Unlikely Tutor Giving Military Afghan Advice," *New York Times*, July 17, 2010, accessed January 4, 2016, http://www.nytimes.com/2010/07/18/world/asia/18tea.html.

56. Bumiller, "Unlikely Tutor Giving Military Afghan Advice."

57. Bumiller, "Unlikely Tutor Giving Military Afghan Advice."

58. "Greg Mortenson," *60 Minutes* (CBS, April 17, 2011), http://www.cbsnews.com/video/watch/?id=7363068n&tag=api.

59. "Jackson Conversations on Leadership with Stan McChrystal and Greg Mortenson," Jackson Institute Conversations on Leadership Series, Yale University, February 21, 2011, accessed January 4, 2016, http://jackson.yale.edu/jackson-conversations-leadership-stan-mcchrystal-greg-mortenson-now-yale-youtube-0.

60. Montgomery McFate and Andrea Jackson, "An Organizational Solution for DoD's Cultural Knowledge Needs," *Military Review* 85, no. 4 (August 2005): 18–21.

61. Greg Mortenson and Susan L. Roth, *Listen to the Wind: The Story of Dr. Greg and Three Cups of Tea* (New York: Dial Books for Young Readers, 2009).

62. Greg Mortenson, *Stones into Schools: Promoting Peace through Education in Afghanistan and Pakistan* (New York: Penguin Books, 2010).

63. David Rieff, *A Bed for the Night: Humanitarianism in Crisis* (New York: Simon and Schuster, 2002); David Rieff, "Moral Blindness: American Troops in Darfur? Is TNR Mad?," *New Republic*, June 5, 2006, 13–15.

64. Trebor Scholz, ed., *Digital Labor: The Internet as Playground and Factory* (New York: Routledge, 2012).

65. See, for instance, Lamia Karim, *Microfinance and Its Discontents: Women in Debt in Bangladesh* (Minneapolis: University of Minnesota Press, 2011).

66. Stephanie Strom, "To Help Donors Choose, Web Site Alters How It Sizes Up Charities," *New York Times*, November 27, 2010, accessed January 4, 2016, http://www.nytimes.com/2010/11/27/business/27charity.html.

67. Donors Choose, homepage, n.d., accessed January 4, 2016, http://www.donorschoose.org.

68. Megan Moodie, "Microfinance and the Gender of Risk: The Case of Kiva.org," *Signs: Journal of Women in Culture and Society* 38, no. 2 (2013): 279–302, doi:10.1086/667448.

69. "Capital One Fuels Kiva's Microlending in U.S. with $500,000 Matching Loan Program," *Business Wire*, February 25, 2013, accessed January 4, 2016, http://www.businesswire.com/news/home/20130225006030/en/Capital-Fuels-Kiva%E2%80%99s-Microlending-U.S.-500000-Matching.

70. Chouliaraki, "Post-Humanitarianism."

71. "Kiva: Loans That Change Lives," Kiva.org, n.d., accessed July 10, 2013, http://www.kiva.org/start.

72. "Kiva: Lending Teams. Connect with Kiva's Lender Community," Kiva.org, n.d., accessed July 17, 2013, http://www.kiva.org/teams?queryString=unhappy+kiva+lenders&search=&category=all&membershipType=all&sortBy=overallLoanedAmount.

73. Nicholas Kristof, "Kristof maintains a twitter account under the handle@Nick Kristof," Twitter post, September 5, 2009, 9:42 AM, https://twitter.com/NickKristof/status/37814237375.

74. Nikolas Rose, John Shotter, and Kenneth Gergen, "Individualizing Psychology," in *Texts of Identity*, vol. 2, ed. John Shotter and Kenneth J. Gergen, 119–32 (London: Sage, 1989).

75. Moodie, "Microfinance and the Gender of Risk."

76. Rachel Silverman, "A New Generation Reinvents Philanthropy: Blogs, Social-Networking Sites Give 20-Somethings a Means to Push, Fund Favorite Causes," *Wall Street Journal*, August 21, 2007, accessed January 4, 2016, http://www.wsj.com/articles/SB118765256378003494.

77. Stephanie Strom, "Confusion on Where Money Lent via Kiva Goes," *New York Times*, November 8, 2009, accessed January 4, 2016, http:www.nytimes.com/2009/11/09/business/global/09kiva.html?mcubz-0.

78. Chouliaraki, "Post-Humanitarianism."

79. Nathan Heller, "California Screaming," *New Yorker*, July 7, 2014, accessed January 4, 2016, http://www.newyorker.com/magazine/2014/07/07/california-screaming.

80. "Kiva: Lending Teams."

81. Didier Fassin and Mariella Pandolfi, eds., *Contemporary States of Emergency: The Politics of Military and Humanitarian Interventions* (New York: Zone Books, 2013).

82. Didier Fassin and Mariella Pandolfi, "Introduction: Military and Humanitarian Government in the Age of Intervention," in Fassin and Pandolfi, eds., *Contemporary States of Emergency*, 15.

83. Fassin and Pandolfi, "Introduction," 12.

3. Muslims, Missionaries, and Humanitarians

1. An interesting sideline to this is the rise and power of the Bharatiya Janata Party (BJP) and the Hindu Right in India, which has turned a blind eye to the burning of churches and attacks on Christian missionaries. In India, anticonversion laws have been designed to create the ideology of a homogenous notion of Hinduism and Hindus as the religion of India, and Christianity and Islam as foreign religions. Several from the US Congress have protested these attacks, but little has come of these protests. In addition, the Modi government has harassed many NGOs, especially those supported by some international funding, in order to prevent any support of opposition to the BJP. Yet, so many religious NGOs operate all over the world, and as the line between secular and religious is harder to maintain, the local and transnational politics of missionary and humanitarian work are ever more contentious—and often involve geopolitical retaliation.

2. Greg Mortenson and David Oliver Relin, *Three Cups of Tea* (New York: Penguin Books, 2006), 243.

3. Mortenson and Relin, *Three Cups of Tea*, 242.

4. See, for instance, Patrick M. Jost and Harjit Singh Sandhu, "The Hawala Alternative Remittance System and Its Role in Money Laundering," US Department of Treasury and INTERPOL/FOPAC, n.d., accessed May 29, 2016, https://www.treasury.gov /resource-center/terrorist-illicit-finance/Documents/FinCEN-Hawala-rpt.pdf.

5. Mortenson and Relin, *Three Cups of Tea*, 243.

6. Mortenson and Relin, *Three Cups of Tea*, 244.

7. Mortenson and Relin, *Three Cups of Tea*, 242.

8. Miriam Jordan and Erica E. Phillips, "Wall Street Journal: Bank Moves Hinder Immigrants," Keith Ellison, June 22, 2012, accessed May 29, 2016, https://ellison.house.gov /media-center/news/wall-street-journal-bank-moves-hinder-immigrants.

9. Peter Waldman and Hugh Pope, " 'Crusade' Reference Reinforces Fears War on Terrorism Is against Muslims," *Wall Street Journal*, September 21, 2001, sec. Front Section, accessed June 3, 2016, http://www.wsj.com/articles/SB1001020294332922160.

10. See Kenton J. Clymer, "Religion and American Imperialism: Methodist Missionaries in the Philippine Islands, 1899–1913," *Pacific Historical Review* 49, no. 1 (1980): 29–50, doi:10.2307/3639303; Anthony J. Dachs, "Missionary Imperialism: The Case of Bechuanaland," *Journal of African History* 13, no. 4 (1972): 647–58; Jeffrey Cox, *Imperial Fault Lines: Christianity and Colonial Power in India, 1818–1940* (Stanford, CA: Stanford University Press, 2002); Joseph L. Grabill, *Protestant Diplomacy and the Near East: Missionary Influence on American Policy, 1810–1927*, Minnesota Archive Editions ed. (Minneapolis: University of Minnesota Press, 1971); Jean Comaroff and John L. Comaroff, *Of Revelation and Revolution*, vol. 1: *Christianity, Colonialism, and Consciousness in South Africa* (Chicago: University of Chicago Press, 1991).

11. Thomas Laqueur, "Body, Details, and the Humanitarian Narrative," in *The New Cultural History*, ed. Lynn Hunt, 186–204 (Berkeley: University of California Press, 1989).

12. Riad Z. Abdelkarim and Basil Z. Abdelkarim, "As American Muslims Face New Raids, Muslim Charities Fight Back," *Washington Report on Middle East Affairs* 21, no. 4 (2002): 80–81.

13. Alan Cooperman, "Muslim Charities Say Fear Is Damming Flow of Money," *Washington Post*, August 9, 2006, A3.

14. For an extended discussion of zakat, see Mona Atia, *Building a House in Heaven: Pious Neoliberalism and Islamic Charity in Egypt* (Minneapolis: University of Minnesota Press, 2013), 12–14.

15. For a comprehensive collection of legal scholarship on this topic, see Marcus Owens, "Symposium: The Anti-Terrorist Financing Guidelines. The Impact on International Philanthropy," *Pace Law Review* 25, no. 2 (2005).

16. William E. Connolly, *Capitalism and Christianity, American Style* (Durham, NC: Duke University Press, 2008).

17. Junaid Rana, *Terrifying Muslims: Race and Labor in the South Asian Diaspora* (Durham, NC: Duke University Press, 2011).

18. Mathijs Pelkmans found that even in Kyrgyzstan, "while 'sectarian' Protestant movements were classified as legitimate denominations, Muslim reformist movements were readily perceived as a threat to the government and suspected of links to terrorist organizations." Mathijs Pelkmans, "The 'Transparency' of Christian Proselytizing in Kyrgyzstan," *Anthropological Quarterly* 82, no. 2 (April 1, 2009): 423–46, 440.

19. There has emerged considerable legal scholarship on this issue, best summarized in Wadie E. Said, *Crimes of Terror: The Legal and Political Implications of Federal Terrorism Prosecutions* (New York: Oxford University Press, 2015); see also Jonathan Benthall, "The Palestinian Zakat Committees 1993–2007 and Their Contested Interpretations," Geneva: Graduate Institute of International and Development Studies, Program for the Study of International Organization(s), 2008, accessed March 31, 2017, http://insanonline.net/images/news_file/10325135848f9981849c65.pdf; David Cole, *Enemy Aliens: Double Standards and Constitutional Freedoms in the War on Terrorism*, new ed. (New York: New Press, 2005). The ACLU report on the topic is also important: American Civil Liberties Union, *Blocking Faith, Freezing Charity: Chilling Muslim Charitable Giving in the "War on Terrorism Financing"* (New York: ACLU, June 2009), https://www.aclu.org/files/pdfs/humanrights/blockingfaith.pdf.

20. Elizabeth Castelli, "Theologizing Human Rights: Christian Activism and the Limits of Religious Freedom," in *Non-Governmental Politics*, ed. Michel Fehre, 673–87 (New York: Zone Books, 2007).

21. Pelkmans, "The 'Transparency' of Christian Proselytizing."

22. George Marsden, ed., *Evangelicalism and Modern America* (Grand Rapids, MI: Eerdmans, 1984).

23. See R. Andrew Chesnut, *Born Again in Brazil: The Pentecostal Boom and the Pathogens of Poverty* (New Brunswick, NJ: Rutgers University Press, 1997).

24. Uta Andrea Balbier, "Billy Graham's Crusade in the 1950s: Neo-Evangelicalism between Civil Religion, Media, and Consumerism," *Bulletin of the GHI*, GHI research (spring 2009): 74, 80.

25. "History," Samaritanspurse.org, n.d., accessed January 4, 2016, http://www.samaritanspurse.org/our-ministry/history.

26. Michael Gryboski, "Franklin Graham: Islam Has Declared War on the World," *Christian Post*, November 18, 2015, accessed January 1, 2016, http://www.christianpost.com/news/franklin-graham-islam-war-world-150362.

27. Laurie Goodstein, "A Nation at War: Missionaries, Groups Critical of Islam Are Now Waiting to Take Aid to Iraq," *New York Times*, April 4, 2003, sec. U.S., accessed January 1, 2016, http://www.nytimes.com/2003/04/04/us/nation-war-missionaries-groups-critical-islam-are-now-waiting-take-aid-iraq.html.

28. Joseph Ax and Jerry Norton, "Darfur Kidnapping Victim Sues Aid Group That Sent Her," *Reuters*, May 19, 2011, accessed January 4, 2016, http://www.reuters.com/article/us-newyork-kidnap-idUSTRE74I70A20110519.

29. David Gonzalez, "U.S. Aids Conversion-Minded Quake Relief in El Salvador," *New York Times*, March 5, 2001, accessed January 4, 2016, http://www.nytimes.com/2001/03/05/world/us-aids-conversion-minded-quake-relief-in-el-salvador.html.

30. Erica Bornstein, *The Spirit of Development: Protestant NGOs, Morality, and Economics in Zimbabwe* (Stanford, CA: Stanford University Press, 2005).

31. Word Vision, homepage, 2015, accessed January 4, 2016, http://www.worldvision.org.

32. "Women's Empowerment," UNDP, accessed May 30, 2016, http://www.undp.org/content/undp/en/home/ourwork/womenempowerment/overview.html.

33. Julie Hearn, "The 'Invisible' NGO: US Evangelical Missions in Kenya," *Journal of Religion in Africa* 32, no. 1 (February 1, 2002): 32–60.

34. Ju Hui Judy Han, "Contemporary Korean/American Evangelical Missions: Politics of Space, Gender, and Difference" (PhD diss., University of California, Berkeley, 2009), http://search.proquest.com/docview/929138797.

35. Pelkmans, "The 'Transparency' of Christian Proselytizing," 438.

36. Mary E. Hancock, "New Mission Paradigms and the Encounter with Islam: Fusing Voluntarism, Tourism and Evangelism in Short-Term Missions in the USA," *Culture and Religion: An Interdisciplinary Journal* 14, no. 3 (2013): 305–23, doi:10.1080/14755610.2012.758160.

37. James Pfeiffer, "Civil Society, NGOs and the Holy Spirit in Mozambique," *Human Organization* 63, no. 4 (2004): 359–72.

38. Scott H. Evertz, "How Ideology Trumped Science: Why PEPFAR Has Failed to Meet Its Potential" (Washington, DC: Council for Global Equality and Center for American Progress, January 2010), accessed January 1, 2016, http://www.globalequality.org/storage/documents/pdf/pepfar_report_final_c.pdf.

39. Pelkmans, "The 'Transparency' of Christian Proselytizing," 436. Barry Yeoman, "The Stealth Crusade," *Mother Jones*, May/June 2002, accessed January 4, 2016, http://www.motherjones.com/politics/2002/05/stealth-crusade. See also Frontiers, homepage, n.d., accessed January 4, 2016, http://frontiers.org; Global Frontier Missions, homepage, 2016, accessed January 4, 2016, http://www.globalfrontiermissions.org.

40. Mpoe Johanna Keikelame, Colleen K Murphy, Karin E Ringheim, and Sara Woldehanna, "Perceptions of HIV/AIDS Leaders about Faith-Based Organisations' Influence on HIV/AIDS Stigma in South Africa," *African Journal of AIDS Research* 9, no. 1 (2010): 63–70, doi:10.2989/16085906.2010.484571; see also the chapter on US missionary work in Uganda in Tom Waidzunas, *The Straight Line: How the Fringe Science of Ex-Gay Therapy Reoriented Sexuality* (Minneapolis: University of Minnesota Press, 2015).

41. Atia, *Building a House in Heaven*. Atia gives the example of the popular television preacher Amr Khaled, who "blends religion, self-reliance, and business principles" (136).

42. Alex de Waal, *Famine Crimes: Politics and the Disaster Relief Industry in Africa*, September 1, 2009, ed. (London: Indiana University Press, 2009), 103. On that same page, however, de Waal states that "Western thinking on famine and relief is founded on the distinctions between charitable and commercial, humanitarian and military, religious and secular, governmental and non-governmental" (103). This sentence is strange, given that in this chapter de Waal describes USAID politics in detail, showing the geopolitics of famine relief at work. In chapter 2 of this book, I argued that humanitarianism is soft

power and tied to both military and war, and in this one I am arguing that soft power links religion and humanitarianism in similar ways.

43. Jonathan Benthall, "Islamic Aid in a North Malian Enclave," *Anthropology Today* 22, no. 4 (2006): 19–21.

44. Jonathan Benthall, *The Palestinian Zakat Committees 1993–2007 and Their Contested Interpretations* (Geneva: Graduate Institute of International and Development Studies, Program for the Study of International Organization[s], 2008), 15, accessed March 31, 2017, http://insanonline.net/images/news_file/10325135848f9981849c65.pdf.

45. Jonathan Benthall and Jerome Bellion-Jourdan, *The Charitable Crescent: Politics of Aid in the Muslim World*, 2nd ed. (London: I. B. Tauris, 2008).

46. Henry A. Giroux, "Beyond Belief: Religious Fundamentalism and Cultural Politics in the Age of George W. Bush," *Cultural Studies ↔ Critical Methodologies* 4, no. 4 (November 1, 2004): 415–25, doi:10.1177/1532708604268219.

47. Sheila Carapico, "Sleeping with the Devil?," *ISIM Review* 20 (2007): 8–9.

48. David E. Kaplan, "Hearts, Minds, and Dollars," *U.S. News and World Report*, April 25, 2005, 22.

49. Kaplan, "Hearts, Minds, and Dollars."

50. Hearn, "The 'Invisible' NGO." Also see Asteris Huliaras, "Evangelists, Oil Companies, and Terrorists: The Bush Administration's Policy towards Sudan," *Orbis* 50, no. 4 (2006): 709–24; Nilay Saiya, "Onward Christian Soldiers: American Dispensationalists, George W. Bush and the Middle East," *Holy Land Studies: A Multidisciplinary Journal* 11, no. 2 (2012): 175–204.

51. Robert Wuthnow, *Saving America? Faith-Based Services and the Future of Civil Society* (Princeton, NJ: Princeton University Press, 2004), 14.

52. Rodney Stark, "Some Basic Facts on America's Armies of Compassion," in *Not by Faith or Government Alone: Rethinking the Role of Faith-Based Organizations* (Waco, TX: Baylor Institute for Studies of Religion, 2008), 11, accessed March 31, 2017, http://www.baylorisr.org/wp-content/uploads/notbyfaith_report1.pdf1.pdf.

53. "Looking Carefully at Charitable Choice," *Southern Communities* 5 (October 31, 2000): 8.

54. Andrea Pallios, "Should We Have Faith in the Faith-Based Initiative? A Constitutional Analysis of President Bush's Charitable Choice Plan," *Hastings Constitutional Law Quarterly* 30, no. 1 (2002): 131–72.

55. Anne Farris, Richard P. Nathan, and David J. Wright, "The Expanding Administrative Presidency: George W. Bush and the Faith-Based Initiative," Roundtable on Religion and Social Welfare Policy (Albany, NY: Nelson A. Rockefeller Institute of Government, August 2004), accessed May 29, 2015, http://www.rockinst.org/pdf/federalism/2004-08-the_expanding_administrative_presidency_george_w_bush_and_the_faith-based_initiative.pdf.

56. All quotations in this paragraph are from George W. Bush, "Rallying the Armies of Compassion," Archives.gov, January 30, 2001, accessed July 31, 2013, http://georgewbush-whitehouse.archives.gov/news/reports/faithbased.html.

57. R. Marie Griffith and Melani McAlister, "Introduction: Is the Public Square Still Naked?," *American Quarterly* 59, no. 3 (2007): 527–63, doi:10.1353/aq.2007.0056.

58. Bob Herbert, "In America; Refusing to Save Africans," *New York Times,* June 11, 2001, sec. Opinion, accessed January 1, 2016, http://www.nytimes.com/2001/06/11/opinion/in-america-refusing-to-save-africans.html.

59. David Kuo, *Tempting Faith: An Inside Story of Political Seduction* (New York: Free Press, 2007).

60. Kuo, *Tempting Faith,* 160.

61. Kuo, *Tempting Faith,* 169.

62. Kuo, *Tempting Faith,* 214.

63. Kuo, *Tempting Faith,* 216.

64. Georgia A. Persons, "Administrative Policy Initiatives and the Limits of Change: Lessons from the Implementation of the Bush Faith-Based and Community Initiative," *Politics and Policy* 39, no. 9 (2011): 949–78, doi:10.1111/j.1747–1346.2011.00332.x.

65. Rebecca Sager, "The 'Purpose Driven' Policy": Explaining State-Level Variation in the Faith-Based Initiatives" (PhD diss., University of Arizona, Tucson, 2006).

66. Sager, "The 'Purpose Driven' Policy," 37–38.

67. Sager, "The 'Purpose Driven' Policy," 126.

68. Sager, "The 'Purpose Driven' Policy," 140.

69. Evidence of this also comes from conservatives who worked in the Bush White House. David Kuo writes in his memoir that though committees making decisions about funding were not explicitly told to only give resources to conservative evangelical Christian churches, they did assume that only those churches could get funding.

70. United States Government Accountability Office, *Faith-Based and Community Initiative: Improvements in Monitoring Grantees and Measuring Performance Could Enhance Accountability* (Washington, DC: United States Government Accountability Office, June 2006), accessed January 4, 2016, http://www.gao.gov/new.items/d06616.pdf.

71. United States Government Accountability Office, *Faith-Based and Community Initiative,* 3.

72. United States Government Accountability Office, *Faith-Based and Community Initiative,* 6.

73. United States Government Accountability Office, *Faith-Based and Community Initiative,* 7.

74. Ben Canada and David M. Ackerman, *Faith-Based Organizations: Current Issues* (Hauppauge, NY: Nova Science Publishers, 2003).

75. American Civil Liberties Union, "Support Civil Rights: Oppose the Faith-Based Initiative," March 12, 2003, accessed December 23, 2013, http://www.aclu.org.

76. Mark Chaves, "Debunking Charitable Choice," *Stanford Social Innovation Review,* summer 2003, accessed January 4, 2016, http://www.ssireview.org/articles/entry/debunking_charitable_choice.

77. Mustapha Bayoumi, *How Does it Feel to Be a Problem? Being Young and Arab in America* (New York: Penguin, 2008).

78. David Theo Goldberg, *The Racial State* (Malden, MA: Blackwell, 2002).

79. Sherene Razack, *Casting Out: The Eviction of Muslims from Western Law and Politics* (Toronto: University of Toronto Press, 2008).

80. Paul Amar, "Introduction: New Racial Missions of Policing: Comparative Studies of State Authority, Urban Governance, and Security Technology in the Twenty-First Century," *Ethnic and Racial Studies* 33, no. 4 (2010): 575–92.

81. Asli Ü Bâli, "Scapegoating the Vulnerable: Preventive Detention of Immigrants in America's 'War on Terror,'" *Studies in Law, Politics and Society* 38 (2006): 25–69.

82. While my chapter will focus only on the criminalization and contestation over humanitarian organizations, there is now a vast literature on the topic of state and non-state violence against Muslims and Arabs—and South Asian groups such as Sikhs—after 9/11. A useful summary of some of this surveillance is provided in Said, *Crimes of Terror*.

83. Said, *Crimes of Terror*, 51.

84. Said, *Crimes of Terror*, 53. For the statute, see "18 U.S. Code § 2339B—Providing Material Support or Resources to Designated Foreign Terrorist Organizations," LII/Legal Information Institute, accessed June 5, 2016, https://www.law.cornell.edu/uscode/text/18/2339B.

85. "18 U.S. Code § 2339B." See also Charles Doyle, "Terrorist Material Support: An Overview of 18 U.S.C 2339A and 2339B," CRS Report for Congress (Washington, DC: Congressional Research Service), accessed May 30, 2016, https://www.fas.org/sgp/crs/natsec/R41333.pdf.

86. American Civil Liberties Union, *Blocking Faith, Freezing Charity*. Also see Laurie Goodstein, "A Nation at War: Muslims Hesitating on Gifts as U.S. Scrutinizes Charities," *New York Times*, April 17, 2003, accessed January 4, 2016, http://www.nytimes.com/2003/04/17/us/nation-war-charities-muslims-hesitating-gifts-us-scrutinizes-charities.html.

87. Erica Caple James, "Governing Gifts: Law, Risk, and the 'War on Terror,'" *UCLA Journal of Islamic and Near Eastern Law* 10 (2010/2011): 65–84.

88. This authorization came from Executive Order No. 13224, 66 Fed. Reg. 49,079 (September 25, 2001), issued by President George W. Bush; and "Continuation of the National Emergency with Respect to Persons Who Commit, Threaten to Commit, or Support Terrorism," 74 Fed. Reg. 48,359 (September 21, 2009), issued by President Barack Obama.

89. Sam Adelsberg, Freya Pitts, and Sirine Shebaya, "The Chilling Effect of the 'Material Support' Law on Humanitarian Aid: Causes, Consequences, and Proposed Reforms," *Harvard National Security Journal* 4, no. 282 (2013): 300–318.

90. Adelsberg, Pitts, and Shebaya, "The Chilling Effect"; Nina J. Crimm, "Symposium: Muslim-Americans' Charitable Giving Dilemma. What about a Terror-Free Donor Advised Fund?," *Roger Williams University Law Review* 13 (2008): 375–410.

91. Stephanie Clifford, "At Trial, Arab Bank's Lawyer Spars with Witness," *New York Times*, September 4, 2014, accessed July 24, 2016, http://www.nytimes.com/2014/09/05/nyregion/at-a-trial-in-brooklyn-arab-banks-lawyer-spars-with-witness.html.

92. James J. Ward, "The Root of All Evil: Expanding Criminal Liability for Providing Material Support to Terror," *Notre Dame Law Review* 84 (2008): 471–510.

93. Global Nonprofit Information Network, "Overview of U.S. Counterterrorism Policies Impacting Charities" (Global Nonprofit Information Network, n.d.).

94. Eric Sandberg-Zakian, "Do the Fifth and Sixth Amendments Prohibit the Designation of U.S. Persons under the International Emergency Economic Powers Act?," *Student Scholarship Papers*, paper no. 103 (April 1, 2010), http://digitalcommons.law.yale .edu/student_papers/103.

95. David Cole and James X. Dempsey, *Terrorism and the Constitution: Sacrificing Civil Liberties in the Name of National Security*, 2nd ed. (New York: New Press, 2006).

96. Michael G. Freedman, "Prosecuting Terrorism: The Material Support Statute and Muslim Charities," *Hastings Constitutional Law Quarterly* 38, no. 4 (2011): 1130–50.

97. Jeff Breinholt, "Resolved, or Is It? The First Amendment and Giving Money to Terrorists," *American University Law Review* 57, no. 5 (June 2008): 1273–90, 1278.

98. Breinholt, "Resolved, or Is It?," 1279.

99. Breinholt, "Resolved, or Is It?," 1281.

100. Crimm, "Symposium," 390.

101. Case No. 3:06MJ7019, United States District Court for the Northern District of Ohio, Western Division, 594 F. Supp. 2nd 855; 2009 US Dist. LEXIS 9055 (2009).

102. KindHearts for Charitable Humanitarian Development, Inc. v. Timothy Geithner, 647 F. Supp. 2d 857–910 (2010).

103. Said, *Crimes of Terror*, 49–50.

104. Ward, "The Root of all Evil," 471–510.

105. Caroline Preston, "Charity Leaders See Broad Impact from Ruling on Muslim Charity," *Chronicle of Philanthropy* 21, no. 5 (2008), accessed January 4, 2016, https:// philanthropy.com/article/Charity-Leaders-See-Broad/173727.

106. Eric Sandberg-Zakian, "Counterterrorism, the Constitution, and the Civil-Criminal Divide: Evaluating the Designation of U.S. Persons under the International Emergency Economic Powers Act," *Harvard Journal on Legislation* 48 (November 2011): 95.

107. Laura Donohue, "Constitutional and Legal Challenges to the Anti-Terrorist Finance Regime," *Wake Forest Law Review* 43, no. 3 (2008): 643–97.

108. Dave Eggers, *Zeitoun*, repr. ed. (New York: Vintage, 2010).

109. Sally Howell, "(Re)Bounding Islamic Charitable Giving in the Terror Decade," UCLA *Journal of Islamic and Near Eastern Law* 10, no. 1 (2010–2011): 35–64; "Raided Muslim Charity Sues Bank."

110. See Al-Haramain Islamic Found., Inc. v. US Dep't of the Treasury (*Al-Haramain II*), No. 07-1155-KI, 2009 WL 3756363, at 1 (D. Or. Nov. 5, 2009); Islamic Am. Relief Agency I, 394 F. Supp. 2d 34 (D. D.C. 2005); Holy Land Found. for Relief and Dev. v. Ashcroft (*Holy Land II*), 333 F. 3d 156 (D.C. Cir. 2003); KindHearts v. Geithner (*KindHearts I*), 647 F. Supp. 2d 857 (N.D. Ohio 2009).

111. Peter Margulies, "Advising Terrorism: Material Support, Safe Harbors, and Freedom of Speech," *Hastings Law Journal* 63, no. 2 (January 1, 2012): 461.

112. Margulies, "Advising Terrorism."

113. Holder v. Humanitarian Law Project, 130 S. Ct. (2010), 2735.

114. Despite these legal decisions and government attacks, many non-Muslim US organizations have also come to support and work with Muslim agencies, challenging government practices.

115. Crimm, "Symposium," 410.

116. Matthew Levitt, *Hamas: Politics, Charity, and Terrorism in the Service of Jihad*, annotated ed. (New Haven: Yale University Press, 2006), 2–3.

117. Benthall, *The Palestinian Zakat Committees.*

118. Margulies, "Advising Terrorism," 461n28. The footnote cites *Kilburn v. Socialist People's Libyan Aran Jamahiriay*, 376. F. 3d 1123 (C.C. Cir 2004), for this precedent.

119. Holder v. Humanitarian Law Project, 130 S. Ct. 2705, 2712, 2723 (2010). This is Chief Justice Roberts, writing for a 6–4 majority.

120. Norman I. Silber, "Charity Considered as a Terrorist Tool," *Hofstra Horizons*, spring 2002, accessed January 4, 2016, http://www.hofstra.edu/pdf/about/administration/provost/hofhrz/hofhrz_s02_silber.pdf.

121. Silber, "Charity Considered as a Terrorist Tool."

122. Silber, "Charity Considered as a Terrorist Tool."

123. Al-Mabarrat Foundation, homepage, 2014, accessed January 1, 2016, http://www.almabarrat.org/.

124. Howell, "(Re)bounding Islamic Charitable Giving in the Terror Decade," 35.

125. Laurie Goodstein, "U.S. Muslims Taken Aback by a Charity's Conviction," *New York Times*, November 26, 2008, A23, accessed January 4, 2016, http://www.nytimes.com/2008/11/26/us/26charity.html.

126. James, "Governing Gifts."

127. Goodstein, "U.S. Muslims Taken Aback by a Charity's Conviction."

128. William Fisher, "Muslim Charities Negotiate a Minefield," *IPS: Inter Press Service*, August 29, 2008, sec. International, accessed January 4, 2016, http://www.ipsnews.net/2008/08/politics-us-muslim-charities-negotiate-a-minefield.

129. Fisher, "Muslim Charities Negotiate a Minefield."

130. United States Department of the Treasury, *U.S. Department of the Treasury Anti-Terrorist Financing Guidelines: Voluntary Best Practices for U.S.-Based Charities* (Washington, DC: United States Department of the Treasury, 2005), http://www.treasury.gov/press-center/press-releases/Documents/0929%20finalrevised.pdf.

131. United States Department of the Treasury, *U.S. Department of the Treasury Anti-Terrorist Financing Guidelines*, 14.

132. United States Department of the Treasury, *U.S. Department of the Treasury Anti-Terrorist Financing Guidelines*, 14. See also Levitt, *Hamas* (documenting the logistical and financial support Hamas charities provide for the group's political and terrorist activities); Heather Timmons, "British Study Charitable Organizations for Links to Plot," *New York Times*, August 25, 2006, accessed January 5, 2016, http://www.nytimes.com/2006/08/25/world/europe/25britain.html?_r=0 (describing the risks inherent in delivering charitable aid and resources to high-risk areas where terrorist organizations are known to operate); Robert F. Worth and Hassan M. Fattah, "Relief Agencies Find Hezbollah Hard to Avoid," *New York Times*, August 23, 2006, accessed

January 5, 2016, http://www.nytimes.com/2006/08/23/world/middleeast/23lebanon
.html (describing Hezbollah's efforts to cultivate support by controlling the provision
of charitable resources and services across southern Lebanon); Laila Bokhair, *Political Struggle over Earthquake Victims* (Kjeller, Norway: Norwegian Defense Research
Establishment, November 23, 2005) (documenting the efforts of terrorist organizations
such as Lashkar-e-Taiba and Jaish-e-Mohammed to provide humanitarian aid after the
South Asia earthquake); Christopher Kremmer, "Charities Linked to Extremists Lead
Quake Relief," *Age*, November 21, 2005, accessed January 5, 2016, http://www.theage
.com.au/news/world/charities-linked-to-extremists-lead-quake-relief/2005/11/20
/1132421545811.html (reporting that in addition to providing relief in South Asia, terrorist organizations are recruiting and indoctrinating orphan children in their extensive
network of orphanages); Evan Kohlmann, *The Role of Islamic Charities in International
Terrorist Recruitment and Financing* (Copenhagen: Danish Institute for International
Studies, 2006), http://www.tenc.net/archive/DIIS%20WP%202006-7.pdf (tracing the
historical link between charitable organizations and terrorist activities from the Soviet–
Afghan war through to the present); BBC News, "Faith, Hate and Charity: Transcript,"
BBC One, Recorded from Transmission, July 30, 2006 (reporting on one of Britain's
leading Islamic charities, Interpol, and illustrating Interpol's use of a network of charities
in Gaza and the West Bank to support and fund Hamas, which the US Government and
the European Union have labeled a terrorist organization).

133. United States Department of the Treasury, *Response to Comments Submitted on
the U.S. Department of the Treasury Anti-Terrorist Financing Guidelines: Voluntary Best
Practices for U.S.-Based Charities* (Washington, DC: United States Department of the
Treasury, December 1, 2010), https://www.treasury.gov/resource-center/terrorist-illicit
-finance/Documents/response.pdf.

134. Armand Mattelart, *The Globalization of Surveillance*, trans. Susan Taponier and
James A. Cohen (Cambridge: Polity, 2010).

135. Matthew Levitt, "Hezbollah's West Bank Terror Network," *Middle East Intelligence Bulletin* (August–September 2003), accessed April 15, 2017, http://www
.washingtoninstitute.org/policy-analysis/view/hezbollahs-west-bank-terror-network.
This article by Levitt is based on unnamed intelligence sources, including Israeli ones.

136. David Murakami Wood and Stephen Graham, "Permeable Boundaries in the
Software-Sorted Society: Surveillance and Differentiations of Mobility," in *Mobile
Technologies of the City*, ed. Mimi Sheller and John Urry (New York: Routledge, 2006),
188.

137. Aloke Chakravarty, "Feeding Humanity, Starving Terror: The Utility of Aid in a
Comprehensive Antiterrorism Financing Strategy," *Western New England Law Review*
32, no. 2 (2010): 295–338.

138. "Financing Terrorism: Looking in All the Wrong Places," *Economist*, October 20,
2005, accessed January 5, 2016, http://www.economist.com/node/5053373?story_id
=5053373.

139. "Financing Terrorism: Looking in All the Wrong Places."

140. Ben Protess and Stephanie Clifford, "Suit Accuses Banks of Role in Financing
Terror Attacks," *New York Times*, November 11, 2014, B1, B5.

141. Mattelart, *The Globalization of Surveillance*, 156.

142. Mattelart, *The Globalization of Surveillance*.

143. Suzanne Malveaux and Jessica Yelin, "Obama Overhauls Faith-Based Agency," CNN, February 5, 2009, accessed June 3, 2013, http://politicalticker.blogs.cnn.com/2009 /02/05/obama-overhauls-faith-based-agency/.

144. Barack Obama, "Remarks by the President at Points of Light 20th Anniversary, College Station, Texas," presented at the Points of Light 20th Anniversary, College Station, Texas, October 16, 2009, WhiteHouse.gov, accessed June 3, 2016, https://www .whitehouse.gov/photos-and-video/video/president-obama-points-light-forum -texas#transcript.

145. Thanks to Cathy Hannabach for this point.

4. "Security Moms" and "Security Feminists"

1. Valerie Amos and Pratibha Parmar, "Challenging Imperial Feminism," *Feminist Review*, no. 17 (1984): 3–19.

2. Cindy Sheehan is a white, US woman who vocally protested George W. Bush's Iraq War after her son was killed while fighting as a US soldier. In her memoir, Sheehan, too, presents herself as one of many naive Americans who had not questioned the rationale for the war until her son was killed. Her voice became a rallying cry for a short-lived antiwar movement. Sheehan is part of a long history of women in twentieth-century peace movements who participated in national and international projects, culminating in numerous protests against US foreign policy and its military and nuclear power. Opposition to war, which in part enabled Barack Obama to win the presidency, has grown largely in response to the war's failures, massive expenditures, and corruption, as well as the loss of American soldiers' lives. Yet, the war on terror has continued. Sheehan disappeared quickly from public view after the Bush presidency, though she remains active in the Peace and Freedom Party and in a variety of leftist causes. Calling herself a "Peace Mom," Sheehan runs a radio show and website and has written a memoir, *Peace Mom*, about her time in the media spotlight.

3. Joshua Reves, "If You See Something, Say Something: Lateral Surveillance and the Uses of Responsibility," *Surveillance and Society* 10, nos. 3/4 (2012): 235–48.

4. Amy Kaplan, *The Anarchy of Empire in the Making of U.S. Culture* (Cambridge, MA: Harvard University Press, 2005).

5. Lila Abu-Lughod, *Do Muslim Women Need Saving?* (Cambridge, MA: Harvard University Press, 2015), 32.

6. Gayatri Chakravorty Spivak, "Can the Subaltern Speak?," in *Marxism and the Interpretation of Culture*, ed. Cary Nelson and Lawrence Grossberg, 271–313 (Urbana: University of Illinois Press, 1988).

7. More recently, this project has extended to rescuing LGBT people from their "traditional cultures" and incorporating them into new forms of global modernity. The nineteenth century saw the imposition of British colonial antisodomy laws that criminalized all sexual practices that did not conform to heterosexuality. American evangelists, such as those I describe in chapter 3, have been active in many parts of the world spreading

newer versions of homophobia and heteronormativity. In doing so they, along with the enthusiastic nationalisms of many modern nation-states, continue the project of normalizing heteronormativity for postcolonial and postconflict social formations. See Jasbir K. Puar on what she calls "homonationalism": Jasbir K. Puar, *Terrorist Assemblages: Homonationalism in Queer Times* (Durham, NC: Duke University Press, 2007).

8. Joseph S. Nye, *Soft Power: The Means to Success in World Politics* (New York: Public Affairs, 2004); Melani McAlister, *Epic Encounters: Culture, Media, and U.S. Interests in the Middle East since 1945* (Berkeley: University of California Press, 2001); Colin S. Gray, *Hard Power and Soft Power: The Utility of Military Force as an Instrument of Policy in the 21st Century* (Carlisle, PA: Strategic Studies Institute, 2011); Leigh Armistead, *Information Operations: Warfare and the Hard Reality of Soft Power* (Lincoln, NE: Potomac Books, 2004); Roberto J. González "Human Terrain: Past, Present, and Future, Applications," *Anthropology Today* 24, no. 1 (February 1, 2008): 21–26, doi:10.1111/j.1467-8322.2008.00561.x; American Anthropological Association, "AAA Opposes US Military's Human Terrain System Project," n.d., accessed February 4, 2016, http://www.aaanet .org/issues/AAA-Opposes-Human-Terrain-System-Project.cfm; Maja Zehfuss, "Culturally Sensitive War? The Human Terrain System and the Seduction of Ethics," *Security Dialogue* 43, no. 2 (April 1, 2012): 175–90, doi:10.1177/0967010612438431. See also the US military's Human Terrain website: http://humanterrainsystem.army.mil/about.html (accessed August 8, 2014). This program was ended by the US Army in 2014 and the website is no longer available.

9. See Simone Browne for the long history of surveillance of African American communities: Simone Browne, *Dark Matters: On the Surveillance of Blackness* (Durham, NC: Duke University Press, 2015).

10. Carrie Rentschler and Carol A. Stabile, "States of Insecurity and the Gendered Politics of Fear," *NWSA Journal* 17, no. 3 (2005): vii–xxv.

11. Browne, *Dark Matters*; Kathleen M. Blee, *Women of the Klan: Racism and Gender in the 1920s*, with a New Preface ed. (Berkeley: University of California Press, 2008).

12. Miranda Joseph, *Debt to Society: Accounting for Life under Capitalism* (Minneapolis: University of Minnesota Press, 2014); Joseph J. Fischel, *Sex and Harm in the Age of Consent* (Minneapolis: University of Minnesota Press, 2016); Setha M. Low, *Behind the Gates: Life, Security, and the Pursuit of Happiness in Fortress America* (New York: Routledge, 2004).

13. For two very different accounts, one with a longer historical arc and one on the recent wars, see Junaid Rana, *Terrifying Muslims: Race and Labor in the South Asian Diaspora* (Durham, NC: Duke University Press, 2011); and Browne, *Dark Matters*.

14. Carole Pateman and Charles Mills, *The Contract and Domination* (Cambridge: Polity, 2007).

15. Shelley Mallett, "Understanding Home: A Critical Review of the Literature," *Sociological Review* 52, no. 1 (February 1, 2004): 62–89.

16. Vicki Bell, "The Vigilant(e) Parent and the Paedophile: The News of the World Campaign 2000 and the Contemporary Governmentality of Child Sexual Abuse," *Feminist Theory* 3, no. 1 (2002): 83–102.

17. Bell, "The Vigilant(e) Parent and the Paedophile," 92.

18. Bell, "The Vigilant(e) Parent and the Paedophile," 100.

19. Another important moment in the United Kingdom was the News Corp scandal when Rupert Murdoch–owned newspapers were found to be hacking the phones of a murdered girl, Milly Dowler, as well as the phones of deceased military personnel. The ensuing scandal scaled down Murdoch's ambitions in the United Kingdom and brought to light collaborations between high-ranking police and reporters spying on celebrities and the British royal family.

20. Fischel, *Sex and Harm in the Age of Consent*.

21. Puar, *Terrorist Assemblages*.

22. Karen Tumulty and Viveca Novak, "Goodbye, Soccer Mom. Hello, Security Mom," *Time*, May 25, 2003, accessed February 4, 2016, http://content.time.com/time /magazine/article/0,9171,454487,00.html.

23. Michelle Malkin, "Candidates Ignore Security Moms at Their Peril," *USA Today*, July 20, 2004, accessed February 4, 2016, http://www.usatoday.com/news/opinion /editorials/2004-07-20-malkin_x.htm.

24. Malkin's website is available at http://www.michellemalkin.com.

25. Malkin, "Candidates Ignore Security Moms at Their Peril."

26. Malkin, "Candidates Ignore Security Moms at Their Peril."

27. Malkin, "Candidates Ignore Security Moms at Their Peril."

28. Malkin, "Candidates Ignore Security Moms at Their Peril."

29. For an interesting take on this security pedagogy, see the viral video *Kony 2012*, made by Invisible Children, Inc. In the video, Invisible Children director and founder Jason Russell gives his four-year-old son an education in humanitarian violence, telling him about the violence enacted by Joseph Kony and the Lord's Resistance Army in Uganda, the Democratic Republic of the Congo, and South Sudan. In a context of US culture, such violent pedagogy seems to be normative across media spheres.

30. The literature on American nationalism is a long one and includes the following works, some from the liberal postwar American intellectual history tradition, and some more recent influenced by imperial, colonial, and postcolonial historiography: Merle Eugene Curti, *The Roots of American Loyalty* (New York: Columbia University Press, 1946); Richard Hofstadter, "Cuba, the Philippines, and Manifest Destiny," in *The Paranoid Style in American Politics and Other Essays* (New York: Vintage Books, [1952] 2008); Jack Citrin, Ernst B. Haas, Christopher Muste, and Beth Reingold, "Is American Nationalism Changing? Implications for Foreign Policy," *International Studies Quarterly* 38, no. 1 (March 1, 1994): 1–31; Michael Kazin and Joseph Anthony McCartin, *Americanism: New Perspectives on the History of an Ideal* (Chapel Hill: University of North Carolina Press, 2006); Kaplan, *The Anarchy of Empire in the Making of U.S. Culture*; Hans Kohn, *American Nationalism: An Interpretative Essay* (New York: Macmillan, 1957); David Waldstreicher, *In the Midst of Perpetual Fetes: The Making of American Nationalism, 1776–1820* (Chapel Hill: University of North Carolina Press, 1997); John Bodnar, *Remaking America: Public Memory, Commemoration, and Patriotism in the Twentieth Century* (Princeton, NJ: Princeton University Press, 1993); Donald E. Pease, *Cultures of*

United States Imperialism (Durham, NC: Duke University Press, 1994); Matthew Frye Jacobson, *Barbarian Virtues: The United States Encounters Foreign Peoples at Home and Abroad, 1876–1917* (New York: Hill and Wang, 2001).

31. Michelle Malkin, http://michellemalkin.com (accessed November 8, 2016).

32. Michelle Malkin, "A National Security Mom Manifesto," michellemalkin.com, July 20, 2004, accessed February 4, 2016, http://michellemalkin.com/2004/07/20/a-national-security-mom-manifesto.

33. John Mueller and Mark G. Stewart, "Balancing the Risks, Benefits, and Costs of Homeland Security," *Homeland Security Affairs: The Journal of the NPS Center for Homeland Defense and Security* 7, article 16 (August 2011), https://www.hsaj.org/articles/43.

34. Malkin, "A National Security Mom Manifesto."

35. Sandra Gunning, *Race, Rape, and Lynching: The Red Record of American Literature, 1890–1912* (New York: Oxford University Press, 1996); Crystal N. Feimster, *Southern Horrors: Women and the Politics of Rape and Lynching* (Cambridge, MA: Harvard University Press, 2011).

36. This rhetoric of safety doesn't just apply to white women here, since Malkin is Asian American. For the history of lynching during Jim Crow, see Feimster, *Southern Horrors*.

37. Kate Crawford and Jason Schultz, "Big Data and Due Process: Toward a Framework to Redress Predictive Privacy Harms," *Boston College Law Review* 55, no. 93 (2014): 93–128, http://papers.ssrn.com/abstract=2325784.

38. Lloyd Grove, "Michelle Malkin Has Feelings, Too," *Daily Beast*, September 22, 2009, accessed February 4, 2016, http://www.thedailybeast.com/articles/2009/09/22/michelle-malkin-has-feelings-too.html.

39. See, for instance, Malkin's website, http://michellemalkin.com. Her books are well known for their right-wing philosophy, and, like Ann Coulter, she often deploys unsubstantiated evidence to attack Democrats and liberals. Many of Malkin's arguments are based on specious evidence and have been refuted by scholars. For instance, her book on Japanese internment during World War II has Mohammed Atta on the cover, for some reason. See Michelle Malkin, *In Defense of Internment: The Case for Racial Profiling in World War II and the War on Terror* (Washington, DC: Regnery, 2004), and *Invasion: How America Still Welcomes Terrorists, Criminals and Other Foreign Menaces to Our Shores* (Washington, DC: Regnery, 2002).

40. Anthony S. Wang, "Demystifying the Asian American Neo-Conservative: A Strange and New Political Animal," *Asian American Law Journal* 5, no. 8 (1998): 213–46. Many of these conservative Asian Americans are East Asian conservative Protestants who belong to Korean and Chinese churches, or conservative Catholics. A few South Asians became prominent through participation in right-wing politics, such as Nikki Haley and Bobby Jindal. Vietnamese Americans form another group whose allegiance to the American nation comes from their refugee status after the Vietnam War and their anticommunist politics—which are changing as the new generation comes of age. On this topic, see Mimi Thi Nguyen, *The Gift of Freedom: War, Debt, and Other Refugee Passages* (Durham, NC: Duke University Press, 2012).

41. Ellen Goodman, "The Myth of 'Security Moms,'" *Boston Globe*, October 7, 2004, accessed February 4, 2016, http://www.boston.com/news/nation/articles/2004/10/07/the_myth_of_security_moms.

42. For critical debates on the term, see Linda Basch, "Human Security, Globalization, and Feminist Visions," *Peace Review* 16, no. 1 (2004): 5–12, doi:10.1080/104026504 2000210085; Roland Paris, "Human Security: Paradigm Shift or Hot Air?," *International Security* 26, no. 2 (October 1, 2001): 87–102; Mohammed Nuruzzaman, "Paradigms in Conflict: The Contested Claims of Human Security, Critical Theory and Feminism," *Cooperation and Conflict* 41, no. 3 (2006): 285–303; Natasha Marhia, "Some Humans Are More Human than Others: Troubling the 'Human' in Human Security from a Critical Feminist Perspective," *Security Dialogue* 44, no. 1 (February 1, 2013): 19–35; Ryerson Christie, "Critical Voices and Human Security: To Endure, to Engage or to Critique?," *Security Dialogue* 41, no. 2 (April 1, 2010): 169–90.

43. Tumulty and Novak, "Goodbye, Soccer Mom."

44. Jeri Thompson, "Security Moms Are Back," *American Spectator*, September 21, 2012, accessed February 4, 2016, http://spectator.org/blog/30573/security-moms-are-back.

45. Jacques Donzelot, *The Policing of Families* (Baltimore: Johns Hopkins University Press, 1997).

46. Thomas Piketty, *Capital in the Twenty-First Century* (Cambridge, MA: Belknap Press, 2014).

47. Cindi Katz, "The State Goes Home: Local Hypervigilance of Children and the Global Retreat from Social Reproduction," *Social Justice* 28, no. 3 (2001): 47–56.

48. Lisa McGirr, *Suburban Warriors: The Origins of the New American Right* (Princeton, NJ: Princeton University Press, 2002).

49. Kaplan, *Anarchy of Empire*.

50. David J. Armor, "Race and Gender in the U.S. Military," *Armed Forces and Society* 23, no. 1 (1996): 7–27, doi:10.1177/0095327X9602300101; Sara L. Zeigler and Gregory G. Gunderson, *Moving beyond GI Jane: Women and the U.S. Military* (Lanham, MD: University Press of America, 2005); Karen O. Dunivin, "Military Culture: Change and Continuity," *Armed Forces and Society* 20, no. 4 (1994): 531–47; Judith Stiehm, *It's Our Military Too: Women and the U.S. Military* (Philadelphia: Temple University Press, 1996); Sheila Jeffreys, "Double Jeopardy: Women, the US Military and the War in Iraq," *Women's Studies International Forum* 30, no. 1 (2007): 16–25, doi:10.1016/j.wsif.2006.12.002.

51. James Castonguay, "Fictions of Terror: Complexity, Complicity and Insecurity in *Homeland*," *Cinema Journal* 54, no. 4 (summer 2015): 139–45.

52. Senate Select Committee on Intelligence, "Committee Study of the Central Intelligence Agency's Detention and Interrogation Program" (Washington, DC: US Senate, December 9, 2014), https://www.intelligence.senate.gov/sites/default/files/documents/CRPT-113srpt288.pdf.

53. Elizabeth P. Macintosh, *Sisterhood of Spies: The Women of the OSS* (Annapolis, MD: Naval Institute Press, 1998); Amy J. Martin, "America's Evolution of Women and

Their Roles in the Intelligence Community," *Journal of Strategic Security* 8, no. 5 (fall 2015): 99–109.

54. The BBC television series *The Bletchley Files* is an excellent example of a recent media text that celebrates the detective abilities of women who worked in British intelligence during World War II as code breakers. The show presents these code breakers as neglected by war historians and popular culture because they were women working in intelligence services.

55. Maureen Dowd, "Good Riddance, Carrie Mathison," *New York Times*, April 4, 2015, accessed February 4, 2016, http://www.nytimes.com/2015/04/05/opinion /sunday/maureen-dowd-good-riddance-carrie-mathison.html.

56. Wendy Brown, *Walled States, Waning Sovereignty* (New York: Zone Books, 2014).

57. Timothy Melley, "Covert Spectacles and the Contradictions of the Democratic Security State," *StoryWorlds: A Journal of Narrative Studies* 6, no. 1 (2014): 61–82.

58. Bigelow shot many of the scenes depicting Pakistan in Chandigarh, India. See Ankur Batra and Jaspreet, "Kathryn Bigelow Shoots in Chandigarh," *Times of India*, March 2, 2012, accessed February 4, 2016, http://timesofindia.indiatimes.com /entertainment/english/hollywood/news/Kathryn-Bigelow-shoots-in-Chandigarh /articleshow/12097543.cms.

59. Melley, "Covert Spectacles," 67.

60. See, for instance, Robert J. Corber, "Cold War Femme: Lesbian Visibility in Joseph L. Mankiewicz's *All about Eve*," GLQ: *A Journal of Lesbian and Gay Studies* 11, no. 1 (2005): 1–22.

61. Melley, "Covert Spectacles."

62. Larry Gross, "Some Ways into Zero Dark Thirty," *Film Comment*, December 18, 2012, accessed February 4, 2016, http://www.filmcomment.com/entry/review-zero -dark-thirty-kathryn-bigelow.

63. Peter Bergen, "A Feminist Film Epic and the Real Women of the CIA," CNN, December 13, 2012, accessed February 4, 2016, http://www.cnn.com/2012/12/13/opinion /bergen-feminist-epic/index.html.

64. Zillah Eisenstein, "Dark Zero-Feminism," *Amass* 17, no. 3 (2013): 44–45.

65. Marouf Hasian, "*Zero Dark Thirty* and the Critical Challenges Posed by Populist Postfeminism during the Global War on Terrorism," *Journal of Communication Inquiry* 37, no. 4 (2013): 322–43, 337, doi:10.1177/0196859913505616.

66. Hasian, "*Zero Dark Thirty*," 332.

67. Peter L. Bergen, *Manhunt: The Ten-Year Search for bin Laden from 9/11 to Abbottabad* (New York: Broadway Books, 2013).

68. Bergen, "Feminist Film Epic."

69. Bergen, "Feminist Film Epic."

70. Bergen, "Feminist Film Epic."

71. Greg Miller, "In 'Zero Dark Thirty,' She's the Hero; in Real Life, CIA Agent's Career Is More Complicated," *Washington Post*, December 10, 2012, accessed April 4, 2017, https://www.washingtonpost.com/world/national-security/in-zero-dark-thirty

-shes-the-hero-in-real-life-cia-agents-career-is-more-complicated/2012/12/10/cedc227e
-42dd-11e2-9648-a2c323a991d6_story.html?utm_term=.fb0d275217e1.

72. Paul Harris, "Valerie Plame Welcomes New Breed of Fictional Female Spy in
Zero Dark Thirty," *Guardian*, December 15, 2012, accessed February 4, 2016, http://
www.theguardian.com/world/2012/dec/16/valerie-plame-female-spy-homeland-zero
-dark-thirty.

73. *Charlie Rose*, "Zero Dark Thirty," December 6, 2012, accessed April 4, 2017,
https://charlierose.com/videos/20079.

74. Senate Select Committee on Intelligence, "Committee Study of the Central Intelligence Agency's Detention and Interrogation Program."

75. "Glenn Greenwald and Peter Maas, " Meet Alfreda Frances Bikowsky, the Senior
Officer at the Center of the CIA's Torture Scandal," *The Intercept*, December 10, 2014,
accessed March 25, 2017, https://theintercept.com/2014/12/19/senior-cia-officer
-center-torture-scandals-alfreda-bikowsky/; Mia De Graaf, "Who Is the CIA's Queen
of Torture? Al Qaeda Expert Who Tortured Suspects, Lied to the Senate about Her
Results and Lost Key Information on 9/11 Was Mentioned 36 Times in Torture Report,"
Daily Mail, December 19, 2014, accessed February 4, 2016, http://www.dailymail.co.uk
/news/article-2881475/Who-CIA-s-queen-torture-Al-Qaeda-expert-tortured-suspects
-lied-Senate-results-lost-key-information-9-11-mentioned-36-times-torture-report.html;
Brad Knickerbocker, "CIA Analyst at the Center of Torture Report Is Outed: She's Not
'Maya,'" *Christian Science Monitor*, December 21, 2014, accessed April 4, 2017, http://
www.csmonitor.com/USA/Politics/DC-Decoder/2014/1221/CIA-analyst-at-the-center
-of-torture-report-is-outed.-She-s-not-Maya-video; Alex Johnson, " 'Rectal Hydration':
Inside the CIA's Interrogation of Khalid Sheikh Mohammed," NBC, December 9, 2014,
accessed February 4, 2016, http://www.nbcnews.com/storyline/cia-torture-report
/rectal-hydration-inside-cias-interrogation-khalid-sheikh-mohammed-n265016.

76. Jane Mayer, *The Dark Side: The Inside Story of How the War on Terror Turned into a
War on American Ideals,* repr. ed. (New York: Anchor, 2009), 273.

77. Joshua Rothman, "Jane Mayer's Reporting on Torture," *New Yorker*, December 13,
2014, accessed February 4, 2016, http://www.newyorker.com/books/double-take/jane
-mayers-reporting-torture. According to Mayer, Khalid Mohammed was also subjected
to numerous other tortures and was water-boarded 183 times.

78. Mayer, *The Dark Side*, 281.

79. Mayer, *The Dark Side*, 281–82.

80. Gina M. Bennett, *National Security Mom: Why Going "Soft" Will Make America
Strong* (Deadwood, OR: Wyatt-MacKenzie, 2008).

81. National Intelligence Estimate, *Trends in Global Terrorism: Implications for the
United States*, NIE-2006-02R (Washington, DC: Office of the Director of National Intelligence, 2006). A declassified and heavily redacted version is available at http://www
.governmentattic.org/5docs/NIE-2006-02R.pdf (accessed February 4, 2016).

82. See the website for the book: http://www.nationalsecuritymom.com/ (accessed
June 8, 2016).

83. Bennett, *National Security Mom*, 129.

84. Bennett, *National Security Mom*, 34.

85. Central Intelligence Agency, "Agency Officer Featured on Oprah Winfrey Show," CIA.gov, December 24, 2008, accessed June 8, 2016, https://www.cia.gov/news-information/featured-story-archive/2008-featured-story-archive/agency-officer-featured-on-oprah.html.

86. Bennett, *National Security Mom*, 2.

87. Bennett, *National Security Mom*, 3.

88. Continuing her parenting-as-security approach, Bennett also wrote a children's book, *How Kids Can Be Good Citizens: Lessons for Keeping America Strong and Safe* (Deadwood, OR: Wyatt-MacKenzie, 2013), which was accompanied by a website selling the book, activities, and games. The website teaches kids Morse code, how to use a Cipher Disk and Cipher Wheel to encrypt (Make Your Own Secret Codes!) and decode information about the National Security Agency (How Can I Work for NSA), how to say "Hello" in different languages, and how to identify security badges from different government services. Colorful links connect kids to the US Department of Energy's website, the CIA's kids page, and the National Counterterrorism Center's kids page. Unfortunately, many of the links seem outdated and do not work, suggesting that the website is no longer maintained or may not have been well used. See Bennett's website, http://www.nationalsecuritymom.com (accessed January 21, 2016).

89. Central Intelligence Agency, "Agency Officer Featured on Oprah Winfrey Show."

90. Wilson Center, "Book Discussion: National Security Mom: Why 'Going Soft' Will Make America Strong," March 16, 2009, accessed January 21, 2016, https://www.wilsoncenter.org/event/book-discussion-national-security-mom-why-going-soft-will-make-america-strong. All quotes are from the webcast recap on the site.

5. Digital Natives

1. Bernadette Murray, "DigitalSecuritymom," *Digital Security Mom*, October 27, 2011, accessed July 29, 2014, http://digitalsecuritymom.com/archives/10#comment-4093.

2. Caren Kaplan, Erik Loyer, and Ezra Claytan Daniels, "Precision Targets: GPS and the Militarization of Everyday Life," *Canadian Journal of Communication* 38, no. 3 (2013): 397–420, http://cjc-online.ca/index.php/journal/article/view/2655.

3. Gary Marx and Valerie Steeves, "From the Beginning: Children as Subjects and Agents of Surveillance," *Surveillance and Society* 7, nos. 3/4 (June 17, 2010): 192–230.

4. Ellen Seiter, *The Internet Playground: Children's Access, Entertainment, and Mis-Education*, 2nd ed. (New York: Peter Lang, 2007).

5. Carole Pateman and Charles Mills, *The Contract and Domination* (Cambridge: Polity, 2007).

6. Thomas Piketty, *Capital in the Twenty-First Century* (Cambridge, MA: Belknap Press, 2014).

7. Roger N. Lancaster, *Sex Panic and the Punitive State* (Berkeley: University of California Press, 2011).

8. Gary Marx, "The Surveillance Society: The Threat of 1984-Style Techniques," *Futurist*, June 1985, 21–26.

9. David Lyon, *Surveillance Society: Monitoring Everyday Life* (Buckingham, England: Open University Press, 2001); David Lyon, *Surveillance as Social Sorting: Privacy, Risk, and Digital Discrimination* (London: Psychology Press, 2003).

10. Natasha Singer, "Mapping, and Sharing, the Consumer Genome," *New York Times*, June 16, 2012, accessed May 11, 2017, http://www.nytimes.com/2012/06/17/technology/acxiom-the-quiet-giant-of-consumer-database-marketing.html.

11. Monica Davey, "Chicago Police Try to Predict Who May Shoot or Be Shot," *New York Times*, May 23, 2016, accessed May 23, 2016, http://www.nytimes.com/2016/05/24/us/armed-with-data-chicago-police-try-to-predict-who-may-shoot-or-be-shot.html. This article mentions that the information gathered comes from encounters with police rather than from other sites, though it does mention that the Chicago police has been accused of racial profiling in the past.

12. Ross MacIejewski, Ryan Hafen, Stephen Rudolph, Stephen G. Larew, Michael A. Mitchell, William S. Cleveland, and David S. Ebert, "Forecasting Hotspots: A Predictive Analytics Approach," *IEEE Transactions on Visualization and Computer Graphics* 17, no. 4 (April 2011): 440–53, doi:10.1109/TVCG.2010.82.

13. Kenneth Cukier and Viktor Mayer-Schoenberger, "Rise of Big Data: How It's Changing the Way We Think about the World," *Foreign Affairs* 92, no. 3 (June 2013): 28–40.

14. Ben Popper, "Harlem Crew Territories circa 2010," December 10, 2014, accessed May 17, 2016, http://apps.voxmedia.com/graphics/theverge-harlem-crew-map.

15. Muslim American Civil Liberties Coalition, the Creating Law Enforcement Accountability and Responsibility Project, and the Asian American Legal Defense and Education Fund, "Mapping Muslims: NYPD Spying and Its Impact on American Muslims," n.d., accessed May 23, 2016, http://www.law.cuny.edu/academics/clinics/immigration/clear/Mapping-Muslims.pdf.

16. Colleen McCue, "Data Mining and Predictive Analytics: Battlespace Awareness for the War on Terrorism," *Defense Intelligence Journal* 13, no. 1 (2005): 47–63.

17. Muslim American Civil Liberties Coalition, the Creating Law Enforcement Accountability and Responsibility Project, and the Asian American Legal Defense and Education Fund, "Mapping Muslims."

18. Greg Elmer, *Profiling Machines: Mapping the Personal Information Economy* (Cambridge, MA: MIT Press, 2003).

19. See for instance, the research by boyd and Hargittai, who dispute that younger generations do not care about privacy: danah boyd and Eszter Hargittai, "Facebook Privacy Settings: Who Cares?," *First Monday* 15, no. 8 (July 27, 2010), http://firstmonday.org/ojs/index.php/fm/article/view/3086.

20. Marx and Steeves, "From the Beginning."

21. The case of Rutgers student Tyler Clementi, an eighteen-year-old white, gay teen who committed suicide in October 2010, is instructive here. Clementi's roommate, a South Asian student, Dharun Ravi, spied on Clementi kissing another man, and his attempt to further spy on Clementi led to charges that he had caused Clementi's suicide. There is no doubt that Ravi's spying and other behavior were morally dubious and destructive, but some activists' claims and the bereaved parents' assertions that it

caused his roommate's suicide have to be understood also in terms of the imbrication of race in this case. There were many in the LGBT community, such as Dan Savage, who felt that Ravi had been scapegoated, and it is possible to see Ravi's race as a factor in such scapegoating, given that gay teen suicide rates have a long and sad history. See Dan Savage, "Who Killed Tyler Clementi?," *The Stranger*, October 2, 2010, accessed May 12, 2016, http://slog.thestranger.com/slog/archives/2010/10/02/before-we-crucify-those -two-teenagers-who-streamed-tyler-clementis-having-sex-over-the-internet.

22. John G. Palfrey and Urs Gasser, *Born Digital: Understanding the First Generation of Digital Natives* (New York: Basic Books, 2008), 4.

23. Cathy Hannabach, *Blood Cultures: Medicine, Media, and Militarisms* (New York: Palgrave Macmillan, 2015).

24. Marx and Steeves, "From the Beginning," 192–230.

25. Gina M. Bennett, *National Security Mom: Why Going "Soft" Will Make America Strong* (Deadwood, OR: Wyatt-MacKenzie, 2008).

26. Bennett, *National Security Mom*.

27. Gill Valentine and Sarah Holloway, "On-Line Dangers? Geographies of Parents' Fears for Children's Safety in Cyberspace," *Professional Geographer* 53, no. 1 (2001): 75.

28. The Internet Society, "A Brief History of the Internet and Related Networks," n.d., accessed July 10, 2016, http://www.internetsociety.org/internet/what-internet/history -internet/brief-history-internet-related-networks.

29. Torin Monahan, *Surveillance in the Time of Insecurity* (New Brunswick, NJ: Rutgers University Press, 2010), 11.

30. The "hacker" is an important example of this fear of the tech-savvy youth who must be rehabilitated to surveil for the state. My thanks to Rebecca Wexler for this important example and point.

31. Danielle J. Garber, "COPPA: Protecting Children's Personal Information on the Internet," *Journal of Law and Policy* 10 (2002–1): 129, 151–52.

32. Alice Miller, *For Your Own Good: Hidden Cruelty in Child-Rearing and the Roots of Violence*, 3rd ed. (New York: Farrar, Straus and Giroux, 2002). Miller sees this Christian tradition as a universal, though I would argue that her account of parental violence is shared by some (though not all) non-Christian cultures.

33. Philippe Aries, *Centuries of Childhood: A Social History of Family Life* (New York: Vintage, 1965).

34. Justine Cassell and Meg Cramer, "High Tech or High Risk: Moral Panics about Girls Online," in *Digital Youth, Innovation and the Unexpected*, ed. Tara McPherson, 53–76 (Cambridge, MA: MIT Press, 2008).

35. Marc Prensky, "Digital Natives, Digital Immigrants," *On the Horizon* 9, no. 5 (2001): 1–6. Also see Prensky's website, where he is described as involved in selling educational products: http://marcprensky.com/marcs-bio (accessed February 20, 2016).

36. Prensky, "Digital Natives, Digital Immigrants," 1.

37. Prensky, "Digital Natives, Digital Immigrants," 1.

38. Marc Prensky, "Do They Really *Think* Differently?," *On the Horizon* 9, no. 6 (December 2001): 1–9.

39. See Ellen Johanna Helsper and Rebecca Eynon, "Digital Natives: Where Is the Evidence?," *British Educational Research Journal* 36, no. 3 (June 17, 2009): 503–20, doi:10.1080/01411920902989227.

40. Prensky, "Digital Natives, Digital Immigrants," 2.

41. Prensky, "Digital Natives, Digital Immigrants," 2.

42. Jane Hill, "Language, Race and White Public Space," *American Anthropologist* 100, no. 3 (September 1998): 680–89.

43. Mari J. Matsuda, "Voices of America: Accent, Antidiscrimination Law, and a Jurisprudence for the Last Reconstruction," *Yale Law Journal* 100, no. 5 (1991): 1329–1407, doi:10.2307/796694.

44. Leti Volpp, " 'Obnoxious to Their Very Nature': Asian Americans and Constitutional Citizenship," *Citizenship Studies* 5, no. 1 (February 1, 2001): 57–71, doi:10.1080/13621020020025196.

45. Prensky, "Digital Natives, Digital Immigrants," 2.

46. Prensky, "Digital Natives, Digital Immigrants," 3.

47. Prensky, "Digital Natives, Digital Immigrants," 3.

48. Prensky, "Digital Natives, Digital Immigrants," 5.

49. Prensky, "Digital Natives, Digital Immigrants," 5.

50. Prensky, "Digital Natives, Digital Immigrants," 6.

51. See Susan L. Robertson, " 'Remaking the World': Neoliberalism and the Transformation of Education and Teachers' Labor," in *The Global Assault on Teaching, Teachers, and Their Unions: Stories for Resistance*, ed. Mary Compton and Lois Weiner, 11–27 (New York: Palgrave Macmillan, 2008).

52. Bernadette Murray, "AppCertain's New Curfew Mode Is a Dream Come True for Parents," *Digital Security Mom*, September 11, 2013, http://digitalsecuritymom.com/archives/339.

53. For more on content as digital labor used by corporations and capital, see Trebor Scholz, ed., *Digital Labor: The Internet as Playground and Factory* (New York: Routledge, 2013).

54. See, for instance, the film *We Break Things*, Rebecca Wexler, dir. (2014). Also on changing ontologies of hackers, see Helen Nissenbaum, "Hackers and the Contested Ontology of Cyberspace," *New Media and Society* 6, no. 2 (April 1, 2004): 195–217, doi:10.1177/1461444804041445.

55. See, for instance, Sara Yin, "7 Hackers Who Got Legit Jobs from Their Exploits," *PCMag*, June 28, 2011, accessed April 6, 2017, http://www.pcmag.com/slideshow/story/266255/7-hackers-who-got-legit-jobs-from-their-exploits.

56. See Philip Jenkins, *Beyond Tolerance: Child Pornography Online* (New York: NYU Press, 2001).

57. Judith Levine, *Harmful to Minors: The Perils of Protecting Children from Sex* (Boston: Da Capo, 2003).

58. Giselinde Kuipers, "The Social Construction of Digital Danger: Debating, Defusing and Inflating the Moral Dangers of Online Humor and Pornography in the Netherlands and the United States," *New Media and Society* 8, no. 3 (2006): 379–400, doi:10.1177/1461444806061949.

59. Valentine and Holloway, "On-Line Dangers?"; Neil Postman, *The Disappearance of Childhood* (New York: Vintage / Random House, 1994); Catharine Lumby, *Bad Girls: The Media, Sex and Feminism in the 90s* (St. Leonards, NSW, Australia: Allen and Unwin, 1997), especially the chapter "New Media, Old Fears," 136–53.

60. In May 2016, I conducted a Google search for "keeping black children safe on the Internet," which returned hundreds of thousands of results, almost none of which focused on African American children. Another search for "keeping African American children safe on the Internet" returned one key article from 1999, from the National Leadership Network of Conservative African Americans; while replicating much of this literature, it added that African American children need to have access to black history, and the Cyber Youth Network was a great resource for this information. Tara Wall, "Keeping Kids Safe on the Internet," National Leadership Network of Conservative African Americans, December 1999, accessed May 24, 2016, https://www.nationalcenter.org/NVWallInternet1299.html. It is also notable that fears concerning the safety of African American youth have been expressed through the language of a "talk" and the "letter" (written by African American parents to their children) that warn children to keep themselves safe from racial violence. Such a discourse emerges from concerns about widespread Internet surveillance by the state and refuses the language of the dysfunctional black family. See, for instance, Ta-Nehisi Coates, *Between the World and Me* (New York: Spiegel and Grau, 2015).

61. Joseph J. Fischel, "Pornographic Protections? Itineraries of Childhood Innocence," *Law, Culture and the Humanities* 12, no. 2 (2016): 206–20.

62. Monahan, *Surveillance in the Time of Insecurity*.

63. Kaplan, Loyer, and Daniels, "Precision Targets."

64. Somini Sengupta, "The Pentagon as Silicon Valley Incubator," *New York Times*, August 23, 2013, accessed August 23, 2013, http://www.nytimes.com/2013/08/23/technology/the-pentagon-as-start-up-incubator.html.

65. Tonya Rooney, "Trusting Children: How Do Surveillance Technologies Alter a Child's Experience of Trust, Risk and Responsibility?," *Surveillance and Society* 7, nos. 3/4 (2010): 344–55.

66. Kaplan, Loyer, and Daniels, "Precision Targets."

67. Kaisa Aunola and Jari-Erik Nurmi, "The Role of Parenting Styles in Children's Problem Behavior," *Child Development* 76, no. 6 (2005): 1144–59, doi:10.1111/j.1467-8624.2005.00840.x-i1.

68. Lancaster, *Sex Panic and the Punitive State*. Also see Jenkins, *Beyond Tolerance*.

69. E. B. Dowdell, "Use of the Internet by Parents of Middle School Students: Internet Rules, Risky Behaviours and Online Concerns," *Journal of Psychiatric and Mental Health Nursing* 20, no. 1 (2013): 9–16, doi:10.1111/j.1365-2850.2011.01815.x.

70. Matthew S. Eastin, Bradley S. Greenberg, and Linda Hofschire, "Parenting the Internet," *Journal of Communication* 56, no. 3 (2006): 486–504, doi:10.1111/j.1460-2466.2006.00297.x.

71. While the company has removed this page from which I quoted (http://www.f.secure.com/en/web/home_us/news-info/securitystories/view/story/91771/Parenting%20the%digital2odigital%20natives [accessed August 14, 2013]), F Secure

now seems to be less alarmist, saying that the software helps parents monitor their children and better utilize their time and that they do not turn parents into spies. F-Secure, "Protecting your Children," n.d., accessed June 20, 2016, https://www.f-secure.com/en/web/home_global/digital-parenting.

72. Care.com, "New Study Finds Bullying and CyberBullying Is Parent's #1 Fear More than Kidnapping, Domestic Terrorism, and Suicide," October 19, 2019, accessed July 2, 2016, http://www.care.com/press-release-parent-fears-survey-p1186-q3645292.html.

73. "Friend Verifier the First Facebook App That Scans Your Friends for Registered Sex Offenders," PRWeb, March 9, 2012, accessed July 2, 2016, http://www.prweb.com/releases/2012/3/prweb9262666.htm.

74. Dowdell, "Use of the Internet by Parents of Middle School Students."

75. M. Valcke, S. Bonte, B. De Wever, and I. Rots, "Internet Parenting Styles and the Impact on Internet Use of Primary School Children," *Computers and Education* 55, no. 2 (September 2010): 454–64, http://doi.org/10.1016/j.compedu.2010.02.009.

76. *Sky Mall Catalog* (fall 2010): 54.

77. Spector Pro, "Unmask Your Child's Online Identity," pc *World*, December 2010, 67.

78. Khaled A. Beydoun, "Between Muslim and White: The Legal Construction of Arab American Identity," *New York University Annual Survey of American Law* 69, no. 1 (2013): 29–76.

79. Beydoun, "Between Muslim and White."

80. Marx and Steeves, "From the Beginning."

81. Shirley R. Steinberg, *Kinderculture: The Corporate Construction of Childhood* (Boulder, CO: Westview, 2011), http://public.eblib.com/EBLPublic/PublicView.do?ptiID=665864.

82. KidsWatch™: The Leader in Parental Control Software, accessed February 29, 2012, http://www.kidswatch.com.

83. Net Nanny, "Net Nanny Is the Most Effective and Flexible Filtering Software Available Today," accessed February 29, 2012, http://www.netnanny.com/features/internet-filter.

84. Amy Adele Hasinoff, *Sexting Panic: Rethinking Criminalization, Privacy, and Consent* (Urbana: University of Illinois Press, 2015).

85. Entertainment Software Rating Board (ESRB), accessed July 2, 2016, http://www.esrb.org.

86. Davey Winder, "Does Parental Control Software Work?," *Alphr*, December 24, 2009, accessed May 12, 2016, http://www.alphr.com/features/354349/does-parental-control-software-work.

87. Winder, "Does Parental Control Software Work?"

88. The term "distro" is shorthand for "distribution systems," which are Linux-related operating systems that include software of various kinds. Since many of these systems are open-source, they are believed to be more clandestine and, therefore, outside the knowledge of anyone who is not familiar with the technology.

89. Winder, "Does Parental Control Software Work?"

90. Qian (Emily) Wang, Michael D. Myers, and David Sundaram, "Digital Natives and Digital Immigrants: Towards a Model of Digital Fluency," *Business and Information Systems Engineering* 5, no. 6 (December 2013): 409–19.

91. Lynne Wrennall, "Surveillance and Child Protection: Demystifying the Trojan Horse," *Surveillance and Society* 7, nos. 3/4 (July 6, 2010): 304–24.

92. Elizabeth M. Losh, *Virtualpolitik: An Electronic History of Government Media-Making in a Time of War, Scandal, Disaster, Miscommunication, and Mistakes* (Cambridge, MA: MIT Press, 2009).

93. Barbara Starr and Holly Yan, "Man behind NSA Leaks Says He Did It to Safeguard Privacy, Liberty," CNN, June 10, 2013, accessed August 28, 2014, http://www.cnn.com/2013/06/10/politics/edward-snowden-profile/index.html; Barton Gellman and Laura Poitras, "U.S., British Intelligence Mining Data from Nine U.S. Internet Companies in Broad Secret Program," *Washington Post*, June 6, 2013, accessed April 6, 2017, https://www.washingtonpost.com/investigations/us-intelligence-mining-data-from-nine-us-internet-companies-in-broad-secret-program/2013/06/06/3a0coda8-cebf-11e2-8845-d970ccb04497_story.html?utm_term=.06ad1df98511.

94. Joanna Stern, "Dissecting Big Tech's Denial of Involvement in NSA's PRISM Spying Program," ABC News, June 7, 2013, accessed August 28, 2014, http://abcnews.go.com/Technology/nsa-prism-dissecting-technology-companies-adamant-denial-involvement/story?id=19350095.

95. Federal Trade Commission, *Privacy Online: A Report to Congress*, June 1998, accessed July 30, 2014, http://www.ftc.gov/sites/default/files/documents/reports/privacy-online-report-congress/priv-23a.pdf, 32.

96. Federal Trade Commission, *Privacy Online*, 37.

97. Federal Trade Commission, *Privacy Online*, 38.

98. Federal Trade Commission, *Privacy Online*, 41.

99. These included the following: Online Privacy Protection Act, S. 809, 106th Congress (1999), sponsored by Senator Conrad Burns (R), https://www.congress.gov/106/bills/s809/BILLS-106s809is.pdf; Electronic Rights for the 21st Century Act, S. 854, 106th Congress, and the Electronic Privacy Bill of Rights Act, H.R. 3321, 106th Congress (1999), sponsored by Senator Patrick Leahy (D), https://www.congress.gov/106/bills/hr3321/BILLS-106hr3321ih.pdf; Secure Online Communication Enforcement Act of 2000, S. 2063, 106th Congress (1999), introduced by Senator Robert Torricelli (D), https://www.congress.gov/106/bills/s2063/BILLS-106s2063is.pdf.

100. Michael Birnhack and Niva Elkin-Koren, "The Invisible Handshake: The Reemergence of the State in the Digital Environment," *Virginia Journal of Law and Technology* 8, no. 6 (2003): 1–57.

101. Tracey DiLascio, "How Safe Is the Safe Harbor? U.S. and E.U. Data Privacy Law and the Enforcement of the FTC's Safe Harbor Program," *Boston University International Law Journal* 22 (fall 2004): 399–424.

102. DiLascio, "How Safe Is the Safe Harbor?," 407–8. See also Federal Trade Commission, "The FTC's First Five Years Protecting Consumers Online," December 1999,

accessed May 12, 2016, https://www.ftc.gov/sites/default/files/documents/reports /protecting-consumers-online/fiveyearreport.pdf.

103. Children's Online Privacy Protection Rule ("COPPA"), 16 CFR 312, http://www .ftc.gov/ogc/coppa1.htm.

104. A "safe harbor" provision appears usually with a somewhat vague standard and says that certain agreed-upon behaviors will not constitute a violation of the rule. For approval of industry-approved guidelines, see Federal Trade Commission, "FTC Children's Online Privacy Protection Rule," *Electronic Code of Federal Regulations*, Title 16: Commercial Practices, accessed July 12, 2016, http://www.ecfr.gov/cgi-bin /text-idx?SID=4939e77c77a1a1a08c1cbf905fc4b409&node=16%3A1.0.1.3.36&rgn=div5.

105. Tara Wheatland, "*Ashcroft v. ACLU*: In Search of Plausible, Less Restrictive Alternatives," *Berkeley Technology Law Journal* 20 (2005): 371.

106. Reno v. American Civil Liberties Union, 521 US 844 (1997).

107. Federal Trade Commission, "COPPA Safe Harbor Program," accessed May 12, 2016, https://www.ftc.gov/safe-harbor-program.

108. Federal Trade Commission, "FTC Announces Settlements with Web Sites That Collected Children's Personal Data without Parental Permission," April 19, 2001, accessed April 6, 2017, https://www.ftc.gov/news-events/press-releases/2001/04/ftc -announces-settlements-web-sites-collected-childrens-personal.

109. Joseph A. Zavaletta, "COPPA, Kids, Cookies & Chat Rooms: We're from the Government and We're Here to Protect Your Children," *Santa Clara Computer and High-Technology Law Journal* 17 (2000–2001): 249–72.

110. Zavaletta, "COPPA, Kids, Cookies & Chat Rooms," 271.

111. Garber, "COPPA," 129.

112. Garber, "COPPA."

113. Lauren A. Matecki, "Update: COPPA Is Ineffective Legislation—Next Steps for Protecting Youth Privacy Rights in the Social Networking Era," *Northwestern Journal of Law and Social Policy* 5 (2010): 369–402.

114. In its 2011 testimony to Congress seeking changes to the COPPA rule, the FTC stated that it had brought seventeen COPPA enforcement actions, had helped consumers and businesses comply with the rule, and had created consumer education portal and materials. Federal Trade Commission, "FTC Testifies on Protecting Children Online in a Fast-Changing Marketplace, and Proposed Changes to COPPA Rule," October 5, 2011, accessed July 30, 2014, http://www.ftc.gov/news-events/press-releases/2011 /10/ftc-testifies-protecting-children-online-fast-changing.

115. Benjamin Edelman, "Adverse Selection in Online 'Trust' Certifications and Search Results," *Electronic Commerce Research and Applications* 10, no. 1 (2011): 17–25.

116. Zavaletta, "COPPA, Kids, Cookies & Chat Rooms."

117. Federal Trade Commission, "Prepared Statement of the Federal Trade Commission on Reauthorization before the Subcommittee on Consumer Affairs, Foreign Commerce and Tourism of the Committee on Commerce, Science, and Transportation, United States Senate," July 17, 2002, accessed April 6, 2017, https://www.ftc.gov /sites/default/files/documents/public_statements/prepared-statement-federal-trade -commission-prepaid-calling-cards/p074406prepaidcallingcards.pdf.

118. Electronic Privacy Information Center, "EPIC to FTC: 'Parental Control' Software Firm Gathers Data for Marketing," Epic.org, September 29, 2009, accessed July 2, 2015, https://epic.org/2009/09/epic-to-ftc-parental-control-s.html. See also EPIC, "Complaint, Request for Investigation, Injunction, and Other Relief," Epic.org, September 25, 2009, accessed July 2, 2015, https://epic.org/privacy/ftc/Echometrix%20 FTC%20Complaint%20final.pdf.

119. Federal Trade Commission, "Prepared Statement of the Federal Trade Commission on 'Protecting Children's Privacy in an Electronic World' before the House Committee on Energy and Commerce, Subcommittee on Commerce, Manufacturing and Trade," October 5, 2011, accessed July 30, 2014, http://www.ftc.gov/sites/default /files/documents/public_statements/prepared-statement-federal-trade-commission -protecting-childrens-privacy-electronic-world/111005coppatestimony.pdf.

120. A cookie is a message that a web server gives to a web browser to identify users and save information about the user that can be recalled if he or she visits the site again. Cookies can gather web-surfing information or web-surfing preferences of users.

121. Federal Trade Commission, "Children's Online Privacy Protection Rule," 2012, accessed August 10, 2013, http://www.ftc.gov/os/2012/12/121219copparulefrn.pdf.

122. danah boyd, Urs Gasser, and John Palfrey, "How the COPPA, as Implemented, Is Misinterpreted by the Public: A Research Perspective," Statement to the United States Senate, Subcommittee on Consumer Protection, Product Safety, and Insurance of the Committee on Commerce, Science and Transportation, Berkman Center for Internet and Society, April 28, 2010, accessed August 10, 2013, http://cyber.law .harvard.edu/publications/2010/COPPA_Implemented_Is_Misinterpreted_by _Public.

123. boyd, Gasser, and Palfrey, "How the COPPA, as Implemented, Is Misinterpreted by the Public."

124. Matecki, "Update: COPPA Is Ineffective Legislation."

125. Anil Kalhan, "Immigration Policing and Federalism through the Lens of Technology, Surveillance, and Privacy," *Ohio State Law Journal* 74, no. 6 (2013): 1105–65.

126. Executive Office of the President, *Big Data: Seizing Opportunities, Preserving Values* (Washington, DC: White House, May 2014), http://www.whitehouse.gov/sites /default/files/docs/big_data_privacy_report_5.1.14_final_print.pdf.

127. The White House, "Consumer Data Privacy in a Networked World: A Framework for Protecting Privacy and Promoting Innovation in the Global Digital World," *Journal of Privacy and Confidentiality* 4, no. 2 (2012): 95–142, also available at http:// repository.cmu.edu/cgi/viewcontent.cgi?article=1096&context=jpc.

128. Daniel J. Solove, *Nothing to Hide: The False Tradeoff between Privacy and Security* (New Haven, CT: Yale University Press, 2011).

129. B. Coleman and Clay Shirky, *Hello Avatar: Rise of the Networked Generation* (Cambridge, MA: MIT Press, 2011).

130. Benjamin Shmueli and Ayelet Blecher-Prigat, *Privacy for Children*, SSRN Scholarly Paper (Rochester, NY: Social Science Research Network), January 24, 2011, http:// papers.ssrn.com/abstract=1746540.

131. Christine Catalfamo, "Stand Your Ground: Florida's Castle Doctrine for the Twenty-First Century," *Rutgers Journal of Law and Public Policy* 4 (2006–7): 527.

132. Daniel J. Solove, Marc Rotenberg, and Paul M. Schwartz, *Privacy, Information, and Technology* (New York: Wolters Kluwer Law and Business, 2011).

133. Samuel D. Warren and Louis D. Brandeis, "The Right to Privacy," *Harvard Law Review* 4, no. 5 (December 15, 1890): 193–220.

134. Singer, "Mapping, and Sharing, the Consumer Genome."

135. Garber, "COPPA: Protecting Children's Personal Information on the Internet," 148.

136. Garber, "COPPA: Protecting Children's Personal Information on the Internet," 129, 148.

137. Mark Andrejevic, *iSpy: Surveillance and Power in the Interactive Era* (Lawrence: University Press of Kansas, 2007), 2.

138. Shmueli and Blecher-Prigat, *Privacy for Children*.

139. Will Thomas DeVries, "Protecting Privacy in the Digital Age," *Berkeley Technology Law Journal* 18, no. 1 (2003): 283.

140. Peter Swire, "The Second Wave of Global Privacy Protection: Symposium Introduction," *Ohio State Law Journal* 74, no. 6 (2013): 841–52.

141. Kalhan, "Immigration Policing and Federalism through the Lens of Technology, Surveillance, and Privacy," 1109.

142. William G. Staples, *Everyday Surveillance: Vigilance and Visibility in Postmodern Life*, 2nd ed. (Lanham, MD: Rowman and Littlefield, 2000), 68.

143. Monahan, *Surveillance in the Time of Insecurity*.

144. Monahan, *Surveillance in the Time of Insecurity*, 2.

145. Monahan, *Surveillance in the Time of Insecurity*, 5.

146. For instance, to be the "good Muslim" or the unthreatening African American. See Mahmood Mamdani, *Good Muslim, Bad Muslim: America, the Cold War, and the Roots of Terror* (New York: Three Leaves, 2005).

147. Jay Caspian Kang, "Should Reddit Be Blamed for the Spreading of a Smear?," *New York Times*, July 25, 2013, accessed June 2, 2015, http://www.nytimes.com/2013/07/28/magazine/should-reddit-be-blamed-for-the-spreading-of-a-smear.html.

148. Will Oremus, "Don't Blame Reddit for Smearing Sunil Tripathi: Blame 'Retweets Aren't Endorsements,'" *Slate*, July 26, 2013, accessed June 2, 2015, http://www.slate.com/blogs/future_tense/2013/07/26/reddit_sunil_tripathi_and_retweets_aren_t_endorsements_who_s_to_blame.html.

149. Christine Haughney, "New York Post Sued over Boston Bombing Article," *New York Times*, June 6, 2013, accessed June 2, 2016, http://www.nytimes.com/2013/06/07/business/media/new-york-post-sued-over-boston-bombing-article.html.

150. Alexis Kleinman, "Reddit User Who Started FindBostonBombers Quits Reddit," *Huffington Post*, April 23, 2013, accessed July 16, 2016, http://www.huffingtonpost.com/2013/04/23/reddit-boston-ama_n_3138623.html.

151. Maeve Duggan and Aaron Smith, "6% of Online Adults Are Reddit Users," Pew Research Center's Internet and American Life Project, July 3, 2013, http://www.pewinternet.org/files/old-media/Files/Reports/2013/PIP_reddit_usage_2013.pdf.

152. Kang, "Should Reddit Be Blamed for the Spreading of a Smear?"

153. Kang, "Should Reddit Be Blamed for the Spreading of a Smear?"

154. Lisa Nakamura, Peter Chow-White, and Alondra Nelson, eds., *Race after the Internet* (New York: Routledge, 2011).

155. Kang, "Should Reddit Be Blamed for the Spreading of a Smear?"

156. Henry Jenkins, Sam Ford, and Joshua Green, *Spreadable Media: Creating Value and Meaning in a Networked Culture* (New York: New York University Press, 2013); Wendy Hui Kyong Chun, *Control and Freedom: Power and Paranoia in the Age of Fiber Optics* (Cambridge, MA: MIT Press, 2008).

157. Erin Maher, "Men Are from Reddit, Women Are from Tumblr" (undergraduate thesis, Yale University, 2014), 20.

158. Maher, "Men Are from Reddit, Women Are from Tumblr," 21.

159. Maher, "Men Are from Reddit, Women Are from Tumblr," 29.

160. Moustafa Bayoumi, *How Does It Feel to Be a Problem? Being Young and Arab in America* (New York: Penguin, 2008); Junaid Rana, *Terrifying Muslims: Race and Labor in the South Asian Diaspora* (Durham, NC: Duke University Press, 2011); Leti Volpp, "The Citizen and the Terrorist," *UCLA Law Review* 49 (2001): 1575; Zareena Grewal, *Islam Is a Foreign Country: American Muslims and the Global Crisis of Authority* (New York: NYU Press, 2013).

161. Muneer Ahmad, "Homeland Insecurities: Racial Violence the Day after September 11," *Social Text* 20, no. 3 (2002): 101–15; Rana, *Terrifying Muslims*.

162. See, for instance, the company Datafloq touting the use of such analytics in Israel: Errol Van Engelen, "Big Data Will Effectively Fight Terrorism in the World," n.d., accessed July 2, 2015, https://datafloq.com/read/big-data-will-effectively-fight -terrorism/785. There are a number of other companies offering such technology.

Coda

1. While most gun deaths do not come from these "mass shootings" as they are called, the spectacle of power and violence in such shootings are central to the kind of project of security and insecurity that I trace in this book.

2. There is a considerable literature on first-person shooter games, much of which focuses on their psychological effects on players. On the link between empire and these games, and the connections to military training, see Johan Höglund, "Electronic Empire: Orientalism Revisited in the Military Shooter," *Game Studies* 8, no. 1 (September 2008), http://gamestudies.org/0801/articles/hoeglund.

3. Max Fisher, "What Makes America's Gun Culture Totally Unique in the World, in Four Charts," *Washington Post*, December 15, 2012, accessed June 14, 2016, https://www.washingtonpost.com/news/worldviews/wp/2012/12/15/what -makes-americas-gun-culture-totally-unique-in-the-world-as-demonstrated-in-four -charts/.

4. Susan Musarrat Akram and Kevin R. Johnson, "Race, Civil Rights, and Immigration Law after September 11, 2001: The Targeting of Arabs and Muslims," *New York University Annual Survey of American Law* 58 (January 17, 2003): 327–55.

5. Jennifer D. Carlson, "States, Subjects and Sovereign Power: Lessons from Global Gun Cultures," *Theoretical Criminology* (November 2013): 1–19.

6. Julia Jones and Eve Bower, "American Deaths in Terrorism vs. Gun Violence in One Graph," CNN, updated Decmber 30, 2015, accessed June 30, 2016, http://www.cnn .com/2015/10/02/us/oregon-shooting-terrorism-gun-violence/index.html.

7. "Behind the Bloodshed: The Untold Story of America's Mass Killings," *USA Today*, August 6, 2016, accessed June 30, 2016, http://usatoday30.usatoday.com/news/nation /mass-killings/index.html.

8. If the term "shooter" is used for nonwhite males, such as Micah Johnson, an African American ex-reservist who shot and killed five police officers in Dallas in 2016 during a march against police violence, it reveals his connection to the military and thus to an exceptionalism gone wrong.

9. Alanne Orjoux, "Accused South Carolina Church Shooter Dylann Roof to Face More Charges," CNN, July 7, 2015, accessed June 15, 2016, http://www.cnn.com/2015 /07/07/us/south-carolina-church-shootings-indictment/; Jacqueline Alemany, "Donald Trump: Obama 'Was More Angry at Me than at the Shooter,'" CBS News, June 15, 2016, accessed June 15, 2016, http://www.cbsnews.com/news/trump-obama -was-more-angry-at-me-than-at-the-shooter/; Jessica Simeone, Tasneem Nashrulla, Ema O'Connor, and Tamerra Griffin, "These Are the Victims of the Charleston Church Shooting," *BuzzFeed*, June 18, 2015, accessed April 17, 2017, http://www.buzzfeed .com/jessicasimeone/these-are-the-victims-of-the-charleston-church-shooting/; Michael R. Sisak, "Shooters Sometimes Exploit Limited Weapons Laws, Blind Spots," AP News, June 14, 2016, accessed June 15, 2016, http://bigstory.ap.org/article/041af8c3 b88341c6b91ae69a8e00def6/shooters-sometimes-exploit-limited-weapons-laws-blind -spots.

10. Ihekwoaba Onwudiwe, "Defining Terrorism, Racial Profiling and the Demonisa- tion of Arabs and Muslims in the USA," *Safer Communities* 4, no. 2 (April 1, 2005): 4–11.

11. Ben Saul, *Defining Terrorism in International Law* (New York: Oxford University Press, 2008). Also see this opinion piece in more popular media: Umar Nasser, "Why Are Only Muslims Called Terrorists?," *Huffington Post*, UK ed., December 21, 2015, accessed July 21, 2016, http://www.huffingtonpost.co.uk/umar-nasser/why-are-only -muslims-called-terrorists_b_8833150.html; Sudha Setty, "What's in a Name? How Nations Define Terrorism Ten Years after 9/11," *University of Pennsylvania Journal of International Law* 33, no. 1 (2011): 1–63.

12. David B. Sugarman and Susan L. Frankel, "Patriarchal Ideology and Wife-Assault: A Meta-Analytic View," *Journal of Family Violence* 11, no. 1 (1996): 23.

13. Among many other such articles, see, for instance, Glenn Greenwald, "Why Is Boston 'Terrorism' but Not Aurora, Sandy Hook, Tucson and Columbine?," *Guard- ian*, April 22, 2013, sec. Opinion, accessed July 2, 2016, https://www.theguardian.com /commentisfree/2013/apr/22/boston-marathon-terrorism-aurora-sandy-hook; Jessica Valenti, "Why Don't Americans Call Mass Shootings 'Terrorism'? Racism," *Guard- ian*, June 19, 2015, sec. Opinion, accessed July 2, 2016, https://www.theguardian.com /commentisfree/2015/jun/19/american-mass-shootings-terrorism-racism.

14. Aaron Winter, *American Terror: From Oklahoma City to 9/11 and After* (New York: Routledge, 2010), https://repository.abertay.ac.uk/jspui/handle/10373/1283.

15. Zack Beauchamp, "Deaths from Gun Violence vs. Deaths from Terrorism, in One Chart," *Vox*, October 1, 2015, accessed July 2, 2016, http://www.vox.com/2015/10/1/9437187/obama-guns-terrorism-deaths.

16. Phillip Martin, "Conservative Politicians Downplay Terrorism Threat from the Far Right," *Huffington Post*, January 3, 2016, accessed June 15, 2016, http://www.huffingtonpost.com/phillip-martin/right-wing-terrorism_b_8907358.html.

17. Muneer Ahmad, "Homeland Insecurities: Racial Violence the Day after September 11," *Social Text* 20, no. 3 (2002): 101–15; Leti Volpp, "The Citizen and the Terrorist," *UCLA Law Review* 49 (2001): 1575.

18. See the essays in the *Sikh Formations* special issue titled "Reflections on the Oak Creek Tragedy," *Sikh Formations* 8, no. 3 (2012).

19. The Orlando massacre was similarly at a club, a space where LGBT people could express their sexuality and where they might have felt safe from the homophobia of the streets.

20. Martin, "Conservative Politicians Downplay Terrorism Threat from the Far Right."

21. Philip Martin, "How Do We Define Domestic Terrorism? The Legal Meaning of a Loaded Term," PRI, July 21, 2015, accessed June 15, 2016, https://www.pri.org/stories/2015-07-21/how-do-we-define-domestic-terrorism-legal-meaning-loaded-term.

22. U.S.C. § 2331: Definitions, accessed June 15, 2016, http://codes.lp.findlaw.com/uscode/18/I/113B/2331.

23. American Civil Liberties Union, "How the USA Patriot Act redefines 'domestic terrorism,'" n.d., accessed July 5, 2016, https://www.aclu.org/how-usa-patriot-act-redefines-domestic-terrorism.

24. Emma Green, "The Politics of Mass Murder," *Atlantic*, June 13, 2016, accessed June 16, 2016, http://www.theatlantic.com/politics/archive/2016/06/orlando-political-reactions-homophobia-gun-rights-extremism/486752/.

25. Mujib Mashal, "Omar Mateen's Father Calls Shooting 'An Act of Terrorism,'" *New York Times*, June 13, 2016, accessed July 14, 2016, http://www.nytimes.com/live/orlando-nightclub-shooting-live-updates/father-of-omar-mateen-speaks-to-media/.

26. Juan Cole, "Omar Mateen and Rightwing Homophobia: Hate Crime or Domestic Terrorism?," *Informed Comment* (blog), June 13, 2016, accessed July 14, 2016, http://www.juancole.com/2016/06/rightwing-homophobia-terrorism.html.

27. Stephen Donnan, "The Orlando Shootings Were Homophobic Terrorism, Whether You Like to Admit That or Not," *Huffington Post*, June 13, 2016, accessed June 29, 2016, http://www.huffingtonpost.co.uk/stephen-donnan/orlando-homophobic-terrorism_b_10431788.html.

28. Haeyoun Park and Iaryna Mykhyalyshyn, "L.G.B.T. People Are More Likely to Be Targets of Hate Crimes than Any Other Minority Group," *New York Times*, June 16, 2016, accessed June 15, 2016, http://www.nytimes.com/interactive/2016/06/16/us/hate-crimes-against-lgbt.html.

29. Jasbir K. Puar and Amit S. Rai, "Monster, Terrorist, Fag: The War on Terrorism and the Production of Docile Patriots," *Social Text* 20, no. 3 (2002): 117–48, doi:10.1215/01642472-20-3_72-117.

30. Mark Mazzetti, Eric Lichtblau, and Alan Blinder, "Omar Mateen, Twice Scrutinized by F.B.I., Shows Threat of Lone Terrorists," *New York Times,* June 13, 2016, accessed July 14, 2016, http://www.nytimes.com/2016/06/14/us/politics/orlando -shooting-omar-mateen.html.

31. Matthew Teague, Spencer Ackerman, and Michael Safi, "Orlando Nightclub Shooter Omar Mateen Was Known to FBI, Agent Says," *Guardian,* June 12, 2016, sec. US news, accessed May 11, 2017, https://www.theguardian.com/us-news/2016/jun/12 /omar-mateen-orlando-nightclub-attack-shooter-named.

32. Alex Emmons, "Orlando Shooter Wasn't the First Murderer Employed by Global Mercenary Firm," *Intercept,* July 14, 2016, accessed July 12, 2016, https://theintercept .com/2016/06/14/orlando-shooter-wasnt-the-first-murderer-employed-by-global -mercenary-firm/.

33. Marcus Power, "Digitized Virtuosity: Video War Games and Post-9/11 Cyber-Deterrence," *Security Dialogue* 38, no. 2 (June 1, 2007): 271–88, doi:10.1177/0967010607078552.

34. See Winter, *American Terror.*

35. Carl Schmitt, *Political Theology: Four Chapters on the Concept of Sovereignty,* ed. George Schwab (Chicago: University of Chicago Press, 2006).

36. Karen R. Jones and John Wills, *The American West: Competing Visions* (Edinburgh: Edinburgh University Press, 2009).

37. Though with some female figures such as Annie Oakley.

38. William Hosley, *Colt: The Making of an American Legend* (Amherst: University of Massachusetts Press, 1996).

39. Russell S. Gilmore, "Another Branch of Manly Sport," in *Guns in America: A Historical Reader,* ed. Jan E. Dizard, Robert Muth, and Stephen P. Andrews, 105–21 (New York: NYU Press, 1999).

40. Adam Winkler, *Gunfight: The Battle over the Right to Bear Arms in America* (New York: W. W. Norton and Company, 2013).

41. Douglas A. Blackmon, *Slavery by Another Name: The Re-Enslavement of Black Americans from the Civil War to World War II,* repr. ed. (New York: Anchor, 2009).

42. Although after his presidency, Reagan expressed support for the Brady Bill for a national background check and waiting period for buying guns, named after his press secretary, Jim Brady, who had been wounded in the assassination attempt on Reagan.

43. Winkler, *Gunfight.*

44. Michelle Alexander, *The New Jim Crow: Mass Incarceration in the Age of Colorblindness* (New York: New Press, 2012), 136.

45. District of Columbia v. Heller, 554 U.S. 570 (2008).

46. Nicholas Riccardi, "Have Gun, Will Show It," *Los Angeles Times,* June 7, 2008, accessed June 15, 2016, http://articles.latimes.com/2008/jun/07/nation/na -opencarry7.

47. Todd C. Frankel, "Why the CDC Still Isn't Researching Gun Violence, Despite the Ban Being Lifted Two Years Ago," *Washington Post*, January 14, 2015, accessed June 16, 2015, https://www.washingtonpost.com/news/storyline/wp/2015/01/14/why-the-cdc-still-isnt-researching-gun-violence-despite-the-ban-being-lifted-two-years-ago/. See also Arthur L. Kellermann and Frederick P. Rivara, "Silencing the Science on Gun Research," *JAMA* 309, no. 6 (2013): 549–50, doi:10.1001/jama.2012.208207.

48. The Protection of Lawful Commerce in Arms Act, 15 U.S.C. §§ 7901–3.

49. Jennifer Mascia, "The Making of the Default Proceed Gun Sale Loophole," *Trace*, July 21, 2015, accessed July 14, 2016, https://www.thetrace.org/2015/07/brady-bill-amendment-default-proceed-loophole-amendment-nra/.

50. James Comey, "Statement by FBI Director James Comey Regarding Dylann Roof Gun Purchase," FBI Press Statement, Washington, DC, July 10, 2015, accessed June 13, 2016, https://www.fbi.gov/news/pressrel/press-releases/statement-by-fbi-director-james-comey-regarding-dylann-roof-gun-purchase.

51. For more on the complex relation between the US government and white, Christian militias, see Winter, *American Terror*.

52. Nate Silver, "Party Identity in a Gun Cabinet," *New York Times*, December 18, 2012, accessed June 15, 2016, http://fivethirtyeight.blogs.nytimes.com/2012/12/18/in-gun-ownership-statistics-partisan-divide-is-sharp/.

53. Michael S. Schmidt, "F.B.I. Confirms a Sharp Rise in Mass Shootings since 2000," *New York Times*, September 24, 2014, accessed June 15, 2016, http://www.nytimes.com/2014/09/25/us/25shooters.html.

54. The Data Team, "To Keep and Bear Arms," *Economist*, August 10, 2015, accessed June 15, 2016, http://www.economist.com/blogs/graphicdetail/2015/08/graphics-americas-guns.

55. Scott Martelle, "We All Pay: The High Costs of Gun Violence," *Los Angeles Times*, April 17, 2015, accessed June 15, 2016, http://www.latimes.com/opinion/opinion-la/la-ol-gun-violence-financial-cost-nra-20150417-story.html.

56. Nicholas Fandos, "U.S. Foreign Arms Deals Increased Nearly $10 Billion in 2014," *New York Times*, December 25, 2015, accessed May 11, 2017, http://www.nytimes.com/2015/12/26/world/middleeast/us-foreign-arms-deals-increased-nearly-10-billion-in-2014.html.

57. Kate Stohr, "Here Are All the Congresspeople Who Took NRA Money and Tweeted Prayers for Orlando," *Fusion*, June 13, 2016, accessed April 12, 2017, http://fusion.net/here-are-all-the-congresspeople-who-took-nra-money-and-1793857464; Karen Sullivan, "Charlotte Community Responds to Orlando Killings with Prayers, Support," *Charlotte Observer*, June 12, 2016, accessed June 16, 2016, http://www.charlotteobserver.com/news/local/article83306577.html.

58. The nonprofit NGO the Southern Poverty Law Center has been most assiduous and effective in monitoring neo-Nazi organizations and bankrupting some of them.

59. Erica Goode and Serge F. Kovaleski, "Wisconsin Killer Fed and Was Fueled by Hate-Driven Music," *New York Times*, August 6, 2012, sec. U.S., A1, accessed June 15, 2016, http://www.nytimes.com/2012/08/07/us/army-veteran-identified-as-suspect-in-wisconsin-shooting.html.

60. Frances Robles, "Dylann Roof Had A R-15 Parts during Police Stop in March, Record Shows," *New York Times*, June 26, 2015, accessed June 15, 2016, http://www .nytimes.com/2015/06/27/us/dylann-roof-was-questioned-by-police-in-march-record -shows.html.

61. Jelani Cobb, "Terrorism in Charleston," *New Yorker*, June 29, 2015, accessed June 29, 2016, http://www.newyorker.com/magazine/2015/06/29/terrorism-in -charleston.

62. Ned Resnikoff, "Repeated Attempts to Pass Hate Crime Bill in South Carolina Have Failed," *Al Jazeera America*, June 18, 2015, accessed June 15, 2016, http://america .aljazeera.com/articles/2015/6/18/south-carolina-lacks-hate-crimes-law.html.

63. Katy Pal Sian, "Gurdwaras, Guns and Grudges in 'Post-Racial' America," *Sikh Formations* 8, no. 3 (December 1, 2012): 293–97, doi:10.1080/17448727.2012.752676.

64. Neel Ahuja, "Unmodeling Minorities: The Sikh Temple Massacre and the Question of Security," *Sikh Formations* 8, no. 3 (2012): 309–12.

65. Frances Robles, "Dylann Roof Photos and a Manifesto Are Posted on Website," *New York Times*, June 20, 2015, accessed June 15, 2016, http://www.nytimes.com/2015 /06/21/us/dylann-storm-roof-photos-website-charleston-church-shooting.html.

66. Ahuja, "Unmodeling Minorities."

67. Emma Green, "The Trouble with Wearing Turbans in America," *Atlantic*, January 27, 2015, accessed June 14, 2016, http://www.theatlantic.com/politics/archive/2015 /01/the-trouble-with-wearing-turbans-in-america/384832/.

68. Violence between Sikhs and Muslims is part of the history of Partition, which is sometimes carried over into diaspora community formations. See Katy P. Sian, *Unsettling Sikh and Muslim Conflict: Mistaken Identities, "Forced" Conversions, and Postcolonial Formations* (Lanham, MD: Lexington Books, 2013).

69. George Morgan and Scott Poynting, eds., *Global Islamophobia: Muslims and Moral Panic in the West* (Farnham, England: Ashgate, 2013).

70. Volpp, "The Citizen and the Terrorist," 1575.

71. The targeting of women has a history as long as the nation, with slavery, sexual violence, and misogyny adding to the mix. The N R A's famous "woman turned zombie" for target practice is but one piece of evidence of the widespread misogyny of neo-Nazi and white Christian groups. See Erin Durkin and Daniel Beekman, "N R A Blasted for Endorsing Target That Looks like Woman and Bleeds," *NY Daily News*, May 7, 2013, accessed June 15, 2016, http://www.nydailynews.com/news/national/nra-blasted -support-target-woman-bleeds-article-1.1337783.

72. A few texts (out of many) include Kevin R. Johnson, " 'Aliens' and the U.S. Immigration Laws: The Social and Legal Construction of Nonpersons," *University of Miami Inter-American Law Review* 28, no. 2 (1996): 263–92; Lisa Lowe, *Immigrant Acts: On Asian American Cultural Politics* (Durham, NC: Duke University Press, 1996); Bill Ong Hing, *Making and Remaking Asian America through Immigration Policy, 1850–1990* (Stanford, CA: Stanford University Press, 1993); Karen Leonard, *Making Ethnic Choices: California's Punjabi Mexican Americans* (Philadelphia: Temple University Press, 1994); Nayan Shah, *Stranger Intimacy: Contesting Race, Sexuality, and the Law in the North American West* (Berkeley: University of California Press, 2012).

73. For more on violence against Sikhs, see "History of Hate: Crimes against Sikhs Since 9/11," *Huffington Post*, August 7, 2012, accessed June 13, 2016, http://www .huffingtonpost.com/2012/08/07/history-of-hate-crimes-against-sikhs-since-911_n _1751841.html.

74. Melani McAlister, *Epic Encounters: Culture, Media, and U.S. Interests in the Middle East since 1945* (Berkeley: University of California Press, 2001); Junaid Rana, *Terrifying Muslims: Race and Labor in the South Asian Diaspora* (Durham, NC: Duke University Press, 2011).

75. Zareena Grewal, *Islam Is a Foreign Country: American Muslims and the Global Crisis of Authority* (New York: NYU Press, 2013).

76. U.S. Army, "America's Army," accessed July 16, 2016, https://www.americasarmy .com/.

77. Allen Robertson, "Games without Tears, Wars without Frontiers," in *War, Technology, Anthropology*, ed. Koen Stroken, Critical Interventions: A Forum for Social Analysis, vol. 13, 83–93 (New York: Berghahn Books, 2012).

78. Nina B. Huntemann and Matthew Thomas Payne, eds., *Joystick Soldiers: The Politics of Play in Military Video Games* (New York: Routledge, 2009).

79. Michael Thomsen, "The Unsettling Realism of 2012's Two Big First-Person Shooter Games," *Atlantic*, December 26, 2012, accessed July 15, 2016, http://www .theatlantic.com/entertainment/archive/2012/12/the-unsettling-realism-of-2012s-two -big-first-person-shooter-games/265812/.

80. Jennifer Terry, "Killer Entertainments," *Vectors* 3, no. 1 (fall 2007), http://www .vectorsjournal.org/projects/index.php?project=86&thread=DesignersStatement.

81. Adrienne Shaw, *Gaming at the Edge: Sexuality and Gender at the Margins of Gamer Culture* (Minneapolis: University of Minnesota Press, 2015).

82. Alexander R. Galloway, "Social Realism in Gaming," *Game Studies* 4, no. 1 (November 2004), http://gamestudies.org/0401/galloway/. Galloway redefines "realism" to understand how representation and reality work together in games, though he problematically argues that a gamer playing a game created by Hezbollah can be considered a realist experience while an American youth playing a Special Forces game cannot.

83. Gerald A. Voorhees, Joshua Call, and Katie Whitlock, eds., *Guns, Grenades, and Grunts: First-Person Shooter Games* (London: Bloomsbury Academic, 2012); Patrick Crogan, *Gameplay Mode: War, Simulation, and Technoculture* (Minneapolis: University of Minnesota Press, 2011).

84. Henry Jenkins, *Fans, Bloggers, and Gamers: Exploring Participatory Culture* (New York: New York University Press, 2006).

85. Victoria Simpson Beck, Stephanie Boys, Christopher Rose, and Eric Beck, "Violence against Women in Video Games: A Prequel or Sequel to Rape Myth Acceptance?," *Journal of Interpersonal Violence* 27, no. 15 (2012): 3016–31.

86. Nick Wingfield, "Feminist Critics of Video Games Facing Threats in 'GamerGate' Campaign," *New York Times*, October 15, 2014, accessed June 15, 2016, http://www .nytimes.com/2014/10/16/technology/gamergate-women-video-game-threats-anita -sarkeesian.html.

87. Luke Malone, "A Breakdown of Anita Sarkeesian's Weekly Rape and Death Threats," *Vocativ*, January 28, 2015, accessed July 15, 2016, http://www.vocativ.com/culture/society/anita-sarkeesian-threats/.

88. Amanda Hess and Belle Boggs, "A Former FBI Agent on Why It's So Hard to Prosecute Gamergate Trolls," *Slate*, October 17, 2014, accessed June 15, 2016, http://www.slate.com/blogs/xx_factor/2014/10/17/gamergate_threats_why_it_s_so_hard_to_prosecute_the_people_targeting_zoe.html.

89. The Southern Poverty Law Center found that Thomas Mair, who killed British Labour MP Jo Cox in 2016, belonged to such groups and had connections with the US-based neo-Nazi group National Alliance. "Nazi Regalia Discovered at House of Jo Cox Killing Suspect," *Guardian*, June 17, 2016, sec. UK news, accessed May 11, 2017, https://www.theguardian.com/uk-news/2016/jun/17/jo-cox-suspect-thomas-mair-bought-gun-manuals-from-us-neo-nazis-group-claims.

AAA Commission on the Engagement of Anthropology with the US Security and Intelligence Communities (CEAUSSIC). "Final Report on the Army's Human Terrain System Proof of Concept Program." American Anthropological Association, October 14, 2009. http://s3.amazonaws.com/rdcms-aaa/files/production/public/FileDownloads/pdfs/cmtes/commissions/CEAUSSIC/upload/CEAUSSIC_HTS_Final_Report.pdf.

Abdelkarim, Riad Z., and Basil Z. Abdelkarim. "As American Muslims Face New Raids, Muslim Charities Fight Back." *Washington Report on Middle East Affairs* 21, no. 4 (May 2002): 80–81.

Abu-Lughod, Lila. *Do Muslim Women Need Saving?* Paperback ed. Cambridge, MA: Harvard University Press, 2015.

———. "Do Muslim Women Really Need Saving? Anthropological Reflections on Cultural Relativism and Its Others." *American Anthropologist* 104, no. 3 (2002): 783–90.

Adams, Vincanne. *Markets of Sorrow, Labors of Faith: New Orleans in the Wake of Katrina.* Durham NC: Duke University Press, 2013.

Adams, Vincanne, Taslim Van Hattum, and Diana English. "Chronic Disaster Syndrome: Displacement, Disaster Capitalism, and the Eviction of the Poor from New Orleans." *American Ethnologist* 36, no. 4 (2009): 615–36.

Adelsberg, Sam, Freya Pitts, and Sirine Shebaya. "The Chilling Effect of the 'Material Support' Law on Humanitarian Aid: Causes, Consequences, and Proposed Reforms." *Harvard National Security Journal* 4, no. 282 (2013): 300–318.

Agamben, Giorgio. *Homo Sacer: Sovereign Power and Bare Life.* Translated by Daniel Heller-Roazen. Stanford, CA: Stanford University Press, 1998.

Ahmad, Muneer. "Homeland Insecurities: Racial Violence the Day after September 11." *Social Text* 20, no. 3 (2002): 101–15.

Ahuja, Neel. "Unmodeling Minorities: The Sikh Temple Massacre and the Question of Security." *Sikh Formations* 8, no. 3 (2012): 309–12.

Akram, Susan Musarrat, and Kevin R. Johnson. "Race, Civil Rights, and Immigration Law after September 11, 2001: The Targeting of Arabs and Muslims." *New York University Annual Survey of American Law* 58 (January 17, 2003): 327–55.

Alemany, Jacqueline. "Donald Trump: Obama 'Was More Angry at Me than at the Shooter.'" CBS *News*, June 15, 2016. Accessed June 15, 2016. http://www.cbsnews.com/news/trump-obama-was-more-angry-at-me-than-at-the-shooter/.

Alexander, Michelle. *The New Jim Crow: Mass Incarceration in the Age of Colorblindness.* New York: New Press, 2012.

Al-Haramain Islamic Found., Inc. v. US Dep't of the Treasury (*Al-Haramain II*), No. 07-1155-KI, 2009 WL 3756363, at 1 (D. Or. Nov. 5, 2009).

Ali, Nosheen. "Books vs. Bombs? Humanitarian Development and the Narrative of Terror in Northern Pakistan." *Third World Quarterly* 31, no. 4 (June 1, 2010): 541–59. doi:10.1080/01436591003701075.

Álvarez, Sonia E. "Advocating Feminism: The Latin American Feminist NGO 'Boom.'" *International Feminist Journal of Politics* 1, no. 2 (1999): 181–209.

Al-Yahya, Khalid, and Nathalie Fustier. "Saudi Arabia as a Global Humanitarian Donor." In *Gulf Charities and Islamic Philanthropy in the "Age of Terror" and Beyond,* edited by Robert Lacey and Jonathan Benthall, 169–97. Berlin: Gerlach Press, 2014.

Amar, Paul, ed. *Global South to the Rescue: Emerging Humanitarian Superpowers and Globalizing Rescue Industries.* New York: Routledge, 2012.

———. "Introduction: New Racial Missions of Policing. Comparative Studies of State Authority, Urban Governance, and Security Technology in the Twenty-First Century." *Ethnic and Racial Studies* 33, no. 4 (2010): 575–92.

———. *The Security Archipelago: Human-Security States, Sexuality Politics, and the End of Neoliberalism.* Durham, NC: Duke University Press Books, 2013.

American Anthropological Association. "AAA Opposes US Military's Human Terrain System Project." n.d. Accessed February 4, 2016. http://www.aaanet.org/issues/AAA-Opposes-Human-Terrain-System-Project.cfm.

American Civil Liberties Union (ACLU). "Blocking Faith, Freezing Charity: Chilling Muslim Charitable Giving in the 'War on Terrorism Financing.'" New York: ACLU, June 2009. https://www.aclu.org/files/pdfs/humanrights/blockingfaith.pdf.

———. "How the USA Patriot Act Redefines 'Domestic Terrorism.'" N.d. Accessed July 5, 2016. https://www.aclu.org/how-usa-patriot-act-redefines-domestic-terrorism.

———. "Support Civil Rights: Oppose the Faith-Based Initiative." March 12, 2003. Accessed December 23, 2013. https://www.aclu.org.

Amoore, Louise, and Marieke Goede. "Governance, Risk and Dataveillance in the War on Terror." *Crime, Law and Social Change* 43, nos. 2/3 (April 2005): 149–73.

Amos, Valerie, and Pratibha Parmar. "Challenging Imperial Feminism." *Feminist Review,* no. 17 (1984): 3–19. doi:10.2307/1395006.

Andrejevic, Mark. *iSpy: Surveillance and Power in the Interactive Era.* Lawrence: University Press of Kansas, 2007.

Apuzzo, Matt, and Adam Goldman. *Enemies Within: Inside the NYPD's Secret Spying Unit and bin Laden's Final Plot against America.* New York: Touchstone, 2013.

Arena, John. *Driven from New Orleans: How Nonprofits Betray Public Housing and Promote Privatization.* Minneapolis: University of Minnesota Press, 2012.

Aries, Philippe. *Centuries of Childhood: A Social History of Family Life.* New York: Vintage, 1965.

Armistead, Leigh. *Information Operations: Warfare and the Hard Reality of Soft Power.* Lincoln, NE: Potomac Books, 2004.

Armor, David J. "Race and Gender in the U.S. Military." *Armed Forces and Society* 23, no. 1 (October 1, 1996): 7–27. doi:10.1177/0095327X9602300101.

Associated Press. "90 Nations Offer Aid to Help U.S. with Katrina." NBC, September 7, 2005. Accessed December 8, 2015. http://www.nbcnews.com/id/9231819/ns/us_news-katrina_the_long_road_back/t/nations-offer-aid-help-us-katrina/.

Atia, Mona. *Building a House in Heaven: Pious Neoliberalism and Islamic Charity in Egypt.* Minneapolis: University of Minnesota Press, 2013.

Aunola, Kaisa, and Jari-Erik Nurmi. "The Role of Parenting Styles in Children's Problem Behavior." *Child Development* 76, no. 6 (November 1, 2005): 1144–59. doi:10.1111/j.1467-8624.2005.00840.x-i1.

Ax, Joseph, and Jerry Norton. "Darfur Kidnapping Victim Sues Aid Group That Sent Her." *Reuters*, May 19, 2011. Accessed January 4, 2016. http://www.reuters.com/article/us-newyork-kidnap-idUSTRE74I70A20110519.

Bajpai, Shailaja. "Apocalypse Now." *Indian Express.* September 5, 2005. Accessed April 23, 2012. http://www.indianexpress.com/full_story.php?content_id=77565&title=Apocalypse Now.

Balbier, Uta Andrea. "Billy Graham's Crusade in the 1950s: Neo-Evangelicalism between Civil Religion, Media, and Consumerism." *Bulletin of the GHI.* GHI Research (spring 2009): 71–80.

Bâli, Asli Ü. "Scapegoating the Vulnerable: Preventive Detention of Immigrants in America's 'War on Terror.' " *Studies in Law, Politics, and Society* 38 (2006): 25–69.

Ball, Kirstie, and Frank Webster, eds. *The Intensification of Surveillance: Crime, Terrorism and Warfare in the Information Age.* London: Pluto, 2003.

Barkan, Joshua. *Corporate Sovereignty: Law and Government under Capitalism.* Minneapolis: University of Minnesota Press, 2013.

Barnett, Michael, and Janice Gross Stein. *Sacred Aid: Faith and Humanitarianism.* New York: Oxford University Press, 2012.

Barsky, Lauren, Joseph Trainor, and Manuel Torres. *Disaster Realities in the Aftermath of Hurricane Katrina: Revisiting the Looting Myth.* Quick Response Report. Boulder, CO: National Hazards Center, University of Colorado at Boulder, 2006. Accessed March 30, 2017. http://udspace.udel.edu/handle/19716/2367.

Barthwal-Datta, Monika. *Understanding Security Practices in South Asia: Securitization Theory and the Role of Non-State Actors.* New York: Routledge, 2012.

Basch, Linda. "Human Security, Globalization, and Feminist Visions." *Peace Review* 16, no. 1 (2004): 5–12. doi.org/10.1080/1040265042000210085.

Batra, Ankur, and Jaspreet. "Kathryn Bigelow Shoots in Chandigarh." *Times of India*, March 2, 2012. Accessed May 11, 2017. http://timesofindia.indiatimes.com

/entertainment/english/hollywood/news/Kathryn-Bigelow-shoots-in-Chandigarh
/articleshow/12097543.cms.

Bauman, Zygmunt, and David Lyon. *Liquid Surveillance*. Cambridge: Polity, 2013.

Bayoumi, Moustafa. *How Does It Feel to Be a Problem? Being Young and Arab in America*.
New York: Penguin, 2008.

BBC News. "Faith, Hate and Charity: Transcript." BBC One, Recorded from Transmission. July 30, 2006.

Beauchamp, Zack. "Deaths from Gun Violence vs. Deaths from Terrorism, in One
Chart." *Vox*, October 1, 2015. Accessed July 2, 2016. http://www.vox.com/2015/10/1
/9437187/obama-guns-terrorism-deaths.

Beck, Victoria Simpson, Stephanie Boys, Christopher Rose, and Eric Beck. "Violence
against Women in Video Games: A Prequel or Sequel to Rape Myth Acceptance?"
Journal of Interpersonal Violence 27, no. 15 (2012): 3016–31.

"Behind the Bloodshed: The Untold Story of America's Mass Killings." *USA Today*, August 6, 2016. Accessed June 30, 2016. http://usatoday30.usatoday.com/news/nation
/mass-killings/index.html.

Belew, Wendell. "The Impact of US Laws, Regulations and Policies on Gulf Charities."
In *Gulf Charities and Islamic Philanthropy in the "Age of Terror" and Beyond*, edited by
Jonathan Benthall and Robert Lacey, 231–57. Berlin: Gerlach Press, 2014.

Bell, Steve. Cartoon in *Guardian*, September 2005. Accessed December 8, 2015. https://
www.theguardian.com/cartoons/stevebell/0,7371,1566268,00.html.

Bell, Vicki. "The Vigilant(e) Parent and the Paedophile: The News of the World Campaign
2000 and the Contemporary Governmentality of Child Sexual Abuse." *Feminist
Theory* 33, no. 1 (2002): 83–102.

Benedetti, Carlo. "Islamic and Christian Inspired Relief NGOs: Between Tactical Collaboration and Strategic Diffidence?" *Journal of International Development* 18 (n.d.):
849–59.

Bennett, Gina M. *How Kids Can Be Good Citizens: Lessons for Keeping America Strong
and Safe*. Deadwood, OR: Wyatt-MacKenzie, 2013.

———. *National Security Mom: Why Going Soft Will Make America Strong*. Deadwood,
OR: Wyatt-MacKenzie, 2009.

Benthall, Jonathan. "Islamic Aid in a North Malian Enclave." *Anthropology Today* 22,
no. 4 (2006): 19–21.

———. *The Palestinian Zakat Committees 1993–2007 and Their Contested Interpretations*.
Geneva: Graduate Institute of International and Development Studies, Program
for the Study of International Organization(s), 2008. Accessed March 31, 2017.
http://insanonline.net/images/news_file/10325135848f9981849c65.pdf.

Benthall, Jonathan, and Jerome Bellion-Jourdan. *The Charitable Crescent: Politics of Aid
in the Muslim World*. 2nd ed. London: I. B. Tauris, 2008.

Benthall, Jonathan, and Robert Lacey, eds. *Gulf Charities and Islamic Philanthropy in the
"Age of Terror" and Beyond*. Berlin: Gerlach Press, 2014.

Bergen, Peter L. "A Feminist Film Epic and the Real Women of the CIA." *CNN*, December 13, 2012. Accessed February 4, 2016. http://www.cnn.com/2012/12/13/opinion
/bergen-feminist-epic/index.html.

———. *Manhunt: The Ten-Year Search for bin Laden from 9/11 to Abbottabad*. New York: Broadway Books, 2013.

Berlant, Lauren. *Cruel Optimism*. Durham, NC: Duke University Press, 2011.

Bernal, Victoria, and Inderpal Grewal. "Feminisms and the NGO Form." In *Theorizing NGOs: States, Feminisms, and Neoliberalism*, edited by Victoria Bernal and Inderpal Grewal, 301–10. Durham NC: Duke University Press, 2014.

———. "Introduction." In *Theorizing NGOs: States, Feminisms, and Neoliberalism*, edited by Victoria Bernal and Inderpal Grewal, 1–18. Durham, NC: Duke University Press, 2014.

Bernstein, Richard. "The View from Abroad." *New York Times*, September 4, 2005. Accessed December 8, 2015. http://www.nytimes.com/2005/09/04/weekinreview/04bern.html.

Beydoun, Khaled A. "Between Muslim and White: The Legal Construction of Arab American Identity." *New York University Annual Survey of American Law* 69, no. 1 (2013): 29–76.

Bialasiewicz, Kayuza, David Campbell, Stuart Elden, Stephen Graham, Alex Jeffrey, and Alison J. Williams. "Performing Security: The Imaginative Geographies of Current US Strategy." *Political Geography* 26 (2007): 405–22.

Biebricher, Thomas, and Frieder Vogelmann. "Governmentality and State Theory: Reinventing the Reinvented Wheel?" *Theory and Event* 15, no. 3 (2012).

Bigo, Didier. "Globalized (in)Security: The Field and the Ban-Opticon." Accessed July 18, 2016. http://www.people.fas.harvard.edu/~ces/conferences/muslims/Bigo.pdf.

———. "Security and Immigration: Towards a Governmentality of Unease." *Alternatives: Global, Local, Political* 27 (2002): 63–92.

Bigo, Didier, and Anastassia Tsoukala, eds. *Terror, Insecurity and Liberty: Illiberal Practices of Liberal Regimes after 9/11*. New York: Routledge, 2008.

Birnhack, Michael, and Niva Elkin-Koren. "The Invisible Handshake: The Reemergence of the State in the Digital Environment." *Virginia Journal of Law and Technology* 8, no. 6 (2003): 1–57.

Bjork, Kjell, and Richard Jones. "Overcoming Dilemmas Created by the 21st Century Mercenaries: Conceptualising the Use of Private Security Companies in Iraq." *Third World Quarterly* 26, nos. 4–5 (2005): 777–96. doi:10.1080/01436590500128014.

Blackmon, Douglas A. *Slavery by Another Name: The Re-Enslavement of Black Americans from the Civil War to World War II*. Repr. ed. New York: Anchor, 2009.

Blee, Kathleen M. *Women of the Klan: Racism and Gender in the 1920s*. With a New Preface ed. Berkeley: University of California Press, 2008.

Blumenthal, Sidney. "Breach of a Myth." *Salon*, September 15, 2005. Accessed December 8, 2015. http://www.salon.com/2005/09/15/bush_myth.

Bodnar, John. *Remaking America: Public Memory, Commemoration, and Patriotism in the Twentieth Century*. Princeton, NJ: Princeton University Press, 1993.

Bokhair, Laila. *Political Struggle over Earthquake Victims*. Norwegian Defense Research Establishment. Kjeller, Norway, November 23, 2005.

Bokhari, Yusra, Nasim Chowdhury, and Robert Lacey. "A Good Day to Bury a Bad Charity: The Rise and Fall of the Al-Haramain Islamic Foundation." In *Gulf Charities* and Islamic Philanthropy in the "Age of Terror" and Beyond, edited by Robert Lacey and Jonathan Benthall, 199–229. Berlin: Gerlach Press, 2014.

Boltanski, Luc. *Distant Suffering: Morality, Media and Politics.* Cambridge: Cambridge University Press, 1999.

Bonilla-Silva, Eduardo. *White Supremacy and Racism in the Post–Civil Rights Era.* Boulder, CO: Lynn Rienner, 2001.

Borah, Porismita. "Comparing Visual Framing in Newspapers: Hurricane Katrina versus Tsunami." *Newspaper Research Journal* 30, no. 1 (2009): 50–57.

Bornstein, Erica. *Disquieting Gifts: Humanitarianism in New Delhi.* Stanford, CA: Stanford University Press, 2012.

———. *The Spirit of Development: Protestant NGOs, Morality, and Economics in Zimbabwe.* Stanford, CA: Stanford University Press, 2005.

Bornstein, Erica, and Peter Redfield, eds. *Forces of Compassion: Humanitarianism between Ethics and Politics.* Santa Fe, NM: SAR Press, 2011.

Borradori, Giovanna. *Philosophy in a Time of Terror: Dialogues with Jürgen Habermas and Jacques Derrida.* New ed. Chicago: University of Chicago Press, 2004.

boyd, danah, and Eszter Hargittai. "Facebook Privacy Settings: Who Cares?" *First Monday* 15, no. 8 (July 27, 2010). http://dx.doi.org/10.5210/fm.v15i8.3086.

boyd, danah, Urs Gasser, and John Palfrey. "How the COPPA, as Implemented, Is Misinterpreted by the Public: A Research Perspective." Statement to the United States Senate, Subcommittee on Consumer Protection, Product Safety, and Insurance of the Committee on Commerce, Science and Transportation, Berkman Center for Internet and Society, April 28, 2010. Accessed August 10, 2013. http://cyber.law.harvard.edu/publications/2010/COPPA_Implemented_Is_Misinterpreted_by_Public.

Breinholt, Jeff. "Resolved, or Is It? The First Amendment and Giving Money to Terrorists." *American University Law Review* 57, no. 5 (June 2008): 1273–90.

Brickhouse Security. "GPS Tracking Device For Kids | Child GPS," n.d. http://www.brickhousesecurity.com/category/gps+tracking/gps+tracking+devices+for+children.do.

Broder, John M. "Amid Criticism of Federal Efforts, Charges of Racism Are Lodged." *New York Times,* September 5, 2005. Accessed December 8, 2015. http://www.nytimes.com/2005/09/05/national/nationalspecial/05race.html.

Bromwich, David. "It's Time to Rethink American Exceptionalism." *Nation,* October 24, 2014, accessed December 7, 2015, http://www.thenation.com/article/its-time-rethink-american-exceptionalism.

Brown, Wendy. "American Nightmare: Neoliberalism, Neoconservatism, and De-Democratization." *Political Theory* 34, no. 6 (December 2006): 690–714.

———. *Walled States, Waning Sovereignty.* New York: Zone Books, 2014.

Browne, Simone. *Dark Matters: On the Surveillance of Blackness.* Durham, NC: Duke University Press Books, 2015.

Brzezinski, Zbigniew. *Strategic Vision: America and the Crisis of Global Power.* New York: Basic Books, 2012.

Bumiller, Elisabeth. "Unlikely Tutor Giving Military Afghan Advice." *New York Times,* July 17, 2010. Accessed January 4, 2016. http://www.nytimes.com/2010/07/18/world/asia/18tea.html.

Bumiller, Kristen. *In an Abusive State: How Neoliberalism Appropriated the Feminist Movement against Sexual Violence*. Durham, NC: Duke University Press, 2008.

Burchell, Graham, Colin Gordon, and Peter Miller, eds. *The Foucault Effect: Studies in Governmentality*. Chicago: University of Chicago Press, 1991.

Burton, Antoinette. *Burdens of History: British Feminists, Indian Women, and Imperial Culture, 1865–1915*. Chapel Hill: University of North Carolina Press, 1994.

Bush, George W. "Rallying the Armies of Compassion." Archives.gov, January 30, 2001. Accessed July 31, 2013. http://georgewbush-whitehouse.archives.gov/news/reports/faithbased.html.

Butler, Judith. *Precarious Life: The Powers of Mourning and Violence*. London: Verso, 2006.

Buzan, Barry, Ole Wæver, and Jaap de Wilde. *Security: A New Framework for Analysis*. Boulder, CO: Lynne Rienner, 1997.

Calhoun, Craig. "The Idea of Emergency: Humanitarian Action and Global (Humanitarian) Order." In *Contemporary States of Emergency: The Politics of Military and Humanitarian*, edited by Didier Fassin and Mariella Pandolfi, 29–58. New York: Zone Books, 2013.

Callenbach, Ernest. "*When the Levees Broke: A Requiem in Four Acts*." *Film Quarterly* 60, no. 2 (2006): 4–10.

Camp, Jordan T. *Incarcerating the Crisis: Freedom Struggles and the Rise of the Neoliberal State*. Oakland: University of California Press, 2016.

———. "'We Know This Place': Neoliberal Racial Regimes and the Katrina Circumstance." *American Quarterly* 61, no. 3 (2009): 693–717.

Campbell, David. "The Biopolitics of Security: Oil, Empire, and the Sports Utility Vehicle." *American Quarterly* 57, no. 3 (2005): 943–72.

———. *Writing Security: United States Foreign Policy and the Politics of Identity*. Minneapolis: University of Minnesota Press, 1992.

Canada, Ben, and David M. Ackerman. *Faith-Based Organizations: Current Issues*. Hauppauge, NY: Nova Science Publishers, 2003.

"Capital One Fuels Kiva's Microlending in U.S. with $500,000 Matching Loan Program." *Business Wire*, February 25, 2013. Accessed January 4, 2016. http://www.businesswire.com/news/home/20130225006030/en/Capital-Fuels-Kiva%E2%80%99s-Microlending-U.S.-500000-Matching.

Carafano, James Jay. *Private Sector, Public Wars: Contractors in Combat. Afghanistan, Iraq, and Future Conflicts*. Westport, CT: Greenwood Publishing Group, 2008.

Carapico, Sheila. "Sleeping with the Devil?" *ISIM Review* 20 (2007): 8–9.

Carby, Hazel V. *Cultures in Babylon: Black Britain and African America*. London: Verso, 1999.

Care.com. "New Study Finds Bullying and CyberBullying Is Parent's #1 Fear More Than Kidnapping, Domestic Terrorism, and Suicide." October 19, 2019. Accessed July 2, 2016. http://www.care.com/press-release-parent-fears-survey-p1186-q3645292.html.

Carlson, Jennifer D. "States, Subjects and Sovereign Power: Lessons from Global Gun Cultures." *Theoretical Criminology* (November 2013): 1–19.

Carmola, Kateri. *Private Security Contractors and New Wars: Risk, Law, and Ethics*. New York: Routledge, 2010.

Cassell, Justine, and Meg Cramer. "High Tech or High Risk: Moral Panics about Girls Online." In *Digital Youth, Innovation and the Unexpected*, edited by Tara McPherson, 53–76. Cambridge, MA: MIT Press, 2008.

Castelli, Elizabeth. "Theologizing Human Rights: Christian Activism and the Limits of Religious Freedom." In *Non-Governmental Politics*, edited by Michel Fehre, 673–87. New York: Zone Books, 2007.

Castonguay, James. "Fictions of Terror: Complexity, Complicity and Insecurity in *Homeland*." *Cinema Journal* 54, no. 4 (summer 2015): 139–45.

Catalfamo, Christine. "Stand Your Ground: Florida's Castle Doctrine for the Twenty-First Century." *Rutgers Journal of Law and Public Policy* 4 (2006–7): 504–45.

"Celebrity Charities: Facts and Daily News." Look to the Stars, n.d. Accessed July 10, 2013. https://www.looktothestars.org/.

Central Intelligence Agency. "Agency Officer Featured on Oprah Winfrey Show." CIA.gov, December 24, 2008. Accessed June 8, 2016. https://www.cia.gov/news -information/featured-story-archive/2008-featured-story-archive/agency-officer -featured-on-oprah.html.

Chakravarty, Aloke. "Feeding Humanity, Starving Terror: The Utility of Aid in a Comprehensive Antiterrorism Financing Strategy." *Western New England Law Review* 32, no. 2 (2010): 295–338.

Chalfin, Brenda. *Neoliberal Frontiers: An Ethnography of Sovereignty in West Africa*. Chicago: University of Chicago Press, 2010.

Challand, Benoit. "Islamic Charities on a Fault Line: The Jordanian Case." In *Gulf Charities and Islamic Philanthropy in the "Age of Terror" and Beyond*, edited by Robert Lacey and Jonathan Benthall, 53–75. Berlin: Gerlach Press, 2014.

Charlie Rose. "Zero Dark Thirty." December 6, 2012. Accessed April 4, 2017, https:// charlierose.com/videos/20079.

Chaves, Mark. "Debunking Charitable Choice." *Stanford Social Innovation Review*, summer 2003. Accessed January 4, 2016. http://www.ssireview.org/articles/entry /debunking_charitable_choice.

Chen, Kuan-Hsing, and David Morley, eds. *Stuart Hall: Critical Dialogues in Cultural Studies*. London: Routledge, 1996.

Chesnut, R. Andrew. *Born Again in Brazil: The Pentecostal Boom and the Pathogens of Poverty*. New Brunswick, NJ: Rutgers University Press, 1997.

Chouliaraki, Lilie. "Introduction: The Soft Power of War." In *The Soft Power of War*, edited by Lilie Chouliaraki. Philadelphia: John Benjamins, 2007.

———. "Post-Humanitarianism: Humanitarian Communication beyond a Politics of Pity." *International Journal of Cultural Studies* 13, no. 2 (2010): 107–26.

Christie, Ryerson. "Critical Voices and Human Security: To Endure, to Engage or to Critique?" *Security Dialogue* 41, no. 2 (April 1, 2010): 169–90. doi:10.1177/0967010610361891.

Chun, Wendy Hui Kyong. *Control and Freedom: Power and Paranoia in the Age of Fiber Optics*. Cambridge, MA: MIT Press, 2008.

Citrin, Jack, Ernst B. Haas, Christopher Muste, and Beth Reingold. "Is American Nationalism Changing? Implications for Foreign Policy." *International Studies Quarterly* 38, no. 1 (March 1, 1994): 1–31. doi:10.2307/2600870.

Clarke, Kamari Maxine. *Fictions of Justice: The ICC and the Challenge of Legal Pluralism in Sub-Saharan Africa.* Cambridge: Cambridge University Press, 2009.

Clarke, Roger. "Information Technology and Dataveillance." *Communications of the ACM* 31, no. 5 (1988): 498–512.

Clifford, Stephanie. "At Trial, Arab Bank's Lawyer Spars with Witness." *New York Times,* September 4, 2014. Accessed July 24, 2016. http://www.nytimes.com/2014/09/05 /nyregion/at-a-trial-in-brooklyn-arab-banks-lawyer-spars-with-witness.html.

Clinton, Bill. *Giving: How Each of Us Can Change the World.* New York: Random House, 2007.

Clymer, Kenton J. "Humanitarian Imperialism: David Prescott Barrows and the White Man's Burden in the Philippines." *Pacific Historical Review* 45, no. 4 (1976): 495–517.

———. "Religion and American Imperialism: Methodist Missionaries in the Philippine Islands, 1899–1913." *Pacific Historical Review* 49, no. 1 (1980): 29–50. doi:10.2307/3639303.

Coates, Ta-Nehisi. *Between the World and Me.* New York: Spiegel and Grau, 2015.

Cobb, Jelani. "Terrorism in Charleston." *New Yorker,* June 29, 2015. Accessed June 29, 2016. http://www.newyorker.com/magazine/2015/06/29/terrorism-in-charleston.

Colapinto, John. "Looking Good." *New Yorker,* March 26, 2012. Accessed January 4, 2016. http://www.newyorker.com/reporting/2012/03/26/120326fa_fact_colapinto.

Cole, David. *Enemy Aliens: Double Standards and Constitutional Freedoms in the War on Terrorism.* New ed. New York: New Press, 2005.

Cole, David, and James X. Dempsey. *Terrorism and the Constitution: Sacrificing Civil Liberties in the Name of National Security.* 2nd ed. New York: New Press, 2006.

Cole, Juan. "Omar Mateen and Rightwing Homophobia: Hate Crime or Domestic Terrorism?" *Informed Comment* (blog), June 13, 2016. Accessed July 14, 2016. http://www .juancole.com/2016/06/rightwing-homophobia-terrorism.html.

Coleman, B., and Clay Shirky. *Hello Avatar: Rise of the Networked Generation.* Cambridge, MA: MIT Press, 2011.

Comaroff, Jean, and John L. Comaroff, eds. *Millennial Capitalism and the Culture of Neoliberalism.* Durham, NC: Duke University Press, 2001.

———. *Of Revelation and Revolution.* Vol. 1: *Christianity, Colonialism, and Consciousness in South Africa.* Chicago: University of Chicago Press, 1991.

———. *Theory from the South: Or, How Euro-America Is Evolving toward Africa.* Boulder, CO: Routledge, 2011.

Comey, James. "Statement by FBI Director James Comey Regarding Dylann Roof Gun Purchase." FBI Press Statement, Washington, DC, July 10, 2015. Accessed June 13, 2016. https://www.fbi.gov/news/pressrel/press-releases/statement-by-fbi-director-james -comey-regarding-dylann-roof-gun-purchase.

Connolly, William E. *Capitalism and Christianity, American Style.* Durham, NC: Duke University Press, 2008.

Considine, Craig. "Why White Men Are 'Gunmen' and Muslim Men Are 'Terrorists.'" *Huffington Post,* March 12, 2015. Accessed May 11, 2017. http://www.huffingtonpost .com/craig-considine/why-white-men-are-gunmen-_b_8704740.html.

Cooke, Miriam. "Saving Brown Women." *Signs: Journal of Women in Culture and Society* 28, no. 1 (September 2002): 468–70. doi:10.1086/340888.

Cooper, Anderson. *Dispatches from the Edge: A Memoir of War, Disasters, and Survival.* New York: HarperCollins, 2007.

Cooper, Helene. "Shadow of Hurricane Katrina Hangs over Obama after Spill." *New York Times*, April 30, 2010. Accessed December 8, 2015. http://www.nytimes.com /2010/05/01/us/politics/01obama.html.

Corber, Robert J. "Cold War Femme: Lesbian Visibility in Joseph L. Mankiewicz's *All about Eve.*" GLQ: *A Journal of Lesbian and Gay Studies* 11, no. 1 (2005): 1–22.

Covington, Jeanette. *Crime and Racial Constructions: Cultural Misinformation about African Americans in Media and Academia.* Lanham, MD: Lexington Books, 2010.

Cox, Jeffrey. *Imperial Fault Lines: Christianity and Colonial Power in India, 1818–1940.* Stanford, CA: Stanford University Press, 2002.

Crawford, Kate, and Jason Schultz. "Big Data and Due Process: Toward a Framework to Redress Predictive Privacy Harms." *Boston College Law Review* 55, no. 93 (2014): 93–128. http://papers.ssrn.com/abstract=2325784.

Crimm, Nina J. "Symposium: Muslim-Americans' Charitable Giving Dilemma. What about a Terror-Free Donor Advised Fund?" *Roger Williams University Law Review* 13 (2008): 375–410.

Crogan, Patrick. *Gameplay Mode: War, Simulation, and Technoculture.* Minneapolis: University of Minnesota Press, 2011.

Cukier, Kenneth, and Viktor Mayer-Schoenberger. "Rise of Big Data: How It's Changing the Way We Think about the World." *Foreign Affairs* 92, no. 3 (June 2013): 28–40.

Curti, Merle Eugene. *The Roots of American Loyalty.* New York: Columbia University Press, 1946.

Dachs, Anthony J. "Missionary Imperialism: The Case of Bechuanaland." *Journal of African History* 13, no. 4 (October 1972): 647–58. doi:10.1017/S0021853700011981.

Dao, James. "Ad Campaign for Marines Cites Chaos as a Job Perk." *New York Times*, March 9, 2012. Accessed January 4, 2016. http://www.nytimes.com/2012/03/10/us /marines-marketing-campaign-uses-chaos-as-a-selling-point.html.

The Data Team. "To Keep and Bear Arms." *Economist*, August 10, 2015. Accessed June 15, 2016. http://www.economist.com/blogs/graphicdetail/2015/08/graphics-americas -guns.

Davey, Monica. "Chicago Police Try to Predict Who May Shoot or Be Shot." *New York Times*, May 23, 2016. Accessed May 23, 2016. http://www.nytimes.com/2016/05/24 /us/armed-with-data-chicago-police-try-to-predict-who-may-shoot-or-be-shot .html.

Dean, Jodi. *Democracy and Other Neoliberal Fantasies: Communicative Capitalism and Left Politics.* Durham, NC: Duke University Press, 2009.

Dear, Michael. "Remembering Katrina but Please, No Photos of Dead People." *Space and Culture* 9, no. 1 (2006): 89–91.

Debord, Guy. *Society of the Spectacle.* Detroit: Black and Red, 2000.

De Graaf, Mia. "Who Is the CIA's Queen of Torture? Al Qaeda Expert Who Tortured Suspects, Lied to the Senate about Her Results and Lost Key Information on 9/11 Was Mentioned 36 Times in Torture Report." *Daily Mail*, December 19, 2014. Accessed February 4, 2016. http://www.dailymail.co.uk/news/article-2881475/Who

-CIA-s-queen-torture-Al-Qaeda-expert-tortured-suspects-lied-Senate-results-lost
-key-information-9-11-mentioned-36-times-torture-report.html.

Denning, Michael. "Wageless Life." *New Left Review* 2, no. 66 (2010): 79–97.

DeVries, Will Thomas. "Protecting Privacy in the Digital Age." *Berkeley Technology Law Journal* 18, no. 1 (January 2003): 283–311.

de Waal, Alex. *Famine Crimes: Politics and the Disaster Relief Industry in Africa*. September 1, 2009, ed. London: Indiana University Press, 2009.

Diefendorf, Jeffry M. "Reconstructing Devastated Cities: Europe after World War II and New Orleans after Katrina." *Journal of Urban Design* 14, no. 3 (2009): 377–97.

DiLascio, Tracey. "How Safe Is the Safe Harbor: U.S. and E.U. Data Privacy Law and the Enforcement of the FTC's Safe Harbor Program." *Boston University International Law Journal* 22 (2004): 399–424.

Dillon, Michael. "Network Society, Network-Centric Warfare and the State of Emergency." *Theory, Culture and Society* 19, no. 4 (August 1, 2002): 71–79. doi:10.1177/0263276402019004005.

Dinmore, Guy. "City of Rape, Rumour and Recrimination." *Financial Times*, September 5, 2005. Accessed May 24, 2016. http://www.ft.com/cms/s/0/06483632-1daa-11da-b40b-00000e2511c8.html?ft_site=falcon&desktop=true#axzz4cotXuwmZ.

Dionne, E. J. "End of the Bush Era." *Washington Post*, September 13, 2005. Accessed December 8, 2015. http://www.washingtonpost.com/wp-dyn/content/article/2005/09/12/AR2005091201433.html.

Dodds, Klaus. "Steve Bell's Eye: Cartoons, Geopolitics and the Visualization of the 'War on Terror.'" *Security Dialogue* 38, no. 2 (2007): 157–77.

Donnan, Stephen. "The Orlando Shootings Were Homophobic Terrorism, Whether You Like to Admit That or Not." *Huffington Post*, June 13, 2016. Accessed June 29, 2016. http://www.huffingtonpost.co.uk/stephen-donnan/orlando-homophobic-terrorism_b_10431788.html.

Donohue, Laura. "Constitutional and Legal Challenges to the Anti-Terrorist Finance Regime." *Wake Forest Law Review* 43 (2008): 643–97.

Donzelot, Jacques. *The Policing of Families*. Baltimore: Johns Hopkins University Press, 1997.

Dowd, Maureen. "Good Riddance, Carrie Mathison." *New York Times*, April 4, 2015. Accessed February 4, 2016. http://www.nytimes.com/2015/04/05/opinion/sunday/maureen-dowd-good-riddance-carrie-mathison.html.

Dowdell, E. B. "Use of the Internet by Parents of Middle School Students: Internet Rules, Risky Behaviours and Online Concerns." *Journal of Psychiatric and Mental Health Nursing* 20, no. 1 (2013): 9–16. doi:10.1111/j.1365-2850.2011.01815.x.

Doyle, Charles. "Terrorist Material Support: An Overview of 18 U.S.C. 2339A and 2339B." CRS Report for Congress. Washington DC: Congressional Research Service. Accessed May 30, 2016. https://www.fas.org/sgp/crs/natsec/R41333.pdf.

Drezner, Daniel W. "Post-Katrina American Foreign Policy." *Foreign Policy Blogs*, September 10, 2005. Accessed December 8, 2015. http://drezner.foreignpolicy.com/posts/2005/09/09/post_katrina_american_foreign_policy.

D'Souza, Dinesh. *The End of Racism*. New York: Free Press, 1995.

Duffield, Mark. *Global Governance and the New Wars: The Merging of Development and Security*. 2nd new ed. New York: Zed Books, 2014.

Duggan, Maeve, and Aaron Smith. "6% of Online Adults Are Reddit Users." Pew Research Center's Internet and American Life Project, July 3, 2013. http://www .pewinternet.org/files/old-media/Files/Reports/2013/PIP_reddit_usage_2013 .pdf.

Dunivin, Karen O. "Military Culture: Change and Continuity." *Armed Forces and Society* 20, no. 4 (July 1, 1994): 531–47. doi:10.1177/0095327X9402000403.

Durham, Frank. "Media Ritual in Catastrophic Time: The Populist Turn in Television Coverage of Hurricane Katrina." *Journalism* 9, no. 1 (2008): 95–116.

Durkin, Erin, and Daniel Beekman. "NRA Blasted for Endorsing Shooting Target That Looks like Woman and Bleeds." *NY Daily News*, May 7, 2013. Accessed June 15, 2016. http://www.nydailynews.com/news/national/nra-blasted-support-target-woman -bleeds-article-1.1337783.

Dyson, Michael Eric. *Come Hell or High Water: Hurricane Katrina and the Color of Disaster*. New York: Civitas, 2006.

Eastin, Matthew S., Bradley S. Greenberg, and Linda Hofschire. "Parenting the Internet." *Journal of Communication* 56, no. 3 (2006): 486–504. doi:10.1111/j.1460-2466.2006.00297.x.

Edelman, Benjamin. "Adverse Selection in Online 'Trust' Certifications and Search Results." *Electronic Commerce Research and Applications*, Special Section: Service Innovation in E-Commerce, 10, no. 1 (January 2011): 17–25. doi:10.1016/j. elerap.2010.06.001.

Edwards, George E. "International Human Rights Law Violations before, during, and after Hurricane Katrina: An International Law Framework for Analysis." *Thurgood Marshall Law Review* 31 (2006): 353.

Eggers, Dave. *Zeitoun*. Repr. ed. New York: Vintage, 2010.

"18 U.S. Code § 2339B—Providing Material Support or Resources to Designated Foreign Terrorist Organizations." LII / Legal Information Institute. Accessed June 5, 2016. https://www.law.cornell.edu/uscode/text/18/2339B.

Eisenstein, Zillah. "Dark Zero-Feminism." *Amass* 17, no. 3 (2013): 44–45.

Electronic Privacy Information Center (EPIC). "Complaint, Request for Investigation, Injunction, and Other Relief." *Epic.org*. September 25, 2009. Accessed July 2, 2015. https://epic.org/privacy/ftc/Echometrix%20FTC%20Complaint%20final.pdf.

———. "EPIC to FTC: 'Parental Control' Software Firm Gathers Data for Marketing." *Epic.org*, September 29, 2009. Accessed July 2, 2015. https://epic.org/2009/09/epic -to-ftc-parental-control-s.html.

Electronic Rights for the 21st Century Act, S. 854, 106th Congress, Electronic Privacy Bill of Rights Act, H.R. 3321, 106th Congress (1999), sponsored by Senator Patrick Leahy (D). https://www.congress.gov/106/bills/hr3321/BILLS-106hr3321ih.pdf.

Elmer, Greg. "Panopticon-Discipline-Control." In *Routledge Handbook of Surveillance Studies*, edited by David Lyon, Kristen Ball, and Kevin D. Iaggerty. Oxon, England: Routledge, 2012.

———. *Profiling Machines: Mapping the Personal Information Economy*. Cambridge, MA: MIT Press, 2003.

Elshtain, Jean Bethke. *Women, Militarism, and War: Essays in History, Politics, and Social Theory*. Savage, MD: Rowman and Littlefield, 1989.

Emerson, Michael O., and Christina Smith. *Divided by Faith: Evangelical Religion and the Problem of Race in America*. Oxford: Oxford University Press, 2000.

Emmons, Alex. "Orlando Shooter Wasn't the First Murderer Employed by Global Mercenary Firm." *Intercept*, June 14, 2016. Accessed July 12, 2016. https://theintercept .com/2016/06/14/orlando-shooter-wasnt-the-first-murderer-employed-by-global -mercenary-firm/.

Engle, Karen " 'Calling in the Troops': The Uneasy Relationship among Women's Rights, Human Rights, and Humanitarian Intervention." *Harvard Human Rights Journal* 20 (2007): 189–226.

———. "Constructing Good Aliens and Good Citizens: Legitimizing the War on Terror(ism)." *University of Colorado Law Review* 75, no. 1 (winter 2004): 59–114.

Engelhardt, Tom. *Shadow Government: Surveillance, Secret Wars, and a Global Security State in a Single-Superpower World*. Chicago: Haymarket Books, 2014.

Enloe, Cynthia. *Bananas, Beaches and Bases: Making Feminist Sense of International Politics*. 2nd ed. Berkeley: University of California Press, 2000.

———. *Maneuvers: The International Politics of Militarizing Women's Lives*. Berkeley: University of California Press, 2000.

Escobar, Arturo. *Encountering Development: The Making and Unmaking of the Third World*. Princeton, NJ: Princeton University Press, 2011.

Evertz, Scott H. "How Ideology Trumped Science: Why PEPFAR Has Failed to Meet Its Potential." Council for Global Equality, Center for American Progress, January 2010. Accessed January 1, 2016. http://www.globalequality.org/storage/documents/pdf /pepfar_report_final_c.pdf.

Executive Office of the President. *Big Data: Seizing Opportunities, Preserving Values*. Washington, DC: White House, May 2014. http://www.whitehouse.gov/sites /default/files/docs/big_data_privacy_report_5.1.14_final_print.pdf.

Fabian, Johannes. *Time and the Other: How Anthropology Makes Its Object*. 2nd ed. New York: Columbia University Press, 2002.

Fandos, Nicholas. "U.S. Foreign Arms Deals Increased Nearly $10 Billion in 2014." *New York Times*, December 25, 2015. Accessed May 11, 2017. http://www.nytimes.com /2015/12/26/world/middleeast/us-foreign-arms-deals-increased-nearly-10-billion-in -2014.html.

Farris, Anne, Richard P. Nathan, and David J. Wright. "The Expanding Administrative Presidency: George W. Bush and the Faith-Based Initiative." The Roundtable on Religion and Social Welfare Policy. Albany, NY: Nelson A. Rockefeller Institute of Government, August 2004. Accessed May 29, 2015. http://www.rockinst.org/pdf /federalism/2004-08-the_expanding_administrative_presidency_george_w_bush _and_the_faith-based_initiative.pdf.

Fassin, Didier. *Humanitarian Reason: A Moral History of the Present*. Berkeley: University of California Press, 2012.

Fassin, Didier, and Mariella Pandolfi, eds. *Contemporary States of Emergency: The Politics of Military and Humanitarian Interventions*. New York: Zone Books, 2013.

———. "Introduction: Military and Humanitarian Government in the Age of Intervention." In *Contemporary States of Emergency: The Politics of Military and Humanitarian Interventions*, edited by Didier Fassin and Mariella Pandolfi, 9–28. New York: Zone Books, 2013.

Federal Trade Commission. "Children's Online Privacy Protection Rule." 2012. Accessed August 10, 2013. http://www.ftc.gov/os/2012/12/121219copparulefrn.pdf.

———. "COPPA Safe Harbor Program." Accessed May 12, 2016. https://www.ftc.gov/safe-harbor-program.

———. "FTC Announces Settlements with Web Sites That Collected Children's Personal Data without Parental Permission." April 19, 2001. Accessed July 2, 2014. https://www.ftc.gov/news-events/press-releases/2001/04/ftc-announces-settlements-web-sites-collected-childrens-personal

———. "The FTC's First Five Years Protecting Consumers Online." December 1999. Accessed May 12, 2016. https://www.ftc.gov/sites/default/files/documents/reports/protecting-consumers-online/fiveyearreport.pdf.

———. "FTC Testifies on Protecting Children Online in a Fast-Changing Marketplace, and Proposed Changes to COPPA Rule." October 5, 2011. Accessed July 30, 2014. http://www.ftc.gov/news-events/press-releases/2011/10/ftc-testifies-protecting-children-online-fast-changing.

———. "Prepared Statement of the Federal Trade Commission on 'Protecting Children's Privacy in an Electronic World' before the House Committee on Energy and Commerce, Subcommittee on Commerce, Manufacturing and Trade." October 5, 2011. Accessed July 30, 2014, http://www.ftc.gov/sites/default/files/documents/public_statements/prepared-statement-federal-trade-commission-protecting-childrens-privacy-electronic-world/111005coppatestimony.pdf.

———. "Prepared Statement of the Federal Trade Commission on Reauthorization before the Subcommittee on Consumer Affairs, Foreign Commerce and Tourism of the Committee on Commerce, Science, and Transportation, United States Senate." July 17, 2002. Accessed July 2, 2016. https://www.ftc.gov/sites/default/files/documents/public_statements/prepared-statement-federal-trade-commission-prepaid-calling-cards/p074406prepaidcallingcards.pdf.

———. *Privacy Online: A Report to Congress.* June 1998. Accessed July 30, 2014. http://www.ftc.gov/sites/default/files/documents/reports/privacy-online-report-congress/priv-23a.pdf.

Feimster, Crystal N. *Southern Horrors: Women and the Politics of Rape and Lynching.* Cambridge, MA: Harvard University Press, 2011.

Ferguson, James. *The Anti-Politics Machine: Development, Depoliticization, and Bureaucratic Power in Lesotho.* Minneapolis: University of Minnesota Press, 1994.

"Financing Terrorism: Looking in all the Wrong Places." *Economist*, October 20, 2005. Accessed January 5, 2016. http://www.economist.com/node/5053373?story_id=5053373.

Fischel, Joseph J. "Pornographic Protections? Itineraries of Childhood Innocence." *Law, Culture and the Humanities* 12, no. 2 (2016): 206–20.

———. *Sex and Harm in the Age of Consent.* Minneapolis: University of Minnesota Press, 2016.

Fisher, Julie. *Nongovernments: NGOs and the Political Development of the Third World.* West Hartford, CT: Kumarian, 1998.

Fisher, Max. "What Makes America's Gun Culture Totally Unique in the World, in Four Charts." *Washington Post*, December 15, 2012. Accessed June 14, 2016. https://www.washingtonpost.com/news/worldviews/wp/2012/12/15/what-makes-americas-gun-culture-totally-unique-in-the-world-as-demonstrated-in-four-charts/.

Fisher, William. "Muslim Charities Negotiate a Minefield." *IPS: Inter Press Service.* August 29, 2008, sec. International, accessed January 4, 2016, http://www.ipsnews.net/2008/08/politics-us-muslim-charities-negotiate-a-minefield.

Fisher, William F. "Doing Good? The Politics and Antipolitics of NGO Practices." *Annual Review of Anthropology* (1997): 439–64.

Forero, Juan, and Steven R. Weisman. "U.S. Allies, and Others, Send Offers of Assistance." *New York Times*, September 4, 2005, sec. International/Americas. Accessed March 31, 2017. http://www.nytimes.com/2005/09/04/international/americas/04offers.html.

Forte, Maximilian C. "The Human Terrain System and Anthropology: A Review of Ongoing Public Debates." *American Anthropologist* 113, no. 1 (March 1, 2011): 149–53. doi:10.1111/j.1548–1433.2010.01315.x.

Fotel, Trine, and Thyra Uth Thomsen. "The Surveillance of Children's Mobility." *Surveillance and Society* 1, no. 4 (2003): 535–54.

Foucault, Michel. *The History of Sexuality*, vol. 1: *An Introduction.* Reissue ed. New York: Vintage, 1990.

———. *Power.* New York: New Press, 2001.

———. *Security, Territory, Population: Lectures at the Collège de France 1977–1978.* Edited by Michel Senellart. New York: Palgrave Macmillan, 2009.

———. *"Society Must Be Defended": Lectures at the Collège de France, 1975–1976.* Repr. ed. New York: Picador, 2003.

Frankel, Todd C. "Why the CDC Still Isn't Researching Gun Violence, Despite the Ban Being Lifted Two Years Ago." *Washington Post*, January 14, 2015. Accessed June 16, 2015, https://www.washingtonpost.com/news/storyline/wp/2015/01/14/why-the-cdc-still-isnt-researching-gun-violence-despite-the-ban-being-lifted-two-years-ago/.

Freedman, Michael G. "Prosecuting Terrorism: The Material Support Stature and Muslim Charities." *Hastings Constitutional Law Quarterly* 38, no. 4 (2011): 1130–50.

Freeman, Dena, ed. *Pentecostalism and Development: Churches, NGOs and Social Change in Africa.* New York: Palgrave MacMillan, 2012.

"Friend Verifier the First Facebook App That Scans Your Friends for Registered Sex Offenders." PRWeb, March 9, 2012. Accessed June 13, 2016. http://www.prweb.com/releases/2012/3/prweb9262666.htm.

Fry, Katherine. "Television News Hero for New Orleans, Hero for the Nation." *Space and Culture* 9, no. 1 (2006): 83–85.

F-Secure. "Protecting your Children." N.d. Accessed June 20, 2016. https://www.f-secure.com/en/web/home_global/digital-parenting.

———. "Protect Your Life on Every Device." N.d. Accessed June 20, 2016. https://www.f-secure.com/en_US/web/home_us/safe?icid=1535.

Fuller, William P., and Barnett F. Baron. "How War on Terror Hits Charity." *Christian Science Monitor* 95, no. 170 (July 29, 2003): 11.

Galloway, Alexander R. "Social Realism in Gaming." *Game Studies* 4, no. 1 (November 2004). http://gamestudies.org/0401/galloway/.

Garber, Danielle J. "COPPA: Protecting Children's Personal Information on the Internet." *Journal of Law and Policy* 10 (2002): 129–87.

Garcia, Courtney. "September 11 Attacks, Katrina Top List of Memorable TV Moments." *Reuters*, July 11, 2012. Accessed December 8, 2015. http://www.reuters.com/article /2012/07/11/entertainment-us-memorablemoments-idUSBRE86A0EG20120711.

Geisler, Charles, Gayatri Menon, and Shelley Feldman, eds. *Accumulating Insecurity: Violence and Dispossession in the Making of Everyday Life.* London: University of Georgia Press, 2011.

Gellman, Barton, and Laura Poitras. "U.S., British Intelligence Mining Data from Nine U.S. Internet Companies in Broad Secret Program." *Washington Post*, June 6, 2013. Accessed May 17, 2016. https://www.washingtonpost.com/investigations/us-intelligence -mining-data-from-nine-us-internet-companies-in-broad-secret-program/2013/06 /06/3a0c0da8-cebf-11e2-8845-d970ccb04497_story.html?utm_term=.06ad1df98511.

Ghandour, Abdel-Rahman. "Humanitarianism, Islam and the West: Contest or Cooperation?" *Humanitarian Exchange* 25 (n.d.): 14–17.

Gilmore, Russell S. "Another Branch of Manly Sport." In *Guns in America: A Historical Reader,* edited by Jan E. Dizard, Robert Muth, and Stephen P. Andrews, 105–21. New York: NYU Press, 1999.

Gingrich, Newt. *A Nation like No Other: Why American Exceptionalism Matters.* Washington, DC: Regnery, 2011.

Giroux, Henry A. "Beyond Belief: Religious Fundamentalism and Cultural Politics in the Age of George W. Bush." *Cultural Studies ↔ Critical Methodologies* 4, no. 4 (November 1, 2004): 415–25. doi:10.1177/1532708604268219.

———. "Reading Hurricane Katrina: Race, Class, and the Biopolitics of Disposability." *College Literature* 33, no. 3 (2006): 171–96.

———. "Zero Tolerance, Domestic Militarization, and the War against Youth." *Social Justice* 30, no. 2 (92) (January 1, 2003): 59–65.

Glanz, James, Jeff Larson, and Andrew W. Lehren. "Spy Agencies Tap Data Streaming from Phone Apps." *New York Times*, January 28, 2014.

Glasser, Ira. "Struggle for a New Paradigm: Protecting Free Speech and Privacy in the Virtual World of Cyberspace." *Nova Law Review* 23, no. 2 (1999): 627–56.

Glauber, Bill. "Oak Creek Officer Shot during Sikh Temple Rampage Retiring." *Milwaukee-Wisconsin Journal Sentinel*, May 15, 2013. Accessed May 11, 2017. http:// www.jsonline.com/news/milwaukee/oak-creek-officer-shot-during-sikh-temple -rampage-retiring-bk9v6rd-207601521.html.

Global Nonprofit Information Network. "Overview of U.S. Counterterrorism Policies Impacting Charities." N.d. Accessed May 8, 2012. http://www.internationaldonors .org/advocacy/pdf/gnin_091508-1.pdf.

Goffin, Alvin M. *The Rise of Protestant Evangelism in Ecuador, 1895–1990.* Gainesville: University Press of Florida, 1994.

Goldberg, David Theo. *The Racial State*. Malden, MA: Blackwell, 2002.

Gonzalez, David. "U.S. Aids Conversion-Minded Quake Relief in El Salvador." *New York Times*, March 5, 2001. Accessed January 4, 2016. http://www.nytimes.com/2001/03/05/world/us-aids-conversion-minded-quake-relief-in-el-salvador.html.

González, Roberto J. "'Human Terrain': Past, Present, and Future Applications." *Anthropology Today* 24, no. 1 (February 1, 2008): 21–26. doi:10.1111/j.1467-8322.2008.00561.x.

Goode, Erica, and Serge F. Kovaleski. "Wisconsin Killer Fed and Was Fueled by Hate-Driven Music." *New York Times*, August 6, 2012, sec. U.S., A1. Accessed June 15, 2016. http://www.nytimes.com/2012/08/07/us/army-veteran-identified-as-suspect-in-wisconsin-shooting.html.

Goodman, Ellen. "The Myth of 'Security Moms.'" *Boston Globe*, October 7, 2004. Accessed February 4, 2016. http://www.boston.com/news/nation/articles/2004/10/07/the_myth_of_security_moms/.

Goodstein, Laurie. "A Nation at War: Missionaries; Groups Critical of Islam Are Now Waiting to Take Aid to Iraq." *New York Times*, April 4, 2003, sec. U.S. Accessed January 1, 2016. http://www.nytimes.com/2003/04/04/us/nation-war-missionaries-groups-critical-islam-are-now-waiting-take-aid-iraq.html.

———. "A Nation at War: Muslims Hesitating on Gifts as U.S. Scrutinizes Charities." *New York Times*, April 17, 2003. Accessed January 4, 2016. http://www.nytimes.com/2003/04/17/us/nation-war-charities-muslims-hesitating-gifts-us-scrutinizes-charities.html.

———. "U.S. Muslims Taken Aback by a Charity's Conviction." *New York Times*, November 26, 2008, A23. Accessed January 4, 2016. http://www.nytimes.com/2008/11/26/us/26charity.html.

Gordon, Colin. "Governmental Rationality: An Introduction." In *The Foucault Effect: Studies in Governmentality*, edited by Graham Burchell, Colin Gordon, and Peter Miller, 1–52. Chicago: University of Chicago Press, 1991.

Gotham, Kevin Fox. "Critical Theory and Katrina: Disaster, Spectacle and Immanent Critique." *City: Analysis of Urban Trends, Culture, Theory, Policy, Action* 11, no. 1 (2007): 81–99.

Gottschalk, Marie. *Caught: The Prison State and the Lockdown of American Politics*. Rev ed. Princeton, NJ: Princeton University Press, 2016.

———. "Democracy and the Carceral State in America." *Annals of the American Academy of Political and Social Science* 651, no. 1 (January 1, 2014): 288–95. doi:10.1177/0002716213503787.

Grabill, Joseph L. *Protestant Diplomacy and the Near East: Missionary Influence on American Policy, 1810–1927*. Minnesota Archive Editions ed. Minneapolis: University of Minnesota Press, 1971.

Graham, Stephen. "'Homeland' Insecurities? Katrina and the Politics of 'Security' in Metropolitan America." *Space and Culture* 9, no. 1 (2006): 63–67.

Gray, Colin S. *Hard Power and Soft Power: The Utility of Military Force as an Instrument of Policy in the 21st Century*. Carlisle, PA: Strategic Studies Institute, 2011.

Gray, Herman. *Watching Race: Television and the Struggle for Blackness*. Minneapolis: University of Minnesota Press, 2004.

Green, Emma. "The Politics of Mass Murder." *Atlantic*, June 13, 2016. Accessed June 16, 2016. http://www.theatlantic.com/politics/archive/2016/06/orlando-political -reactions-homophobia-gun-rights-extremism/486752/.

———. "The Trouble with Wearing Turbans in America." *Atlantic*, January 27, 2015. Accessed June 14, 2016. http://www.theatlantic.com/politics/archive/2015/01/the -trouble-with-wearing-turbans-in-america/384832/.

Greenwald, Glenn. "Why Is Boston 'Terrorism' but Not Aurora, Sandy Hook, Tucson and Columbine?" *Guardian*, April 22, 2013, sec. Opinion. Accessed July 2, 2016. https://www.theguardian.com/commentisfree/2013/apr/22/boston-marathon -terrorism-aurora-sandy-hook.

Greenwald, Glenn, and Peter Maas. "Meet Alfreda Frances Bikowsky, the Senior Officer at the Center of the CIA's Torture Scandal." *The Intercept*, December 10, 2014. Accessed March 25, 2017. https://theintercept.com/2014/12/19/senior-cia-officer -center-torture-scandals-alfreda-bikowsky/.

"Greg Mortenson." *60 Minutes*, CBS, April 17, 2011. http://www.cbsnews.com/video /watch/?id=7363068n&tag=api.

Grewal, Inderpal. "Outsourcing Patriarchy: Feminist Encounters, Transnational Mediations and the Crime of 'Honour Killings.'" *International Feminist Journal of Politics* 15, no. 1 (March 1, 2013): 1–19. doi:10.1080/14616742.2012.755352.

———. *Transnational America: Feminisms, Diasporas, Neoliberalisms*. Durham, NC: Duke University Press, 2005.

Grewal, Zareena. *Islam Is a Foreign Country: American Muslims and the Global Crisis of Authority*. New York: NYU Press, 2013.

Griffith, R. Marie, and Melani McAlister. "Introduction: Is the Public Square Still Naked?" *American Quarterly* 59, no. 3 (2007): 527–63. doi:10.1353/aq.2007.0056.

Gross, Larry. "Some Ways into Zero Dark Thirty." *Film Comment*, December 18, 2012. Accessed February 4, 2016. http://www.filmcomment.com/entry/review-zero-dark -thirty-kathryn-bigelow.

Grove, Lloyd. "Michelle Malkin Has Feelings, Too." *Daily Beast*, September 22, 2009. Accessed February 4, 2016. http://www.thedailybeast.com/articles/2009/09/22 /michelle-malkin-has-feelings-too.html.

Gryboski, Michael. "Franklin Graham: Islam Has Declared War on the World." *Christian Post*, November 18, 2015. Accessed January 1, 2016. http://www.christianpost.com /news/franklin-graham-islam-war-world-150362/.

Guérin, Isabelle. "Juggling with Debt, Social Ties, and Values: The Everyday Use of Microcredit in Rural South India." *Current Anthropology* 55, no. S9 (August 1, 2014): S40–S50. doi:10.1086/675929.

Gunning, Sandra. *Race, Rape, and Lynching: The Red Record of American Literature, 1890–1912*. New York: Oxford University Press, 1996.

Gusterson, Hugh, and Catherine Besteman, eds. *The Insecure American: How We Got Here and What We Should Do about It*. Berkeley: University of California Press, 2009.

Haass, Richard. "Storm Warning: How the Flood Compromises U.S. Foreign Policy." *Slate*, September 9, 2005. Accessed December 8, 2015. http://www.slate.com/articles /news_and_politics/foreigners/2005/09/storm_warning.html.

Hadar, Leon. "America's Eroding Credibility: Fallout from Baghdad and New Orleans Makes It Difficult for Bush Administration to Mobilise Support." *Business Times Singapore*, September 14, 2005.

Hall, Stuart. "Encoding/Decoding." In *Culture, Media, Language: Working Papers in Cultural Studies*, 128–38. London: Hutchinson, 1973.

———. "The Neoliberal Revolution." In *The Neoliberal Crisis*, edited by Jonathan Rutherford and Sally Davison, 8–26. Soundings Ebook. Lawrence Wishart, n.d. http://www.lwbooks.co.uk/ebooks/The_Neoliberal_crisis.pdf.

———. "The Television Discourse: Encoding and Decoding." *Education and Culture* 25 (1974): 8–14.

Hall, Stuart, Chas Critcher, Tony Jefferson, John Clarke, and Brian Roberts. *Policing the Crisis: Mugging, the State, and Law and Order*. London: Macmillan, 1978.

Halley, Janet. *Split Decisions: How and Why to Take a Break from Feminism*. Princeton, NJ: Princeton University Press, 2008

Hallsworth, Simon, and John Lea. "Emerging Contours of the Security State." *Theoretical Criminology* 15, no. 2 (2011): 141–57.

Hammond, Laura. "The Power of Holding Humanitarianism Hostage." In *Humanitarianism in Question: Politics, Power, Ethics*, edited by Michael Barnet and Thomas G. Weiss, 172–95. Ithaca, NY: Cornell University Press, 2008.

Han, Ju Hui Judy. "Contemporary Korean/American Evangelical Missions: Politics of Space, Gender, and Difference." PhD dissertation, University of California, Berkeley, 2009. http://search.proquest.com/docview/929138797.

Hancock, Mary E. "New Mission Paradigms and the Encounter with Islam: Fusing Voluntarism, Tourism and Evangelism in Short-Term Missions in the USA." *Culture and Religion: An Interdisciplinary Journal* 14, no. 3 (2013): 305–23. doi:10.1080/14755610.2012.758160.

Hannabach, Cathy. *Blood Cultures: Medicine, Media, and Militarisms*. New York: Palgrave Macmillan, 2015.

Hansen, Thomas Blom, and Finn Stepputat. "Introduction." In *Sovereign Bodies: Citizens, Migrants, and States in the Postcolonial World*, edited by Thomas Blom Hansen and Finn Stepputat, 1–38. Princeton, NJ: Princeton University Press, 2005.

———, eds. *Sovereign Bodies: Citizens, Migrants, and States in the Postcolonial World*. Princeton, NJ: Princeton University Press, 2005.

Harden, Monique, Nathalie Walker, and Kali Akuno. "Racial Discrimination and Ethnic Cleansing in the United States in the Aftermath of Hurricane Katrina: A Report to the United Nations' Committee for the Elimination of Racial Discrimination." Advocates for Environmental Human Rights and Peoples' Hurricane Relief Fund. Accessed May 28, 2016. http://www.ushrnetwork.org/sites/ushrnetwork.org/files/cerd2008hurricanekatrinaracialdiscriminationandethniccleansingintheunitedstates.pdf.

Hardt, Michael, and Antonio Negri. *Empire*. Cambridge, MA: Harvard University Press, 2000.

Harris, Cheryl I. "Whiteness as Property." *Harvard Law Review* 106, no. 8 (1993): 1707–91.

Harris, Paul. "Valerie Plame Welcomes New Breed of Fictional Female Spy in Zero Dark Thirty." *Guardian*, December 15, 2012, sec. World News. Accessed February 4,

2016. http://www.theguardian.com/world/2012/dec/16/valerie-plame-female-spy
-homeland-zero-dark-thirty.

Harrison, Faye. "The Gendered Politics and Violence of Structural Adjustment." In *Situated Lives: Gender and Culture in Everyday Life*, edited by Louise Lamphere, Helena Ragoné, and Patricia Zavella, 451–68. New York: Routledge, 1997.

Harvey, David. *A Brief History of Neoliberalism*. Oxford: Oxford University Press, 2007.

Hasian, Marouf. "*Zero Dark Thirty* and the Critical Challenges Posed by Populist Postfeminism during the Global War on Terrorism." *Journal of Communication Inquiry* 37, no. 4 (October 1, 2013): 322–43. doi:10.1177/0196859913505616.

Hasinoff, Amy Adele. *Sexting Panic: Rethinking Criminalization, Privacy, and Consent*. Urbana: University of Illinois Press, 2015.

Haughney, Christine. "New York Post Sued over Boston Bombing Article." *New York Times*, June 6, 2013. Accessed June 2, 2016. http://www.nytimes.com/2013/06/07/business/media/new-york-post-sued-over-boston-bombing-article.html.

Hearn, Julie. "African NGOs: The New Compradors?" *Development and Change* 38, no. 6 (2007): 1095–110.

———. "The 'Invisible' NGO: US Evangelical Missions in Kenya." *Journal of Religion in Africa* 32, no. 1 (February 1, 2002): 32–60.

Heefner, Gretchen. *The Missile Next Door: The Minuteman in the American Heartland*. Cambridge, MA: Harvard University Press, 2012.

Heller, Nathan. "California Screaming." *New Yorker*, July 7, 2014. Accessed January 4, 2016. http://www.newyorker.com/magazine/2014/07/07/california-screaming.

Helsper, Ellen Johanna, and Rebecca Eynon. "Digital Natives: Where Is the Evidence?" *British Educational Research Journal* 36, no. 3 (June 17, 2009): 503–20. doi:10.1080/01411920902989227.

Heng, Yee-Kuang, and Ken McDonagh. "The Other War on Terror Revealed: Global Governmentality and the Financial Action Task Force's Campaign against Terrorist Financing." *Review of International Studies* 34, no. 3 (July 2008): 553–73.

Herbert, Bob. "In America: Refusing to Save Africans." *New York Times*, June 11, 2001, sec. Opinion. Accessed January 1, 2016. http://www.nytimes.com/2001/06/11/opinion/in-america-refusing-to-save-africans.html.

Herbert, Melissa S. *Camouflage Isn't Only for Combat: Gender, Sexuality, and Women in the Military*. New York: NYU Press, 1998.

Hess, Amanda, and Belle Boggs. "A Former FBI Agent on Why It's So Hard to Prosecute Gamergate Trolls." *Slate*, October 17, 2014. Accessed June 15, 2016. http://www.slate.com/blogs/xx_factor/2014/10/17/gamergate_threats_why_it_s_so_hard_to_prosecute_the_people_targeting_zoe.html.

Hill, Jane. "Language, Race and White Public Space." *American Anthropologist* 100, no. 3 (September 1998): 680–89.

Hindle, Charlotte, Rachel Collinson, Mike Richard, Korina Miller, Sarah Wintle, and Nate Cavalieri. *Volunteer: A Traveller's Guide to Making a Difference around the World*. 3rd ed. Melbourne, Australia: Lonely Planet, 2013.

Hing, Bill Ong. *Making and Remaking Asian America through Immigration Policy, 1850–1990*. Stanford, CA: Stanford University Press, 1993.

"History of Hate: Crimes against Sikhs since 9/11." *Huffington Post*, August 7, 2012. Accessed June 13, 2016. http://www.huffingtonpost.com/2012/08/07/history-of-hate-crimes-against-sikhs-since-911_n_1751841.html.

Hofstadter, Richard. "Cuba, the Philippines, and Manifest Destiny." In *The Paranoid Style in American Politics and Other Essays*. New York: Vintage Books, [1952] 2008.

Höglund, Johan. "Electronic Empire: Orientalism Revisited in the Military Shooter." *Game Studies* 8, no. 1 (September 2008). http://gamestudies.org/0801/articles/hoeglund.

Hoogensen, Gunhild, and Kirsti Stuvøy. "Gender, Resistance and Human Security." *Security Dialogue* 37, no. 2 (June 1, 2006): 207–28. doi:10.1177/0967010606066436.

Hosley, William. *Colt: The Making of an American Legend*. Amherst: University of Massachusetts Press, 1996.

Howard, Philip N., John N. Carr, and Tema J. Milstein. "Digital Technology and the Market for Political Surveillance." *Surveillance and Society* 3, no. 1 (2005): 59–73.

Howell, Sally. "(Re)bounding Islamic Charitable Giving in the Terror Decade." UCLA *Journal of Islamic and Near Eastern Law* 10, no. 1 (2010–2011): 35.

Huliaras, Asteris. "Evangelists, Oil Companies, and Terrorists: The Bush Administration's Policy towards Sudan." *Orbis* 50, no. 4 (2006): 709–24.

Huntemann, Nina B., and Matthew Thomas Payne, eds. *Joystick Soldiers: The Politics of Play in Military Video Games*. New York: Routledge, 2009.

Ilgen, Thomas L. "Reconfigured Sovereignty in the Age of Globalization." In *Reconfigured Sovereignty: Multi-Layered Governance in the Global Age*, edited by Thomas L. Ilgen, 6–35. Aldershot, England: Ashgate, 2003.

———, ed. *Reconfigured Sovereignty: Multi-Layered Governance in the Global Age*. Aldershot, England: Ashgate, 2003.

Incite! Women of Color against Violence. *The Revolution Will Not Be Funded: Beyond the Non-Profit Industrial Complex*. Cambridge, MA: South End Press, 2009.

The Inter-American Commission of Human Rights General Situation Hearing on Natural Disaster and Human Rights. *When Disaster Strikes: A Human Rights Analysis of the 2005 Gulf Coast Hurricanes*. Berkeley, CA: International Human Rights Clinic, Boalt Hall School of Law, March 6, 2006. https://www.academia.edu/10149179/When_Disaster_Strikes_A_Human_Rights_Analysis_of_the_2005_Gulf_Coast_Hurricanes_Submitted_to_the_Inter-American_Commission_of_Human_Rights.

The Internet Society. "A Brief History of the Internet and Related Networks." N.d. Accessed July 10, 2016. http://www.internetsociety.org/internet/what-internet/history-internet/brief-history-internet-related-networks.

Jabri, Vivian. *War and the Transformation of Global Politics*. New York: Palgrave Macmillan, 2007.

Jackson, Linda A., Yong Zhao, Anthony Kolenic, Hiram E. Fitzgerald, Rena Harold, and Alexander Von Eye. "Race, Gender, and Information Technology Use: The New Digital Divide." *CyberPsychology and Behavior* 11, no. 4 (August 1, 2008): 437–42. doi:10.1089/cpb.2007.0157.

"Jackson Conversations on Leadership with Stan McChyrstal and Greg Mortenson." Jackson Institute Conversations on Leadership Series. Yale University, February 21,

2011. Accessed January 4, 2016. http://jackson.yale.edu/jackson-conversations
-leadership-stan-mcchrystal-greg-mortenson-now-yale-youtube-0.

Jacobson, Matthew Frye. *Barbarian Virtues: The United States Encounters Foreign Peoples at Home and Abroad, 1876–1917*. New York: Hill and Wang, 2001.

Jaitla, Punnu. "Thoughts on the Creation of 'Enemies Within.'" *Sikh Formations* 8, no. 3 (December 1, 2012): 319–22. doi:10.1080/17448727.2012.752678.

James, Allison. *Constructing Childhood: Theory, Policy and Social Practice*. New York: Palgrave Macmillan, 2004.

James, Erica Caple. "Governing Gifts: Law, Risk, and the 'War on Terror.'" *UCLA Journal of Islamic and Near Eastern Law* 10 (2010/2011): 65–84.

Jayasinghe, Saroj. "Erosion of Trust in Humanitarian Agencies: What Strategies Might Help?" *Global Health Action* 4 (January 2011): 1–5. doi:10.3402/gha.v4i0.8973.

Jeffery, Patricia, and Amrita Basu, eds. *Appropriating Gender: Women's Activism and Politicized Religion in South Asia*. New York: Routledge, 1998.

Jeffreys, Sheila. "Double Jeopardy: Women, the US Military and the War in Iraq." *Women's Studies International Forum* 30, no. 1 (January 2007): 16–25. doi:10.1016/j.wsif.2006.12.002.

Jelinek, Pauline. "New Ads Pitch Marine Corps' Kinder, Gentler Side." *Washington Times*, March 8, 2012. Accessed January 4, 2016. http://www.washingtontimes.com/news/2012/mar/8/new-ads-pitch-marine-corps-kinder-gentler-side/.

Jenkins, Henry. *Fans, Bloggers, and Gamers: Exploring Participatory Culture*. New York: New York University Press, 2006.

Jenkins, Henry, Sam Ford, and Joshua Green. *Spreadable Media: Creating Value and Meaning in a Networked Culture*. New York: NYU Press, 2013.

Jenkins, Pamela. "Gender and the Landscape of Community Work before and after Katrina." In *The Women of Katrina: How Gender, Race, and Class Matter in an American Disaster*, edited by Emmanuel David and Elaine Enarson, 169–78. Nashville: Vanderbilt University Press, 2011.

Jenkins, Philip. *Beyond Tolerance: Child Pornography Online*. New York: NYU Press, 2001.

Johnson, Alex. "'Rectal Hydration': Inside the CIA's Interrogation of Khalid Sheikh Mohammed." NBC, December 9, 2014. Accessed February 4, 2016. http://www.nbcnews.com/storyline/cia-torture-report/rectal-hydration-inside-cias-interrogation-khalid-sheikh-mohammed-n265016.

Johnson, Cedric, ed. *The Neoliberal Deluge: Hurricane Katrina, Late Capitalism, and the Remaking of New Orleans*. Minneapolis: University of Minnesota Press, 2011.

Johnson, Kevin R. "'Aliens' and the U.S. Immigration Laws: The Social and Legal Construction of Nonpersons." *University of Miami Inter-American Law Review* 28, no. 2 (1996): 263–92.

Johnson, Lyman. "Law and Legal Theory in the History of Corporate Responsibility: Corporate Personhood." SSRN Scholarly Paper. Rochester, NY: Social Science Research Network, 2012. http://papers.ssrn.com/abstract=2070939.

Johnson, Michael P. "Patriarchal Terrorism and Common Couple Violence: Two Forms of Violence against Women." *Journal of Marriage and Family* 57, no. 2 (May 1995): 283–94.

Jones, Bradley A. "Hurricane Katrina, the Politics of Pity, and the News Media." PhD dissertation, University of Michigan, 2011.

Jones, Julia, and Eve Bower. "American Deaths in Terrorism vs. Gun Violence in One Graph." *CNN*, updated December 30, 2015. Accessed June 30, 2016. http://www.cnn .com/2015/10/02/us/oregon-shooting-terrorism-gun-violence/index.html.

Jones, Karen R., and John Wills. *The American West: Competing Visions*. Edinburgh: Edinburgh University Press, 2009.

Jopson, Barney. "Uber and Airbnb Urge Watchdog to Back Off." *Financial Times*, June 10, 2015. Accessed May 11, 2017. https://www.ft.com/content/fd65c05a-0eaf-11e5 -9ae0-00144feabdc0.

Jordan, Miriam, and Erica E. Phillips. "Wall Street Journal: Bank Moves Hinder Immigrants." Keith Ellison, June 22, 2012. Accessed May 29, 2016. https://ellison.house.gov /media-center/news/wall-street-journal-bank-moves-hinder-immigrants.

Joseph, Miranda. *Debt to Society: Accounting for Life under Capitalism*. Minneapolis: University of Minnesota Press, 2014.

Jost, Patrick M., and Harjit Singh Sandhu. "The Hawala Alternative Remittance System and Its Role in Money Laundering." US Department of Treasury and INTERPOL/ FOPAC, n.d. Accessed May 29, 2016. https://www.treasury.gov/resource-center /terrorist-illicit-finance/Documents/FinCEN-Hawala-rpt.pdf.

Kalhan, Anil. "Immigration Policing and Federalism through the Lens of Technology, Surveillance, and Privacy." *Ohio State Law Journal* 74, no. 6 (2013): 1105–65.

Kamat, Sangeeta. *Development Hegemony: NGOs and the State in India*. New York: Oxford University Press, 2002.

———. "The Privatization of Public Interest: Theorizing NGO Discourse in a Neoliberal Era." *Review of International Political Economy* 11, no. 1 (2004): 155–76.

Kang, Jay Caspian. "Should Reddit Be Blamed for the Spreading of a Smear?" *New York Times*, July 25, 2013, sec. Magazine. Accessed June 2, 2015. http://www.nytimes .com/2013/07/28/magazine/should-reddit-be-blamed-for-the-spreading-of-a-smear .html.

Kaplan, Amy. *The Anarchy of Empire in the Making of U.S. Culture*. Cambridge, MA: Harvard University Press, 2005.

———. " 'Left Alone with America': The Absence of Empire in the Study of American Culture." In *Cultures of United States Imperialism*, edited by Amy Kaplan and Donald E. Pease, 3–21. Durham, NC: Duke University Press, 1993.

Kaplan, Amy, and Donald E. Pease, eds. *Cultures of United States Imperialism*. Durham, NC: Duke University Press, 1994.

Kaplan, Caren. "Desert Wars: Virilio and the Limits of 'Genuine Knowledge.' " In *Virilio and Visual Culture*, edited by John Armitage and Ryan Bishop, 69–85. Edinburgh: Edinburgh University Press, 2013.

———. *Questions of Travel: Postmodern Discourses of Displacement*. Durham, NC: Duke University Press, 1996.

Kaplan, Caren, Erik Loyer, and Ezra Claytan Daniels. "Precision Targets: GPS and the Militarization of Everyday Life." *Canadian Journal of Communication* 38, no. 3 (September 16, 2013): 397–420. http://cjc-online.ca/index.php/journal/article/view /2655.

Kaplan, David E. "Hearts, Minds, and Dollars." *U.S. News and World Report* 138, no. 15 (April 25, 2005): 22.

Kaplan, E. Ann. "Global Trauma and Public Feelings: Viewing Images of Catastrophe." *Consumption, Markets and Culture* 11, no. 1 (2008): 3–24.

Karim, Lamia. *Microfinance and Its Discontents: Women in Debt in Bangladesh.* Minneapolis: University of Minnesota Press, 2011.

Karnani, Aneel. "Microfinance Misses Its Mark (SSIR)." *Stanford Social Innovation Review.* Accessed May 29, 2016. http://ssir.org/articles/entry/microfinance_misses_its_mark.

Karush, Sarah. "FBI Investigation of Islamic Charity Has Muslims Hesitant about Giving." *New York Sun*, September 25, 2006. Accessed January 4, 2016. http://www.nysun .com/national/fbi-investigation-of-islamic-charity-has-muslims/40279.

"'Katrinagate' Fury Spreads to US Media." *TVNZ*, September 6, 2005. Accessed November 5, 2014. http://www.news24.com/World/Archives/HurricaneWatch /Katrinagate-fury-spreads-20050906.

Katz, Cindi. "The State Goes Home: Local Hypervigilance and the Global Retreat from Social Reproduction." *Social Justice* 28, no. 3 (2001): 47–56.

Katz, Elihu, and Tamar Liebes. "No More Peace!" In *Media Events in a Global Age*, edited by Nick Couldry, Andreas Hepp, and Friedrich Krotz, 32–42. New York: Routledge, 2009.

Kaur, Valarie. "Tragedy Returns to Oak Creek." *Salon*, August 17, 2013. Accessed May 11, 2017. http://www.salon.com/2012/08/17/tragedy_returns_to_oak_creek/.

Kazin, Michael, and Joseph Anthony McCartin. *Americanism: New Perspectives on the History of an Ideal.* Chapel Hill: University of North Carolina Press, 2006.

Kazzarato, Maurizio. "Neoliberalism in Action: Inequality, Insecurity and the Reconstitution of the Social." *Theory, Culture and Society* 26, no. 6 (n.d.): 109–33.

Keikelame, Mpoe Johannah, Colleen K. Murphy, Karin E. Ringheim, and Sara Woldehanna. "Perceptions of HIV/AIDS Leaders about Faith-Based Organisations' Influence on HIV/AIDS Stigma in South Africa." *African Journal of AIDS Research* 9, no. 1 (2010): 63–70. doi:10.2989/16085906.2010.484571.

Keller, Bill. "The Return of America's Missionary Impulse." *New York Times*, April 15, 2011. Accessed January 4, 2016. http://www.nytimes.com/2011/04/17/magazine /mag-17Lede-t.html.

Kellermann, Arthur L., and Frederick P. Rivara. "Silencing the Science on Gun Research." *JAMA* 309, no. 6 (February 13, 2013): 549–50. doi:10.1001/ jama.2012.208207.

Kelsey, Nola Lee. *700 Places to Volunteer before You Die: A Traveler's Guide.* Hot Springs, SD: Dog's Eye View Media, 2010.

Kennedy, Denis. "Selling the Distant Other: Humanitarianism and Imagery. Ethical Dilemmas of Humanitarian Action." *Journal of Humanitarian Assistance*, February 28, 2009. http://sites.tufts.edu/jha/archives/411.

Kennedy, John F. *A Nation of Immigrants.* Rev. ed. New York: Harper Perennial, 2008.

Kennedy, Randall. *Race, Crime, and the Law.* Repr. ed. New York: Vintage, 1998.

Khalili, Laleh. *Time in the Shadows: Confinement in Counterinsurgencies.* Stanford, CA: Stanford University Press, 2012.

Kidd, Thomas S. *American Christians and Islam: Evangelical Culture and Muslims from the Colonial Period to the Age of Terrorism*. Princeton, NJ: Princeton University Press, 2009.

Kiely, Ray. *Empire in the Age of Globalisation: US Hegemony and Neo-Liberal Disorder*. London: Pluto, 2005.

King, Rita J. "Big, Easy Money: Disaster Profiteering on the American Gulf Coast." *CorpWatch*, August 15, 2006. Accessed December 8, 2016. http://www.corpwatch.org/article.php?id=14004.

Kinsey, Christopher. *The Corporate Soldiers and International Security: The Rise of Private Military Companies*. New York: Routledge, 2006.

Kiva. "Lending Teams. Connect with Kiva's Lender Community." n.d. Accessed July 17, 2013. http://www.Kiva.org/teams?queryString=unhappy+kiva+lenders&search=&category=all&membershipType=all&sortBy=overallLoanedAmount.

Klein, Naomi. *The Shock Doctrine: The Rise of Disaster Capitalism*. New York: Metropolitan Books, 2007.

Kleinman, Alexis. "Reddit User Who Started FindBostonBombers Quits Reddit." *Huffington Post*, April 23, 2013. Accessed July 16, 2016. http://www.huffingtonpost.com/2013/04/23/reddit-boston-ama_n_3138623.html.

Knickerbocker, Brad. "CIA Analyst at the Center of Torture Report Is Outed: She's Not 'Maya.'" *Christian Science Monitor*, December 21, 2014. Accessed April 4, 2017. http://www.csmonitor.com/USA/Politics/DC-Decoder/2014/1221/CIA-analyst-at-the-center-of-torture-report-is-outed.-She-s-not-Maya-video.

Kohlmann, Evan. *The Role of Islamic Charities in International Terrorist Recruitment and Financing*. Copenhagen: Danish Institute for International Studies, 2006. http://www.tenc.net/archive/DIIS%20WP%202006-7.pdf.

Kohn, Hans. *American Nationalism: An Interpretative Essay*. New York: Macmillan, 1957.

Koonz, Claudia. *Mothers in the Fatherland: Women, the Family and Nazi Politics*. New York: St. Martin's, 1987.

Krakauer, Jon. *Three Cups of Deceit: How Greg Mortenson, Humanitarian Hero, Lost His Way*. New York: Anchor, 2011.

Kremmer, Christopher. "Charities Linked to Extremists Lead Quake Relief." *Age*, November 21, 2005. Accessed January 5, 2016. http://www.theage.com.au/news/world/charities-linked-to-extremists-lead-quake-relief/2005/11/20/1132421545811.html.

Kristof, Nicholas. "Kristof Maintains a Twitter Account under the Handle @NickKristof." Twitter post. September 5, 2009, 9:42 AM, https://twitter.com/NickKristof/status/37814237375.

Kromm, Chris, and Sue Sturgis. "Hurricane Katrina and the Guiding Principles on Internal Displacement: A Global Human Rights Perspective on a National Disaster." *Southern Exposure* 36, no. 1. (January 2008).

Kuipers, Giselinde. "The Social Construction of Digital Danger: Debating, Defusing and Inflating the Moral Dangers of Online Humor and Pornography in the Netherlands and the United States." *New Media and Society* 8, no. 3 (June 1, 2006): 379–400. doi:10.1177/1461444806061949.

Kumar, Deepa. *Islamophobia and the Politics of Empire*. Chicago: Haymarket Books, 2012.

Kumar, Deepa, and Arun Kundnani. "Homeland and the Imagination of National Security." *Jacobin*, November 11, 2013. https://www.jacobinmag.com/2013/11/homeland-and-the-imagination-of-national-security/.

Kuo, David. *Tempting Faith: An Inside Story of Political Seduction*. New York: Free Press, 2007.

Lancaster, Roger N. *Sex Panic and the Punitive State*. Berkeley: University of California Press, 2011.

Lang, Sabine. "The NGOization of Feminism." In *Transitions, Environments, Translations: Feminisms in Contemporary Politics*, edited by Cora Kaplan, Debra Keates, and Joan Wallach Scott, 101–20. New York: Routledge, 1997.

Laqueur, Thomas. "Body, Details, and the Humanitarian Narrative." In *The New Cultural History*, edited by Lynn Hunt, 186–204. Berkeley: University of California Press, 1989.

Larner, Wendy. "Neo-Liberalism: Policy, Ideology, Governmentality." *Studies in Political Economy* 63 (2000): 5–25. http://spe.library.utoronto.ca/index.php/spe/article/viewArticle/6724.

Larrinaga, Miguel de, and Marc G. Doucet, eds. *Security and Global Governmentality: Globalization, Governance and the State*. New York: Routledge, 2010.

Laska, Shirley. "The 'Mother of All Rorschach's': Katrina Recovery in New Orleans." *Sociological Inquiry* 78, no. 4 (2008): 580–91.

Lee, Spike. *If God Is Willing and da Creek Don't Rise*. Documentary film. HBO, 2010.

———. *When the Levees Broke: A Requiem in Four Acts*. Documentary film. HBO, 2006.

Lefebvre, Henri. *The Production of Space*. Translated by Donald Nicholson-Smith. Oxford: Blackwell, 1992.

Leonard, Karen. *Making Ethnic Choices: California's Punjabi Mexican Americans*. Philadelphia: Temple University Press, 1994.

Levine, Judith. *Harmful to Minors: The Perils of Protecting Children from Sex*. Boston: Da Capo, 2003.

Levitt, Matthew. *Hamas: Politics, Charity, and Terrorism in the Service of Jihad*. Annotated ed. New Haven: Yale University Press, 2006.

———. "Hezbollah's West Bank Terror Network." *Middle East Intelligence Bulletin* (August–September 2003). Accessed April 15, 2017. http://www.washingtoninstitute.org/policy-analysis/view/hezbollahs-west-bank-terror-network.

———. *Targeting Terror: U.S. Policy toward Middle Eastern State Sponsors and Terrorist Organizations, Post–September 11*. Washington, DC: Washington Institute for Near East Policy, 2003.

———. "Tightened Security." *Chronicle of Philanthropy* 22, no. 14 (June 17, 2010): 6.

Levitt, Matthew, and Michael Jacobson. *The Money Trail: Finding, Following and Freezing Terrorist Finances*. Policy Focus #89. Washington, DC: Washington Institute for Near East Policy, 2008.

Li, Darryl. "Afterword: Capital, Migration, Intervention: Rethinking Gulf Islamic Charities." In *Gulf Charities and Islamic Philanthropy in the "Age of Terror" and*

Beyond, edited by Jonathan Benthall and Robert Lacey, 375–89. Berlin: Gerlach Press, 2014.

Liebes, Tamar. "Television's Disaster Marathons: A Danger to Democratic Processes?" In *Media, Ritual and Identity*, edited by James Curran and Tamar Liebes, 71–86. New York: Routledge, 2002.

Lipset, Seymour Martin. *American Exceptionalism: A Double-Edged Sword*. New York: W. W. Norton and Company, 1997.

Lisheron, Mark. "The Ties That Bind." *American Journalism Review*, August/September 2006. Accessed April 7, 2017. http://ajrarchive.org/Article.asp?id=4163.

Litt, Jacquelyn, Althea Skinner, and Kelley Robinson. "The Katrina Difference: African American Women's Networks and Poverty in New Orleans after Katrina." In *The Women of Katrina: How Gender, Race and Class Matter in an American Disaster*, edited by Emmanuel David and Elaine Enarson, 130–41. Nashville: Vanderbilt University Press, 2011.

"Looking Carefully at 'Charitable Choice.'" *Southern Communities* (October 31, 2000): 8.

Losh, Elizabeth M. *Virtualpolitik: An Electronic History of Government Media-Making in a Time of War, Scandal, Disaster, Miscommunication, and Mistakes*. Cambridge, MA: MIT Press, 2009.

Low, Setha M. *Behind the Gates: Life, Security, and the Pursuit of Happiness in Fortress America*. New York: Routledge, 2004.

Lowe, Jeffrey S., and Todd C. Shaw. "After Katrina: Racial Regimes and Human Development Barriers in the Gulf Coast Region." *American Quarterly* 61, no. 3 (2009): 803–27.

Lowe, Lisa. *Immigrant Acts: On Asian American Cultural Politics*. Durham, NC: Duke University Press, 1996.

———. *The Intimacies of Four Continents*. Durham, NC: Duke University Press, 2015.

Lubiano, Wahneema. "Race, Class, and the Politics of Death: Critical Responses to Hurricane Katrina." *Transforming Anthropology* 14, no. 1 (2006): 31–34.

Lumby, Catharine. *Bad Girls: The Media, Sex and Feminism in the 90s*. St. Leonards, NSW, Australia: Allen and Unwin, 1997.

Lyon, David. *The Electronic Eye: The Rise of Surveillance Society*. Minneapolis: University of Minnesota Press, 1994.

———. *Identifying Citizens: ID Cards as Surveillance*. Cambridge: Polity, 2009.

———. *Surveillance as Social Sorting: Privacy, Risk, and Digital Discrimination*. London: Psychology Press, 2003.

———. *Surveillance Society: Monitoring Everyday Life*. Buckingham, England: Open University Press, 2001.

———. *Theorizing Surveillance: The Panopticon and Beyond*. Devon, England: Willan, 2006.

MacIejewski, Ross, Ryan Hafen, Stephen Rudolph, Stephen G. Larew, Michael A. Mitchell, William S. Cleveland, and David S. Ebert. "Forecasting Hotspots: A Predictive Analytics Approach." *IEEE Transactions on Visualization and Computer Graphics* 17, no. 4 (April 2011): 440–53. doi:10.1109/TVCG.2010.82.

Macintosh, Elizabeth P. *Sisterhood of Spies: The Women of the OSS*. Annapolis, MD: Naval Institute Press, 1998.

Maclellan, Nic. "From Fiji to Fallujah: The War in Iraq and the Privatisation of Pacific Security." *Pacific Journalism Review* 12, no. 2 (September 2006): 47–65.

Maher, Erin. "Men Are from Reddit, Women Are from Tumblr." Undergraduate thesis. Yale University, 2014.

Mahmood, Cynthia Keppley. "Gun Cultures, Majority Nationalism, and the Prominence of Fear: Reflections on Anti-Sikh Hate Crimes." *Sikh Formations* 8, no. 3 (December 1, 2012): 275–79. doi:10.1080/17448727.2012.752675.

Mahrouse, Gada. "Feel Good Tourism: An Ethical Option for Socially-Conscious Westerners?" *ACME: An International E-Journal for Critical Geographies* 15, no. 3 (2011): 372–91. acme-journal.org/index.php/acme/article/view/903.

Malkin, Michelle. "A National Security Mom Manifesto." michellemalkin.com, July 20, 2004. Accessed February 4, 2016. http://michellemalkin.com/2004/07/20/a-national-security-mom-manifesto.

———. "Candidates Ignore Security Moms at Their Peril." *USA Today*, July 20, 2004. Accessed February 4, 2016. http://usatoday30.usatoday.com/news/opinion/editorials/2004-07-20-malkin_x.htm.

———. *In Defense of Internment: The Case for Racial Profiling in World War II and the War on Terror*. Washington, DC: Regnery, 2004.

———. *Invasion: How America Still Welcomes Terrorists, Criminals and Other Foreign Menaces to Our Shores*. Washington, DC: Regnery, 2002.

Mallett, Shelley. "Understanding Home: A Critical Review of the Literature." *Sociological Review* 52, no. 1 (February 1, 2004): 62–89. doi:10.1111/j.1467–954X.2004.00442.x.

Malone, Luke. "A Breakdown of Anita Sarkeesian's Weekly Rape and Death Threats." *Vocativ*, January 28, 2015. Accessed July 15, 2016. http://www.vocativ.com/culture/society/anita-sarkeesian-threats/.

Malveaux, Suzanne, and Jessica Yelin. "Obama Overhauls Faith-Based Agency." *CNN*, February 5, 2009. Accessed June 3, 2013. http://politicalticker.blogs.cnn.com/2009/02/05/obama-overhauls-faith-based-agency/.

Mamdani, Mahmood. *Good Muslim, Bad Muslim: America, the Cold War, and the Roots of Terror*. New York: Three Leaves, 2005.

Margulies, Peter. "Advising Terrorism: Material Support, Safe Harbors, and Freedom of Speech." *Hastings Law Journal* 63, no. 2 (January 1, 2012): 455–519.

Marhia, Natasha. "Some Humans Are More Human than Others: Troubling the 'Human' in Human Security from a Critical Feminist Perspective." *Security Dialogue* 44, no. 1 (February 1, 2013): 19–35. doi:10.1177/0967010612470293.

Marichal, José. *Facebook Democracy: The Architecture of Disclosure and the Threat to Public Life*. New York: Routledge, 2016.

Marsden, George, ed. *Evangelicalism and Modern America*. Grand Rapids, MI: Eerdmans, 1984.

Martelle, Scott. "We All Pay: The High Costs of Gun Violence." *Los Angeles Times*, April 17, 2015. Accessed June 15, 2016. http://www.latimes.com/opinion/opinion-la/la-ol-gun-violence-financial-cost-nra-20150417-story.html.

Martin, Amy J. "America's Evolution of Women and Their Roles in the Intelligence Community." *Journal of Strategic Security* 8, no. 5 (2015): 99–109.

Martin, Phillip. "Conservative Politicians Downplay Terrorism Threat from the Far Right." *Huffington Post*, January 3, 2016. Accessed June 15, 2016. http://www.huffingtonpost.com/phillip-martin/right-wing-terrorism_b_8907358.html.

———. "How Do We Define Domestic Terrorism? The Legal Meaning of a Loaded Term." PRI, July 21, 2015. Accessed June 15, 2016. https://www.pri.org/stories/2015-07-21/how-do-we-define-domestic-terrorism-legal-meaning-loaded-term.

Martino, John. *War/Play: Video Games and the Militarization of Society*. New York: Peter Lang, 2015.

Marx, Gary. "The Surveillance Society: The Threat of 1984-Style Techniques." *Futurist*, June 1985, 21–26.

Marx, Gary, and Valerie Steeves. "From the Beginning: Children as Subjects and Agents of Surveillance." *Surveillance and Society* 7, nos. 3/4 (June 17, 2010): 192–230.

Mascia, Jennifer. "The Making of the Default Proceed Gun Sale Loophole." *Trace*, July 21, 2015. Accessed July 14, 2016. https://www.thetrace.org/2015/07/brady-bill-amendment-default-proceed-loophole-amendment-nra/.

Mashal, Mujib. "Omar Mateen's Father Calls Shooting 'An Act of Terrorism.'" *New York Times*, June 13, 2016. Accessed July 14, 2016. http://www.nytimes.com/live/orlando-nightclub-shooting-live-updates/father-of-omar-mateen-speaks-to-media/.

Matecki, Lauren A. "Update: COPPA Is Ineffective Legislation—Next Steps for Protecting Youth Privacy Rights in the Social Networking Era." *Northwestern Journal of Law and Social Policy* 5 (2010): 369–402.

Matsuda, Mari J. "Voices of America: Accent, Antidiscrimination Law, and a Jurisprudence for the Last Reconstruction." *Yale Law Journal* 100, no. 5 (1991): 1329–1407. doi:10.2307/796694.

Mattelart, Armand. *The Globalization of Surveillance*. Translated by Susan Taponier and James A. Cohen. Cambridge: Polity, 2010.

Mayer, Jane. *The Dark Side: The Inside Story of How the War on Terror Turned into a War on American Ideals*. Repr. ed. New York: Anchor, 2009.

Mazzetti, Mark, Eric Lichtblau, and Alan Blinder. "Omar Mateen, Twice Scrutinized by F.B.I., Shows Threat of Lone Terrorists." *New York Times*, June 13, 2016. Accessed July 14, 2016. http://www.nytimes.com/2016/06/14/us/politics/orlando-shooting-omar-mateen.html.

Mbembe, Achille. "The Banality of Power and the Aesthetics of Vulgarity in the Postcolony." *Public Culture* 4, no. 2 (1992): 1–30.

———. "Necropolitics." *Public Culture* 15, no. 1 (December 21, 2003): 11–40. doi:10.1215/08992363-15-1-11.

———. *On the Postcolony*. Berkeley: University of California Press, 2001.

McAlister, Melani. *Epic Encounters: Culture, Media, and U.S. Interests in the Middle East since 1945*. Berkeley: University of California Press, 2001.

———. "Guess Who's Coming for Dinner: American Missionaries, the Problem of Racism, and Decolonization in the Congo." *OAH Magazine of History* 26 (2012): 33–37.

———. "What Is Your Heart For? Affect and Internationalism in the Evangelical Public Sphere." *American Literary History* 20, no. 4 (2008): 870–95.

McCarthy, Cameron, et al. "Danger in the Safety Zone: Notes on Race, Resentment, and the Discourse of Crime, Violence and Suburban Security." *Cultural Studies* 11, no. 2 (2006): 274–95.

McCoy, Alfred W. *Policing America's Empire: The United States, the Philippines, and the Rise of the Surveillance State*. Madison: University of Wisconsin Press, 2009.

McCue, Colleen. "Data Mining and Predictive Analytics: Battlespace Awareness for the War on Terrorism." *Defense Intelligence Journal* 13, no. 1 (2005): 47–63.

McEnaney, Laura. *Civil Defense Begins at Home*. Princeton, NJ: Princeton University Press, 2000.

McFate, Montgomery, and Andrea Jackson. "An Organizational Solution for DoD's Cultural Knowledge Needs." *Military Review* 85, no. 4 (August 2005): 18–21.

McGirr, Lisa. *Suburban Warriors: The Origins of the New American Right*. Princeton, NJ: Princeton University Press, 2002.

McMillon, Bill, Doug Cutchins, and Anne Geissinger. *Volunteer Vacations: Short-Term Adventures That Will Benefit You and Others*. 11th ed. Chicago: Chicago Review Press, 2012.

McNeill, Jena, James Jay Carafano, Matt A. Mayer, and Richard Weitz. "Accepting Disaster Relief from Other Nations: Lessons from Katrina and the Gulf Oil Spill." Heritage Foundation, February 2011. Accessed October 24, 2014. http://www .heritage.org/research/reports/2011/02/accepting-disaster-relief-from-other-nations -lessons-from-katrina-and-the-gulf-oil-spill.

McPherson, Tara, ed. *Digital Youth, Innovation, and the Unexpected*. Cambridge, MA: MIT Press, 2008.

Melley, Timothy. "Covert Spectacles and the Contradictions of the Democratic Security State." *StoryWorlds: A Journal of Narrative Studies* 6, no. 1 (2014): 61–82.

Miller, Alice. *For Your Own Good: Hidden Cruelty in Child-Rearing and the Roots of Violence*. 3rd ed. New York: Farrar, Straus and Giroux, 2002.

Miller, Greg. "In 'Zero Dark Thirty,' She's the Hero; in Real Life, CIA Agent's Career Is More Complicated." *Washington Post*, December 10, 2012. Accessed February 4, 2016. https://www.washingtonpost.com/world/national-security/in-zero-dark -thirty-shes-the-hero-in-real-life-cia-agents-career-is-more-complicated/2012/12/10 /cedc227e-42dd-11e2-9648-a2c323a991d6_story.html?utm_term=.fb0d275217e1.

Miller-Davenport, Sarah. " 'Their Blood Shall Not Be Shed in Vain': American Evangelical Missionaries and the Search for God and Country in Post–World War II Asia." *Journal of American History* 99, no. 4 (March 2013): 1109–32.

Minear, Larry, and Thomas G. Weiss. *Mercy under Fire: War and the Global Humanitarian Community*. Boulder, CO: Westview, 1995.

Mirzoeff, Nicholas. "War Is Culture: Global Counterinsurgency, Visuality, and the Petraeus Doctrine." *PMLA* 124, no. 5 (October 1, 2009): 1737–46. doi:10.1632/ pmla.2009.124.5.1737.

Mishra, Smeeta. " 'Saving' Muslim Women and Fighting Muslim Men: Analysis of Representations in *The New York Times*." *Global Media Journal* 6, no. 1 (fall

2007). http://www.globalmediajournal.com/open-access/saving-muslim-women
-and-fighting-muslim-men-analysis-of-representations-in-the-new-york-times
.pdf.

Mitchell, Kimberly J., David Finkelhor, and Janis Wolak. "The Exposure of Youth
to Unwanted Sexual Material on the Internet: A National Survey of Risk, Impact, and Prevention." *Youth and Society* 34, no. 3 (March 1, 2003): 330–58.
doi:10.1177/0044118X02250123.

Mitchell, Timothy. "The Limits of the State: Beyond Statist Approaches and
Their Critics." *American Political Science Review* 85, no. 1 (1991): 77–96.
doi:10.2307/1962879.

Moallem, Minoo. *Between Warrior Brother and Veiled Sister: Islamic Fundamentalism and
the Politics of Patriarchy in Iran.* 1st paperback ed. Berkeley: University of California
Press, 2005.

Monahan, Torin. *Surveillance and Security: Technological Politics and Power in Everyday
Life.* New York: Routledge, 2006.

———. *Surveillance in the Time of Insecurity.* New Brunswick, NJ: Rutgers University
Press, 2010.

Monahan, Torin, and Rodolfo D. Torres. *Schools under Surveillance: Cultures of Control
in Public Education.* New Brunswick, NJ: Rutgers University Press, 2010.

Moodie, Megan. "Microfinance and the Gender of Risk: The Case of Kiva.org." *Signs: Journal of Women in Culture and Society* 38, no. 2 (January 2013): 279–302. doi:10.1086/667448.

Morgan, George, and Scott Poynting, eds. *Global Islamophobia: Muslims and Moral
Panic in the West.* Farnham, England: Ashgate, 2013.

Mortenson, Greg. *Stones into Schools: Promoting Peace through Education in Afghanistan
and Pakistan.* New York: Penguin Books, 2010.

Mortenson, Greg, and David Oliver Relin. *Three Cups of Tea.* New York: Penguin,
2006.

Mortenson, Greg, and Susan L. Roth. *Listen to the Wind: The Story of Dr. Greg and Three
Cups of Tea.* New York: Dial Books for Young Readers, 2009.

Muehlebach, Andrea. "Complexio Oppositorum: Notes on the Left in Neoliberal Italy."
Public Culture 21, no. 3 (2009): 495–515.

Mueller, John, and Mark G. Stewart. "Balancing the Risks, Benefits, and Costs of
Homeland Security." *Homeland Security Affairs: The Journal of the NPS Center for
Homeland Defense and Security* 7, article 16 (August 2011). https://www.hsaj.org
/articles/43.

Murray, Bernadette. "AppCertain's New Curfew Mode Is a Dream Come True for
Parents." *Digital Security Mom,* September 11, 2013. http://digitalsecuritymom.com
/archives/339.

———. "DigitalSecuritymom." *Digital Security Mom,* October 27, 2011. Accessed July 29,
2014. http://digitalsecuritymom.com/archives/10#comment-4093.

Murray, Charles. *American Exceptionalism: An Experiment in History.* Washington, DC:
AEI Press, 2013.

Murunga, Ambrose. "Press Dismay at Katrina Chaos." *BBC,* September 3, 2005. Accessed
December 8, 2015. http://news.bbc.co.uk/2/hi/americas/4211320.stm.

Muslim American Civil Liberties Association, the Creating Law Enforcement Accountability and Responsibility Project, and the Asian American Legal Defense and Education Fund. "Mapping Muslims: NYPD Spying and Its Impact on American Muslims." The Creating Law Enforcement Accountability and Responsibility Project. New York: CUNY School of Law, n.d. Accessed May 23, 2016, http://www.law.cuny.edu/academics/clinics/immigration/clear/Mapping-Muslims.pdf.

Musto, Jennifer. *Control and Protect: Collaboration, Carceral Protection, and Domestic Sex Trafficking in the United States.* Repr. ed. Oakland: University of California Press, 2016.

Nakamura, Lisa, Peter Chow-White, and Alondra Nelson, eds. *Race after the Internet.* New York: Routledge, 2011.

Nasser, Umar. "Why Are Only Muslims Called Terrorists?" *Huffington Post,* UK ed., December 21, 2015. Accessed July 21, 2016. http://www.huffingtonpost.co.uk/umar-nasser/why-are-only-muslims-called-terrorists_b_8833150.html.

National Intelligence Estimate (NIE). *Trends in Global Terrorism: Implications for the United States.* NIE 2006-02R. Washington, DC: Office of the Director of National Intelligence, 2006. Accessed February 4, 2016. http://www.governmentattic.org/5docs/NIE-2006-02R.pdf.

"Nazi Regalia Discovered at House of Jo Cox Killing Suspect." *Guardian,* June 17, 2016, sec. UK news. Accessed May 11, 2017. https://www.theguardian.com/uk-news/2016/jun/17/jo-cox-suspect-thomas-mair-bought-gun-manuals-from-us-neo-nazis-group-claims.

Nellis, Ashley Marie. "Gender Differences in Fear of Terrorism." *Journal of Contemporary Criminal Justice* 25, no. 3 (August 1, 2009): 322–40. doi:10.1177/1043986209335012.

Net Nanny. "Net Nanny Is The Most Effective and Flexible Filtering Software Available Today." Accessed February 29, 2012. http://www.netnanny.com/features/internet-filter.

Nguyen, Mimi Thi. *The Gift of Freedom: War, Debt, and Other Refugee Passages.* Durham, NC: Duke University Press, 2012.

Nissenbaum, Helen. "Hackers and the Contested Ontology of Cyberspace." *New Media and Society* 6, no. 2 (April 1, 2004): 195–217. doi:10.1177/1461444804041445.

———. "Philanthropy: College Students Get $100,000 to Give Away to Charity." *Huffington Post,* January 25, 2012. Accessed May 13, 2017. http://www.huffingtonpost.com/2012/01/25/lessons-in-giving-classro_n_1231527.html.

———. "Sexually Active Teens." July 2014. http://www.childtrends.org/?indicators=sexually-active-teens.

———. "Social Media and the Search for the Boston Bombing Suspects." *CBS News 48 Hours,* April 24, 2013. Accessed May 13, 2017. http://www.cbsnews.com/news/social-media-and-the-search-for-the-boston-bombing-suspects/.

Nuruzzaman, Mohammed. "Paradigms in Conflict: The Contested Claims of Human Security, Critical Theory and Feminism." *Cooperation and Conflict* 41, no. 3 (September 1, 2006): 285–303. doi:10.1177/0010836706066560.

Nussbaum, Emily. "Kids, the Internet, and the End of Privacy: The Greatest Generation Gap since Rock and Roll." *New York Magazine,* February 12, 2007.

Nye, Joseph S. "Public Diplomacy and Soft Power." *Annals of the American Academy of Political and Social Science* 616, no. 1 (March 1, 2008): 94–109. doi:10.1177/0002716207311699.

———. *Soft Power: The Means to Success in World Politics*. New York: Public Affairs, 2004.

Obama, Barack. "Remarks by the President at Points of Light 20th Anniversary, College Station, Texas." Presented at the Points of Light 20th Anniversary, College Station, Texas, October 16, 2009.

Ochieng, Phillip. "Katrina and the Poverty of Development." *Daily Nation*, September 11, 2005. Accessed May 23, 2016. http://www.nation.co.ke/oped/-/1192/81058/-/we8vorz/-/index.html.

O'Dougherty, Maureen. "Public Relations, Private Security: Managing Youth and Race at the Mall of America." *Environment and Planning D: Society and Space* 24, no. 1 (2006): 131–54.

Ong, Aihwa. *Flexible Citizenship: The Cultural Logics of Transnationality*. Durham, NC: Duke University Press, 1999.

———. *Neoliberalism as Exception: Mutations in Citizenship and Sovereignty*. Durham, NC: Duke University Press, 2006.

———. "Powers of Sovereignty: State, People, Wealth, Life." *Focaal—Journal of Global and Historical Anthropology* 64 (2012): 24–35.

Online Privacy Protection Act, S. 809, 106th Congress (1999), sponsored by Senator Conrad Burns (R). https://www.congress.gov/106/bills/s809/BILLS-106s809is.pdf.

Onwudiwe, Ihekwoaba. "Defining Terrorism, Racial Profiling and the Demonisation of Arabs and Muslims in the USA." *Safer Communities* 4, no. 2 (April 1, 2005): 4–11. doi:10.1108/17578043200500009.

Oremus, Will. "Don't Blame Reddit for Smearing Sunil Tripathi: Blame 'Retweets Aren't Endorsements.'" *Slate*, July 26, 2013. Accessed June 2, 2015. http://www.slate.com/blogs/future_tense/2013/07/26/reddit_sunil_tripathi_and_retweets_aren_t_endorsements_who_s_to_blame.html.

Oren, Michael B. *Power, Faith, and Fantasy: America in the Middle East: 1776 to the Present*. Reprint. W. W. Norton and Company, 2008.

Orjoux, Alanne. "Accused South Carolina Church Shooter Dylann Roof to Face More Charges." cnn, July 7, 2015. Accessed June 15, 2016. http://www.cnn.com/2015/07/07/us/south-carolina-church-shootings-indictment/.

Ortblad, Vanessa. "Criminal Prosecution in Sheep's Clothing: The Punitive Effects of ofac Freezing Sanctions." *Journal of Criminal Law and Criminology* 98, no. 4 (2008): 1439–66.

Osuri, Goldie. "India First and the bjp Anti-Conversion Platform: Goldie Osuri." *Kafila*, October 12, 2013. Accessed May 13, 2017. https://kafila.online/2013/10/12/india-first-and-the-bjp-anti-conversion-platform-goldie-osuri/

———. *Religious Freedom in India: Sovereignty and (Anti) Conversion*. New York: Routledge, 2012.

Owens, Marcus. "Symposium: The Anti-Terrorist Financing Guidelines: The Impact on International Philanthropy." *Pace Law Review* 25, no. 2 (2005): 193ff.

Palfrey, John G., and Urs Gasser. *Born Digital: Understanding the First Generation of Digital Natives*. New York: Basic Books, 2008.

Pallios, Andrea. "Should We Have Faith in the Faith-Based Initiative? A Constitutional Analysis of President Bush's Charitable Choice Plan." *Hastings Constitutional Law Quarterly* 30, no. 1 (2002): 131–72.

Parenti, Christian. *The Soft Cage: Surveillance in America from Slavery to the War on Terror*. Repr. ed. New York: Basic Books, 2004.

"Parents Blame Technology: Bullying and Cyberbullying Are Parent's #1 Fear More than Kidnapping, Domestic Terrorism and Suicide." *Families Online Magazine*, March 23, 2014. http://www.familiesonlinemagazine.com/parents-blame-technology -bullying-and/.

Paris, Roland. "Human Security: Paradigm Shift or Hot Air?" *International Security* 26, no. 2 (October 1, 2001): 87–102. doi:10.1162/016228801753191141.

Park, Haeyoun, and Iaryna Mykhyalyshyn. "L.G.B.T. People Are More Likely to Be Targets of Hate Crimes than Any Other Minority Group." *New York Times*, June 16, 2016. Accessed June 15, 2016. http://www.nytimes.com/interactive/2016/06/16/us /hate-crimes-against-lgbt.html.

Pateman, Carole. *The Sexual Contract*. Stanford, CA: Stanford University Press, 1988.

Pateman, Carole, and Charles Mills. *The Contract and Domination*. Cambridge: Polity, 2007.

Pease, Donald E. *The New American Exceptionalism*. Minneapolis: University of Minnesota Press, 2009.

Pelkmans, Mathijs. "The 'Transparency' of Christian Proselytizing in Kyrgyzstan." *Anthropological Quarterly* 82, no. 2 (April 1, 2009): 423–45.

Persons, Georgia A. "Administrative Policy Initiatives and the Limits of Change: Lessons from the Implementation of the Bush Faith-Based and Community Initiative." *Politics and Policy* 39, no. 6 (2011): 949–78. doi:10.1111/j.1747-1346.2011.00332.x.

Pettegrew, John. " 'The Soldier's Faith': Turn-of-the-Century Memory of the Civil War and the Emergence of Modern American Nationalism." *Journal of Contemporary History* 31, no. 1 (January 1, 1996): 49–73.

Pfeiffer, James. "Civil Society, NGOs and the Holy Spirit in Mozambique." *Human Organization* 63, no. 4 (2004): 359–72.

Phillips, Layli. *The Womanist Reader: The First Quarter Century of Womanist Thought*. New York: Routledge, 2006.

Pieterse, Jan Nederveen. "Neoliberal Empire." *Theory, Culture and Society* 21, no. 3 (2004): 119–40.

Piketty, Thomas. *Capital in the Twenty-First Century*. Cambridge, MA: Belknap Press, 2014.

Pinker, Steven. *The Better Angels of Our Nature: Why Violence Has Declined*. New York: Viking, 2011.

"Polishing the U.S. Image." *Newsday*, September 10, 2005. Accessed December 8, 2015. http://www.newsday.com/opinion/polishing-the-u-s-image-1.694159.

Popper, Ben. "Harlem Crew Territories circa 2010." Vox Media, December 10, 2014. Accessed May 17, 2016. http://apps.voxmedia.com/graphics/theverge-harlem-crew-map.

Poster, Mark. *The Mode of Information: Poststructuralism and Social Context.* Chicago: University of Chicago Press, 1990.

———. *The Second Media Age.* Cambridge: Polity, 1995.

Postman, Neil. *The Disappearance of Childhood.* New York: Vintage / Random House, 1994.

Power, Marcus. "Digitized Virtuosity: Video War Games and Post-9/11 Cyber-Deterrence." *Security Dialogue* 38, no. 2 (June 1, 2007): 271–88. doi:10.1177/0967010607078552.

Powers, Shawn. "The Aftermath of Katrina: An Update of Media Coverage, International Reactions, and Public Diplomacy." USC Center on Public Diplomacy, September 20, 2005. Accessed April 23, 2012. https://uscpublicdiplomacy.org/pdin_monitor_article/aftermath-katrina-update-media-coverage-international-reactions-and-public.

Prensky, Marc. "Digital Natives, Digital Immigrants." *On the Horizon* 9, no. 5 (October 2001): 1–6.

———. "Do They Really Think Differently?" *On the Horizon* 9, no. 6 (December 2001): 1–9.

"Press Dismay at Katrina Chaos." BBC, September 3, 2005. Accessed December 8, 2015. http://news.bbc.co.uk/2/hi/americas/4211320.stm.

Preston, Caroline. "Charity Leaders See Broad Impact from Ruling on Muslim Charity." *Chronicle of Philanthropy*, December 11, 2008. Accessed January 4, 2016, https://philanthropy.com/article/Charity-Leaders-See-Broad/173727.

Privacy Rights Clearinghouse. "Data Brokers and Your Privacy." September 1, 2014. Accessed May 2016. https://www.privacyrights.org/content/data-brokers-and-your-privacy.

Prosser, William. "Privacy." *California Law Review* 48 (1960): 383.

The Protection of Lawful Commerce in Arms Act, 15 U.S.C. §§ 7901–3.

Protess, Ben, and Stephanie Clifford. "Suit Accuses Banks of Role in Financing Terror Attacks." *New York Times*, November 11, 2014.

Puar, Jasbir K. *Terrorist Assemblages: Homonationalism in Queer Times.* Durham, NC: Duke University Press, 2007.

Puar, Jasbir K., and Amit S. Rai. "Monster, Terrorist, Fag: The War on Terrorism and the Production of Docile Patriots." *Social Text* 20, no. 3 (September 21, 2002): 117–48.

Rafael, Vicente L. *White Love and Other Events in Filipino History.* Durham, NC: Duke University Press, 2000.

"Raided Muslim Charity Sues Bank." *Arab-American Business* 7, no. 2 (2006/2007): 10.

Rainie, Lee. "The State of Privacy in Post-Snowden America." *Pew Research Center*, January 20, 2016. http://www.pewresearch.org/fact-tank/2016/01/20/the-state-of-privacy-in-america/.

Ralph, Michael. "'It's Hard Out Here for a Pimp . . . with . . . a Whole Lot of Bitches Jumpin' Ship': Navigating Black Politics in the Wake of Katrina." *Public Culture* 21, no. 2 (2009): 343–76.

Ramirez, Deborah A., Jennifer Hoopes, and Tara Lai Quinlan. "Defining Racial Profiling in a Post–September 11 World." *American Criminal Law Review* 40 (2003): 1195.

Rana, Junaid. *Terrifying Muslims: Race and Labor in the South Asian Diaspora*. Durham, NC: Duke University Press, 2011.

Ravitch, Diane. *The Death and Life of the Great American School System: How Testing and Choice Are Undermining Education*. 1st trade paperback, ed., rev., and exp. ed. New York: Basic Books, 2011.

Razack, Sherene. *Casting Out: The Eviction of Muslims from Western Law and Politics*. Toronto: University of Toronto Press, 2008.

Razack, Sherene, Malinda Smith, and Sunera Thobani, eds. *States of Race: Critical Race Feminism for the 21st Century*. Toronto: Between the Lines, 2010.

Reddy, Chandan. *Freedom with Violence: Race, Sexuality, and the US State*. Durham, NC: Duke University Press, 2011.

"Reflections on the Oak Creek Tragedy." Special issue, *Sikh Formations* 8, no. 3 (2012).

Rentschler, Carrie A. "Risky Assignments: Sexing Security in Hostile Environmental Reporting." *Feminist Media Studies* 7, no. 3 (September 2007): 257–79. doi:10.1080/14680770701477875.

Rentschler, Carrie, and Carol A. Stabile. "States of Insecurity and the Gendered Politics of Fear." *NWSA Journal* 17, no. 3 (2005): vii–xxv.

Resnikoff, Ned. "Repeated Attempts to Pass Hate Crime Bill in South Carolina Have Failed." *Al Jazeera America*, June 18, 2015. Accessed June 15, 2016. http://america.aljazeera.com/articles/2015/6/18/south-carolina-lacks-hate-crimes-law.html.

Reves, Joshua. "If You See Something, Say Something: Lateral Surveillance and the Uses of Responsibility." *Surveillance and Society* 10, nos. 3/4 (2012): 235–48.

Rhodan, Maya. "New Federal Racial Profiling Guidelines Worry Civil Rights Groups." *Time*, December 8, 2014. Accessed December 7, 2015. http://time.com/3623851/justice-department- racial-profiling-muslims-sikhs-aclu.

Riccardi, Nicholas. "Have Gun, Will Show It." *Los Angeles Times*, June 7, 2008. Accessed June 15, 2016. http://articles.latimes.com/2008/jun/07/nation/na-opencarry7.

Rieff, David. *A Bed for the Night: Humanitarianism in Crisis*. New York: Simon and Schuster, 2002.

———. "Moral Blindness: American Troops in Darfur? Is TNR Mad?" *New Republic*, June 5, 2006, 13–15.

Risen, James, and Laura Poitras. "N.S.A. Collecting Millions of Faces from Web Images." *New York Times*, May 31, 2014. Accessed May 17, 2017. http://www.nytimes.com/2014/06/01/us/nsa-collecting-millions-of-faces-from-web-images.html.

Roberts, Dorothy. "Collateral Consequences, Genetic Surveillance, and the New Biopolitics of Race." *Howard Law Journal* 54 (2011): 567.

Robertson, Allen. "Games without Tears, Wars without Frontiers." In *War, Technology, Anthropology*, edited by Koen Stroken, 83–93. Critical Interventions: A Forum for Social Analysis, vol. 13. New York: Berghahn Books, 2012.

Robertson, Linda. "How Shall We Remember New Orleans? Comparing News Coverage of Post-Katrina New Orleans and the 2008 Midwest Floods." In *The Neoliberal Deluge: Hurricane Katrina, Late Capitalism, and the Remaking of New Orleans*, edited by Cedric Johnson, 269–99. Minneapolis: University of Minnesota Press, 2011.

Robertson, Susan L. " 'Remaking the World': Neoliberalism and the Transformation of Education and Teachers' Labor." In *The Global Assault on Teaching, Teachers, and Their Unions: Stories for Resistance,* edited by Mary Compton and Lois Weiner, 11–27. New York: Palgrave Macmillan, 2008. doi:10.1057/9780230611702_2.

Robinson, Kerry H. *Innocence, Knowledge and the Construction of Childhood: The Contradictory Nature of Sexuality and Censorship in Children's Contemporary Lives.* New York: Routledge, 2013.

Robles, Frances. "Dylann Roof Had AR-15 Parts during Police Stop in March, Record Shows." *New York Times,* June 26, 2015. Accessed May 17, 2017. http://www.nytimes .com/2015/06/27/us/dylann-roof-was-questioned-by-police-in-march-record-shows .html.

———. "Dylann Roof Photos and a Manifesto Are Posted on Website." *New York Times,* June 20, 2015. Accessed June 15, 2016. http://www.nytimes.com/2015/06/21 /us/dylann-storm-roof-photos-website-charleston-church-shooting.html.

Rodríguez, Havidán, and Russell Dynes. "Finding and Framing Katrina: The Social Construction of Disaster." Understanding Katrina, Social Science Research Council, June 11, 2006. Accessed December 8, 2015. http://understandingkatrina.ssrc.org /Dynes_Rodriguez/.

Roediger, David. "The Retreat from Race and Class." *Monthly Review* 58, no. 3 (2006). https://monthlyreview.org/2006/07/01/the-retreat-from-race-and-class.

Rohde, Joy. *Armed with Expertise: The Militarization of American Social Research during the Cold War.* Ithaca, NY: Cornell University Press, 2013.

Romero, Mary. "Racial Profiling and Immigration Law Enforcement: Rounding Up of Usual Suspects in the Latino Community." *Critical Sociology* 32, no. 2 (2006): 447–73.

Rooney, Tonya. "Trusting Children: How Do Surveillance Technologies Alter a Child's Experience of Trust, Risk and Responsibility?" *Surveillance and Society* 7, nos. 3/4 (July 6, 2010): 344–55.

Rose, Nikolas. "Community, Citizenship, and the Third Way." *American Behavior Scientist* 43, no. 9 (2000): 1395–411.

———. "Governing 'Advanced' Liberal Democracies." In *Foucault and Political Reason: Liberalism, Neo-Liberalism, and Rationalities of Government,* edited by Andrew Barry, Thomas Osborne, and Nikolas Rose, 37–64. Chicago: University of Chicago Press, 1996.

———. *Governing the Soul: The Shaping of the Private Self.* 2nd ed. London: Free Association Books, 1999.

Rose, Nikolas, John Shotter, and Gergen Kenneth. "Individualizing Psychology." In *Texts of Identity,* vol. 2, edited by John Shotter and Kenneth J. Gergen, 119–32. London: Sage, 1989.

Rose, Nikolas, and Kevin Rozario. " 'Delicious Horrors': Mass Culture, the Red Cross, and the Appeal of Modern American Humanitarianism." *American Quarterly* 55, no. 3 (2003): 417–55.

Rosenblatt, Susannah, and James Rainey. "Katrina Takes a Toll on Truth, News Accuracy." *Los Angeles Times,* September 27, 2005. Accessed April 23, 2012. http://articles .latimes.com/2005/sep/27/nation/na-rumors27.

Rothman, Joshua. "Jane Mayer's Reporting on Torture." *New Yorker*, December 13, 2014. Accessed February 4, 2016. http://www.newyorker.com/books/double-take/jane-mayers-reporting-torture.

Roy, Ananya. *Poverty Capital: Microfinance and the Making of Development*. New York: Routledge, 2010.

Roy, Ananya, Genevieve Negrón-Gonzales, Kweku Opoku-Agyemang, and Clare Talwalker. *Encountering Poverty: Thinking and Acting in an Unequal World*. Oakland: University of California Press, 2016.

Roy, Ravi K., Arthur T. Denzau, and Thomas D. Willett. *Neoliberalism: National and Regional Experiments with Global Ideas*. New York: Routledge, 2006.

Ruddick, Sara. *Maternal Thinking: Toward a Politics of Peace*. Boston: Beacon, 1995.

Russell, Gordon, and James Varney. "From Blue Tarps to Debris Removal: Layers of Contractors Drive Up the Cost of Recovery, Critics Say." *NOLA.com/The Times-Picayune*, August 3, 2015. Accessed May 28, 2016. http://www.nola.com/katrina/index.ssf/2005/12/from_blue_tarps_to_debris_remo.html.

Sager, Rebecca. " 'The 'Purpose Driven' Policy: Explaining State-Level Variation in the Faith-Based Initiative.' " PhD dissertation, University of Arizona, Tucson, 2006.

Said, Wadie E. *Crimes of Terror: The Legal and Political Implications of Federal Terrorism Prosecutions*. New York: Oxford University Press, 2015.

Saito, Natsu Taylor. "Colonial Presumptions: The War on Terror and the Roots of American Exceptionalism." *Georgetown Journal of Law & Modern Critical Race Perspectives*, no. 1 (2008): 67.

———. "The Costs of Homeland Security." *Radical History Review*, no. 93 (2005): 53.

———. "Model Minority, Yellow Peril: Functions of Foreignness in the Construction of Asian American Legal Identity." *Asian Law Journal* 4, no. 1 (1997): 71–95.

Saiya, Nilay. "Onward Christian Soldiers: American Dispensationalists, George W. Bush and the Middle East." *Holy Land Studies: A Multidisciplinary Journal* 11, no. 2 (2012): 175–204.

Samaritan's Purse. "History." N.d. Accessed January 4, 2016. http://www.samaritanspurse.org/our-ministry/history.

Sandberg-Zakian, Eric. "Counterterrorism, the Constitution, and the Civil-Criminal Divide: Evaluating the Designation of U.S. Persons under the International Emergency Economic Powers Act." *Harvard Journal on Legislation* 48 (November 2011): 95.

———. "Do the Fifth and Sixth Amendments Prohibit the Designation of U.S. Persons under the International Emergency Economic Powers Act?" *Student Scholarship Papers*, paper no. 103 (April 1, 2010). http://digitalcommons.law.yale.edu/student_papers/103.

Sassen, Saskia. *Losing Control? Sovereignty in an Age of Globalization*. New York: Columbia University Press, 1996.

———. "Toward a Sociology of Information Technology." *Current Sociology* 50, no. 3 (2002): 382.

Saul, Ben. *Defining Terrorism in International Law*. New York: Oxford University Press, 2008.

Savage, Charlie. "F.B.I. Casts Wide Net under Relaxed Rules for Terror Inquiries, Data Show." *New York Times*, March 26, 2011. Accessed July 6, 2016. http://www.nytimes.com/2011/03/27/us/27fbi.html.

Savage, Dan. "Who Killed Tyler Clementi?" *The Stranger*, October 2, 2010. Accessed May 12, 2016. http://slog.thestranger.com/slog/archives/2010/10/02/before-we-crucify-those-two-teenagers-who-streamed-tyler-clementis-having-sex-over-the-internet.

Scharff, Christina. "Disarticulating Feminism: Individualization, Neoliberalism and the Othering of 'Muslim Women.'" *European Journal of Women's Studies* 18, no. 2 (May 1, 2011): 119–34. doi:10.1177/1350506810394613.

Schmidt, Michael S. "F.B.I. Confirms a Sharp Rise in Mass Shootings since 2000." *New York Times*, September 24, 2014. Accessed June 15, 2016. http://www.nytimes.com/2014/09/25/us/25shooters.html?_r=0.

Schmitt, Carl. *Political Theology: Four Chapters on the Concept of Sovereignty*. Edited by George Schwab. Chicago: University of Chicago Press, 2006.

Scholz, Trebor, ed. *Digital Labor: The Internet as Playground and Factory*. New York: Routledge, 2013.

Scott-Childress, Reynolds J. *Race and the Production of Modern American Nationalism*. New York: Routledge, 2014.

Secure Online Communication Enforcement Act of 2000, S. 2063, 106th Congress (1999), introduced by Senator Robert Torricelli (D). https://www.congress.gov/106/bills/s2063/BILLS-106s2063is.pdf.

Seiter, Ellen. *The Internet Playground: Children's Access, Entertainment, and Mis-Education*. 2nd ed. New York: Peter Lang, 2007.

Senate Select Committee on Intelligence. "Committee Study of the Central Intelligence Agency's Detention and Interrogation Program." Washington, DC: US Senate, December 9, 2014. https://www.intelligence.senate.gov/sites/default/files/documents/CRPT-113srpt288.

Sengupta, Somini. "The Pentagon as Silicon Valley Incubator." *New York Times*, August 23, 2013. Accessed August 23, 2013. http://www.nytimes.com/2013/08/23/technology/the-pentagon-as-start-up-incubator.html.

Setty, Sudha. "What's in a Name? How Nations Define Terrorism Ten Years after 9/11." *University of Pennsylvania Journal of International Law* 33, no. 1 (2011): 1–63. https://www.law.upenn.edu/live/files/139-setty33upajintll12011pdf.

Shah, Nayan. *Stranger Intimacy: Contesting Race, Sexuality, and the Law in the North American West*. Berkeley: University of California Press, 2012.

Shaw, Adrienne. *Gaming at the Edge: Sexuality and Gender at the Margins of Gamer Culture*. Minneapolis: University of Minnesota Press, 2015.

Sheehan, Cindy. *Peace Mom: A Mother's Journey through Heartache to Activism*. New York: Atria Books, 2006.

Sheikh, Anwar. "Who Pays for Welfare in the Welfare State? A Multicountry Study." *Social Research* 70, no. 2 (2003): 531–50.

Shmueli, Benjamin, and Ayelet Blecher-Prigat. "Privacy for Children." SSRN Scholarly Paper. Rochester, NY: Social Science Research Network, January 24, 2011. http://papers.ssrn.com/abstract=1746540.

"Shot Pakistan Schoolgirl Malala Yousafzai Addresses UN." BBC, July 12, 2013, sec. Asia. Accessed May 17, 2017. http://www.bbc.co.uk/news/world-asia-23282662.

Sian, Katy Pal. "Gurdwaras, Guns and Grudges in 'Post-Racial' America." *Sikh Formations* 8, no. 3 (December 1, 2012): 293–97. doi:10.1080/17448727.2012.752676.

———. *Unsettling Sikh and Muslim Conflict: Mistaken Identities, "Forced" Conversions, and Postcolonial Formations.* Lanham, MD: Lexington Books, 2013.

Siegel, Eric. *Predictive Analytics: The Power to Predict Who Will Click, Buy, Lie, or Die.* Hoboken, NJ: Wiley, 2013.

Silber, Norman I. "Charity Considered as a Terrorist Tool." *Hofstra Horizons*, spring 2002. Accessed January 4, 2016. https://www.hofstra.edu/pdf/about/administration/provost/hofhrz/hofhrz_s02_silber.pdf.

Silver, Nate. "Party Identity in a Gun Cabinet." *New York Times*, December 18, 2012. Accessed June 15, 2016. http://fivethirtyeight.blogs.nytimes.com/2012/12/18/in-gun-ownership-statistics-partisan-divide-is-sharp/.

Silverman, Rachel. "A New Generation Reinvents Philanthropy: Blogs, Social-Networking Sites Give 20-Somethings a Means to Push, Fund Favorite Causes." *Wall Street Journal*, August 21, 2007. Accessed January 4, 2016. http://www.wsj.com/articles/SB118765256378003494.

Simeone, Jessica, Tasneem Nashrulla, Ema O'Connor, and Tamerra Griffin. "These Are the Victims of the Charleston Church Shooting." *BuzzFeed*, June 18, 2015. http://www.buzzfeed.com/jessicasimeone/these-are-the-victims-of-the-charleston-church-shooting.

Simon, Jonathan S. "Wake of the Flood: Crime, Disaster, and the American Risk Imaginary after Katrina." *Issues in Legal Scholarship* 6, no. 3 (February 26, 2007): 1–20. http://www.degruyter.com/view/j/ils.2007.6.issue-3/ils.2007.6.3.1094/ils.2007.6.3.1094.xml.

Sinervo, Aviva. "Connections and Disillusion: The Moral Economy of Volunteer Tourism in Cusco, Peru." *Childhoods Today* 5, no. 2 (2011): 1–23. www.childhoodstoday.org/download.php?id=66.

Singer, Natasha. "For Consumers, an 'Open Data' Society Is a Misnomer." *New York Times*, May 25, 2013, BU3.

———. "Mapping, and Sharing, the Consumer Genome." *New York Times*, June 16, 2012. Accessed May 11, 2017. http://www.nytimes.com/2012/06/17/technology/acxiom-the-quiet-giant-of-consumer-database-marketing.html.

———. "You for Sale: A Data Giant Is Mapping, and Sharing, the Consumer Genome." *New York Times*, June 17, 2012.

Singer, Peter W. "The Private Military Industry and Iraq: What We Have Learned and Where to Next?" Policy Paper. Geneva: Geneva Centre for the Democratic Control of Armed Forces, 2004. Accessed April 11, 2017. https://www/files.ethz.ch/isn/14132/PP4_Singer.pdf.

Sisak, Michael. "Shooters Sometimes Exploit Limited Weapons Laws." *AP News*, June 14, 2016. Accessed June 15, 2016. http://bigstory.ap.org/article/041af8c3b88341c6b91ae69a8e00def6/shooters-sometimes-exploit-limited-weapons-laws-blind-spots.

Sjoberg, Laura. *Gendering Global Conflict: Toward a Feminist Theory of War.* New York: Columbia University Press, 2013.

———. *Gender, War, and Conflict.* Cambridge: Polity, 2014.

Social Science Research Council. "Understanding Katrina: Perspectives from the Social Sciences." Accessed April 7, 2017. http://understandingkatrina.ssrc.org.

Solove, Daniel J. *The Digital Person: Technology and Privacy in the Information Age.* New York: NYU Press, 2004.

———. *Nothing to Hide: The False Tradeoff between Privacy and Security.* New Haven, CT: Yale University Press, 2011.

Solove, Daniel J., Marc Rotenberg, and Paul M. Schwartz. *Privacy, Information, and Technology.* New York: Wolters Kluwer Law and Business, 2011.

Sontag, Susan. *Regarding the Pain of Others.* New York: Macmillan, 2003.

Sorkin, Michael, ed. *Indefensible Space: The Architecture of the National Insecurity State.* New York: Routledge, 2008.

Spector Pro. "Unmask Your Child's Online Identity." *PC World,* December 2010, 67.

Spivak, Gayatri Chakravorty. "Can the Subaltern Speak?" In *Marxism and the Interpretation of Culture,* edited by Cary Nelson and Lawrence Grossberg, 271–313. Urbana: University of Illinois Press, 1988.

Staples, William G. *Everyday Surveillance: Vigilance and Visibility in Postmodern Life.* 2nd ed. Lanham, MD: Rowman and Littlefield, 2013.

Stark, Rodney. "Some Basic Facts on America's Armies of Compassion." In *Not by Faith or Government Alone: Rethinking the Role of Faith-Based Organizations,* edited by Baylor Institute for Studies of Religion, 11. Waco, TX: Baylor Institute for Studies of Religion, 2008. http://www.baylorisr.org/wp-content/uploads/notbyfaith_report1.pdf1.pdf.

Starr, Barbara, and Holly Yan. "Man behind NSA Leaks Says He Did It to Safeguard Privacy, Liberty." *CNN,* June 10, 2013. Accessed August 28, 2014. http://www.cnn.com/2013/06/10/politics/edward-snowden-profile/index.html.

Steger, Manfred B., and Ravi K. Roy. *Neoliberalism: A Very Short Introduction.* Oxford: Oxford University Press, 2010.

Steinberg, Shirley R. *Kinderculture: The Corporate Construction of Childhood.* Boulder, CO: Westview, 2011. http://public.eblib.com/EBLPublic/PublicView.do?ptiID=665864.

Stephens, Sharon. *Children and the Politics of Culture.* Princeton, NJ: Princeton University Press, 1995.

Stern, Joanna. "Dissecting Big Tech's Denial of Involvement in NSA's PRISM Spying Program." *ABC News,* June 7, 2013. http://abcnews.go.com/Technology/nsa-prism-dissecting-technology-companies-adamant-denial-involvement/story?id=19350095.

Stiehm, Judith. *It's Our Military Too: Women and the U.S. Military.* Philadelphia: Temple University Press, 1996.

Stohr, Kate. "Here Are All the Congresspeople Who Took NRA Money and Tweeted Prayers for Orlando." *Fusion,* June 13, 2016. Accessed April 11, 2017. http://fusion.net/here-are-all-the-congresspeople-who-took-nra-money-and-1793857464.

Strom, Stephanie. "Confusion on Where Money Lent via Kiva Goes." *New York Times,* November 8, 2009. Accessed January 4, 2016. http://www.nytimes.com/2009/11/09/business/global/09kiva.html?mcubz-0.

———. "To Help Donors Choose, Web Site Alters How It Sizes Up Charities." *New York Times*, November 27, 2010. Accessed January 4, 2016. http://www.nytimes.com /2010/11/27/business/27charity.html.

Sugarman, David B., and Susan L. Frankel. "Patriarchal Ideology and Wife-Assault: A Meta-Analytic View." *Journal of Family Violence* 11, no. 1 (1996): 23.

Sullivan, Karen. "Charlotte Community Responds to Orlando Killings with Prayers, Support." *Charlotte Observer*, June 12, 2016. Accessed June 16, 2016. http://www .charlotteobserver.com/news/local/article83306577.html.

Swire, Peter. "The Second Wave of Global Privacy Protection: Symposium Introduction." *Ohio State Law Journal* 74, no. 6 (2013): 841–52.

Taylor, Clarence. "Hurricane Katrina and the Myth of the Post–Civil Rights Era." *Journal of Urban History* 35, no. 5 (2009): 640–55.

Teague, Matthew, Spencer Ackerman, and Michael Safi. "Orlando Nightclub Shooter Omar Mateen Was Known to FBI, Agent Says." *Guardian*, June 12, 2016, sec. US news. Accessed May 11, 2017. https://www.theguardian.com/us-news/2016/jun/12/omar -mateen-orlando-nightclub-attack-shooter-named.

Teensafe. "Why You Should Track Your Kid's Cell Phone." January 9, 2015. Accessed May 17, 2017. http://www.teensafe.com/blog/track-kids-cell-phone/.

Terry, Jennifer. "Killer Entertainments." *Vectors* 3, no. 1 (fall 2007). http://www .vectorsjournal.org/projects/index.php?project=86&thread=DesignersStatement.

———. "Significant Injury: War, Medicine, and Empire in Claudia's Case." *WSQ: Women's Studies Quarterly* 37, no. 1 (2009): 200–225.

Thobani, Sunera. "Racial Violence and the Politics of National Belonging: The Wisconsin Shootings, Islamophobia and the War on Terrorized Bodies." *Sikh Formations* 8, no. 3 (December 1, 2012): 281–86. doi:10.1080/17448727.2012.752681.

Thompson, Jeri. "Security Moms Are Back." *American Spectator*, September 21, 2012. Accessed February 4, 2016. http://spectator.org/blog/30573/security-moms-are -back.

Thomsen, Michael. "The Unsettling Realism of 2012's Two Big First-Person Shooter Games." *Atlantic*, December 26, 2012. Accessed July 15, 2016. http://www.theatlantic .com/entertainment/archive/2012/12/the-unsettling-realism-of-2012s-two-big-first -person-shooter-games/265812/.

Tickner, Ann. "You Just Don't Understand: Troubled Engagements between Feminists and IR Theorists." *International Studies Quarterly* 41, no. 4 (1997): 611–32.

Ticktin, Miriam. "Where Ethics and Politics Meet." *American Ethnologist* 33, no. 1 (2006): 33–49.

Tierney, Kathleen. "Foreshadowing Katrina: Recent Sociological Contributions to Vulnerability Science." *Contemporary Sociology* 35, no. 3 (2006): 207–12.

Timmons, Heather. "British Study Charitable Organizations for Links to Plot." *New York Times*, August 25, 2006. Accessed January 5, 2016. http://www.nytimes.com /2006/08/25/world/europe/25britain.html?_r=0.

Todd, Robb, and Charles Wolfson. "Katrina's Impact on Foreign Policy." *CBS News*, September 9, 2005. Accessed December 8, 2015. http://www.cbsnews.com/2100-18568 _162-830306.html.

Torres, Nicole I. *Walls of Indifference: Immigration and the Militarization of the US-Mexico Border*. Repr. ed. Boulder, CO: Routledge, 2016.

Trottier, Daniel, and Christian Fuchs, eds. *Social Media, Politics and the State: Protests, Revolutions, Riots, Crime and Policing in the Age of Facebook, Twitter and YouTube*. New York: Routledge, 2014.

Tudesco, James Patrick. "Missionaries and French Imperialism: The Role of Catholic Missionaries in French Colonial Expansion, 1880–1905." PhD dissertation, University of Connecticut, 1980.

Tumulty, Karen, and Viveca Novak. "Goodbye, Soccer Mom. Hello, Security Mom." *Time*, May 25, 2003. Accessed February 4, 2016. http://content.time.com/time/magazine/article/0,9171,454487,00.html.

United Nations Development Programme. "Women's Empowerment." UNDP. Accessed May 30, 2016. http://www.undp.org/content/undp/en/home/ourwork/womenempowerment/overview.html.

United Nations Human Rights Council. *Racism, Racial Discrimination, Xenophobia and Related Forms of Intolerance, Addendum: Mission to the United States of America, Report of the Special Rapporteur on Contemporary Forms of Racism, Racial Discrimination, Xenophobia and Related Intolerance, Doudou Diène*. Geneva: United Nations Human Rights Council, April 28, 2009. http://www2.ohchr.org/english/bodies/hrcouncil/docs/11session/A.HRC.11.36.Add.3.pdf.

United States Census Bureau. "Computer and Internet Use in the United States." Population Characteristics. Washington, DC: United States Census Bureau, May 2013. https://www.census.gov/content/dam/Census/library/publications/2013/demo/p20-569.pdf.

United States Department of the Treasury. *Response to Comments Submitted on the U.S. Department of the Treasury Anti-Terrorist Financing Guidelines: Voluntary Best Practices for U.S.-Based Charities*. Washington, DC: United States Department of the Treasury, December 1, 2010. https://www.treasury.gov/resource-center/terrorist-illicit-finance/Documents/response.pdf.

———. *U.S. Department of the Treasury Anti-Terrorist Financing Guidelines: Voluntary Best Practices for U.S.-Based Charities*. Washington, DC: United States Department of the Treasury, 2005. http://www.treasury.gov/press-center/press-releases/Documents/0929%20finalrevised.pdf.

United States Government Accountability Office. *Disaster Recovery: Federal Contracting in the Aftermath of Hurricanes Katrina and Rita*. Testimony before the United States Senate Committee on Small Business and Entrepreneurship. Washington, DC: United States Government Accountability Office, September 15, 2011. http://www.gao.gov/assets/130/126954.pdf.

———. *Faith-Based and Community Initiative: Improvements in Monitoring Grantees and Measuring Performance Could Enhance Accountability*. Washington, DC: United States Government Accountability Office, June 2006. Accessed January 4, 2016. http://www.gao.gov/new.items/d06616.pdf.

United States House of Representatives Committee on Government Reform—Minority Staff, Special Investigations Division. *Waste, Fraud, and Abuse in Hurricane*

Katrina Contracts. Washington, DC: United States House of Representatives, August 2006. https://www.hsdl.org/?view&did=466563.

United States Senate. *Special Report of the Committee on Homeland Security and Governmental Affairs: Hurricane Katrina: A Nation Still Unprepared*. 2006. https://www.gpo.gov/fdsys/pkg/CRPT-109srpt322/pdf/CRPT-109srpt322.pdf.

U.S.C. § 2331: Definitions. Accessed June 15, 2016. http://codes.lp.findlaw.com/uscode/18/I/113B/2331.

US Navy. "About the Navy." Navy.com, n.d. Accessed July 10, 2013. http://www.navy.com/about/gffg.html.

Valcke, M., S. Bonte, B. De Wever, and I. Rots. "Internet Parenting Styles and the Impact on Internet Use of Primary School Children." *Computers and Education* 55, no. 2 (September 2010): 454–64.

Valenti, Jessica. "Why Don't Americans Call Mass Shootings 'Terrorism'? Racism." *Guardian*, June 19, 2015. Sec. Opinion. Accessed July 2, 2016. https://www.theguardian.com/commentisfree/2015/jun/19/american-mass-shootings-terrorism-racism.

Valentine, Gill, and Sarah Holloway. "On-Line Dangers? Geographies of Parents' Fears for Children's Safety in Cyberspace." *Professional Geographer* 53, no. 1 (2001): 71–83. doi:10.1111/0033–0124.00270.

Van der Linde, Daan. *The Politics of Disaster: A Study into Post-Katrina International Aid*. November 2008. Accessed December 8, 2015. http://www.disasterdiplomacy.org/pb/vanderlinde2008.pdf.

Van Engelen, Errol. "Big Data Will Effectively Fight Terrorism in the World." N.d. Accessed July 2, 2015. https://datafloq.com/read/big-data-will-effectively-fight-terrorism/785.

Van Meter, Jonathan. "Unanchored." *New York Magazine*, September 19, 2005. Accessed December 8, 2015. http://nymag.com/nymetro/news/features/14301.

Vlcek, William. "Alongside Global Political Economy: A Rhizome of Informal Finance." *Journal of International Relations and Development* 13, no. 4 (December 2010): 429–51. doi:10.1057/jird.2010.17.

Vogel, Ann. "Who's Making Global Civil Society: Philanthropy and US Empire in World Society." *British Journal of Sociology* 57, no. 4 (2006): 635–55.

Volpp, Leti. "The Boston Bombers." SSRN Scholarly Paper. Rochester, NY: Social Science Research Network, April 1, 2014. http://papers.ssrn.com/abstract=2419287.

———. "The Citizen and the Terrorist." *UCLA Law Review* 49 (2001): 1575.

———. "'Obnoxious to Their Very Nature': Asian Americans and Constitutional Citizenship." *Citizenship Studies* 5, no. 1 (February 1, 2001): 57–71. doi:10.1080/13621020020025196.

Voorhees, Gerald A., Joshua Call, and Katie Whitlock, eds. *Guns, Grenades, and Grunts: First-Person Shooter Games*. London: Bloomsbury Academic, 2012.

Waidzunas, Tom. *The Straight Line: How the Fringe Science of Ex-Gay Therapy Reoriented Sexuality*. Minneapolis: University of Minnesota Press, 2015.

Waldman, Peter, and Hugh Pope. "'Crusade' Reference Reinforces Fears War on Terrorism Is against Muslims." *Wall Street Journal*, September 21, 2001,

sec. Front Section. Accessed June 3, 2016. http://www.wsj.com/articles
/SB10010202943329221160.

Waldstreicher, David. *In the Midst of Perpetual Fetes: The Making of American National-ism, 1776–1820.* Chapel Hill: University of North Carolina Press, 1997.

Wall, Tara. "Keeping Kids Safe on the Internet: December 1999." National Leadership Network of Conservative African Americans, December 1999. Accessed May 24, 2016. https://www.nationalcenter.org/NVWallInternet1299.html.

Walt, Stephen M. "Delusion Points." *Foreign Policy*, November 8, 2010. Accessed December 8, 2015. http://www.foreignpolicy.com/articles/2010/11/08/delusion_points.

Wang, Anthony S. "Demystifying the Asian American Neo-Conservative: A Strange and New Political Animal." *Asian American Law Journal* 5, no. 8 (1998): 213–46.

Wang, Qian (Emily), Michael D. Myers, and David Sundaram. "Digital Natives and Digital Immigrants: Towards a Model of Digital Fluency." *Business and Information Systems Engineering* 5, no. 6 (December 2013): 409–19. doi:http://dx.doi.org/10.1007/s12599–013–0296-y.

Wang, Rong, Suzanne Bianchi, and Sara Raley. "Teenagers' Internet Use and Family Rules: A Research Note." *Journal of Marriage and Family* 67, no. 5 (December 2005): 1249–58.

Ward, James J. "The Root of All Evil: Expanding Criminal Liability for Providing Mate-rial Support to Terror." *Notre Dame Law Review* 84 (2008): 471–510.

Wark, McKenzie. *Gamer Theory.* Cambridge, MA: Harvard University Press, 2007.

Warren, Samuel D., and Louis D. Brandeis. "The Right to Privacy." *Harvard Law Review* 4, no. 5 (December 15, 1890): 193–220. doi:10.2307/1321160.

Warschauer, Mark. *Technology and Social Inclusion: Rethinking the Digital Divide.* New ed. Cambridge, MA: MIT Press, 2004.

We Break Things. Rebecca Wexler, dir., 2014. Film.

West, Paige. *Rhetoric and Inequality in Papua New Guinea.* New York: Columbia Univer-sity Press, 2016.

Wexler, Laura. *Tender Violence: Domestic Visions in an Age of U.S. Imperialism.* Chapel Hill: University of North Carolina Press, 2000.

Wheatland, Tara. "*Ashcroft v. ACLU*: In Search of Plausible, Less Restrictive Alternatives." *Berkeley Technology Law Journal* 20 (2005): 371–96.

The White House. "Consumer Data Privacy in a Networked World: A Framework for Protecting Privacy and Promoting Innovation in the Global Digital World." Washington, DC: The White House, February 2012. http://repository.cmu.edu/cgi/viewcontent.cgi?article+1096&context=jpc.

White House Report. "Consumer Data Privacy in a Networked World: A Framework for Protecting Privacy and Promoting Innovation in the Global Digital World." *Jour-nal of Privacy and Confidentiality* 4, no. 2 (2012): 95–142.

"Why Does the US Need Our Money?" *BBC*, September 6, 2005, sec. Magazine. Accessed December 8, 2015. http://news.bbc.co.uk/2/hi/uk_news/magazine/4215336.stm.

Williams, Raymond. *Marxism and Literature.* Oxford: Oxford University Press, 1978.

Wilson, William Julius. *When Work Disappears: The World of the New Urban Poor*. New York: Vintage, 1997.

Wilson Center. "Book Discussion: National Security Mom: Why 'Going Soft' Will Make America Strong." March 16, 2009. Accessed January 21, 2016. https://www.wilsoncenter.org/event/book-discussion-national-security-mom-why-going-soft-will-make-america-strong.

Winder, Davey. "Does Parental Control Software Work?" *Alphr*, December 24, 2009. Accessed May 12, 2016. http://www.alphr.com/features/354349/does-parental-control-software-work.

Wingfield, Nick. "Feminist Critics of Video Games Facing Threats in 'GamerGate' Campaign." *New York Times*, October 15, 2014. Accessed June 15, 2016. http://www.nytimes.com/2014/10/16/technology/gamergate-women-video-game-threats-anita-sarkeesian.html.

Winkler, Adam. *Gunfight: The Battle over the Right to Bear Arms in America*. New York: W. W. Norton and Company, 2013.

Winter, Aaron. *American Terror: From Oklahoma City to 9/11 and After*. New York: Routledge, 2010. https://repository.abertay.ac.uk/jspui/handle/10373/1283.

Wolf, Richard. "Obama Goes to La. to Address Oil Spill." *USA Today*, April 4, 2010. Accessed December 8, 2015. http://usatoday30.usatoday.com/news/nation/2010–05–02-obama-spill_N.htm.

Wolfe, Patrick. *Traces of History: Elementary Structures of Race*. London: Verso, 2016.

Woo, Jisuk. "The Right Not to Be Identified: Privacy and Anonymity in the Interactive Media Environment." *New Media and Society* 8, no. 6 (December 1, 2006): 949–67. doi:10.1177/1461444806069650.

Wood, David Murakami, and Stephen Graham. "Permeable Boundaries in the Software-Sorted Society: Surveillance and Differentiations of Mobility." *Mobile Technologies of the City*, edited by Mimi Sheller and John Urry, 188. New York: Routledge, 2006.

Woods, Clyde. "*Les Miserables* of New Orleans: Trap Economics and the Asset Stripping Blues, Part 1." *American Quarterly* 61, no. 3 (2009): 769–96.

Woolf, Virginia. *Three Guineas*. London: Hogarth Press, [c. 1938] 1986.

Worth, Robert F., and Hassan M. Fattah. "Relief Agencies Find Hezbollah Hard to Avoid." *New York Times*, August 23, 2006. Accessed January 5, 2016. http://www.nytimes.com/2006/08/23/world/middleeast/23lebanon.html.

Wrennall, Lynne. "Surveillance and Child Protection: De-Mystifying the Trojan Horse." *Surveillance and Society* 7, nos. 3/4 (July 6, 2010): 304–24.

Wuthnow, Robert. *Boundless Faith: The Global Outreach of American Churches*. University of California Press, 2010.

———. *Saving America? Faith-Based Services and the Future of Civil Society*. Princeton, NJ: Princeton University Press, 2004.

Wuthnow, Robert, and Virginia A. Hodgkinson. *Faith and Philanthropy in America: Exploring the Role of Religion in America's Voluntary Sector*. Jossey-Bass, 1990.

Yeoman, Barry. "The Stealth Crusade." *Mother Jones*, May/June 2002. Accessed January 4, 2016. http://www.motherjones.com/politics/2002/05/stealth-crusade.

Yin, Sara. "7 Hackers Who Got Legit Jobs from Their Exploits." *PCMag*, June 28, 2011. Accessed June 14, 2016. http://www.pcmag.com/slideshow/story/266255/7-hackers -who-got-legit-jobs-from-their-exploits.

Yong, Su-Ting, and Peter Gates. "Born Digital: Are They Really Digital Natives?" *International Journal of E-Education, E-Business, E-Management and E-Learning* 4, no. 2 (April 2014): n/a. doi:http://dx.doi.org/10.7763/IJEEEE.2014.V4.311.

Young, Iris Marion. "The Logic of Masculinist Protection: Reflection on the Current Security State." *Signs: Journal of Women in Culture and Society* 29, no. 1 (2003): 1–25.

Zaborowski, Marcin. "Iraq, Katrina and US Foreign Policy: Implications for the EU." European Union Institute for Security Studies, n.d. Accessed April 23, 2012. http://www .iss.europa.eu/uploads/media/analy111.pdf.

Zavaletta, Joseph A. "COPPA, Kids, Cookies & Chat Rooms: We're from the Government and We're Here to Protect Your Children." *Santa Clara Computer and High-Technology Law Journal* 17 (2000–2001): 249–72.

Zehfuss, Maja. "Culturally Sensitive War? The Human Terrain System and the Seduction of Ethics." *Security Dialogue* 43, no. 2 (April 1, 2012): 175–90. doi:10.1177/0967010612438431.

Zeigler, Sara L., and Gregory G. Gunderson. *Moving beyond G.I. Jane: Women and the U.S. Military*. Lanham, MD: University Press of America, 2005.

Zemach-Bersin, Talya. "Imperial Pedagogies: Education for American Globalism, 1898–1950." PhD dissertation, Yale University, 2015.

Zunz, Olivier. *Philanthropy in America: A History*. Updated ed. with a new preface. Princeton, NJ: Princeton University Press, 2014.

Zurawik, David. "TV Accords More Respect to Victims in U.S." *Baltimore Sun*, September 3, 2005. Accessed November 5, 2014. http://articles.baltimoresun.com/2005–09–03/news/0509030074_1_tsunami- grief-natural-disasters.

Note: Page numbers in italics indicate figures.

Cox, Jo, 259n89
critical race studies, 18, 28–29, 146
cruel optimism, 55
cultural studies, transnational and intersectional, 29
cyberbullying, 151, 162
Cyber Youth Network, 246n60

Daily Nation, 34
Dallas, TX, shooting, 253n8
Daly, Kay R., 125
Danes, Claire, 132
Daniels, Ezra Claytan, 145
dataveillance, 168
dawa movements, 97
Dear, Robert, 187
Debord, Guy, 46
Delay, Tom, 101
Deleuze, Gilles, 24
Democratic Party, 65, 99, 116, 129, 171, 238n39
Democratic Republic of the Congo, 53, 237n29
Department of Defense, 52
Department of Education, 99
Department of Energy, 242n88
Department of Health and Human Services, 100
Department of Homeland Security (DHS), 1, 36, 46, 52, 194
Department of Housing and Urban Development, 100
Department of Justice, 100, 114
Department of Labor, 100
Department of State, 36, 111; Bureau of Intelligence and Research, 140
Department of Treasury, 108, 113, 115; Anti-Terrorist Financing Guidelines, 107; Office of Foreign Assets Control, 106
Derrida, Jacques, 22–23
de Waal, Alex, 97, 228n42
de Wilde, Jaap, 20
diaspora, 23, 200, 257n68
digital enclosure, 178
digital native, figure of, 30, 144–84
digital security mom, figure of, 146, 150, 152, 157–60, 175. *See also* national security mom, figure of; security mom, figure of
Dilulio, John, 101
Dionne, E. J., 41
disaster diplomacy, 35
disciplinary society, 24
Doctors without Borders, 61
domestic violence, 188–89
Donnan, Stephen, 192
donor-advised funds (DAFs), 110–12

DonorsChoose, 80, 83
Doucet, Marc G., 18
Dowd, Maureen, 133–35, 139, 141
Dowler, Milly, 237n19
Drezner, Daniel W., 41
Duffield, Mark, 20
Durham, Frank, 46

eBay, 81
Eberhardt, Isabelle, 72
eBlaster, 166
EchoMetrix, 173–74
Economist, 115
Edward M. Kennedy Serve America Act, 116
Eggers, Dave, 110; *Zeitoun*, 49–50
Egypt, 97
Electronic Privacy Information Center (EPIC), 173
Elkin-Koren, Niva, 171
Elmer, Greg, 24
El Salvador, 95
Emanuel African Methodist Episcopal Church, 189
Emerson, Michael O., 65
empire, 7–10, 13–15, 26, 38, 147, 152, 216n58, 237n30; exceptional citizens saving, 2, 5–6, 117, 149, 185, 189, 203; humanitarianism and, 20, 29–30, 39, 60–73, 75, 78–79, 82, 86–87, 90–91, 96, 117; neoliberal, 5, 28, 31, 116; racialized gender and, 6, 11–12, 18, 21, 31, 47–48, 63, 73, 118–21, 131–34, 139, 148, 153, 184, 189–90, 200–203; soft power and, 11, 17, 28, 71, 86, 117; waning of, 1, 4, 19–22, 50, 57, 186, 189. *See also* colonialism
Enloe, Cynthia, 64
Entertainment Software Association: "safe harbor" program, 172
Entertainment Software Ratings Board (ESRB), "safe harbor" provision, 167, 172
entrepreneurial self, 3
Europe, 9, 16–17, 34, 39–40, 62, 91–92, 98, 115, 140, 148, 154, 175, 190, 192, 206n13; European colonialism, 2, 7–8, 15, 87, 99, 118, 120, 132
European Union (EU), 175, 178, 233n132
exceptional citizens, 16, 21, 50, 52, 152, 154–57, 159, 162, 169, 173, 179–80, 193–94, 201; feminism and, 121, 123–24, 130–31, 138, 140, 143; humanitarianism and, 6, 10, 60, 82–83, 86, 88, 90, 92, 101–2, 108–9, 114, 117; saving the security state, 3–6, 13–14, 117, 119–22, 131, 138–39, 145–46, 149, 185–89, 203; saving US empire, 2, 5–6, 117, 149, 185, 189–90, 203; securitization and, 1–2, 4–6, 23–25, 120, 143

Maher, Erin, 182–83
Mahrouse, Gada, 67
Mair, Thomas, 259n89
Malkin, Michelle, 124–29, 139–40, 142–43, 238n36, 238n39
Mandela, Nelson, 94
Manifest Destiny, 186, 193
Maraini, Fosco, 74
Marshall Plan, 43
Martelle, Scott, 197
Martin, Erik, 181–83
Martin, Trayvon, 183
Marx, Gary, 145, 147, 151
Marx, Karl, 17
masculinity, 11, 18, 25–26, 28, 31, 71, 77, 124, 129, 135–37, 196; citizenship and, 183; colonial, 66; digital native and, 157; hetero-, 73, 187–89, 202–3; militant, 26–27, 193; white, 11, 17–21, 63, 120, 194, 197
Mateen, Omar, 191–93
Matsuda, Mari, 155
Mattelart, Armand, 11–12, 113, 115
Matthews, Jennifer, 137–38
Mayer, Jane, 241n77; *The Dark Side*, 138–39
Mbembe, Achille, 8, 15
McAfee Family Protection, 166
McAlister, Melani, 65, 68, 101
McChrystal, Stanley A., 76–77
McVeigh, Timothy, 187
Medal of Honor: Warfighter, 201
media convergence, 23–25
media studies, 28
Megan's Law, 160
Melley, Timothy, 135
mental illness, 132, 193, 199
Mexico–US border, 126
Michigan, 113
microlending, 29, 79–85
Microsoft, 78, 169; Windows, 167
Middle East, 10, 49, 50, 105, 182, 191; hawala money transfer systems in, 88, 92; humanitarianism in, 90, 92, 96–99; US wars in, 6, 89, 146. *See also individual countries*
"Middle Eastern or North African" (MENA) category, 163
Miller, Alice, 244n32
Miller, George, 102–3
Miller, Greg, 138
Mills, Charles, 26, 122
MinorMonitor, 166
Mirzoeff, Nicholas, 48

misogyny, 89, 133, 183, 193, 202, 257n71
Mississippi, 33, 40, 45, 51. *See also* Hurricane Katrina
Modi, Narendra, 225n1
Moeller, Susan, 38
Mohammed, Khalid Sheikh, 139, 241n77
Moller, Thomas, 19
Mom's Choice Awards, 163
Monahan, Torin, 151
Moodie, Megan, 80, 83
moral economies, 10
moral panics, 6, 30, 47–48, 121–23, 145, 150–51, 157, 168, 172, 175
Mormon Church, 68
Morocco, 181, 183
Mortenson, Greg, 79, 81, 91, 95–96, 109, 143; *Listen to the Wind*, 77; *Stones into Schools*, 77; *Three Cups of Tea*, 71–78, 88–89, 223n51. *See also* Central Asia Institute
motherhood, 180; feminism and, 119–20, 133–34; securitization of, 6, 30, 119–32, 136, 139–43, 146, 150–51, 175; surveillance and, 30, 146, 150, 152, 157–61, 167–68, 175–76. *See also* digital security mom, figure of; national security mom, figure of; security mom, figure of; soccer mom, figure of
Mubarak, Hosni, 97
Muehlebach, Andrea, 63
multiculturalism, 66, 134
Murdoch, Rupert, 237n19
Murray, Bernadette, 152, 158–59; *Digital Security Mom*, 144–45
Murunga, Ambrose, 34
Muslim Advocates, 113
"Muslim-looking" category, 119, 200
Muslims, 65, 72, 118, 130, 139, 176, 178, 180, 199, 231n82, 257n68; charities targeted, 29, 90–115, 117, 227n18, 233n114, 233n132; citizenship of, 13–14, 163; "good Muslim" role, 192, 251n146; racial profiling of, 10–11, 50, 183, 188–93, 198; surveillance of, 119, 121, 127, 148–50, 189, 200–201. *See also* Islam

NAACP, 45, 199
Nagin, Ray, 45, 47
National Counterterrorism Center, 242n88
National Guard, 39
National Leadership Network of Conservative African Americans, 246n60
National Rifle Association (NRA), 195, 257n71
National Security Administration (NSA), 121, 242n88; PRISM, 147–48, 169–70